Struggling
to Be Heard

Edited by
VALERIE OOKA PANG
LI-RONG LILLY CHENG

Struggling
to Be Heard

The Unmet Needs of
Asian Pacific American Children

STATE UNIVERSITY OF NEW YORK PRESS

The editors thank the following for permission to reprint previously published materials:

Reprinted by permission of the publisher from Miramonics, O. B., Nadeau, A., & Commins, N. L., *Restructuring Schools for Linguistic Diversity: Linking Decision Making to Effective Programs*. (New York: Teachers College Press, © 1997 by Teachers College, Columbia University. All rights reserved), pp. 271–298.

"Troubled Southeast Asian Youth: Profile of a Delinquent Population," by Kenji Ima and Jean Nidorf in *Current Issues in Asian and Pacific Education*, edited by Russell Endo, Clara C. Park, and John Nobuya Tsuchida (El Monte, CA: Pacific Asia Press, 1998).

Published by
State University of New York Press, Albany

© 1998 State University of New York

For information, address State University of New York Press,
State University Plaza, Albany, NY 12246

Production by Ruth Fisher
Marketing by Fran Keneston

Library of Congress Cataloging-in-Publication Data

Struggling to be heard : the unmet needs of Asian Pacific American
   children / edited by Valerie Ooka Pang, Li-Rong Lilly Cheng.
       p.   cm. — (SUNY series, the social context of education)
   Includes bibliographical references and index.
       ISBN 0-7914-3839-2 (alk. paper). — ISBN 0-7914-3840-6 (pbk. :
   alk. paper)
       1. Asian Americans—Education—Social aspects—Case studies.
   2. Pacific Islander Americans—Education—Social aspects—Case
   studies. 3. Educational anthropology—United States—Case studies.
   4. Multicultural education—United States—Case studies. I. Pang,
   Valerie Ooka, 1950–   . II. Cheng, Li-Rong Lilly. III. Series:
   SUNY series, social context of education.
   LC2632.S87 1998
   370.117—dc21   97-47482
                                                                        CIP

10 9 8 7 6 5 4 3 2 1

To Jenn, Matt, and Gerry. (V. O. P.)
To Ping and Philip. (L. L. C.)

Contents

Acknowledgments

We thank the many children and their families who have shared their lives, hopes, and struggles. The children have inspired us to continue in our efforts toward social justice; it is through their resilience, patience and courage that we find inspiration. We thank them all. We also want to thank our mentors and the many authors who have been there with us spiritually as we travel through the journey of life.

We thank Christine Sleeter who encouraged us to begin and finish this important book. We also appreciate the generosity of all of the contributors because they have donated the profits of this book to children's organizations. Finally, many thanks to Priscilla Ross, David Ford, and their staff at SUNY Press whose advice was invaluable.

Foreword

Enrique (Henry) T. Trueba

I f one could telescope in seconds the events of the twenty-first century, perhaps one of the most remarkable impressions would be the predominance of Asian people taking control over the most powerful industries, economic institutions, and technological inventions. The rapid development of Japanese, Korean, and Chinese economic and technological power is a fair warning to Western societies (especially to the United States) of the need to understand and recognize Asian cultures, negotiate mutually beneficial economic, political, and military policies, offer assistance in their development of democratic institutions (especially their universities), and cultivate cooperative partnerships in research and development. Obviously, in the light of recent historical events, the importance of Asian American populations who have the knowledge of languages and cultures of Asian nations should receive a long overdue recognition and support.

This volume speaks to the neglect of Asian Pacific Americans in the United States, of their struggles for liberation, hopes, troubles, and personal identities. The military, economic, and political interventions of the United States in Asia (especially in the Southeast) have created permanent links between this nation and hundreds of Asian nations. The cultural contacts between Americans and those groups has had an enormous impact on the education and health of Asian Pacific American children and their families, on many refugee populations, and on the creation of a new cultural environment in America that placed our society in a "post-melting pot" era, or as the authors call it, an era "beyond multiculturalism," one of enhanced ethnic awareness and of determination to participate in the sociopolitical process of maintaining American democracy with its consequences for educational equity and respect for all Americans.

These pages take us through a review of our immediate history and enable us to rethink our attitudes (racial, educational, political, economic, and social) regarding the welfare of Asian Pacific American families. Furthermore, these pages force us to reflect on the painful dilemmas that have to be faced by Asian Pacific Americans in this country. Let me list just a few:

1. The dilemma supporting a decision to pursue total emancipation of one's own ethnic group in order to best fit into American society, versus the decision to create pan-Asian coalitions with greater political power, more organized pressure groups, and more clear equity action targets.
2. The dilemma of either continuing a policy of silent compliance with American societal demands, effectively remaining invisible and enjoying some peace in this country, or becoming a visible political force with a clear commitment to take power within the political machinery and to participate actively in the decision-making process.
3. The dilemma of either keeping silence as the price of peace, and thus accepting the appearance of being colonized, oppressed, and abused by employers, school personnel, public officials, and representatives of traditional institutions (such as banks, hospitals, insurance companies, corporations, etc.), or openly demanding first-class citizenship, fair treatment, justice, and respect.

Ultimately, these dilemmas amount to either accepting U.S. society as a prejudiced and racist society, or viewing it as a society where prejudice and racism are unacceptable and therefore one is expected to fight it at any cost. The opening of many wounds suffered during the immigration experience and the commitment to pursue a distinct cultural identity within the United States are linked by the fundamental belief that our nation is indeed a democratic society, and therefore, that it is all right to keep high expectations, and it is not all right to deny the existence of racism; it is all right to discover the pecking order in the racial/ethnic strata, but it is not all right to pass for Anglo or another ethnic group with higher status; it is good to believe in the contributions of one's own ethnic group to U.S. society, but it is not all right to neglect your ethnic group and ignore its language and culture with the intent of becoming acceptable to mainstream society. In the end, what has made this country unique, the strongest in the world and the most advanced technologically, is the fact that the United states has a way of opening its doors to, and rewarding fully, any ethnic group that wants to make a contribution to the entire society.

The use of stereotypes, ethnic quotas, and racial barriers, in order to neglect Asian Pacific American populations, or to fail to recognize their contributions to America, as in the case of Vietnam veterans (see P. Kiang, 1991: 22–40), forces all Americans (including ethnic subgroups) to look in the mirror and ask themselves: What kind of society do we want to live in? What kind of democracy are we willing to fight and die for? What kind of nation are we creating for our children? The role of Asian Americans in the future of this country is crucial. They will play a very important role in establishing the new boundaries of tolerance in our interaction with foreign nations, in identifying our goals for our economic and technological development, in pursuing aggressive economic growth through fair and practical import/export policies and investment strategies. To the extent that Asian Pacific Americans in the United States retain a clear and strong ethnic identity, and to the extent that they retain their cultural and linguistic heritage, they will be able to play the most delicate and crucial historical role ever given to any other group of Americans, a role that will determine the place of U.S. democratic institutions in the world of the twenty-first century.

I

General Background Information

Introduction

Valerie Ooka Pang
Li-Rong Lilly Cheng

The Quest for Concepts, Competence, and Connections

The Education of Asian Pacific American Children

> We are lightning and justice.
> Our souls become transparent like glass
> revealing tears for war-dead sons
> red ashes of Hiroshima
> jagged wounds from barbed wire.
> We must recognize ourselves at last
> We are a rainforest of color
> and noise.
> We hear everything.
> We are unafraid.
> Our language is beautiful.
>
> —Mirikitani, 1983, p. 191

Teachers often do not understand the needs of Asian Pacific American (APA) students. We present this book in the hope that educators will better understand which concepts and issues are most germane to the APA community, develop competence in providing the best schools for APA students, and make clear connections between culture and education. To many teachers, APA children are invisible; though teachers may notice physical differences, their needs are often overlooked. The APA population continues to grow by leaps and bounds because of high birth rates and continued immigration. It is estimated that, by the year 2020, Asian Pacific American students ages five through seventeen will make up over 8 percent of the school-age population, 4,382,500 (Ong & Hee, 1993), and as their numbers increase, their needs will also continue to become more evident.

We believe educators must challenge a biased educational and social system which often labels APA children as "model minorities." The label acts as an excuse for schools to avoid addressing the social, psychological, and educational needs of APA youth. Some teachers like having Asian Pacific American children in their classes because "they make me look good and do not cause problems" (M. Nakagawa, personal communication, July 12, 1996); unfortunately this teacher may not be attending to her APA students because they are well behaved and do not question her.

The first quest of the authors in this text is to challenge overgeneralized and unsubstantiated concepts many teachers hold about Asian Pacific American students and their communities and substitute more accurate information. Most teachers believe that Asian Pacific American students are welcomed into schools and society in general. Many also believe that Asian Pacific Americans are successful models. However we argue that there is a system in place which subordinates groups like APA from the majority. Social stereotypes serve to confirm those beliefs and dehumanize Asian Pacific Americans. We believe these beliefs serve as barriers which justify why teachers have not developed comprehensive programs for APA students. Too many Asian Pacific American students have been silenced. They are trapped in schools that do not notice them or are placed in programs where students have not developed critical skills (Darder, 1991; Gay, 1993).

We believe it is a struggle to convince many educators to examine the issues covered in this book. Most teachers are anxious to gather information about cultural rituals and traditions, however few teachers examine critical issues like why special education services are not reaching Asian populations because this will call into question their ability as educators. It is much easier to make origami cranes and teriyaki chicken, than to create programs that address teenage suicide or develop collaboration with parents who may speak languages other than English. In order to develop effective programs, it is crucial for educators to understand which implicit cultural values are operating and how those values shape the beliefs and behaviors of people. Advocates for APA students often must swim upstream against the current in their attempt to bring attention to issues like gang involvement, mental health problems, bilingual education, ethnic identity confusion, and relevant curriculum.

Our second quest is for competence. We hope that this book will assist teachers in developing competence in providing Asian Pacific American students with culturally affirming and effective educational learning environments. We encourage each reader to examine her/his own views and to find other professionals to discuss the issues our authors share in this text. It is only through dialogue and soul searching that change can occur. Listen to APA parents and listen carefully to your APA students. Get to know them well enough to be able to understand their viewpoint and perspective. Our book can only provide basic knowledge and direction, however real competence will develop when educators listen to their students and find out what they think and observe how they react in schools. At the same time it is crucial to talk with parents and other community leaders in order to make sure that what one is seeing is what one thinks one is seeing. For example a child, as Tran has written in her chapter, may smile, but that smile may not be one of happiness, but rather of embarrassment.

Our final quest is connection; success is based on networking. We feel fortunate to be able to bring to you an interdisciplinary collaboration of various specialists in Asian Pacific American education. The authors represent specializations in psychology, teacher education, counseling, history, communication disorders, bilingual education, special education, sociology, and social work. Their chapters provide you with a comprehensive view of APA children and their needs. We hope the reader will make connections with APA youth in their classroom and develop programs and practices that meet their specialized needs. Students should be encouraged to develop their talents and clarify personal views; APA voices should be distinctive contributors to our democracy (Darder, 1991). Educational programs should teach children that they can make choices about who they are, what they want to do in life, and how they should view themselves. These connections should affirm students as Asian Pacific Americans who have been members of the U.S. family since before the Revolutionary War. Filipinos have made the continental United States their home since 1763 when sailors jumped from Spanish galleons (Cordova, 1983).

The book is divided into three sections. The initial portion of the book focuses on the cultural background of APA communities. In this section, Leung, Flores, and Tran discuss cultural values found in various communities so that the reader can better understand how belief systems shape how people think, behave, and find meaning in life. Flores carefully describes important issues within the Filipino community and presents an intervention program she and her colleagues developed for Filipino American teenagers utilizing cultural heritage as the foundation. The need for cultural role models and guidance in the Filipino American community are crucial issues at a time when violence, gangs, and suicide are increasing at alarming rates.

To bring information about Chinese American, Japanese American, and Korean American children, Leung's chapter discusses the difference between "macro" or large group patterns and "micro" culture or individual differences within groups. One of the most powerful values in these communities is collectivism; family ties and group harmony are continually encouraged. Leung also pointed to historical differences among Chinese, Japanese, and Korean immigration and how assimilation levels may correspond with historical experiences. His case studies provide examples of real children and how their lives have been shaped by culture.

In presenting information about Southeast Asian American children, Tran carefully outlined how the true heart of Southeast Asian American children is often difficult for mainstream teachers to perceive. Many Southeast Asians respect and highly value education; however, because of their refugee experiences and forced move to the United States, they face many educational, psychological, and social problems in their adjustment to the mainstream culture. Though none of the chapters can paint a comprehensive picture of any one group, they point to patterns or trends in groups. When reading these chapters, a caution is shared with the reader: though there are group trends, an individual within each group can be extremely different from another member. We also wanted to stress that we attempted to present a wide spectrum of information about many groups, however our text does not have specific sections about many APA groups like East Indians and Pacific Islanders.

The second portion of the book focuses on sociocultural aspects of APA communities. Young described the ethnic identity confusion of many APA students. He found many APA children trying to cope with the confusion of a double consciousness. How do young people maintain a strong ethnic identity while assimilating into mainstream culture? Young believed young people develop different identities—which he labeled as "the golden child," "the misfit child," "the good child," and "the hyphenated child"—in order to cope within a bicultural or multicultural environment.

Ethnic identity confusion is also an issue Chun and Sue identify. In their chapter on the mental health of children, they express concern that little attention is paid to the emotional and psychological development of Asian Pacific American students. Chun and Sue's chapter explained that they felt depression, lack of interpersonal skills, anxiety, and posttraumatic stress disorder in refugees were the most pressing mental health issues.

Ima and Nidorf share with us a similar viewpoint. They provide critical information explaining why some APA students join gangs. For many students, gangs provide family relationships that they long for and have lost. Many refugee students have come to the United States without their parents and must rely on older brothers and sisters, who themselves have difficulty surviving. Some of these students may seem like a "model minority" in that they are quiet in school and do their homework, however after school they are involved in gang activity.

Many teachers have little knowledge about the conflicts Asian Pacific American children encounter as they are thrust into mainstream schools. Cheng shared numerous examples of how the implicit view and hidden curriculum of U.S. culture can be confusing to some Asian Pacific American children. Using humor and interesting samples of cultural differences, Cheng carefully explained how we all come to situations with cultural glasses. It is through these glasses that we interpret the language and behaviors of others. Cheng believed that educators must move "beyond multiculturalism" to understand the underlying values and beliefs which tangible and outward behaviors represent.

The last section of the book centers on numerous aspects of schooling. First, Nadeau, a former principal, discusses the practices she instituted with her staff in an elementary school that was over 44 percent Asian Pacific American with three major Asian languages, Hmong, Vietnamese, and Lao. Under her leadership, the school staff became highly effective with their students and this led to many awards including an RJR Nabisco grant and U.S. Department of Education distinguished school honor. Next, Watanabe points out in his chapter that Asian Pacific American students are underserved in special education. He explains why parents are often embarrassed or reluctant to allow their children to participate in programs for children with disabilities. For example, some Lao parents believe a child with special needs is a symbol that God is punishing a person for something done in the past. Teachers will need to understand the fears of parents and other community members in order to be effective.

As the second largest APA group, it is critical for teachers to have an in-depth knowledge of Filipinos. Although their legacy in the United States is rich and over 225 years old, few teachers have an understanding of the impact of Filipino American presence in U.S. history. Cordova has provided an in-depth list of Filipino Americans who have contributed to and continue to have a powerful influence on our society. This list is an important resource for teachers.

Moving to the area of curriculum and instruction, Cheng provides an important chapter presenting her views on assessment and instructional strategies for limited English speaking APA students. Assessment is an extremely complicated process and Cheng gives clear guidelines and practical strategies. In order to provide students with comprehensible input, she offers examples of cultural information that she feels educators should cover in their curriculum. Halloween, idioms, and metaphors are several areas Cheng encourages teachers to include in their linguistic program. Her chapter is followed by a chapter by Fung, who presents important curriculum ideas for use in the classroom. These ideas are culturally relevant and highlight the use of carefully selected Asian Pacific American literature as bridges between what children may already know and new concepts that are being taught. Fung stressed the importance of developmentally appropriate instruction, culturally affirming content, and using multisensory approaches.

Ima shared an ethnographic view of schools. He examined the experiences of secondary Asian newcomer students in one of the largest school districts in the nation. He generally found that schools did not attend to the needs of Asian Pacific American students. Schools fell into four categories: some schools focused on assimilating students into a middle-class, Eurocentric curriculum paying little attention to cultural relevancy, some schools were not equipped or trained to educate newcomer students, other schools focused their attention on "keeping order" though little education occurred, and at some schools parents attempted to become more political in their call for bilingual services however slow the district is to respond.

In Appendix A, Lovelace presents a case study about the media. Her research focuses on creating affirming Asian Pacific American images on Sesame Street. Children's Television Workshop formed an Asian Pacific American Advisory Board to assist them in creating segments that would integrate culturally affirming information. She and her colleagues found APA preschool students responded positively to video segments where Asian cultural activities were presented. Unfortunately, they also discovered that students from other cultural groups did not respond as positively to the segments on Asian Pacific Americans.

The final portion of the book provides recommendations for teachers and other service providers. Kiang has written a powerful chapter describing the importance of guiding and empowering teenage Asian Pacific American students to create organizations that are socially active in society. In this way not only are students able to create their own "voice," but also to develop important participatory skills. He has organized students in calling for culturally relevant curriculum and more sensitivity to Asian issues, and has brought students together in pan Asian conferences. Though students initially felt disempowered by the system, through their collaboration and the direction given by Kiang and his colleagues, APA students realized they could shape their own future.

In the final chapter Pang encourages the reader to focus on the education of the whole child. Too often teachers may channel APA students into math, science, and other technical areas; however teachers should also suggest to students courses in art, creative writing, drama, ensemble, journalism, and sports. She believes it is crucial for APA youth to develop their cognitive talents along with high self esteem, leadership skills, emotional stability, and interpersonal skills.

To us, Asian Pacific American children are cherished hopes. They represent the hope of their families and communities whether they are immigrants or American natives. We believe educators and other service providers must examine the impact of culture on Asian Pacific American students because culture is "not simply a factor, or an influence, or a dimension, but it is in process, in everything that we do, say, or think in or out of school (Spindler & Spindler, 1993: p. 27) We know educators can better guide APA children when the implicit messages of culture are understood. Otherwise the voices of Asian Pacific American youth will continue to be absent in society because the potential growth of APA students is not fully developed. Many "fall through the cracks" in their schools and others continue to hit their heads against the invisible but clearly real "glass ceiling" of society. Few leaders have emerged from the APA community, and the hopes and possibilities of their communities continue to lie dormant.

It is our responsibility as educators to guide all students to be the best they can be. It is our intention to see more programs that nurture the potential growth of Asian Pacific American students, involve their parents, and encourage confidence development. We want our youth to become well-educated adults who are able to make connections throughout the global village. As adult citizens, they will live in a borderless world that looks beyond multiculturalism toward global collaboration (Kanter, 1995). We envision a world where Asian Pacific American students become thinkers, doers, and collaborators in the world community. In order for this to occur, we need more educators to become advocates for Asian Pacific American students and to push the educational and social system to better address the needs of APA youth.

Valerie Ooka Pang
Li-Rong Lilly Cheng

1

Brian P. Leung

Who Are Chinese American, Japanese American, and Korean American Children?

Cultural Profiles

This chapter will focus on three Asian American groups that have some shared similarities, Chinese Americans, Japanese Americans, and Korean Americans. But before our attention is turned to these groups, I'm compelled to introduce a cautionary statement of heterogeneity: intergroup differences as well as intragroup differences are enormous (Trueba, Cheng & Ima, 1993). This recognition must be taken seriously by educators because, although these groups are commonly referred to as "Asian Americans," each group came to the United States with very different characteristics. As importantly, each group's acculturation into the United States took a distinct path, resulting in different behaviors and reactions. Also, individual differences abound in any human group. Therefore, when discussing individual student needs or specific family interactions, careful attention and independent considerations are needed so that students and families are not erroneously assumed to be all alike.

So how do educators sort through the almost infinite amount of information that could characterize different groups of people, and also the almost countless ways that individuals may vary within each group? Like other complex stimuli people encounter, we use broad terms such as *Asian*, *European*, and *Latino* to categorize large groups of humanity to simplify learning. This cognitive structuring of information, which occurs almost naturally in the brain, allows us to learn in a world with an infinite variety of stimuli (Bruner, 1990). Since categorization (aka stereotyping) of people happens, it is imperative that educators encourage this process to: (1) remain continuous, that is, new information be constantly added to existing categories (i.e., a lifelong learner); and (2) be based on substantive attributes, that is, categorize others not on superficial characteristics (e.g., skin color, language, etc.), but rather based on ways that people live (e.g., patterns of interactions, life issues, value orientation, etc.). Substantive categories allow a deeper understanding of others. Categorizations that proceed as a continuous and deliberate process enable educators to feel confident about working with those who are culturally different, yet promote a sense of openness and respect for those they are learning from.

Two sets of substantive categories can be used to facilitate lifelong learning of cultural differences. The first set focuses on group-level patterns (i.e., *macro* in nature): the cultural dimensions of individualism-collectivism and family types. The second set is concerned with individual students and families (i.e., *micro* in nature): the various personal subsystems. Brief descriptions of the immigration histories and educational issues for each of the three groups will follow. Finally, three case studies illustrate the diversity and complexity in the Asian American population.

Macrolevel Patterns

An important group level difference is illustrated by the cultural dimension of individualism-collectivism. This dimension has been identified as central to an understanding of cultural values between groups (Triandis, Brislin & Hui, 1988).

Individualism and Collectivism

Individualism is an orientation characterized by individuals of a group subordinating the goals of the group/collective (e.g., family) to their personal goals. Collectivism, on the other hand, is characterized by individuals subordinating their personal goals to the goals of a collective. This cultural pattern is common in Asia, Africa, South America, and the Pacific; while individualism is the cultural pattern found in most northern and western regions of Europe and in North America (Triandis et al., 1988). There are distinct differences in behaviors between these two orientations.

An individualist can belong to many groups (e.g., family, religious, political, or social groups), yet no one group membership defines his identity or determines his behaviors. A collectivist, however, usually belongs to fewer groups but has higher attachments to these groups and is defined by them. For a collectivist, behavior is largely a function of norms and roles that are determined through tradition or interactions among group members (e.g., family roles); while an individualist essentially defines his own personal behavior. Collectivists are associative within their "in-group," affording much time and devotion; but are dissociative toward their "out-group," which are typically distrusted. By contrast, an individualist tends to have many in-groups, but his relationships with each one may be situationally determined and temporary (e.g., friendship circle). Collectivists are often viewed as cliquish by individualists. Typically, a collectivist has positive attitudes toward vertical relationships (e.g., parent-child, teacher-student) and accepts differences in power. Individualists value horizontal relationships (e.g. friend-friend, spouse-spouse) and are ambivalent about people in authority. While both groups support self-reliance, collectivists are expected to be reliant on the group, whereas individualists rely on the self. Independence is highly valued to an individualist, while interdependence is more important to a collectivist. The top values for collectivists are group harmony, face saving, and modesty in self-achievement. Top values for individualists are freedom, honesty, and individual recognition.

In general, Asian Americans are collectivists. Moreover, insight into Asian American behaviors is possible by understanding deeply rooted socialization practices taught by Confucius (Kitano & Daniels, 1988). In describing values, there are often conflicts and inconsistencies in practice; nonetheless, it is interesting to note that values related to strong family ties and maintaining group harmony are identifiable behavioral tendencies among Asian Americans, even after several generations of living in an individualistic society such as the United States (Nakanishi, 1994).

The "family" is well accepted as the central social unit (rather than the individual) in Asian societies, and filial piety is an attitude prevalent in most Asian Americans (Kitano & Daniels, 1995; Chan, 1991). This practice of reciprocal obligation presupposes that the parents will sacrifice to raise the children, and in turn, the grown children will take care of their parents. Within this most important in-group (i.e., family) and other in-groups, face-saving gestures are of great importance in order to preserve harmony. Face-saving gestures are equally extended to interactions with out-group members and therefore, open disagreements are generally frowned upon or avoided. When disagreements do occur, the tendency is to circumvent them or mediators will work with the parties to soothe the problem (Triandis et al., 1988). Although collectivists believe in equality in distribution of resources based on membership in a group, Asian countries have traditionally been male dominated. Therefore, distribution of finite resources will likely go to males before females.

The above description would suggest the following characteristics for an Asian American student: the student is less likely to express individual thoughts and is dependent on the family for decisions; tends to subordinate wishes (e.g., choice of extracurricular activities, school majors, etc.) to the family; socializes with fewer groups of people; cooperates better with other Asian American students than outside groups. In fact, this student is likely to be a poor "joiner" of new groups. This student will be quiet and not boastful of his/her achievement. This cultural orientation teaches an acceptance of deference (i.e., principal-teacher-student; and parents defer to teachers); is mindful of role definitions (e.g., teacher teaches, students listen and learn, and parents stay out of the way); and creates duty-bound behaviors (e.g., parents work long, hard hours to send children to school). Parents are less likely to openly disagree with teachers in order to save face and promote harmony. They will likely pay more attention to the educational attainment of the boys, rather than the girls, in the family.

It is important to view these behaviors as tendencies of a collectivist culture, not definite behaviors of all Asian American students or families. Furthermore, these behaviors are influenced by cultural orientations, not expressions of weaknesses or personality deficits. One's cultural context has pervasive and profound impact on one's behaviors, and teachers must be encouraged to understand the basis for behaviors for students and their parents. And again, individual differences abound.

Family Type

Another macro pattern to consider in understanding Asian American families is family types. Lee's (1982) topology of families seems applicable to Asian American groups. The family types are: recently arrived immigrant families, immigrant-American families, and immigrant-descendant families.

Recently Arrived Immigrant Families

These families are usually the most "at risk" of the three groups, because they may need basic survival skills (e.g., a command of English, employment) in order to adjust to the new environment. Students in this family group may need intensive ESL or bilingual education services in order to survive in the classroom. Their parents are less able to be highly involved in school due to different expectations of home-school partnership, work demands, or simply a language barrier. These parents also tend to rely heavily on teachers to provide their children with direction. These families may live in ethnic communities and rely primarily on in-language services.

Immigrant-American Families

Such families usually consist of overseas-born parents and their American-born children or overseas-born parents and children who have been in the United States for a long period of time (e.g., twenty years or more). Since these families have been in the country for an extended period, they are more familiar with routines in typical American institutions, including school. These parents are more able to collaborate with teachers in decision making for their children, although there exists a common tendency for cultural conflicts between parents' wishes and their children's (e.g., the selection of an academic major). Both parents and students are likely to experience the turbulence associated with differing rates of acculturation (Nakanishi, 1994). Lack of a common language can complicate communication among family members, as the children learn English much more quickly than their parents. Often, desiring to preserve their cultural heritage, parents enroll their children in language schools within their ethnic communities on weekends or after school (Trueba, Cheng & Ima, 1993). These families, although no longer living within an ethnic community, will usually continue to have frequent contact with its members.

American-born Families

These families consist of American-born parents and their children. Family members speak primarily or only English at home and are quite Westernized in their lifestyle and orientation. These parents can be highly involved in schools because they understand the active role parents can take in school decisions. These families usually live outside of ethnic communities and generally move freely between communities. Basic cultural orientations (e.g., collectivist orientations) are retained but practiced to a lesser degree by these families.

This typology of families, based on life issues, can assist educators in gaining deeper insights into the familial contexts of Asian American students. This insight can guide the teacher toward a more effective choice of strategies for instruction and achieving parent involvement. A mitigating variable is socioeconomic status (SES). A high-SES, recent-immigrant family is more likely to participate in school activities, since they will not be concerned with financial stability (Chan, 1991).

After macrolevel patterns are used to sort through information, we can further refine our understanding about specific students based on microlevel issues.

Microlevel Patterns

In understanding any Asian American student or family, there are at least three subsystems that an educator might explore (Lee, 1982). These include: personal system, family system, and community system.

Personal System

This subsystem is the most obvious when learning about a particular Asian American student. It involves knowing the student's personal characteristics, including such information as language and dialect spoken (e.g., Chinese has over twenty-five different dialects), physical health status (i.e., immigrant children from war-torn countries), years in the United States, and educational history. Additionally, some sense of the student's self-identity is useful to ascertain his self-esteem, especially in psychosocial and interpersonal development. Takaki (1989) pointed out that "physically identifiable" minorities, such as Asian Americans, go through a different acculturation process than those immigrants who are physically unidentifiable from the mainstream (i.e., European). The basis for this difference is due to the superficial characteristics (i.e., skin color, physical features) that many Americans use to identify "foreigners" (Allport, 1954). The physical attributes of Asian Americans lead some to believe they are recent immigrants. These feelings of marginalization often lead to self-hatred and denial of ethnic heritage as the student struggles with finding a sense of belonging (Sue & Zane, 1985). Educators can facilitate an easier transition if they understand the difficulty an Asian American student might confront despite being considered a "model minority" (Divoky, 1988). This is particularly important for native-born students who may not see themselves as *Asians* yet are not fully accepted as *Americans*. Educators need to recognize each student as an individual rather than as a representative from an ethnic group that is stereotypically considered to excel in educational achievement (Sue & Okazaki, 1990).

Family System

As noted earlier, the family is probably the most influential in-group for an Asian American student (Trueba, Cheng & Ima, 1993; Chan, 1991). Therefore, careful consideration of the impact of the student's family on his life is vital to understanding the student. To the extent that the family defines student behaviors, knowing the family's goals and expectations, as well as quality of family communication can help educators understand the behaviors of the student. It is likely that recent-immigrant families will have greater influence on the student than native-born parents. Other important information includes family composition, number of siblings, and living arrangements (it is not uncommon for several families to share a household, especially among recent immigrants), extent of support network (extended family members, sponsors), and the family's acculturation and adjustment process (family members may experience varying degrees of acculturation). A particularly sensitive but critical piece of information relates to the family's financial situation. This aspect defines lifestyle, including leisure activity, and other family responsibilities (Lee, 1982). Educators can better understand the student if they appreciate the context that shapes his perceptions and motivations in achievement situations.

Community System

An Asian American student's involvement with the ethnic community tells a great deal about his/her identity. Information regarding the extent of contact and interactions within this subsystem will help educators clarify the student's sense of self. Ethnic communities have traditionally provided safety and security for immigrants, continuing to serve as a focal point for not only residential, but also social and business opportunities of many Asian American families (Fong, 1994; Chan, 1991). Information about social institutions within ethnic communities, where families might seek services (e.g., native health services, language schools), can help educators to better recognize the opportunities and constraints that frame the life of an Asian American student (Trueba, Cheng & Ima, 1993).

Cultural influences are highly influential in shaping the behaviors of Asian American students and families, yet these influences are often elusive to grasp. The discussion of both the macro (group-level) and micro (individual-level) patterns are intended to facilitate substantive categories in order for educators to sort through the myriad of information that they may encounter about Asian Americans. When categorization of information proceeds along substantive rather than superficial issues, it will not only further the educator's continuous understanding of the Asian American students and their families, it will also minimize overgeneralization of global information of the three Asian American groups discussed next.

Brief Historical Information about
Chinese, Japanese, and Korean Students

There is a great deal of material written about these three Asian American groups; therefore, the discussion to follow is very brief and will focus on immigration histories, which provide the sociopolitical context for Asians in the United States, and educational issues, which allow educators to develop appropriate expectations for the students they work with.

It is important to note that anti-Asian sentiments were pervasive and prevailed for many decades in the United States. These racist sentiments translated into local, state, and federal legislation that not only restricted immigration but allowed overt discriminatory practices to occur (e.g., denial of legal due process, owning property, enjoying rights afforded all citizens of this country). These practices greatly affected the relationships between Asian Americans and the greater American society (Wei, 1993; Chan, 1991).

Chinese American

Among Asian groups the Chinese have had one of the longest legacies in the United States, having had documentation of small contingents here as early as 1785 (Sung, 1967). Significant numbers of Chinese were seen in the United States, especially in California, by the latter part of the 1800s, due mostly to the attraction of jobs (e.g., intercontinental railroad, farms, etc.) and special opportunities (e.g., gold rush). Most of these were peasants who intended to raise enough money to return to China, but many never did return (Sung, 1967). Due to unfamiliarity with Western cultures as well as personal preferences, the Chinese lived their own cultural and social experiences. Since Chinese immigrants were a source of cheap labor, they were initially welcomed; however, their isolation made them easy political targets for labor union agitation. Strong anti-Chinese sentiment led to The Chinese Exclusion Act in 1882, despite protests from the Chinese government which was itself too weak to mount any significant pressure. This exclusion act, not repealed until 1943, shaped both the psyches and the demographics of the Chinese in this country (Kitano & Daniels, 1995). This federal act sanctioned local, regional, and state overt discriminatory practices that included extreme housing segregation and a denial of legal due process. Moreover, this law barred future immigration, which created a bachelor society in the Chinese community. This prevailed for decades until the 1950s, when the Chinese population finally regained its numbers (Kitano & Daniels, 1988).

This immigration history suggests that some Chinese families have been in the United States for over five generations. Yet, the bulk of Chinese Americans were part of the largely unacculturated "bachelor society" that dominated the Chinatowns of America until World War II (Kitano & Daniels, 1988). After the immigration restrictions were lifted in the 1940s, over a million Chinese immigrated to the United States, mostly from China and Hong Kong in the 1950s to 1970s, and more recently, from Taiwan. The U.S. Census of 1990 showed that there are 1.6 million ethnic Chinese living in the United States, with over 40 percent living in California. Better economic opportunities and better schooling for their children were primary reasons for the vast majority of Chinese to immigrate to America. Educational attainment remains a paramount goal of Chinese parents for their children.

When interacting with Chinese immigrant students, teachers may expect to see the highest level of formal education in Chinese children from Hong Kong (with a British system of education) and Taiwan. Children from the People's Republic of China (PRC), due to the practice of teaching political ideals rather than basic skills and due to having fewer schools, will have the least amount of formal education. Chinese children from Vietnam, especially those coming here after 1975, will tend to have minimal schooling due to the war that raged on in the 1970s. Exposure to English, especially oral, will likely be highest among the Chinese children from Hong Kong, since English is taught in schools and used within the business world in Hong Kong (Pang, 1995). It is important for educators to recognize that the quality of education varies a great deal within any of the countries mentioned. Quality standards are few and accountability is generally absent. Overall, educational opportunities are highly related to family financial situations.

Korean American

The first Koreans arrived in the United States via Hawaii, primarily as laborers, during the early 1900s. During the early to mid-1900s, Koreans entered with Japanese passports, creating a difficulty in accounting for clear immigration patterns until the 1950s, when Korea was given a separate quota for immigration (Kim, 1978; Lee, 1975). Most Koreans entered through the West Coast and settled in Los Angeles. Anti-Asian sentiments followed the Koreans, much like with other Asian groups, which resulted in many immigrants settling in close-knit communities. The Korean community was generally not visible due to its small size until after World War II, when Korean immigration increased rapidly as a result of federal legislation eliminating the national origin quota in 1965 (Lehrer, 1988). There are currently close to one million Koreans in the United States, with over 30 percent living in California (Bureau of the Census, 1990). Kim (1978) identified three primary reasons for Korean immigration: educational opportunities, economic improvement, and family reunion. It is important to note that Korean immigrants are generally well educated. However, due to limited English proficiency, many are not able to obtain comparable positions in America. Many professionals (e.g., doctors, engineers) take up jobs not commensurate with their educational background or many simply operate small family businesses (Kwak & Lee, 1991). This often leads to a lower standard of living than the family might have been accustomed to, and generally requires that the Korean parent spend very long hours outside the home. Issues of after-school child care and developing family relationships become the unique needs of Korean immigrant families in the United States (Nah, 1993).

The education system in Korea is patterned after the American system, with elementary, junior high, and senior high schools (California State Department of Education, 1983). Although school is not compulsory after elementary school, there is a high percentage of students who enter high school. Education is viewed as critical to financial security as well as a measure of personal worth. Korean parents are fully supportive of schools and generally want their children to attain the highest education possible. These parents have high respect for teachers and administrators. They tend to believe in assisting the school by deferring to teachers, listening and following their professional judgments. Parents' deference to teachers often leads them to expect that teachers will manage their children's education with complete success (California State Department of Education, 1983). It is therefore important to use overt methods to involve parents, such as using in-language material, meeting them in community institutions (e.g., church), and networking among Korean families.

Japanese American

While the first Japanese immigrants, like the Chinese, were also peasants seeking better economic opportunities, they arrived in Hawaii as contract laborers for sugar plantations. By 1900, persons of Japanese ancestry comprised 39.7 percent of the total population of the Islands (Ichihashi as cited in O'Brien & Fugita, 1991). The descents of these early settlers now constitute the largest ethnic community in Hawaii and dominate politics and public bureaucracies (Kitano as cited in O'Brien & Fugita). In the late 1800s and early 1900s, the Japanese were welcomed on the mainland (California) as replacement for the declining number of Chinese laborers due to the Chinese Exclusion Act, but they too quickly became targets of restrictive immigration legislation. The so-called Gentlemen's Agreement between Washington and Tokyo and the Exclusion Act of 1924 effectively stopped immigration from 1931 to 1940 (O'Brien & Fugita, 1991). However, the delay in Japanese immigration restriction, unlike the Chinese, allowed females to also immigrate, which led to a firm demographic foundation for a native-born, citizen generation of Japanese, the Nisei (Tamura, 1991). By the 1940s, two thirds of the Japanese in this country were native born. The acculturation process of the overall Japanese Americans were clearly farther advanced than the Chinese Americans.

Despite a generally hostile atmosphere (i.e., unlike European immigrants, first-generation Japanese immigrants, the Issei, could never become naturalized citizens), the Issei were able to establish an economic niche in the agricultural economy, particularly in California with a growing native-born population. However, rejected by White Americans, Japanese Americans developed their own social organizations (e.g., social clubs, athletic leagues, church groups) within their own community (Kitano & Daniels, 1995; O'Brien & Fugita, 1991).

World War II, particularly the attack on Pearl Harbor, became the central event in the history of Japanese Americans in the United States. Almost as soon as bombs were dropped on Pearl Harbor, the generally hostile atmosphere toward Japanese Americans became brutal. The wartime internment, with property seizure, of all Japanese persons remains as the single most significant event that has affected the psychosocial adjustment of Japanese Americans to this day (O'Brien & Fugita, 1991; Broom & Kitsuse, 1973). The extreme anti-Japanese sentiments immobilized the entire Japanese American community. In response to these pressures, Japanese American closed language schools and Buddhist temples and buried or otherwise destroyed family treasures such as samurai swords, Japanese flags, and family photographs. Speak-English campaigns were started for the Issei, and Nisei were discouraged from speaking Japanese (Ogawa, 1978). The recovery of a sense of community and pride of heritage would be a slow and painful process for many Japanese Americans, especially for the Nisei.

Since most Japanese Americans are native born, their involvement in and expectations of schools are based primarily on their own experiences. Compared with the other two Asian groups mentioned in this chapter, they are more likely to fully participate in home-school collaboration because they are the most acculturated of any Asian American community.

Conclusion

Culture has a pervasive and profound influence on how we all behave. One's culture, however, is *not* based solely on one's national origin. An important contributing factor is one's history as an immigrant. A knowledge of both the sociopolitical histories and cultural orientations provide the context for educators to better understand their interactions with Asian families and students. I hope that a better understanding will lead to meaningful adaptation of curriculum and services for students and families. This chapter emphasizes that culture (i.e., ways of living) is never static. People are constantly evolving due to interactions with the environment. The best use of cultural information continuously modifies existing categories (and stereotypes) in an effort to better understand individual students and their families.

This chapter suggests that the investigative process of Asian American groups begin with an understanding of the notion of *collectivism*. Educators need to recognize social behaviors influenced by this important cultural dimension. Expectations and frustrations can be tempered by teachers who tend to be more individualistic, to facilitate communication. Beyond the broad group-level understanding, educators can focus on individual-level variables, such as knowing the subsystems in which students and families live. The subsystem *context* can often provide educators a good sense of the needs of these families. The prevailing perception that all Asian Americans are successful sadly relegates those less successful ones to inadequate attention and services. Utilizing macro and micro information suggested in this chapter, service providers can work with Asian Americans "one person at a time." This is the best approach to combat the "model minority myth" (Nakanishi, 1994; Divoky, 1988), which prevents many people from seeing each Asian American as an individual.

Case Studies

The following case studies depict families the author has personally interacted with as a school psychologist. Names and circumstances have been altered to provide anonymity. These cases seek to illustrate the complexities and diversities among the three types of Asian American families: *recent immigrants*, *immigrant American*, and *immigrant descendant*.

Recent Immigrant

Nancy, a fourteen-year-old Korean American girl, was referred to me when the family relocated to my school district. She had been diagnosed as having Downs Syndrome and was in a class for "trainable mentally retarded" students in an urban school district nearby. The family had immigrated to the United States from Peru five years earlier. Nancy was the youngest of three girls, all born in Peru. Her sisters were ages sixteen and seventeen.

The multidisciplinary team assessment of Nancy was routine for the most part: She had a significantly low nonverbal intelligence score concurrent with clear deficiencies in overall adaptive behavior. Her functional academic skills were minimal. Her overall language skills, however, were more difficult to assess. Through an interpreter, we learned that although Korean was the primary language spoken at home, Nancy had only minimal receptive language in Korean because her primary caretakers had been her sisters and Spanish-speaking housekeepers. Her parents worked long hours both in Peru and now in the United States running a dry cleaning business.

We discovered that communication within the family was rather complex. The parents spoke mostly Korean and very little Spanish or English. The oldest girl had the best command of both Korean and Spanish and was speaking a good deal of English. The middle girl was fluent in Spanish, had receptive skills in Korean, and preferred to speak English. Nancy's most proficient language was Spanish (approximately six-yr. level in expressive and eight-yr. level in receptive language), and she was now beginning to learn English. This meant that the parents had to communicate with Nancy through her sisters or by gesturing. The fact that all three girls were speaking yet another language that the parents did not understand further complicated the family communication.

The parents were very supportive of all services provided by the school. Our difficulty in serving Nancy revolved around the language of instruction and recommendation for primary language support. We had one Spanish-speaking special education teacher but we weren't sure which language to support, Spanish or Korean? What language should be recommended for home use?

After considerable discussion, the Individualized Education Program Team (IEPT) recommended English instruction and (primary) language support at home in whichever language was most comfortable for her caretakers. Since her primary caretakers were now her sisters, they chose English. We recommended English at school since that appeared to be her emerging language and language of choice. Moreover, when Nancy has to care for her own needs, English will likely be the most useful language for her. We regretted that her sisters did not want to speak Korean at home, thus contributing to further distancing between Nancy and her parents; however, we did not feel we could dictate the language used by her sisters at home. For Nancy's schooling, other functional skills were easily identified as part of her IEP, and she was placed in an appropriate special education placement. But I detected some uneasiness from the parents, especially the mother, during our meetings about Nancy.

Many immigrant Asian parents attribute the cause of a child with disabilities as personal punishment for past transgressions (i.e., from previous generations). Whether or not this attribution is made, there is a sense of shame associated with having a child with disabilities, and no one feels this more than the mother. I believe that this was the case with Nancy's parents. The team tried very hard to be supportive of the parents, the mother in particular; but at the IEP meeting, the parents just wanted "what was best" for Nancy and didn't appear receptive to exploring this issue. Without excellent rapport with the family, we decided to wait before we explored this cultural reaction with them.

Immigrant American

I met Victor, a five-year-old Chinese American boy, through the School Study Team at a different school. He was referred by his kindergarten teacher in November for testing, because he was having difficulties retaining what was taught (e.g., the alphabet, colors, etc.). Victor was new to the school, as his family had just moved into the area.

Victor was born and raised in the United States. He is the third of four children of Chinese parents who immigrated from Hong Kong five years ago. He had two older and one younger siblings. The family has lived in Chinatown since their immigration. Although the parents had finally made enough money to move out of Chinatown, they commuted back to Chinatown to work as a cook and a seamstress, with long and late hours.

The primary caretaking belonged to the sixty-seven-year-old paternal grandmother who immigrated with the family and lived with them. Because of filial piety, she lived with her oldest son's family. As is also common in these immigrant families, the older siblings shared in some household chores and cared for the younger kids.

Victor's teacher was very surprised that Victor was Limited English Proficient (LEP) on the language testing; after all, wasn't he born and raised in the United States? In reality, this is not at all uncommon for young children in many working-class immigrant-American homes, where both the parents and the primary caretaker (e.g., grandmother) came to the United States with no proficiency in English. Additionally, the family had lived in an ethnic enclave, Chinatown, where day-to-day living did not depend on using English. Although both parents had expressed an interest in learning English, their long working hours limited the opportunities. The grandmother had no reason to learn English. All of the children were exposed solely to Chinese at home and in most social encounters, except for school.

A home visit confirmed that the language-use pattern in this immigrant-American family was similar to the previous casestudy with a recent-immigrant family. The older children were using more English than Chinese. They responded to their parents in English, even when the parents asked in Chinese; and they conversed with each other and their friends in English. Although they had to use Chinese with their grandmother, talking with her became less important as they got older. Victor was much more dependent on the grandmother and so, used more Chinese.

This type of combination language use describes the home life of many immigrant families in the United States. Children assimilate much quicker than adults, and language is one of the fastest transition areas because it facilitates the children's interaction with the "outside" environment. This serves to separate families. Because Chinese is less used in the home, natural cultural transmission from one generation to another is sadly disrupted and the adults lose their children quickly to a world that they are not familiar with. This common differing assimilation rate among family members is often exacerbated by families who try to provide a better environment for themselves by moving away from ethnic communities and into suburban communities. The children are then further removed from their ethnic histories.

According to my observations, Victor's difficulties in his English-only instruction class were related to his limited English proficiency. The School Study Team recommended that the teacher provide Victor with more context and visual aids to help him understand what was taught in class, and to give him some time to feel comfortable with English. As Victor is exposed to more English in school and in his new neighborhood, he, too, will lose Chinese quickly, much like his older siblings and countless other children of immigrant families.

Such is the cost associated with assimilation for immigrant families. Many Chinese immigrant-American families attempt to reintroduce their children to their ethnic background and language by sending them to Chinese schools on weekends. However, the desire to be like their peers and the absence of a need to speak Chinese are reasons for much failure of these children to retain language or knowledge of their ethnic backgrounds.

Immigrant Descendant

I met Vivian's parents by invitation of the principal at a teacher conference requested by her parents. Her parents were upset at Vivian's teacher. She was doing a world history month in her (fifth-grade) class and asked the five "Oriental" students, including Vivian, to work together and prepare to tell the class about Oriental customs in their homes (e.g., food, dress, dance). Vivian was a third-generation (sansei) Japanese American, whose parents were born and raised in California, her grandparents were from Hawaii.

When the "Oriental" group met together to discuss and plan their presentation, Vivian felt embarrassed and out of place. She was embarrassed because as the only American-born student in the group, she had never considered herself an Oriental, and she didn't want to be "one of the Orientals." She had not interacted much with these Asian students and her friends were mostly White students. Furthermore, she didn't know much about Japanese customs, let alone Oriental customs!

She went home and told her parents about the assignment and her uneasiness with the group and her parents concurred. They were upset that the teacher had failed to recognize the differences in Asian groups and had simply lumped everyone together. They also did not want to be called "Orientals."

In the last two decades, most people with Asian heritage have identi-fied themselves as Asian Americans rather than Orientals. The latter term was used exclusively to describe people of Asian/Pacific heritage from the early to mid 1900s in the United States. In the late 1960s into the 1970s, there was a great "awakening" among American minority groups spurred by the Civil Rights movement. Asian Americans disliked the term *Oriental* as it carried many negative connotations (e.g., Yellow Peril) and conveyed a foreign and exotic mystique. Asian Americans wanted to be perceived as an integral part of the American fabric. The change of terms was a socio-political move that sought to change the image of Asians in the United States. However, many older Asian Americans still use the term *Oriental* to describe themselves, as do other older non-Asian Americans, like Vivian's teacher.

Moreover, Asian Americans' self-identity in the United States has fol-lowed the predictable patterns of other physically identifiable minorities (e.g., Latinos). As noted earlier in this chapter, physically identifiable minorities must assimilate differently than those who are not "identifiable" (e.g., European immigrants). They must adapt through greater behavior changes than the nonidentifiable and can expect challenges to personal alliances due to "looking different." Since many native borns feel they belong here, there is a tendency for some to not want to be lumped together with immigrant Asians. This tendency reflects a manifestation of self-hatred seen in acculturation patterns. This feeling may well have been a part of Vivian's parents' reactions.

I began this joint conference by restating the (good) intention of the assignment and the fact that it had upset Vivian and her parents. I then proceeded to discuss the differences among various "Asian" groups and the need to treat each separately. The teacher readily admitted not realizing the differences and agreed wholeheartedly to trying to reshape the assign-ment. The use of the term *Asian* was also introduced to the teacher, but I suspect that she has used *Oriental* too long to make the switch easily.

This conference presented an opportunity for the teacher to learn first hand about the multicultural nature of her students, especially the differ-ences within large categories like Asians. The principal also saw the oppor-tunity and as a direct result of this parent conference, scheduled a staff development discussion about the differences within the rapidly changing student population in his school.

2

Penelope V. Flores

Filipino American Students

Actively Carving a Sense of Identity

> There is a true yearning to respond to
> The singing River and the wise Rock.
> So say the Asian, the Hispanic, the Jew,
> The African, the Native American, the Sioux,
> The Catholic, the Muslim, the French, the Greek,
> The Irish, the Rabbi, the Priest, the Sheikh,
> The Gay, the Straight, the Preacher,
> The privileged, the homeless, the Teacher,
> They all hear
> The speaking of the Tree
>
> —Maya Angelou, Poet Laureate
> "On the Pulse of Morning"

At the inauguration of Bill Clinton as president of the United States, poet laureate Maya Angelou was invited to give testament to America's diverse population. Angelou's words soared. Her inspired testament to the American pulse was moving. Some Asian Pacific Americans observed that she named Asians first, followed by many other cultural groups. In one particular classroom in San Francisco, Filipino American children were excited, until one student asked: "Does one think of the Filipinos whenever one hears the word *Asian*?" An active discussion followed. "Asians are Chinese, Japanese, Korean, Cambodian, East Indian, Vietnamese, Hmong, Laotian, Pacific Islanders. Filipinos are

27

Asians, aren't they?" Unfortunately in this classroom, students had little knowledge of Filipino Americans except that the Philippines is geographically and physically part of Asia.

Perusing the research literature of the 1950s and '60s (Aguilar, 1988), Asians were lumped together as a monolithic presence and the Filipinos within that Asian group were scarcely mentioned. May (1987) observed the invisibility of the Filipinos and noted that even the subject of the Philippines as a topic was also a forgotten endeavor. Luckily, new scholars are correcting this situation (Tachiki et al., 1971).

The chapter will focus on two issues. In the first section, the chapter will discuss the invisibility of Filipino Americans to many Americans even though it is the largest and fastest-growing segment of the Asian Pacific American population. When teachers and other professionals have little knowledge of Filipino Americans, they may not be able to understand how difficult it is for Filipino youth to carve a positive sense of self because of the Philippine-U.S. colonial relationship. Research tells us that the schools' hidden curriculum and recent immigrants' experience interact in many unanticipated ways (Gay, 1983; Davidman and Davidman, 1997). Among the many factors that influence how Filipino youth construct their self-identity is through the process of becoming bicultural, bilingual Americans. In the second section, using essays from high school students, the chapter focuses on the complex question, What does it mean to be a Filipino American?

Philippine-U.S. Colonial Relations

The Philippines was *Hispanicized* (from 1521 to 1898) by more than three hundred years of Spanish colonization (Corpuz, 1989) and for nearly fifty years (from 1898 to 1946) was a formal colony of the United States (Miller, 1982). The unique relationship between the American and Filipino people developed during this half-century. There was little national attention to the Philippines as the United States entered the Spanish-American war in Cuba in 1898. One of the reasons for U.S. involvement in the war was to free Cuba from Spanish colonization. Filipino leaders also believed the United States had no intentions of colonizing the Philippines either. They thought that the Philippine nationalist movement led by Emilio Aguinaldo would be given a role in the capture of Manila and the formation of the Philippine government. Instead the United States fought Filipino nationalists where Filipinos were described as "Injuns" and "savages" that had to be "pacified" (Miller, 1984). It was clear that during that war, Filipinos' aspirations for nationhood stood in the way of America's "manifest destiny"; it was a strange ironic reversal of circumstances.

English as the Medium of Instruction in Philippine Schools

As part of the colonization of the Philippines, their schools were patterned after the U.S. public education system. After the guns died down in the battle of Manila Bay, Corpuz (1989), U.S. soldiers set up schools in the barracks. The battle for the minds and souls of the Filipinos simultaneously began. Later (in 1901), a load of American teachers arrived in Manila on board the steamship USS Thomas and were sent out to the provinces to set up schools in English (Fee, 1910). The legacy of that event endures to the present. The language of schools as well as business, the courts, and government is English. An interesting footnote reveals that the first textbooks shipped to the Philippines consisted of all the condemned basal text readers the administration could find in the state of California (Philippine Commission Report, 1901). This first international educational recycling event characterizes what Constantino (1975) termed "the miseducation of the Filipinos." True, the Filipinos learned how to read English as in "A is for apple," "S is for snow"; however, pupils had no idea of what an apple tasted like nor had they ever seen or felt snow in the hot and humid tropical Philippine Islands. Through the following decades, the Philippine curricula had undergone several national reforms, but the premise of English as the medium of instruction has remained.

Filipino Immigrant Students and Language Instruction

Many teachers in U.S. schools consistently place Filipino immigrant students in Non-English Proficient (NEP) classes without understanding the students' schooling experience. Filipino immigrants took advantage of change in immigration laws starting in 1965. Most were college-educated professionals. Their families certainly were no strangers to English. This lack of understanding the historical connection of the Philippine educational system with the U.S. educational system is at the heart of many school-related problems (Azores, 1987).

The Filipino Americans will be the Asian majority by the year 2000 based on the U.S. Census of 1990. As of 1995, demographers have noted that Filipinos in the United States have surpassed the Chinese as the largest group among the Asian immigrants. E. San Juan (1994) writes:

By the year 2000 the Filipino body count will surpass the two million mark. We are rapidly becoming the majority (21 percent of the total in 1992) of the Asian American population of nearly 10 million. . . . This third (even fourth) wave of immigration [was] comprised mostly of professionals and technical workers, unlike their predecessors, the farmworkers of

Hawaii and California and Alaskan cannery hands. . . . Over 170,000 Filipinos enter the country legally every year. This doesn't include about 25,000 Filipinos serving in the U.S. Navy. (p. 206)

It almost appears as if there is an "emotional wall" when it comes to Filipino Americans. U.S. policy toward the Philippines has much to contribute to this phenomenon. Sobredo (1997) traces the U.S. government's shift in its immigration and legal treatment of the Filipinos in America. According to Sobredo, when the Philippines was taken and made into a colony of the United States, the Filipinos in America were considered "nationals." Then with the establishment of the Commonwealth of the Philippines in 1935, the Filipinos in America suddenly became "aliens." The recruitment of Filipino laborers in Hawaii, California, and Alaska gave an economic boost to U.S. agribusinesses, and at this point in time, the Filipinos were considered essential to U.S. economy (Lasker, 1931; Sharma, 1984). Also, as a commonwealth, the Filipinos fought side by side with their American counterparts in World War II while Filipinos were patronizingly called "our little brown brothers."

The invisibility of the Filipinos in America is the product of America's internal guilt for subjugating the country in the guise of "manifest destiny." Historians (Miller, 1982; Stanley, 1974) noted that one of America's unspoken imperialist acts in Southeast Asia was to intervene in other nations' internal matters through the use of military force. Imperialism is at the root of internal guilt: the ironic reversal of circumstances that changed the United States from savior to imperialist oppressor and antagonizing Philippine nationalists. Americans raise an invisible curtain toward Filipino Americans because the United States was once a colonizer of the Philippines (Zwick, 1992). Even when the Philippines became an independent country, it was treated as a neocolony of the United States. For example, the Filipino people act as a colonized people. When the country came out of World War II ruined psychologically and economically, the Philippines voted to amend their constitution to allow U.S. businesses to have parity with Philippine citizens in harnessing the natural resources of the country. This Parity Law, passed in 1946, coincided with the year of Philippine independence (Corpuz, 1989).

In World War II, many Filipinos were inducted into the U.S. Army and fought side by side with U.S. service people at the battle of Corregidor. They trekked the Death March from Bataan to Capas. Other countries in Europe whose nationals were incorporated into the U.S. Army and fought with the Americans were honored by the U.S. government. Not so with the Filipinos. The promise of citizenship and benefits to the veteran soldiers (in the Philippines) were denied again and again. Similarly, the Filipinos in America who were inducted into the U.S. Army and who fought the same war were not allowed citizenship in their own country of birth upon their return.

Alabado (1996) in his memoirs of the Bataan March, decries the unequal treatment given to the Filipino veterans who served in the U.S. Army. World War II veterans (if they happened to be Filipinos) were denied their contributions and accomplishments, while veterans (if they happened to be Europeans) were honored everywhere; just read about the fiftieth-anniversary celebrations of D Day in 1995 newspapers. This U.S. internal guilt tends to be reflected in the Filipino-U.S. relations in the most unlikely places: schools, institutions, and local government, where the Filipinos' empowerment ratio is nonexistent. Promises were given; promises were broken.

The Impact of Filipinos in U.S. Schools

Today, Filipino American students are impacting schools in many parts of California, Washington, and Hawaii. In the San Francisco Unified School District alone, Filipino enrollment figures have grown at an accelerating rate. Many newly arrived students are labeled Limited English Proficient (LEP).

Many newcomers find this labeling pernicious and offensive. Reports however show that some Filipinos turn this labeling process to their advantage (Trueba, 1989). A look at the percentage of Filipinos officially labeled LEPs in schools is instructive. The enrollment figures show a decrease over time. In comparing the 1990 Limited English Proficient (LEP) figures for Latinos and Filipinos, using LEP as an indicator, Filipinos appear to have become more assimilated into the mainstream of the English speaking society. For example, Trueba reported that in 1980 that there were 33,200 Filipinos ages five through fourteen classified as LEP. This figure is 1.4 percent of the total linguistic minority population composed of other language-speaking groups, such as Spanish, French, German, Italian, Polish, Chinese, Greek, Japanese, Vietnamese, Navajo, Portuguese, Yiddish, Korean, and others. In 1990 the number was 35,000 or 1.2 percent of the total linguistic minority population. By the year 2000, the projected number is 38,000 or 1.1 percent. This trend indicates an actual decrease in percentage of LEPs over time. Although the percentage figure is not much, it is clear to see what is really happening. The initial LEP placement was not the right classification for the "newcomers." In contrast, the corresponding percentage figure for Spanish speaking population is 72.2 percent in 1980, 74.8 percent in 1990, and 77.4 percent projected for the year 2000. For the Spanish speakers, the percentage of LEPs increased over time (Trueba, 1989).

In general, Filipinos remain bilinguals of varying degrees. Filipinos living in families comprised of two or more members tend to speak Tagalog or a Philippine language at home. For example, in 1990, there were 168,000 Filipinos between the ages of five and seventeen, of whom 104,000 spoke English at home compared to 64,000 who spoke one of the Philippine dialects/or languages at home. Contrary to the beliefs of some teachers, at home Filipino families with school-aged children do speak English to their children. It shows also that Filipino parents help their children in the assimilation process by consciously making the effort of speaking English to their children at home. Yet, in many school districts where Filipinos are a large minority, the school administrators are unaware or else choose to disregard or remain unaware of parental efforts.

Filipinos
Products of the National Bilingual School Policy

What is generally ignored is the fact that the Filipinos come from a country with a clear national bilingual education policy. Philippine immigrants speak at least two or even three languages: their native tongue, a Philippine lingua franca (e.g., Tagalog, Ilocano, or Cebuano), and English, which is the official language of the school and government (*Manila Bulletin,* 1995). There is definitely a marked difference in how bilingualism is viewed between the United States and the Philippines. In the Philippines, to speak English, Pilipino,* and another lingua franca is a mark of prestige and academic distinction. When a Filipino student comes to the United States, the fact that he/she is an English/Pilipino bilingual/trilingual immediately raises the flag among school administrators and is immediately labeled "at risk." In short, in Philippine schools, being an English, Spanish-Pilipino bilingual is considered an advantage, whereas in the United States, being a Filipino or Spanish bilingual is seen as a disadvantage; unless the other language is German, French, Italian, or Russian. In general, society looks differently against those who speak English with an accent, especially when the accent is coming from a non-Romance or non-Anglo Saxon language.

Bilingualism among Filipinos differs by age cohorts. A look at the figures of Filipinos ages eighteen and beyond is reported by Trueba. In 1990s there were a total of 423,000 Filipinos ages eighteen and older. Of this number, only 64,000 speak English at home leaving 359,000 who speak a Philippine language at home. The data suggest that the older the Filipino Americans, the more likely they are to speak the national language called Pilipino or a Philippine language at home. Sibayan (1978), who studied the topology of the Philippine bilinguals, noted that Filipino bilinguals use Pilipino or a Pilipino dialect within the domains of the home and familiar situations regardless of English proficiency. In a recent U.S. example, in an oral history project of preserving the stories of Filipinos and their experience of World War II in the Philippines, the interviewees (both Filipinos) communicated in English

---

* In this chapter I use the term *Filipino* in referring to the people, and the term *Pilipino* in referring to the language.

throughout the interview. However, in one particular instance when they uncovered a shared common experience—of something emotionally personal—both interviewer and interviewee suddenly switched to Tagalog (Duggins, 1995). This illustrates that Pilipino usage is applied to separate domains and has little to do with the English proficiency of the speakers.

The Hidden Curriculum

Many students from culturally diverse communities experience difficulties in schools (Gay, 1983). The Filipino Americans are no exceptions. The failure and success of Filipino American bilingual depends not only on labels attached to them, but also to their knowledge of the hidden curriculum. Though it is rarely discussed, the "hidden curriculum" is a powerful force in schools.

A component of the hidden curriculum is the labeling process. What happens to students when they are identified and categorized as possessing limited English language potential? The blow to one's self-esteem can be severe when labeled LEP. In addition, what if the student's environment is unsafe, debilitating, and unsupportive? Some Filipino Americans have overcome tremendous problems, but to expect everyone to do so ignores the fact that having positive self-esteem is almost impossible for many young immigrant Filipino youth, given the deplorable conditions under which many are forced to live. The inequities in the society and the continuing invisibility of the Filipino Americans in the American consciousness perpetuates learned helplessness among recent Filipino American youths, especially those who are living in low socioeconomic-status families. Students often internalize that there is nothing much they can do.

A second important question is, What values do the identified students have in common with their teachers? Many teachers of Filipino Americans share very few values with their pupils. When students speak ungrammatically, wear old ethnic clothes, or appear to be less familiar with books and school activities, teachers and other students may assume that these students are not bright (Gage & Berliner, 1991). Teachers may avoid calling on students to protect them from the embarrassment of giving wrong answers or because they simply make teachers uncomfortable. The recent immigrant and LEP-labeled Filipino student may come to believe that he or she isn't very good at schoolwork. Of the many Filipino American students who quit school, the majority come from economically struggling families (Azores, 1987).

It is also pertinent to ask, Who are those students being identified and relegated to slower and lower-track classes? Are Latinos, African Americans, and Filipinos more likely to be assigned disproportionately to remedial classes? These groups' ethnic cultures are constantly being devalued. As Davidman and Davidman (1997) suggested: "Teachers should have increased awareness of the influential relationship between some individuals and their ethnic or cultural group" (p. 3). When the Filipino culture is invisible or, as Fallows (1987) writes, is a "damaged culture," what message does it convey to the student and the school?

Albert Shanker once said that schools socialize immigrant children into the American society, but schools also mirror the inequalities of society. Seen this way, the assimilation process does not come easy for many Filipino immigrants where the environment is characterized by residential segregation, teacher insensitivity, and school administrators setting up structurally self-defeating tracking systems.

Filipino immigrants assimilate into American society at different rates. The rate of assimilation depends on how much knowledge family members have about industrialization. Thus, families coming from the urban centers of Manila, those from the more affluent cities and suburbs, the progressive capital cities, and the industrialized provincial towns in the Philippines, tend to more successfully assimilate into the schooling process. In contrast, the less acquainted a family is with the pluralistic, complex, technologically sophisticated society, the greater the time is needed for assimilation (Bello, 1992).

If there is one phrase that characterizes the Filipino Americans, it is that their identity is "perpetually under siege" (Cablas, 1991), be it in the schools they attend or the community where they reside. This "under seige mentality" among Filipino students may be extremely difficult to overcome. Schools consider bilingual Filipinos "disadvantaged" or "at risk." Like a self-fulfilling prophecy, the students could run true to form and play the part.

The next section of this chapter looks closely into how students who live under difficult environmental conditions define themselves, by analyzing the essays of a selected group of high school students from Seattle, California, and Hawaii.

Filipino American Students' Identity Construction

The Philippine Renaissance Project, 1995

There are several high schools in California, Washington, and Hawaii with large Filipino populations. Many problems arise among Filipino groups. Neighborhood gangs in Daly City, California, are closely monitored in Jefferson High School by Al Sinor, the school vice principal. He observes that the Filipino "barkada" (a Filipino term denoting a socially close-knit group of people who share common interests and who hang out together) does not carry the current violent ethos of the "Crips and Blood" gangs. These barkadas were beginning to affect many Filipino residential communities. My colleagues and I were deeply concerned about the Filipino youth, so in October of 1994 we formed the Philippine Renaissance Project (PRP) (*Manila Bulletin*, 1994). The project objectives were:

1. to provide a vehicle for Filipino youth in the United States at the middle and high school levels to develop cultural and historical awareness of their roots, the Philippines;
2. to inform, educate, and mobilize the Filipino community in support of the education of their children and in becoming a national force for parental involvement;
3. to raise the self-esteem of Filipino American students in their respective school districts; and
4. to provide a vehicle for Filipino American and mainstream communities to develop awareness and interest in the Filipino American culture.

Several high schools formed teams and competed in a local Philippine TV quiz show (Channel 26 in the San Francisco Bay area). The materials for the quiz show covered Philippine history, Philippine literature, Philippine society and culture, and Filipino American history and literature. By the beginning of the school year, school teams from the Bay Area and Northern California, Southern California, Central California, Seattle, and Honolulu were formed. The students focused on Philippine history, culture, and society skills. One of PRP's board members, Dr. Michael Crilly, superintendent of Jefferson Unified School District whose high schools' enrollments are predominantly Filipino, suggested that students who did not want to compete on television also be given a chance to participate. The students wrote essays on the topic "What it Means to Be a Filipino."

The different regions in the West Coast had their elimination rounds by January and February of 1995. By mid-May, each region had finalists. The face-off was held on June 12, 1995, before thousands of people who attended the Fiesta Filipina Celebration of Philippine Independence at Fort Mason, San Francisco.

Finalists at the Independence Day Face-Off

Northern California was represented by Vallejo Senior High School. Central California was represented by Luther Burbank High School in Sacramento. Southern California was represented by John Marshall High School in Los Angeles. Washington State was represented by Ingraham High School in Seattle, and Hawaii was represented by Farrington High School in Honolulu. Besides cash prizes, the top prize was a week's trip to the Philippines, all expenses paid (for the 4–team member accompanied by the school coach and a school administrator). The winning team (John Marshall HS of Los Angeles) were the official guests of the

Philippine National Centennial Commission of the 100th Year of Philippine Independence and met with President Fidel Ramos.

The essay winners earned trophies; their winning entries were published in *Heritage*, a monthly Philippine literary magazine based in Los Angeles and in the *Manila Bulletin USA*, a weekly newspaper with a 250,000 circulation nationwide.

The Sample Essays

Of the initial essay entries numbering 105, one-fourth or twenty-five papers reached the semifinalist stage. Out of this, fourteen entries were declared winners—first, second, and third place (two tied for third), plus ten honorable mentions. These winning essays provided the raw data in this study.

The essays showed insight into the Filipino dream, Filipino American experience, Filipino American identity, and racism. On the aggregate, the collective entries gave much more information than any survey or instrument. The high school students' words were simple and straightforward; their messages rang true, clear, and loud.

One limitation of the data is that the entries were not representative of all Filipino high school students but were written by highly articulate, self-selected students who were confident and courageous enough to join an open national essay contest.

Procedure

A content analysis of the essays was conducted using the *emic* approach: one that represents the perspective of the members of a given group in contrast to the *etic*, which represents an analytical standpoint from outside the particular culture (Pike, 1954). The integrity of the written material was kept and no attempt was made to correct grammar, punctuation, and spelling. These were the best of the students' works and therefore the quality of the essays were of great merit.

Findings

The frustrations, the loss of self-esteem, and the active social construction of identity were seen from the winning essays.

On the American Dream

The beckoning power of the American dream was one aspect of the Filipino family's quest for more opportunities not found in the mother country. Several students talked of the push-and-pull factors influencing their parents' plan to immigrate. Several essays described the hope, anticipation, and hardships of that decision.

(My father) as a young boy heard about a place across the Pacific. A place called the "Land of Everything." The more he learned about this land of freedom, riches, success, and of course more opportunity, the more he worked harder to reach this dream.

It was evident that many letters written by earlier immigrants painted an exaggerated picture of life in America. Propaganda about the "land of opportunity" filtered down to the furthest Philippine barrios. The idea of U.S. immigration was a consistent dream to many.

In December 1971, the dream of my parents was fulfilled. They arrived in Seattle, Washington, with only seventy-five dollars in . . . their pockets and a small suitcase.

This Filipino experience validates the common experience of majority of immigrants from other countries.

Experience with Racism

The students knew about institutional and systemic racism and were able to recognize and articulate their feelings about it eloquently. But it ended right there; statements of facts without any critical analysis.

My dad worked as a busboy in a nearby restaurant, while my mother worked as a secretary. Neither of them worked in their respective fields. My father graduated with a civil engineering degree from a Philippine university; my mother was a credentialed high school math teacher.

Very powerful statements. It meant that his parents were professionals and were underemployed for having no U.S.experience. It appears that high school students are not encouraged to question the morality of such a society that permits the undervaluing of individual personal worth and previous Philippine experience.

One student wrote about his sufferings as a minority. He painfully talked about the racism and injustice experienced by a member of his family member.

Every night before I go to sleep, I always look for and wish on one of the brightest stars in the sky, and dream to become a Surgeon General one day, and not to let innocent people experience what my grandfather did.

He revealed how his grandfather was shot in a race riot and bled to death without medical care. This ambitious senior high school student continues his essay in an altruistic, deterministic, but with an activist moral stance:

> I know that I will become a surgeon one of these days. I may not be able to help all the people in America but at least I could do something to help a few others.

He presents himself as a role model, substantiating the fact that many Filipino youth have none:

> I will become a role model for younger Filipinos; I can embody the message that you can become whatever you want if you put your mind to it.

Some essays rationalized a lot about racism and were ambivalent about it. Indeed, students must learn to live with people of other races amid the self-loathing forced on them by society.

> The United States is the world's melting pot. With its many different races, it is difficult for America to be one unified nation.

> We have many different races including Hawaiian, Samoan, Chinese, Japanese, Filipino, and many others. We do not always get along, though we get along well enough to live in the same community. If Hawaii were not such an "Aloha state," there would be nothing but racial fights.

On Institutional Racism

One essay captured an offspring looking through his father's lenses on the sensitive subject of racism. Many Filipinos would not really know how to deal with it. Many were never able to articulate the complexity of both asserting race and at the same time challenging its categorization of people by skin color.

> My father never faced racism or never even heard of the term. He said that he would describe himself as "a naive young man who just stepped out of college and into the real world. . . . Now, still working with the same company, he says the only way he could really handle racism is just to laugh about it or ignore it.

This parent never made it past the "glass ceiling." This "naive" father, who must have been overwhelmed by the flip side of the American dream, did not have the courage to tell his son there never was a place for him in

America except at home with the family. He just laughed it off.

Other students justified school clubs that tend to segregate the minority students. Students want and need friendly relationships with other people. This is what McKeachie (1961) calls the "affiliation motive."

> Racial clubs do not seem like a good idea because you are separating people from learning other cultures but there is a purpose for these clubs.

It is heartening to note that the students were thinking about race and community building as a necessary first step to dismantling institutional racism in U.S. schools and society.

> It is important to get along with other people but it is also important to still know your cultural roots.

On the Filipinos' Immutable Characteristics

Perhaps because of the LEP labels they receive in school, many Filipino bilingual students suffer from lack of self-esteem. It is likely that as adolescents, they become overly concerned with their differences especially those personal immutable physical attributes with which they are born. In addition, their parents' accents may be regarded as legitimate identifiers of their own LEP categories and a constant reminder of their "inferior" status. This is especially true among the essays submitted by the high school students in Hawaii.

In the Filipino Hawaiian migration history, laborers from predominantly rural Philippines, especially in the hard-pressed provinces in the Ilocos and Visayan regions, were recruited to work in the Hawaiian sugar cane plantations in the mid 1900s. A majority who came had little formal education (Lasker, 1931; Anderson, 1984). Today, high school students in Hawaii still deal with the Filipino accent. They mock or are ashamed of the heritage that produced that accent.

> When I was younger, I was ashamed of letting my peers know that I was Filipino, and the fact that I looked more Hawaiian helped me conceal this fact.

By coincidence, another essay from the same school served as a cross reference:

> One of my friends is Filipino-German-Japanese-Hawaiian. This person is half-Filipino but acts as if he is pure Hawaiian. Sometimes he makes fun of the race by making fun of the accent. When he does this, all my friends remind him that he shouldn't tease the race because he is part of it.

Another student was really bothered by the Filipino accent:

> Many people stereotyped Filipinos as people who talked with a farcical accent. If people asked me what nationality I was then I would tell them everything but Filipino.

The author had a culturally centered, sensitive, and wise grandmother who straightened her out:

> When my grandmother heard about this she was very disappointed. She told me that the Filipino accent is what makes the race so special. My grandmother said that I should be proud of the accent because no other race has that accent. . . . As my grandmother's teachings were etched into my brain, I started to be proud of the Filipino race and I found myself wanting to tell people that I was Filipino.

A majority of the students realized that living in a multicultural world is not easy. They must learn to integrate with the outside environment and at the same time look inwardly toward their own psyches:

> It becomes even more important to remember where you came from, your background, and to take pride in being a Filipino to become a good citizen in America.

The complexity was stated simplistically, revealing facets of the same feeling by several students:

> Don't judge a book by its cover. Don't look at the outside of a person but their inside, at their personality.

> To appreciate other cultures, the initial action must start from within one's self.

> If you continue to learn about your culture, you'll be able to understand more about your background. If you understand more about your culture, you'll be able to relate some cultures to your own.

One student took a hard look at the media and how it influences or reinforces people's prejudices:

> I feel TV and the media have a strong effect on the way people think. . . . Many times we are prejudiced toward a person's race because of what we see in the media or the movies. . . . So, I feel that the media could greatly help to promote peace and harmony in a multiracial community.

A veritable treasure, the essays contained pearls of wisdom revealing feelings about carving one's identity and underscoring the concomitant frustrations society inflicts on its young. It appears that the Filipino high school students in the sample are bothered by the perceived down-grading. The lingering effects of the racism encountered by the early Filipino immigrants still haunt the children of the second and third generations.

Implications for Teachers in Mainstream America

Filipino Americans comprise the largest Asian Pacific American community today. Demographic projections indicate that the Filipino American populations will consistently increase because of immigration and high growth rates. Unfortunately, many Filipino Americans still struggle to be heard. For example, there are few Filipino teachers and professors. Filipinos are not getting equal access to opportunity and empowerment. Hard questions must be asked why this is so.

As one educator stated: "Filipino students in higher education have become among the endangered species" (Cablas, 1991). The leakage or dropout rates in the educational pipeline, from high school to a community or two-year college and on to higher education or a four-year college, has been studied in the University of California system (Hsia & Hirano-Nakanishi, 1995). The findings reveal that the largest numbers of dropouts are Filipinos. As Wong (1994) reports, Filipino high school dropout rates are the highest among Asians. Teachers must attend carefully to the articulation process because they play an important part in the attrition rate. Thus, when teachers criticize, allow put-downs in class, and place increased emphasis on social comparisons, especially in classes with ethnically diverse students, they must be sensitive to how these actions may have negative effects on students.

School districts must address the problem of Filipino dropouts; this must be done systematically and through the development of a well-thought-out plan. An estimated one million Filipino Americans are categorized as LEPs. These labels can seriously damage the self-esteem of students. Needs of students must be examined carefully by every teacher, and teachers need to be trained in how to reach their diverse students (Pang, 1994). Substantial cuts in state funding to teacher training institutions must be reversed.

Another implication for teaching Filipino children is for teachers to understand the social ills of a fast-growing immigrant group caught in a maelstrom of cultural and social problems. Why do more immigrant students drop out of school? Research shows that gangs, drugs, teenage pregnancy, broken homes, AIDS, and falling academic performance are greater problems encountered by Filipinos relative to other Asian Americans (Aguilar, 1994).

Teachers who understand the needs of Filipino Americans must be included in the current dialogue of race. The passage in California of Proposition 187 in November 1994 denies schooling to children of illegal immigrants. On the heels of Proposition 187, the University of California Board of Regents began dismantling Affirmative Action programs in the summer of 1995. The chilling effect was felt on Latinos and African Americans in the 1997 admission figures released by Chancellor Tien of UC Berkeley. Discussions of race in the United States are often cast solely in black and white terms, and often conducted only by Blacks and Whites. Kurashige (1992) writes: "The public view of Asian Americans is a lot like that of Casper the Ghost: we're either white or we're invisible."

Mainstream society constantly ignores the needs of Filipinos. Worse, the Filipinos have, as a colonized nation, decades of internalized racism to overcome. Filipino Americans fighting racism require a positive reclamation of their Filipino roots (as the students' essays revealed). This assertion of the Filipino Americans' unacknowledged contributions to U.S. society can be remedied only if schools enrich their curriculum. The school curriculum can describe how some Filipino Americans view the actions of the United States as imperialistic while explaining how crucial alliances across cultures can be developed.

A sensitive area teachers need to review is criticism of Filipino American parents. Educators must understand the dynamics of the Filipino American family and have more sensitivity to the Filipino American parenting style (Flores, 1994). For example, raising a child to be independent early is part of the American parenting style but this is in conflict with the views of many Filipino parents. Doi (1971) calls this the "dependency theory," where the mother-offspring relations is strengthened throughout the childhood years. The Philippines is a place where family ties are incredibly strong and where families typically operate as a unit to maximize collective resources and to promote collective ends (May, 1996). Some educators continue to characterize Filipino American parents as "uninvolved."

Educators need to find a way to affirm the heritage of their Filipino American students and explicitly critique the corporate values of U.S. businesses and U.S. foreign policy that create only occasional possibilities for many Filipinos to move up the socioeconomic ladder. The Filipinos are among the many peoples in the world for whom education is seen as the one and only key to upward mobility and where education is considered the key to success in all fields of endeavors (Andres, 1987). The paradox is that the families' high aspirations for their children clash with the reality of occupying the lowest rung of society. The average Filipino householders tend to hold two jobs, a necessity for survival in a society where the immigrants are more likely to be underemployed or paid less, given the same educational and work qualifications as others.

It is easy to suggest teaching strategies on how to teach Filipino students, but many of the causes of the problems are beyond the control of the typical teacher. The school structure forces Filipino immigrant students to take courses that are inappropriate and do not allow for their individual needs or level of achievement. This kind of structure breeds failure and threatens self-esteem. Schools tend to be impersonal and overcrowded, have low expectations, and give scanty emphasis on basic skills, as the San Francisco Unified School District Report Cards in 1996 show.

Conclusion

Filipino Americans defy stereotypes and categorization. Because of this, educators need to reexamine their own personal feelings, prejudices, and expectations concerning immigrant Filipino parents, and through them understand the first- and second-generation Filipinos. In 1992 there were 5,195,777 Filipino children enrolled in California's public schools from grades K–12, indicating an accelerating rate of increase from the 1985 enrollment figures. By 1995, these figures had risen. No one predicted in 1970 that Filipino Americans would nearly triple in 1985 and that the next Filipino American generation in 1995 would be younger. Many Filipino Americans see themselves as marginal to the Asian American struggle. Some are struggling to assert their Filipino heritage, often without understanding a larger context in which they might see connections to other issues and communities.

As we approach the twenty-first century, there is growing concern about Filipino American students because educators have little knowledge of how U.S. imperialism and past colonial relations in the Philippines continues to impact their self-concept development. Students need programs that not only assist them in creating positive views of themselves as Filipino Americans, but also foster understanding of the process of assimilation and colonialism. Filipino American students are at risk of falling through the cracks of the educational system because they are often neglected or forgotten. They must be heard.

3

MyLuong T. Tran

Behind the Smiles

The True Heart of Southeast Asian American Children

t was the beginning of the year and the students were excited about their new class. The teacher asked the fifth graders to get to know each other by introducing themselves. Everyone was busily sharing with each other. Suddenly the teacher turned to Kim Lan, a Southeast Asian girl and said, " Aren't you from Indonesia?" Then another student interjected, "Aren't you Viet-na-nese?" Kim Lan was startled and hurt because her teacher assumed she was from Indonesia instead of Vietnam. She felt bad because her classmate referred to her as Vietnanese instead of Vietnamese. "Don't they know about Vietnam?" she thought.

The purpose of this chapter is threefold: First, to move away from the misconception that all Southeast Asians are members of a single ethnic group; second, to describe the general cultural and linguistic characteristics of individual ethnic groups; and third, to focus on linguistic and cultural factors that may create misunderstanding and conflict in interpersonal interactions.

Immigration Patterns of Southeast Asians

Since the end of the Vietnam War in 1975, Southeast Asian people have fled their homelands of Vietnam, Laos, and Cambodia in three waves of refugee exodus. The first wave (1975) of refugees included employees and military personnel of the South Vietnamese government, those employed by Americans in Vietnam, and members of the Vietnamese middle class, mainly professionals such as medical doctors, educators, engineers, and business people. In general they had a high level of education and were well-to-do members of the Vietnamese society.

The new Vietnamese refugees made sociocultural adjustments with few difficulties, and many of their children have since become professionals themselves. As new members of the U.S. population, they advanced economically and contributed to society. Most of the Vietnamese from the first wave owned their own homes and cars, and lived comfortably. By 1990, especially in California, Texas, and New York, they had established themselves and initiated sociocultural activities in order to preserve and promote the Vietnamese language and cultural heritage.

The second wave of refugees entered the United States between 1975 and 1978 (Keiter, 1990). Many were Vietnamese, most of whom were immediate family members or relatives of first-wave immigrants. Laotians, Cambodians, and Hmong, who had been associated with the U.S. military in their countries, immigrated to the United States to escape reeducation camps or the harsh life in "new economic zones."

The third wave of refugees occurred between 1978 and 1980. This period saw the exodus of "boat people" from Vietnam, Laos, and Cambodia who had to stay "in limbo" in refugee camps. Some of these individuals escaped desperate conditions of refugee camps when they were admitted to the United States. The majority were farmers, fishermen, and rural folks and did not have any affiliation with the U.S. government. They came with little or no formal education (Huang, 1989).

In the fourth wave, from 1980 to 1990, the Southeast Asian refugees were mostly released prisoners from reeducation camps who had since joined their families in the U.S. due to the Orderly Departure Program (ODP). In addition, many Amerasian children, whose fathers were military servicemen during the Vietnam War, migrated to the United States.

Geographical and Cultural Backgrounds
of Southeast Asian Students

Southeast Asians came from three countries, Vietnam, Laos, and Cambodia. These countries are located between China in the north and India in the southwest. The refugees who arrived in the United States from these nations are the Vietnamese, Chinese from Vietnam, Laotians, Cambodians, Hmong, Mien, and Meo. These ethnic groups have distinct cultures and languages. Though the Vietnamese culture shares many similarities with the Chinese because China occupied Vietnam for thousands of years, the East Indian culture has had considerable influence on Laotian and Cambodian cultures and languages.

The Hmong are the most recent arrivals in Southeast Asia. From a homeland in Central China, the Hmong have, over the centuries, moved southward to escape persecution. About 150 years ago, they began to settle the mountaintops of northern Vietnam, Laos, and Thailand (Walsh, 1981). Most of the Hmong in the United States have come from Laos (Chan, 1994).

Not only does diversity exist among these ethnic groups, but it also exists within ethnic groups. For example, the Laotians who populate Laos are not homogeneous; they include the Lao, the Hmong, the Khmu, the Tai, and the Iu-Mien. The Laotian languages are also diverse. Therefore, the right question to ask a Laotian, should be, Are you a Lao or a Hmong or a Khmu, etc.? (Luangpraseut, 1989).

Buddhism is a strong influence in several ethnic groups. For example, though the Vietnamese, Laotians, and Cambodians are three distinct national and ethnic groups, many share common value orientations that stem from Buddhism. As a religious ideology, Buddhism dictates philosophical and religious beliefs as well as moral codes that govern Southeast Asian behaviors and attitudes, and shape their world views. Some of the shared values are:

- hard work and education;
- strong sense of collective responsibility and cooperation;
- family orientation; and
- filial piety, respect for authority and propriety.

These values provide teachers with important cultural threads and can be used to better understand the behaviors and motivational patterns of Southeast Asian students.

Implications for Schools

As a result of their socialization processes, the Southeast Asian students bring to school cultural orientations and values that may directly influence their behaviors and attitudes in school: Because their parents value hard work, they expect their children to emulate this aspect of work ethic. In response, the children work hard in school. Earning good grades in school, for example, is a way to show their appreciation for their parents' many sacrifices in their upbringing and education.

At a very young age, the Southeast Asian children are instilled with a sense of respect for the parents and other authority figures. Consequently, they may transfer this value—filial piety, that is respect (along with love and care)—to their teachers, school staff, and administrators.

On the other hand, the concept of collective responsibility may influence their behaviors in their decision making and choosing of a career at the expense of their own professional preferences. Thus, one of the Southeast Asian salient cultural values—collective responsibility—dictates that they need to think of the family well-being first and of themselves second. Individualism in the Southeast Asian values hierarchy is a lower priority. Thus, if a Southeast Asian student would like to become a teacher, but his/her parents want him/her to become a medical doctor, to later financially support the family, a "filial" son or daughter who respect and obey the parents, will comply with their wishes. In other words, in school, Southeast Asian students' qualifications for a specific career orientation might be in conflict with that of the family's career expectation of their children. A Southeast Asian student might be labeled "untrustworthy" if one makes his/her own career choice and, consequently, would bring great parental disappointment.

In brief, hard work, filial piety, and collective responsibility are important values that are interwoven and directly influence the Southeast Asian students' behaviors and values orientation as well as their perceptions of their school and teachers.

Worldview
Southeast Asian Perspectives

People have different worldviews, which are often shaped by culture. One's worldview is the complex set of interrelated beliefs, values, and attitudes providing a person with a frame of reference that influences his/her perception, thinking, encoding, and other communicative behaviors (Samovar, 1981). Therefore, it is helpful for teachers to understand the frame of reference and cultural value systems their Southeast Asian students bring to the classroom.

Laos, Cambodia, and Vietnam share similar worldviews because of the common religion, Buddhism. Values derived from Theravada Buddhism include:

• The unity of all life and the ultimate perfectibility and equality of all mankind.
• Detachment from worldly affairs and from the accumulation of wealth.

- One's responsibility for one's own status in life.
- Self-discipline, humility, temperance, and harmonious relationships with others.
- Emphasis on morality, mindfulness, and wisdom rather than book knowledge.
- Filial piety, i.e., respect, love, and care for one's parents.

Because Laotian and Cambodian cultures have been influenced by Hinduism, they differ from the culture of Vietnam, which was influenced by Chinese culture. Some of the differences in cultural perspectives are:

- The Cambodians derived a formal pattern and deference to people of superior rank from Hinduism.
- The Laotians derived their cultural perspectives from Brahmanism, Buddhism, and Animism, leading to beliefs such as magic and the cult of spirits, called Phi (souls) (Luangpraseut, 1989).
- The Vietnamese social and moral values were influenced by Buddhism, Confucianism, and Taoism. More than the Cambodians and the Laotians, the Vietnamese put a high premium on education.

Naming Systems

Before teachers get to know Southeast Asian students, it is recommended that they learn to pronounce their students' names appropriately and avoid putting their students and themselves in an awkward situation. As a part of the cultural heritage of Southeast Asian students, parents instill qualities in their child by choosing meaningful names for each child. But before teachers learn about the variation of names, it is necessary to provide them with a brief discussion on the importance of the Southeast Asian children's names.

When the children become old enough to understand abstract concepts, the Southeast Asian parents usually explain the reason why their children receive certain names. The parents also try to instill moral and aesthetic qualities in their children by giving them names that bear aesthetic and moral values and qualities, such as bravery, courage, strong intellect, virtue, for males; and modesty, chastity, purity, and sweetness for females, to name just a few.

Also, the children are often reminded that they carry significant and beautiful names, so they need to be mindful of their behaviors as well as their manners, especially for the females—noticeably those who come from upper middle and high social classes. So, a great compliment is given to a girl, for example, when someone says her behaviors and countenance match her name. A male is similarly complimented but worded differently.

Such a compliment not only boosts the children's self-esteem because it makes them feel good, but it also reinforces high expectations the parents have for them regarding good conduct and industrious behaviors in school. Consequently, and like a self-fulfilling prophecy, the children, in most cases, try to live up to their names and the expectations of their parents.

In the United States, however, the Southeast Asian students choose to adopt American names to facilitate their teachers' pronunciation of their names and to prevent embarrassment on both the student's and the teacher's part. For example, in a Vietnamese girl's name, Dung, the *D* is pronounced *Z*, so the correct pronunciation is Dzung not the English pronunciation *Dung*, meaning cow manure or horse dung. Thus, imagine your name Dung (in Vietnamese it means "beautiful countenance" for female and "courage" for male) becomes in English "cow manure" or "horse dung." What an insult to an individual!

The name Tung—an evergreen, a tree that grows out of rugged terrain covered with stones—symbolizing spiritual strength and independent character, is used to name both boys and girls.

Vietnamese, Cambodian, Hmong, and Lao names have several similarities and few differences. Some names have three parts and others have only two. Only the Lao use the same naming order as used in English, where the individual name is first and family name follows.

Most Vietnamese names have three parts: Family name, middle name, and given name, written in this order. It may be confusing for a Vietnamese student to be asked to tell you his/her first or last name. Not only is it confusing to refer to names as "first" or "last," but also, in Vietnam, family names are rarely used in daily interpersonal interactions.

Vietnamese are called by their given name and not their family name alone. In formal circumstances, a person is called by his/her full name or first name preceded by a title such as Mr., Mrs., or Reverend Among friends and relatives, a person is called by his/her name without a title. Older relatives are addressed by an affectionate kinship term and not by their first names (Huynh, 1988).

There are few family names in Vietnam. In theory there are one hundred family names, but in practice there are about twenty common names. Some are: Bui, Cao, Dinh, Dang, Ho, Le, Nguyen, Pham, Phan, Tran, Truong, Vo, Vu.

Vietnamese given names always have a meaning. Parents want to instill moral qualities in their children by giving them names of virtues such as Thao (Generosity), Dung (Courage, pronounced Dzung), or Duc (Virtue). Names for girls usually mean something beautiful, sweet, or fragrant such as Hoa (Flower), Lan (Orchid), or Nguyet (Moon). Names for boys usually mean qualities or virtues such as Dung (Courage), Duc (Virtue), or Nhat (Sun).

One of the uses of middle names is to distinguish a male from a female name. The middle name for females is usually Thi, while there are many middle names for males such as Duc, Dinh, Trong, Van, Huu, and Cat. There is now a tendency among the younger generation to drop the middle name Thi. Consequently, it is now more difficult to distinguish a male from a female name (Huynh, 1988).

Cambodian names usually consist of two parts. There are no middle names in Cambodian. The order of the two parts of a Cambodian name is the same as in a Vietnamese name. For example, in the name Pok Borin, the first element (Pok) is the family name and the second (Borin) is the given name. Cambodians are called by their given name with a title (formal) or without a title (informal) but not by the family name. The family name appears in the full name only. Cambodian first names have a meaning. Girls' names often mean something sweet or beautiful such as Bopha (Flower) or Virak (Brave). Like their Vietnamese counterparts, married women in Cambodia keep their maiden names as their legal names (Huynh, 1988).

Among the Southeast Asians only the Lao people follow the order of American names. In Lao, the given name occurs first and the family name last. Like Cambodians, Lao people do not take middle names. Like the Cambodians and Vietnamese, Lao people are called by their given name, with or without a title, but not by their family name. Although Lao is a monosyllabic language, Lao names are polysyllabic because they are borrowed from Sanskrit. If you meet a Southeast Asian with a polysyllabic (long) name, chances are that this person is a Lao (Huynh, 1988).

Hmong names consist of two parts. Like Vietnamese and Cambodian names, the Hmong family name occurs first and the given name occurs last. Hmong people are called by their given name or by their full names. Clan associations are an important aspect of Hmong culture. Some of the most common family names are Cha, Fang, Ly, Thao, Hang, Her, Lo, Moua, Vang, and Yang (Huynh, 1988; Chan, 1994).

Linguistic Backgrounds of Southeast Asians

The Vietnamese, Lao, Hmong, and Cambodian languages share some common linguistic characteristics, but they are distinct languages differing in their writing systems as well as in their spoken form. One aspect these languages have in common is that they are monosyllabic, except for Lao names. All of them except Cambodian (Khmer) are tonal languages, that is, the pitch, or tone, of the word is important to meaning, and in the written forms diacritic marks are used to indicate tone. Though some of the languages have ancient roots, the Hmong written form was not devised until the 1950s when Western missionaries created a written script (Chan, 1994). Some children and adults in the Hmong community may have little knowledge of the Hmong written language because they come from a pre-literate agrarian culture.

The Cambodian and Lao languages derived from Sanskrit, the classi-cal literary language of India. Like the Vietnamese language, Cambodian, or Khmer, belongs to the Mon-Khmer family (Nguyen, 1972). Like Viet-namese, Lao is a tonal, uninflected language, that is it does not express grammatical categories by way of suffixes. (In contrast, English uses suf-fixes such as -ed, -ing, and -s to express grammatical categories.) Cambo-dian, or Khmer, is not tonal, that is, variations in pitch are not part of the basic sound structure of words. Khmer has a monotone but staccato qual-ity, with a rising intonation at the end of each sentence. Khmer has thirty-three consonant symbols, twenty-one dependent vowel symbols, and twelve independent vowel symbols. Two printing styles of Khmer prevail today: Chrieng characters are wedge shaped and are used in regular textbooks, journals, and official documents. Mul Characters, or cursive, have roundish strokes and are used in transcription of Pali text (Pali is the ancient Indic language of Southern India) (Chhim, 1989).

Lao writing is also based on Sanskrit, but it looks somewhat different from Cambodian script. It consists of thirty-two consonant symbols, twenty-eight vowel symbols, and four tone marks.

Table 3.1 illustrates one of the Southeast Asian languages, Viet-namese. Vietnamese is the national language spoken by over fifty-six mil-lion Vietnamese. It has three dialects from Northern, Central, and Southern Vietnam; basically they are different from one another in pro-nunciation. Dr. Huynh noted that "The situation is more comparable to English which has British, American, and Australian varieties than to Chi-nese [which has mutually unintelligible dialects]" (Huynh, 1989).

Vietnamese has thirty-five segmented phonemes, which consist of vow-els (that can occur initially, medially, or finally), semivowels, and conso-nants. All of the consonants except the allophone p occur in the initial position but few consonants (about ten) occur in the final position.

Vietnamese is a tonal language; the pitch change changes in the mean-ing of the word; it is an uninflected language; that is, verbs are invariable. When necessary, grammatical meaning is expressed by function words. In Vietnamese, the same verb form is used for present, past, and future actions or for first, second, and third person—for example, No an com (He eats rice/He ate rice) and Toi an com (I eat rice/I ate rice) (Huynh, 1989).

Vietnamese relies almost entirely on syntax for expressing grammati-cal relationships and meaning. The two syntactic devices are word order and function words. Since words are invariable, they can occupy almost any position in the sentence. The concept of tense, aspect, voice, number,

TABLE 3.1

According to Professor Emeritus Dinh-Hoa Nguyen of Southern Illinois University, Vietnamese is not genetically related to Chinese, but theoretically it was increasingly accepted to belong to the Vietnamese-Muong group of the Mon-Khmer family.

Vietnamese is a monosyllabic, uninflected, and tonal language. The tones are integral parts of Vietnamese words. There are six "tones," as illustrated in these six words:

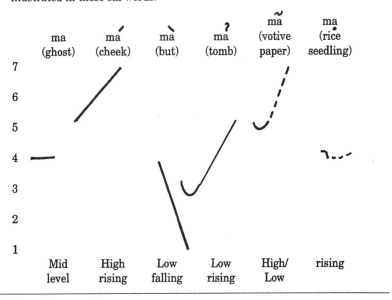

ma (ghost)	má (cheek)	mà (but)	ma? (tomb)	mã (votive paper)	ma (rice seedling)
Mid level	High rising	Low falling	Low rising	High/ Low	rising

(Nguyen, 1972)

negation, interrogation, imperative, and exclamation are all expressed by function words (Huynh, 1989).

Vietnamese writing: Before the seventeenth century, the Vietnamese people, especially the scholars, first used the Chinese writing system. After Vietnam was freed from Chinese occupation, Vietnamese scholars used "demotic language," a version of Chinese created by the Vietnamese to express their ideas and concepts.

In the seventeenth century, Catholic missionaries from Spain, Portugal, Italy, and France used Latinized scripts to represent Vietnamese that became the Vietnamese "national language." Hence, the Vietnamese alphabet consists of twelve vowels, twenty-six consonants, and five tone marks. Alexandre de Rhodes wrote the first Vietnamese dictionary, published in Rome in 1651 (Nguyen, 1972).

Implications

Working Suggestions

Teachers need to be aware of the cultural characteristics of Southeast Asian students because "knowledge that empowers is situated within and interacts with the themes and language of the students" (Shor & Freire, 1987b). The following will examine some similarities and differences in the socialization process.

Similarities:

- The family authority pattern leads to socialization of Southeast Asian children into submission, obedience, and respect for authority figures.
- Good behavior, attitude, and responsibility learned at home are later transferred to relationships with teachers and school personnel.
- The Vietnamese and Chinese Vietnamese share a similar Confucian work ethic exemplified in hard work, thrift, family cohesion, and patience.
- Other common and shared values are importance of family harmony in interactive styles, and an indirect approach to interpersonal relationships.

Differences:

- The students from Cambodia and Laos may come to school with a low level of literacy and a problematic language barrier because of political situations in their countries (Luangpraseut, 1989).
- The Vietnamese have a love of knowledge and learning. A learned and virtuous individual is highly respected in Vietnam, and upward social mobility may be achieved through the pursuit of knowledge and education.
- While the Vietnamese students may be able to function in either a cooperative or a competitive situation in school, the preferred style for the Cambodians, Laotians, or Hmong is cooperation.

Communication

It is said that teaching is, in a sense, sharing common meanings. In order for the teachers of Southeast Asian students to communicate effectively they need knowledge and understanding of their students' cultures and subtle aspects of the students' communicative styles. Although Southeast Asian student socialization processes are not identical, there is one important aspect that is common and prevalent to all three cultures: children have respect for and obedience to authority figures, whether they are parents, teachers, or administrators. In addition, the Southeast Asian students' preference for harmony in their interactive styles, reflects their indirect approach to communicating and relating.

A concrete example may help clarify the supposedly "ambiguous" behaviors and attitudes of Southeast Asian students in general, and of the Vietnamese students, in particular:

Nonverbal Interaction: The Smile

Dr. Huynh commented on this nonverbal language, writing, "for the Vietnamese, the smile is a proper response in most situations in which verbal expression is not needed or not appropriate" (Huynh, 1989). For example, instead of saying "I'm sorry" when coming late to class, the Southeast Asian, especially the Vietnamese, student's "appropriate" behavior is almost always a "smile" instead of a verbal excuse. By the same token, when a student's friend is embarrassed the Vietnamese student will smile. Also, a smile is a sufficient response to a compliment, it may serve as an apology for a minor offense, or as a way of greeting and welcoming someone who comes to one's home. So, when teachers give compliments to the Southeast Asian students in class, it is likely that they will receive a smile in return instead of a thank you.

Nonverbal Interaction
The Meaning of Silence

Silence is considered a desirable trait in the Southeast Asian student cultural value system, and it should not be perceived as a "passive" attitude or behavior. In a verbal society such as that of the United States, "silence" appears to be intolerable, and the art of listening is not highly valued (Pang, 1996). Small wonder many teachers find Southeast Asian students "uninterested," "shy," or even "unmotivated."

At a very early age, the Vietnamese children, for example, were taught to "be seen but not heard," especially when in the presence of people in authority. So, hesitancy or even silence served as a preferred mode of subtle communication or as a response to a verbal compliment.

Hall characterizes the Asian culture as "high context" culture in which much of the interpersonal meanings are shared outside of the explicit verbal messages (Hall, 1976). Consequently, teachers may communicate more effectively with the Southeast Asian students when they take into consideration nonverbal cues as well as the communicative messages that are laden with high context meanings.

When Southeast Asian students need to express disagreement with teachers, they may do so nonverbally with a smile, raising of the eyebrows, or hesitancy. A cultural orientation should not be misinterpreted as lack of motivation, interest, or self-confidence. Hence the "true heart" of the Southeast Asian students may lie hidden in communicative behaviors that are reserved, indirect, subtle, and almost always nonconfrontational.

The practice of "beating around the bush" to avoid a negative answer to a request and the tendency of the Vietnamese student to say yes to every question asked by his/her teacher stems from the preoccupation with "saving face," and is another example of indirect interactive style (Huynh, 1989).

Recommendations for Educators

Teachers' understanding and acknowledgment of the Southeast Asian students' diverse and rich backgrounds is the first step in affirming the student's cultural heritage. But it will be more helpful to the teachers to translate their cultural knowledge of Southeast Asian students into teaching skills. In her insightful and revealing article entitled, "About Teachers and Teaching—Ethnic Prejudice: Still Alive and Hurtful," Pang identified assumptions and stereotypes that commonly occur without either teachers or students being aware of them (Pang, 1988). Some examples of cultural specifics and behaviors that may occur in the classroom are:

- Students may be reluctant to volunteer in class discussions.
- Students may smile when they mean No.
- Students may not always come on time because of different perceptions of time or the underlying assumption that the reality of their lives demands flexibility.
- Students may need more physical space between people when conversing (about one arm's length).
- Students may pay more attention to the other person's feelings than to the content of the conversation. *How* one says something is more important than *what* one says.
- Students may be used to a formal relational style with their teachers.
- Students may want to keep their personal emotions and feelings a private matter.
- Students may be modest or silent to show respect for their teacher.
- Students may learn best by observation and by memorization. Pattern practice and rote learning may be preferred to discovery learning (Cheng, 1987).

Thus, teachers need to understand the cultural characteristics and values of Southeast Asian students, for some may be similar to the American mainstream students, while others are different or may even be in direct conflict.

Concerning cultural value differences and the relationship of culture and communication, Kim wrote, "A central characteristic of Asian culture as it relates to Asian communicative patterns is its basic orientation to the harmonious relationship of the individual to the society. The primary function of communication among Asians therefore is not to enhance the welfare of the individual speaker or listener but to promote social harmony between them." As a result, "the Asian students almost always refrain from disagreeing with persons in positions of authority to avoid confrontation and do not voice negative feelings in order to maintain harmony (Kim, 1978). It would be advisable to avoid labeling Southeast Asian students as "shy" or "passive." They may behave in this way out of being "reserved" and also out of respect for the teacher.

Conclusion

In summary, though a teacher must not use cultural knowledge to stereotype individual students, she/he can utilize culture to better understand, motivate, and communicate with students. In addition, a teacher will be able to minimize cultural conflicts in the classroom and effectively facilitate his/her Southeast Asian students' learning experiences if he/she knows, understands, and values a rich cultural backgrounds that the students bring with them into the classrooms: An educator can

- "walk a mile in his/her students' shoes" and empathize with them once she/he has learned about the students' traumatic experiences in their journey to freedom;
- understand the students' differences in linguistic and cultural orientations that may help lessen his/her frustration in the face of the unknown;
- proactively share with the students different mainstream educational perspectives and values; and
- bring about a crosscultural perspective to create a warm and accepting atmosphere for the Southeast Asian students.

Understanding "the true heart of the Southeast Asian students" means understanding the cultural backgrounds of students from their cultural vantage points without prejudgment or assumptions about cultural differences. A teacher needs to develop empathy and adapt to the various Southeast Asian cultures in the schools with an open mind, a caring attitude, and an honest acceptance of diversity. No amount of cultural knowledge and experience will create a positive and rich experience for any teacher dealing with Southeast Asian students without sincere caring of the students and honest acceptance and valuing of the later's cultural differences.

II

Critical Issues in the Development of Asian Pacific American Children

4

Russell L. Young

Becoming American

Coping Strategies of
Asian Pacific American Children

I n the process of becoming assimilated into mainstream America, the Asian Pacific American child must grapple with the dilemma of ethnic identity. Recent immigrants are uprooted from their Asian or Pacific Island homeland and heritage. U.S.-born children of Asian/Pacific heritage are mistaken as foreigners. They face immense social discrimination and are often not fully accepted as "American." They are expected to assimilate, but face racial discrimination and are rejected by mainstream America and become "hyphenated Americans" (so named because non-White ethnic groups are often stigmitized and not considered Americans).

Like all children, Asian Pacific Americans are faced with the task of coming to terms with who they are. Finding their identity can be emotionally painful because they face the problem of accepting or rejecting their heritage. They are expected to accept being American, and yet often are rejected for assimilating. Asian Pacific American children often lack social role models to emulate. To better understand how Asian Pacific American youth deal with the struggles of ethnic identity formation, the chapter will be divided into two parts. The first part will deal with social theories of ethnic identity. The second part will deal with several social role models that have been created for Asian Pacific American children.

Becoming American

In 1903, W. E. B. DuBois eloquently analyzed the psychology of ethnic identity in *The Souls of Black Folk*:

> The Negro is a sort of seventh son, born with a veil, and gifted with second-sight in this American world—a world which yields him no true self-consciousness, but only lets him see himself through the revelation of the other world. It is a peculiar sensation, this double-consciousness, this sense of always looking at one's self through the eyes of others, of measuring one's soul by the tape of a world that looks on in amused contempt and pity. One ever feels this two-ness—an American, a Negro; two souls, two thoughts, two unreconciled strivings; two warring ideals in one dark body, whose dogged strength alone keeps it from being torn asunder. (p. 3)

Asian Pacific Americans have followed a similar path in defining their own identity in America. There is a double consciousness that arises because of inner conflicts to assimilate into the mainstream while simultaneously maintaining one's ethnic soul. The double consciousness surfaces when Asian Pacific American children realize that the image society portrays of them is not only different, but often of lesser value from their self-perceptions.

Decades ago, sociologists recognized the role of ethnicity in society. Park (1928) believed that the process of civilization could best be studied in the mind of the "Marginal Man" because he represented the interaction of diverse groups to form a new society. Stonequist (1935) further discussed the "Marginal Man" in terms of culture conflict and racial prejudice recognizing that living in two cultures produced dual identities and loyalties. Thus his ambitions run counter to his feelings of self-respect: he would prefer recognition by the dominant race, but resents its arrogance. A sense of superiority to one race is counterbalanced by a sense of inferiority to the other race. Pride and shame, love and hate, and other contradictory sentiments, mingle uneasily in his nature (p. 6).

The Asian Pacific American child must struggle to belong to two or more groups at the same time. However, different values must be resolved within the mind of the child in order to foster a healthy ethnic identity. This can be difficult when negative stereotypes are present in the dominant society, creating a sense of inferiority. These negative stereotypes are perpetuated by a society based on differential power where there is persistent discriminatory treatment toward Asian Pacific American children. These negative views may eventually become internalized (Erickson, 1968; Tajfel, 1978). A sense of inferiority may also arise when a person wishes to assimilate into the dominant society but can't because of racial discrimination (DeVos & Romanucci-Ross, 1975). When a person of color tries to emulate the WASP (White Anglo Saxon Protestant) society, marginality and alienation increase because they encounter discrimination excluding them from social assimilation (Hurh, 1977; Hurh, Kim & Kim, 1978). Ogbu (1987) describes how some African Americans may develop an "oppositional" identity to Whites that is very antisocial. It is essential to replace negative images of self and one's ethnic group (Cross, 1978; Kim, 1981; Tajfel, 1978; Phinney & Alipuria, 1990).

Stages of Ethnic Identity Development

Many theorists have argued that people of color in the United States go through several stages of ethnic identity development in order to rid themselves of negative images of self and ethnic group. Ethnic identity development depends on complex choices people make in relationship to one's own home culture and a more powerful, yet discriminatory, dominant culture (Helms, 1990). Many theories of ethnic identity development arose from the work of the Thomas (1971) and Cross (1971) models of Black ethnic identity development. Generally, theorists believe that one goes from a stage in which ethnicity is not dealt with to one of internal resolution between the conflicting and opposing cultural perspectives.

First Stage
Avoidance

Avoidance occurs in the first stage, where ethnic issues such as alienation, discrimination, racism, and identity are not dealt with. The individual may not have a clear understanding of the issues. An individual has neither engaged in exploration nor made a commitment of identity. Marcia (1980) calls this the diffusion stage. It is also often referred to as the Preencounter Stage (Cross, 1991; Tatum, 1992).

Second Stage
Marginality

The second stage is marked with commitment toward one's identity with little exploration of one's ethnicity. One's ethnic identity is usually based on parental values. Conflict between two cultural worldviews is often denied or not dealt with. Likewise, individuals who have not faced much discrimination may not have had to deal with bicultural conflict (Phinney, 1989). Self-identity may be either positive or negative. Negative views from the dominant culture are often internalized and taken as one's own. For example, an Asian Pacific American child may see his/her highly educated parent working in a field that underutilizes the parent's skills, thus learning that meritorious performance does not always overcome social prejudices. Sue (1977) calls this phenomenon "learned helplessness," where the Asian Pacific American tries hard with little corresponding reward. On the other hand, positive feelings toward one's ethnic group can be fostered from a strong cultural environment (Phinney, 1989).

Third Stage
Self-Identity Exploration

The third stage is marked with active resolution of the conflict between the dominant group and the ethnic group. The individual goes through a period of exploration of heritage and ethnicity. It is marked with experimentation within one's own ethnic community. Experimentation may take the form of language learning, participation in religious activities, or travel to the "old country." There are several reasons why one may be motivated to explore one's roots. Cross (1978) suggests there may be "a shocking personal or social event that temporarily dislodges the person from his old world-view, making the person receptive to a new interpretation of his identity" (p. 17). There may be a conflict of values between the majority culture and those of the minority culture (Arce, 1981). The individual may understand that there are differing standards of beauty (Kim, 1981) or negative stereotypes about other cultural communities (Mendelberg, 1986). The basis of this Immersion/Emersion Stage (Cross, 1991) is the rejection of the negative image imposed by the dominant society through pervasive discriminatory practices. One immerses him/herself into the home culture in hopes of finding a positive self-identity based on congruent cultural values.

Stage Four
Self-Acceptance

The fourth stage finds the individual internalizing and personalizing ethnic identity. The individual no longer needs to experiment with heritage and culture because there is an acceptance of self as a cultural being with ties to both the ancestral and majority culture. A balance is created where the individual sees her/himself as comfortable with multiple roots. The individual understands there is diversity within both the ancestral and majority culture. With this understanding, she/he feels more confident of fitting into society and finding a level of biculturalism.

Complexities of Ethnic Identity Formation

Although there is some agreement that people of color must resolve cultural conflict by going through stages of ethnic identity development, there are varying views of the impact marginality has on one's mental health. Thomas (1971), in describing the Negro-to-Black process of identity development, introduces the concept "negromachy." Negromachy is a form of mental illness caused by wanting to feel a part of society while being made to feel apart from it. The African American remains afflicted until the internal conflict is resolved by progressing through the stages. Sue and Sue (1971) suggest three responses of a Chinese American to marginality. A person who becomes overly Westernized and rejects Asian ways is called a "Marginal Man." A person who is closely allied with his/her own culture is a "Traditionalist." The "Asian American" rebels against parental authority and attempts to reconcile both cultures into their identity. There are no stages in this model.

The disparity in perspective concerning marginality may be explained by the Ogbu and Matute-Bianchi (1986) typology of people of color. Immigrant minorities are people who have moved more or less voluntarily to their host or new society for economic, social, or political reasons. Some Asian and Pacific Islanders fall into this category. Although "immigrant minorities" may be oppressed in the United States, they are "not highly influenced by the dominant group's denigration and rationalization of their subordination and exploitation, partly because they do not consider themselves a part of the stratification system prevailing in their host society; they see themselves as 'strangers' or 'outsiders'" (p. 88). This may explain why many Asian Pacific American children do not always follow the same identity development patterns. These theories are an outgrowth of the civil rights movement where African Americans actively fought oppressive ideologies. An identity theory based on Black integrity rather than inferiority was needed to combat the deficit models of the times.

The ethnic identity theories described would be more applicable to those who are highly influenced by the dominant group's discrimination. These children may not be connected to their ancestral roots or their families may have been separated by war. These children would act more like what Ogbu and Matute-Bianchi (1986) call castelike minorities, where there is a belief that one must circumvent the dominant society's system in order to survive. Ogbu's (1987) "oppositional identity" is an example of a survival skill. These survival skills, often seen by the dominant group as anti social, can become institutionalized cultural practices and beliefs.

Hurh (1980) and Kim (1972) maintain that Americanism (assimilation) and ethnic identity development are not mutually exclusive. Hurh (1980) describes four models of ethnic identity. A person high in cultural assimilation and high in ethnic identity has a pluralist orientation. A person low in cultural assimilation and high in ethnic identity is a traditionalist. A person low in both cultural assimilation and ethnic identity is an isolationist. A person high in cultural assimilation but low in ethnic identity is an integrationist.

Hurh (1980) suggests that people of color who go through the stages of identity development do not necessarily deal with their marginality in a negative manner. Negative images of marginality, such as inferiority complexes or lacking self-confidence (Hurh, 1980), could be replaced at this stage with positive images. Positive images include having a cosmopolitan outlook, objective attitudes, intermediary social roles, high achievement motivation, creativity, and leadership potential.

Generational Differences

One's identity is also closely tied to the amount of contact with the ancestral country, time of arrival, and type of contact with fellow countrymen and women. Hurh (1980) adapted Park's (1950) theory of race relations to the process of establishing a Korean American community. This process has implications to other Asian and Pacific Islander enclaves. According to Hurh (1980), those of the first generation become more culturally assimilated into American society. They may learn the language, behaviors, and lifestyles appropriate to survive. However, there is limited social assimilation due to discrimination. A strong sense of identity based on one's culture serves as a defense mechanism against culture shock and the dominant group's indifference and hostility.

The security of seeing fellow countrymen and women wears off after a period of time. People focus their efforts on building a foundation with certain relatives and friends. Later, an immigrant may even feel an indifference toward people of their country of origin. The heterogeneous nature within culture is more noticeable. For example, some countrymen or women are seen as competitors.

Eventually, one starts to establish him/herself within the community and gains a feeling of success. However, there is a realization that social mobility is often restricted within the community and the "American dream" is still subject to discriminatory policies and practices in society (Greeley, 1971). Limited social assimilation leads one to view the ethnic community as both oppressive and a haven at the same time (Yuan, 1970).

The Asian Pacific Double Consciousness

The Asian Pacific American children must go through life trying to appease many social realities at one time. First, there is the assumed pressure many face to do well in the United States. Success of children gives the family "face." Children represent a future of unlimited possibilities that most first-generation Asian Pacific Americans have been denied. Language, financial, and racial barriers have limited first-generation immigrants and prevented them from attaining the American dream. For many Vietnamese, the hopes and aspirations of the rest of the family rest on the shoulders of the children. The children may have left their parents in Vietnam in order to make a better life abroad (Peters, 1988). Thousands of Chinese children from Taiwan are sent by their parents to complete their education in the United States. These children are often sent as adolescents and may live alone or with friends and relatives that the children hardly know (Young, 1986). The pressure to succeed and not disappoint the family is tremendous. The sense of guilt and anxiety is high. Anger may also be felt by the children who face such tremendous pressure.

Second, many children are expected to succeed in the United States while maintaining their culture. The need to keep the soul or heart of the family culture is important. Many Asians and Pacific Islanders see America as a land of opportunity in the material sense, but lacking spirituality. Children are asked to become Americanized, but on the parents' terms (observing filial piety, yet at the same time speaking fluent English and reading Shakespeare). Unfortunately, many parents, especially those who do not speak English well, become more alienated as their children become more Americanized (National Education Association, 1987). The children are expected to become fully bicultural in order to satisfy the demands of assimilation and upholding traditions. The pressure to be bicultural can be immense and frustrating when there is cultural conflict.

Third, children are faced with stereotypes that limit opportunities for Asians and Pacific Islanders. Perhaps the most popular image to influence Asian Pacific Islander children is that of the model minority. Asian Americans have been portrayed by the media as extraordinary achievers (Sue & Okazaki, 1990). The exaggerated image centers around students overcoming incredible language and cultural barriers to attain and even surpass the educational achievements of their mainstream counterparts.

Like many stereotypes, the model minority resulted from kernels of truth. Many Asian Pacific Islander parents give up everything in their homelands to improve the lives of their children. In some cases, the children do well and go on to establish successful lives in the United States. However, many Asian Pacific American children do not fit into the model minority mold. The image originated from a number of popular magazines (such as *U.S. News and World Report, Newsweek, New York Times, Time*) portraying Asian Americans as extraordinary achievers. However, this portrayal is misleading. Asian Pacific Islander children are very heterogeneous. For example, Asian Americans show not only high educational attainments but relatively higher proportions of individuals with no education compared with Whites (Sue & Padilla, 1986). A bimodal distribution of achievement is found where some Asian Pacific Islander groups (such as Chinese, Filipinos, Koreans, Japanese, and Indian) do well compared to Whites while others (some southeast Asian groups) do poorly (Kan & Liu, 1986). Economically, the successful image does not always hold up because, compared to Whites, many Asian Pacific Islanders (1) live in urban areas, (2) have a higher average number of wage earners per household, and (3) face a "glass ceiling" creating a high percentage of overqualified workers (Nakanishi & Hirano-Nakanishi, 1983).

The model minority image often does more harm than good. If students do not fit the model minority stereotype, teachers may become frustrated or blame the students for their poor performance. The students can internalize these stereotypes and feel unworthy and sense that they are unintelligent. Many Asian Pacific American children are pressured to seek academic excellence or risk losing face and family integrity (National Education Association, 1987). A model minority stereotype may preempt opportunities for Asian and Pacific Islander students to participate in bilingual programs and justify nonaction with youths who genuinely require other types of assistance (Trueba, Cheng & Ima, 1993). The model minority stereotype can have debilitating social effects. First, other minority groups seen as less "successful" are blamed for not being able to do as well as the Asian achievers. Second, Asians become pitted against other ethnic minorities. When the model minority myth is embraced as true, oppression becomes trivialized because it is seen as easily overcome by hard work and cultural values.

Other images of being lazy or too fun-loving can hurt Pacific Island children. Reports of Asian or Pacific Islander gangs has alienated many people from these groups. For example, the Southeast Asian community of San Diego not only has the highest level of academic achievement, but also has the highest rates of juvenile delinquency (Rumbaut & Ima, 1988). This creates misunderstanding in schools when teachers assume that all Southeast Asians can perform well in class.

Fourth, there is often a lack of appropriate role models for Asian Pacific American children. Many schools with a significant Asian or Pacific Islander population do not have Asian Pacific Islander school personnel as positive role models. This is compounded by the feeling among many Asian and Pacific Islander parents that the teaching profession lacks prestige and financial rewards and discriminates against them in the job market (National Education Association, 1987).

Social Roles and Role Models

Many social roles are created in the Asian and Pacific Islander communities among adolescents in their attempt to find a niche in U.S. society. Lack of role models motivates them to find alternate social roles. Having a social role is important in the assimilation process. Often, others of the same ethnicity may be inadequate role models because of a generational difference or lack of Americanization. Those of another ethnicity may take on a gender or career role model, but perceived racial dissimilarity becomes a barrier in being an ethnic role model. Some social roles that Asian Pacific American children conform to are the golden, misfit, obedient, and hyphenated child.

The Golden Child

The "golden child" is expected to conform to the extremely high expectations of their parents and family. The high expectations sometimes take on seemingly unrealistic proportions. Part of the reasoning comes from the sacrifices families often endure for their children's education. Parents will spend money and devote time in pursuit of the best education for their "golden" children. Extracurricular activities (including piano, violin, choir practice), long hours of study, and home tutoring are not only encouraged, but accepted as normal. In many parts of Asia and the Pacific, education is more of a privilege than in America. There is keen competition for promotion from one academic level to the next. Asian and Pacific Island cultures are more group oriented as compared to the focus on individualism in the United States. Hence, the "golden child" brings honor to the entire family when he/she is successful. It is seen as a reflection of the entire family in addition to the individual's achievement. Cultural factors such as respect for education, obedience to teachers, induction of guilt, and high expectations are cited as reasons for higher achievement (Mordkowitz & Ginsburg, 1987). There is some truth to the model minority stereotype, thus perpetuating the golden child role in society. Examples of golden children who have become famous in the United States are ice skater Kristi Yamaguchi, tennis star Michael Chang, and television personality Connie Chung.

The Misfit Child

The "misfit child" follows the path of antisocial behavior. Being a misfit child comes from a lack of well-integrated role models for the adolescents. As a vehicle for assimilation, education has both advantages and limitations. Although Asians and Pacific Islanders may see advanced education as a means of making money or getting a better job (Hirschman &

Wong, 1986), they still face discrimination that may limit opportunities (Sue, 1989). There are many cases of highly educated Asian and Pacific Island immigrants who must take a less prestigious career in the United States because of language, economic, social, or legal barriers. Asian Pacific American children see their parents and others in the communities as underemployed. Their ethnic role models are those that have "learned to be helpless" and accept their fate. This, combined with unattained parental expectations, lead some adolescents to create their own role models. These Asian Pacific American children may turn to peer gangs for acceptance and security (Takaki, 1989). Benjamin Ng, an immigrant from Hong Kong convicted at the age of twenty of murdering thirteen people in Seattle, is an extreme example of a misfit child.

The Obedient Child

Like the golden child, the "obedient child" is heavily influenced by parental expectations. The obedient child is expected to uphold traditional values and be respectful to elders. Parents of an obedient child also want their child to do well in school, but not at the expense of losing their Asian or Pacific Islander "soul." Parents may be aware of the difficulty of growing up within two or more cultures and under various value systems that are often at odds with one another. For example, in many Asian Pacific American cultures it is customary for a son or daughter to stay at home until married. This creates conflict in an American society that values a more independent lifestyle. From an American perspective the obedient child seems spoiled. Traditions, language, religion, and customs may be actively upheld so that the heritage is not lost. Perhaps more important is that as objective markers of ethnicity (language, knowledge of customs) may be lost, it is imperative that subjective markers (self-identifying with ethnic group) be maintained (Isajiw, 1974). Parents may have varying degrees of valuing the maintenance of language and customs, depending on generational differences or ties with the community. However, it is important that the children value being members of the ethnic group. In this way, traditions and customs will be seen as inherently important and will be maintained. To exemplify an obedient child, the author recalls watching a film from Taiwan entitled "The Greatest Love of All." Expecting to see a romantic movie, the author was completely confused by the film until he discovered toward the end that "the greatest love" was the love a son had toward his mother.

The Hyphenated Child

The "hyphenated child" struggles to find a balance between traditional and mainstream values in many ways. Many are as academically successful as the golden child, but also very concerned with the struggle to balance fitting into American society and maintaining one's heritage. Unlike the misfit child, the hyphenated child may have Asian or Pacific Islander role models, yet not be able to identify completely with them. There is a growing concern with the role one plays in society. Often, the hyphenated child may feel obligated to carry on traditional ways and fight discrimination. This may stem from seeing their parents as accepting Americanization at a price of loss of heritage. For example, a Filipino American student wrote of his feelings of both loss and resentment at the fact that his immigrant parents did not do more to instill a sense of Filipino pride. The parents would talk to him in Tagalog until he started to attend school. At this time the teacher told the parents to use English at home. The parents' agreement to do so is still seen as symbolic of backing down to the wishes of a dominant society.

Hyphenated children may fight to maintain a cultural identity because they want to feel proud of themselves in the face of discrimination. They also hope that their parents feel proud as cultural beings instead of blindly accepting assimilation. The energy this child expends to achieve one's goals goes beyond individualized or familial honors and extends to the community. The community might be symbolized by extended family, church, or other social organizations. There is a consciousness that ponders the responsibility of becoming a future Asian or Pacific Islander role model. The hyphenated child struggles with finding a niche in American society that can fairly balance two cultures. This often comes from being the first Asian or Pacific Islander to break into certain domains previously occupied by people of other ethnic groups and being seen as representing the whole cultural group. For example, an acquaintance of the author always insists that the children dress nicely when going out to play because they are the only Chinese family in the neighborhood and it would be a poor reflection on the culture to dress in "ragged" clothes.

Loss of heritage can be especially painful and embarrassing because the student is unable to justify ethnicity on objective grounds (unable to speak the language, for example). The sense of cultural being is based on a subjective feeling of belonging that is constantly challenged. A sense of conflict may arise because of a combination of shame toward home culture, inability to assimilate, being rejected as an American by peers, and discrimination. In order to resolve such conflicts, Asian Pacific American children often actively explore their cultures, especially during the adolescent years. Participation in cultural activities becomes important as a source of pride. The immersion process can be both painful and a relief. It can be painful because children may place guilt on the parents for not actively supporting cultural maintenance or blame White society for supporting an assimilationist policy that considers Asian and Pacific Islanders as inferior.

It can become a relief when a child finally comes to terms with himself or herself as a bicultural being.

With the exception of the hyphenated child, the four discussed social roles could be situated in any of the ethnic identity stages of denial, limited commitment, active resolution, and internalizing. The hyphenated child is described as part of the third stage. The social roles presented are not exhaustive. For example, some Asian Pacific American children follow a path in which they reject their ancestral heritage and become very mainstream. There are also those who face conflicting demands between an Asian Pacific culture and another nonmainstream culture (children of mixed parentage or those that grow up in an ethnic community different from their own).

These models are meant to present several ways that Asian Pacific American children often cope with the conflicting demands placed on them to assimilate by the dominate society versus maintaining their heritage. For the obedient child and the golden child, coping comes in the form of pleasing parental demands first and hopefully becoming acceptable to the larger mainstream society. Problems arise when children are unable to adequately meet parental demands and/or they conflict with the process of assimilating into the larger mainstream society. In these cases, the Asian Pacific American child must go through the third and fourth stages of ethnic identity development. An extreme case of lack of conflict resolution is the misfit child. The misfit child in unable to meet the demands of both the parents and mainstream society. The misfit child may find security and reinforcement for one's identity with peers, albeit often in nonsocial ways.

Coping in Both Worlds

Coping means that there is a psychological movement from being part Asian or Pacific Islander and part American to being full Asian or Pacific Islander and full American. Ethnic identity conflicts are resolved when there is psychological reconciliation upon the creation of self identity.

In many ways, the loss of one's heritage is not the source of an "unhealthy" ethnic identity. Rather, it is the perceived deficiency of self in terms of being a cultural being as well as an empowered American. The Asian Pacific American child will look at objective markers of ethnicity as a measure of how "Asian" or "Pacific Islander" they are. The reality is that there is much diversity within any cultural group, and there are huge variations based on individual, socioeconomic, generational, and geographical differences. An Asian or Pacific Islander growing up in the ancestral country will inevitably be different from one in America. The Asian Pacific American child copes by understanding this diversity and accepting herself or himself as a cultural being. In contrast, problems arise when one (1) believes one's own heritage is inferior, (2) sees oneself as a "deficient" ethnic being, or (3) blames society for the discrimination one faces to the extent that one feels helpless.

Asian Pacific American children discover that they are American with ties to Asian or Pacific cultures. They do not accept that they are somehow inferior or less deserving of civil rights because of their ethnicity. They understand that American society represents a diverse community and nation. They realize that they need not continue to feel like outsiders because America is their home. In other words, using Ronald Takaki's (1989) book title as an analogy, Asian Pacific American children must come to the conclusion that they are no longer strangers from a different shore. They are equally entitled to be called Americans.

In conclusion, Asian Pacific Americans often are faced with differing perspectives on American life from the home and mainstream cultures. Depending on one's degree of internal conflict, social support, and adaptive strategies, they will be challenged to reconcile conflicts encountered when becoming bicultural.

5

Chi-Ah Chun
Stanley Sue

Mental Health Issues Concerning Asian Pacific American Children

Asian American children are often depicted as whiz kids, genius musicians, or computer nerds. Teachers and mental health professionals, as well as the public at large, frequently perceive Asian American children as being well behaved, well adjusted, and high achieving. In short, they are seen as a "model minority." At a quick glance this myth may appear to be grounded in truth. However, the myth of model minority oversimplifies stereotypes that ignore the heterogeneity of Asian Americans. Asian Americans consist of more than twenty different ethnic groups and speak over thirty different languages. They also differ in terms of their migration to the United States. The cultural, linguistic, and historical diversity has implications for distinct social, economical, and psychological conditions for each ethnic group.

The myth of model minority furthermore overlooks the psychological toll that many Asian Americans pay in order to achieve "success." Little is yet known about the mental health status of Asian Americans. This is particularly true in the case of Asian American children. Studies have shown that there are many factors, such as acculturative stress and strong parental pressure for academic achievement, that can place Asian American children at risk for poor psychological adjustment.

It is important that educators be aware of children's mental health issues because such awareness enables educators to identify children who are at risk for poor mental health. Early identification is critical, as it allows for early intervention to take place. The issue of early identification is even more important in the case of Asian American children who tend not to receive the kind of attention or concern that is received by other children due to the widespread stereotype of a well-adjusted, problem-free child and the educators' poor knowledge of Asian American children's mental health status and their risk factors.

The purpose of this chapter is to highlight the mental health issues pertinent to Asian American children. Several questions are addressed. First, what kinds of adjustment and mental health problems are exhibited? Second, what are the familial, educational, and societal influences that promote or detract from their psychological well-being? Third, how can teachers and mental health professionals identify these problems in children? Lastly, what kinds of intervention measures can be used to enhance well-being? Particular attention is placed on the cultural context of the issues, on unique problems of immigrants and refugees, and on intra-Asian differences.

Mental Health Status of Asian American Children

Studies on the utilization pattern of the mental health care delivery system have found that Asian American adults and children are underrepresented in that they use services proportionately less than do other Americans (Bui & Takeuchi, 1992; Sue et al., 1991). Furthermore, those Asian American adults and children who enter the mental health system are more likely to have more serious psychiatric conditions than other ethnic groups (Bui & Takeuchi, 1992; Sue et al., 1991). One implication of these findings is that Asian Americans may be seeking mental health services only after their mental health has seriously deteriorated. Thus, it is simplistic to interpret the low utilization rate of services as a reflection of low mental health needs of Asian Americans.

The literature on Asian American children's mental health is still too scant to draw meaningful conclusions about their mental health needs. Fortunately, the few studies that are available shed some light on the matter. First, some research indicates that Asian American children may have less conduct problems than do Euro Americans (Touliatos & Lindholm,

1980), although some evidence suggests that the low rate may be attributable to Asian American girls rather than boys (L. S. Kim & Chun, 1993).

Second, and contrary to the findings on conduct disorders, studies that measured the level of depression in community samples found that Asian American children and adolescents tend to be more depressed than their Euro American counterparts. Chinese American boys were rated to be more withdrawn and depressed by their parents compared to the American norm (Chang, Morrissey & Koplewicz, 1995). Korean American college students tended to be more depressed than their Euro American counterparts on a self-report measure (Aldwin & Greenberger, 1987). Thus, depression may be a more common phenomenon among Asian Pacific American children and adolescents than among their Euro American peers.

Third, in a community study, Chang and his colleagues asked the parents of Chinese American boys attending a Chinese school in New York to rate their sons on the Child Behavior Checklist. The ratings showed that the Chinese American boys had more interpersonal problems and less social competence than those in the measure's American norm (Chang, Morrissey & Koplewicz, 1995).

Fourth, studies suggest that Asian American children and adolescents tend to be more anxious than their Euro American peers. Onoda (1977) found that third-generation high school students were more anxious and worried than the Euro American high school students. Asian American middle school students reported more test anxiety than Euro American students (Pang, 1991). A higher anxiety level was also found in Chinese American college students compared to students of other ethnicities, for both males and females (D. W. Sue & Kirk, 1972). No information is available on the prevalence of clinical cases of anxiety disorders in Asian American children and adolescents except for posttraumatic stress disorder (PTSD) in refugees.

Fifth, with respect to PTSD, most Southeast Asian refugee children and adolescents have been traumatized in their war-torn homeland, in the refugee camps, and/or on the route to freedom by sea pirates (Nidorf, 1985). Consequently, symptoms of PTSD have been frequently observed in these children and adolescents. Realmuto and his colleagues (1992) found that 37 percent of their Cambodian adolescent sample met the DSM-III-R criteria for PTSD. Kinzie and his colleagues (1989) conducted a three-year longitudinal investigation on the course of symptoms of PTSD in Cambodian refugee adolescents who were traumatized as young children. At time one, about half of the forty-six Cambodian adolescents in the sample met the DSM-III-R criteria of PTSD. Depression, anxiety disorders, and panic attacks were also associated with PTSD in this sample. Three years later, PTSD was once again diagnosed in nearly half of the twenty-seven students remaining in the follow-up sample.

In sum, the patterns of differences in diagnosis and symptom levels seem to suggest that Asian American children and adolescents are not better adjusted than Euro American children and adolescents.

Factors Affecting Mental Health Status of Asian American Children

The mental health status of Asian-American children is affected by a variety of factors. There are general developmental issues that any child or adolescent, regardless of gender, race, or ethnicity, would face in some phases of their development. We have selected those factors that are exacerbated by the differences between the mainstream Euro American and Asian American cultures. Then, there are the factors unique to Asian American children, such as experiences of the children of immigrants and refugees. The factors relevant for these children include premigrational and migrational factors and postmigrational stressors.

Identity Formation

Adolescence is regarded as the critical period of time during which a child develops a sense of who he or she is, separate and independent from his or her own family. Successful resolution of the individuation process results in the formation of stable identity. On the other hand, failure to individuate may result in identity diffusion, based "on a strong previous doubt of one's ethnic and sexual identity" (Erikson, 1980).

Huang (1994) points out that the developmental task of forming a sense of stable identity is unique to individualistic Western cultures. In collectivist societies, adolescence is often not a distinct stage in one's development. Furthermore, individuation is strongly discouraged. Such cultural differences may create a conflict for Asian American adolescents whose parents will often object to their assertion of independence, which is deemed acceptable outside of their home environment. The process of individuation can thus lead not only to confusion but also to a great deal of psychological distress.

The notion of identity is further complicated for Asian American adolescents—or all ethnic minority adolescents for that matter—because of the layer of ethnic identity. Their question of Who am I? needs to address who they are in this multiethnic society. There is a strong pull from the mainstream society for the adolescents to adopt the mainstream beliefs and attitudes which are often counteracted by another strong pull for the adolescents to retain their ethnic heritage. S. Sue and D. W. Sue (1971) identified three types of Chinese American personalities. The Traditionalists are those who conformed to the traditional Asian values. The Marginalists rebelled against the traditional Asian values and adopted the mainstream Western values. The Asian Americans also rebelled against the Asian values but instead of completely discarding them and adopting only the Western values, were able to integrate the two cultures and develop Asian American values. According to S. Sue and D. W. Sue (1971), each of the three personality types has a unique set of conflicts.

Language Barriers

One challenge that almost all Asian American children who have resettled in the United States must face is the task of learning an entirely new language. Fortunately, children who come to the United States at a young age acquire English fairly quickly. However, for children who come at an older age, English acquisition is slower and can be very frustrating (Dao, 1991). Older immigrant children face multiple difficulties because poor English proficiency creates more negative ramifications for them than for the younger children. First, their school material requires more advanced language skills. Thus, these older children encounter more academic difficulties. Second, their interpersonal interactions rely more on the ability to communicate verbally than the younger children. Thus, they are more socially impaired by their poor English skills. The older children are also more aware of and sensitive to the large discrepancy in proficiencies in their native tongue and English. Knowing that they are much more sophisticated thinkers and yet unable to articulate at an age when other people's perception seems to matter the most can destroy their self-esteem, motivation to learn the new language, and interest in school.

A study on Korean American children found a positive association between self-concept and English proficiency (S. P. Kim, 1983). In Korean American children, those with a low self-concept were not very proficient in English and vice versa. There also appears to be a relationship between language difficulties and stress. Increase in English proficiency, however, does not necessarily signify a decrease in stress because the increase in English proficiency can result in a decrease in the children's proficiency in their native language. Many bilingual children are often only moderately proficient in both languages. English as Second Language (ESL) programs for the older children should take these extracurricular factors into account to keep the children motivated to learn the second language.

Acculturation

Acculturation is another major factor that influences Asian American children's mental health. Acculturation refers to the process of change in one's values, beliefs, attitudes, and behaviors to adapt to a new environment (Rogler, Cortes & Malgady, 1991). The process of acculturation can be quite stressful, especially for recent immigrants and refugees who are faced with the task of acculturation in almost every aspect of life (Padilla, 1986). In fact, Padilla and his colleagues (1986) found that *generational status* was a strong predictor of acculturative stress for Mexican American and Japanese American college students. For both ethnic groups, first-generation students perceived greater stress than later-generation students. Such acculturative stress in the face of few personal and environmental resources can lead to poor mental health (Rogler, Gurak & Cooney, 1987).

Several factors appear to play a role in how quickly Asian American children acculturate. Chang, Morrissey, and Koplewicz (1995) found that Chinese American girls become more acculturated the longer they stay in the United States, whereas for Chinese American boys the length of stay in the United States was not associated with acculturation. Age at the time of immigration was also found to affect the process of acculturation. Children who immigrate in their adolescence have greater difficulty adjusting to life in the United States. In other words, the younger the child at the time of immigration the quicker and better the adjustment.

The differential rates of acculturation within the family due to gender and/or age at the time of immigration often exacerbate intergenerational conflict and the cultural gap between children and their parents (Lee, 1988; Uba, 1994). Conflict between parents and children was found to be associated with depression for Asian American children. Bourne (1975) found that Asian American children who experienced cultural conflict were more likely to be depressed. Among Korean American college students, those who had modern values but whose parents had traditional values were more depressed than those whose values were consistent with their parents, modern or traditional (Aldwin & Greenberger, 1987).

Postmigration Changes in the Families

For immigrant and refugee families, several changes often take place after the migration. Due to language difficulties, parents often compromise their authority and become dependent on their children to communicate with the larger society, thus "parentifying" the children (Huang 1989; Huang & Ying, 1989; Nidorf, 1985; Uba, 1994). Temporary parentification can boost the parentified child's self-esteem in the short run; however, long-term parentification can burden the child and change the traditional family structure (Huang & Ying, 1989). The parentified child who is naturally in need of guidance may find him/herself trapped in the position of guiding the entire family. Lack of appropriate guidance and role models for children and adolescents of immigrant and refugee families are implicated in the proliferation of gangs in Asian American communities (Huang, 1989).

Unaccompanied Minors

There are about six thousand refugee children who are unaccompanied by any adult family members. Frequently referred to as unaccompanied minors, these children comprise about 1 percent of the refugee population and are mostly boys (Uba, 1994). About half of the unaccompanied minors have a relative in the United States (Porte & Torney-Purta, 1987). Before coming to the United States, unaccompanied minors have usually stayed longer in refugee camps than other refugee children (Huang, 1989). In the United States, these minors stay with elder siblings or relatives or foster homes and perceive themselves either as a burden or an additional source of income to their caretaker (Chung & Okazaki, 1991). They also report feeling guilty about surviving and feeling responsible for bringing the rest of the family to the United States (Baker, 1982). They struggle to adapt to life in the United States while grieving the absence of their family (Mortland & Egan, 1987). It is, therefore, not surprising that unaccompanied children do not adjust as well as those who came to the U.S. with their parents and are found to be at much higher risk for psychological problems (Harding & Looney, 1977; Porte & Torney-Purta, 1987). Unaccompanied minors frequently report feeling lonely, depressed, angry, homesick, and anxious (Huang, 1989; Uba, 1994). Common major concerns for unaccompanied minors are missing friends and family, problems with foster parents, dealing with the experiences of war trauma, establishing ethnic identity, and becoming biculturally competent (B. Nguyen, personal communication, 1987, cited in Huang, 1989; Daly & Carpenter, 1985).

A study on ethnic matches between unaccompanied minors and their foster homes revealed some promising findings on the adjustment of unaccompanied minors (Porte & Torney-Purta, 1987). Unaccompanied minors who were placed in foster homes of Southeast Asian families were significantly less depressed and had a higher grade point average in school than those placed in foster homes of Euro American families. The minors of Southeast Asian foster homes also reported higher levels of self-efficacy in school and in making friends. They also utilized more active coping skills (e.g., seeking help from others) when feeling sad. For unaccompanied minors in Euro American foster homes, having many friends was associated with a lower level of depression. The customary practice of the social agencies was to place unaccompanied children in Euro American foster homes to facilitate their adjustment to life in the United States. However, these findings clearly suggest that these children fare better in ethnically matched foster homes.

Parachute Children

Recently, another group of unaccompanied minors has been emerging in the United States. These minors are often called "parachute children" because they are dropped off in the United States by their parents. Although it is still a relatively new phenomenon, the number of parachute children in the United States appears to be rapidly rising. Unlike the unaccompanied refugee minors, these children come from wealthy families in Asia and are sent to the United States to pursue higher education. Some of these parachute children are gifted and the purpose for their move to the United States is to receive education that can maximize their potential. However, for many of the parachute children the move to the states is an escape from the extremely competitive educational system in their homeland. Some of these children stay with relatives who live in the United States. Others live by themselves and are unsupervised most of the time, often with a lot of money and time. Because of the lack of parental guidance and support, parachute children are often at high risk for adjustment difficulties, loneliness, depression, poor school attendance, and dropping out of school. The absence of parents or legal guardians in their residence also poses a serious legal problem.

Assessment

Assessment entails gathering and interpreting information to evaluate cognitive, emotional, and/or social functioning. Assessment "gives meanings to the findings within the context of the child's life situation and clinical history" (Sattler, 1992). In school systems, students are constantly evaluated by their teachers, counselors, and/or school psychologists. These evaluations of students have important implications for they are used to determine progress from one class to another, the need for guidance and counseling, eligibility for special education, to indicate achievement, and for other purposes (Sue, 1988). Thus, it is critical that the conclusions drawn from the assessment are accurate and valid.

Choosing Culturally Effective Assessment Techniques

For accurate and valid assessment, culturally appropriate assessment techniques should be administered. According to Nagata (1989), there are several assessment techniques that have been found to be useful in assessing Asian American children. One such technique is conducting behavioral assessments, rather than ambiguous projective tests, because Asian American children tend to respond better in directive and structured settings (Nagata, 1989). Parents can be enlisted to participate in obtaining behavioral data (Kim, 1985, as cited in Nagata). Another useful technique is conducting cross-situational assessment of behavior (Sue & Morishima, 1982). Asian American children tend to show a great deal of cross-situational variability in their behavior. Situations commonly determine their role, which in turn dictates their behavior. For example, an Asian American child who is obedient and quiet in the presence of his teacher, an authority figure, may be loud and aggressive among his peers in the absence of a teacher.

Assessments commonly include psychological testing. An important advantage of using standardized psychological tests is that the findings of the tests allows comparisons of the child's performance or functioning to established norms (Sattler, 1992). However, interpretation of the findings of psychological tests are not simple, especially with Asian American children, because certain tests have inappropriate norms (Saeki, Clark & Azen, 1985, as cited in Nagata, 1989). Thus, selection of psychological tests to be administered to an Asian American child should be done with much care to avoid potential biases.

Treatment

Asian American children not only underutilize the mental health services but are also likely to drop out of treatment (Bui & Takeuchi, 1992; Yeh, Takeuchi & Sue, 1994). Yeh and her colleagues found that Asian American children who sought treatment at a mainstream mental health agency were five times as likely to drop out of treatment after the first session as those who sought treatment at a parallel agency that served mainly Asian Americans. The implication of this finding is that Asian Americans respond better to treatment provided at a parallel agency, at least enough to stay in treatment. Due to lack of systematic investigations, it is difficult to pinpoint what the parallel agencies are doing differently from mainstream agencies that decreases premature termination of treatment of Asian American children.

Initiation of Treatment

The initial contact with the family is critical because of the high rate of premature termination among Asian American children. During the initial session, the therapist needs to establish credibility with both the child and the patients. *Thus, the treatment objectives of the initial session should assist the therapist achieve this goal by giving the child and the parents as many gifts as possible.* Gift giving is providing the client with a benefit (a "gift") from treatment. This gift could take the form of anxiety reduction relieving some depression, feeling less ashamed, or gaining hope. In the process of gift giving, the cultural context and definition of gifts should be considered.

1. Alleviate the child's anxiety and fear about treatment (Gibbs & Huang, 1989): Asian American children may enter treatment with little knowledge about mental health services and feel anxious not knowing what to expect. They may also fear being stigmatized by their peers or fam-

ily members for receiving treatment. Others who have had experiences with the social welfare agency may enter treatment with negative attitudes toward the professionals. Therapists should help clients relieve initial anxiety and fear about entering treatment. If the initial session is conducted with the child and the parents, the parents' feelings and concerns about having their child in treatment should also be addressed.

2. Explain the treatment process (Gibbs & Huang, 1989; Nagata, 1989): It is a standard practice for therapists to explain the treatment process to clients at the beginning of therapy. It is intended to provide a rationale and to alter the clients' expectations so that they fit the treatment process (Sue & Zane, 1987). This step is especially important for Asian American clients because of the general lack of familiarity with mental health services.

3. Set immediate primary goals (Nagata, 1989): During the initial session some primary goals need to be set, based on the available information. Therapists should then allow for the formation of secondary goals as more information is revealed during the course of treatment. It helps, especially at the beginning of treatment, to set culturally congruent treatment goals (Sue & Zane, 1987). If goals go against the cultural norms and practices, clients will either resist treatment or find the goals too difficult to achieve. For example, the goal of improving assertiveness for an Asian American adolescent may be met with strong resistance from his or her parents, which the adolescent may not be ready for. If such culturally incongruent objectives are deemed necessary, then they should be set as secondary goals that will be pursued after the culturally relevant primary goals are achieved.

4. Facilitate the delayed grief process (Huang, 1989): Some Southeast Asian refugee children were not allowed to talk about their traumatic experiences in an attempt to bury the past. As a result, these children were unable to grieve their losses and process their traumatic experiences. Therapists should be aware of the possible denial in the family and help those children process their experiences by allowing them to tell their story (Kinzie, 1981).

5. Establish a working alliance with the parents (Huang & Ying, 1989): To prevent premature termination of treatment, parents need to be engaged in the treatment as partners. The therapist and the parents need to find common ground, a problem that the parents find personally and culturally valid to them (Huang, 1994). This may entail reframing the problem in a way that is consistent with the parents' values and conceptualization of the problem. The sense of partnership in their child's treatment will reduce the parents' concerns or ambivalence about the treatment. The parents will also feel that their authority over the child is respected by the therapist, thus feeling less threatened by the therapist. A

strong working alliance with the parents can minimize the child client's resistance to treatment, whereas a failure to establish such an alliance can result in premature termination, particularly in Asian American families because of the parents' strong control over their child.

Culturally Effective Techniques

Active Exchange

Active exchange refers to the reciprocal relationship between therapists and patients (Huang, 1989). Very similar to Sue and Zane's "gift giving" process of treatment (Sue & Zane, 1987), it emphasizes the need for clients to feel immediate and direct benefits from the treatment. These benefits, just like the gifts in gift giving, include immediate symptom relief, cognitive clarifications, explanation of the treatment process, empathic understanding, and so forth. Active exchange also deals with the pattern of communication in therapy (Huang, 1989). Asian American clients feel uneasy about the one-way communication pattern of psychotherapy. Thus, therapists treating Asian American clients should be willing to reveal some personal information about themselves such as their educational and training background, which balances the clients' problems and secrets to the therapist.

Pacing Disclosure

Asian American clients' difficulty disclosing personal and family problems and secrets is well known. Because of shame and desire to save face, Asian American clients tend to resist therapists' inquiries about their problems and family history (Huang & Ying, 1989). This is especially true in group therapies. Therapists should also keep in mind that disclosure of problems may have different meanings for various family members. Huang (1989) presented a case of a Chinese American family who came to see a therapist for their adolescent son's behavior problems. In this case, during the initial session, the mother and son openly expressed their frustration and anger toward the father. The father remained silent throughout the session. The family did not return for the following sessions because the therapist failed to control the pace of disclosure and the father lost face.

Normalizing the Problem

One gift that therapists can give to the parents of the Asian American child clients is normalizing their child's problem (Sue & Zane, 1987). Normalizing the problem reduces parents' shame and embarrassment and alleviates their distress. Normalizing is more effective when the problem behavior or issue is compared with others of the same ethnic group (Huang, 1994).

Cultural Brokering

Cultural brokering is a useful intervention for cases where the problem of the child client is due to cultural conflicts between the child and the parents, the child and the school, and so forth. In such cases, therapists act as a cultural broker, presenting the cultural viewpoint of the child client and of the parents (Spiegel, 1983, cited in Huang, 1994). The goal of brokering is to help the child and the parents to break the cycle of blame and inadequacy and to "scapegoat" the acculturation process (Huang, 1994).

Culturally Effective Therapy Modalities

Play Therapy

For younger children, play therapy may be an effective therapy. Children find the therapeutic work nonthreatening. It also allows indirect, nonverbal communication for the child without overtly shaming parents (Nagata, 1989). Therapists, however, should explain the rationale and potential benefits of play therapy to the parents at the beginning to increase the credibility of the treatment.

Family Therapy

Family therapy can work well in treating Asian American children (Nagata, 1989). Of the models of family therapy, the strategic-structural model, has been recommended for Asian American families because it focuses on concrete, external stress rather than internal conflicts, teaches problem-solving techniques and active problem management, and helps to achieve concrete, external solutions (for details, see S. C. Kim, 1985). According to S. C. Kim, the goals, processes, and techniques of strategic-structural family therapy are more congruent with the traditional Asian belief and value system, family structure, communication patterns and style, hierarchical interpersonal relationships, and preference for concrete solutions.

General Family Practitioner Model

Hong (1988) proposed that for Asian Americans a general family practitioner approach, different from the traditional family therapy models, might be effective. In this model, members of a family are seen by the same therapist sequentially, often individually over different periods of time, for their individual problems. Thus, the general family practitioner model is not a model of family therapy. In this model, therapy is not terminated but rather temporarily discontinues until another issue develops for the same or another family member. Furthermore, the model focuses not only on therapeutic work but also preventive and normal developmental issues such as "psychological checkups" at critical life events. The therapist becomes the resource person or consultant who provides help and guidance for the entire family.

Final Comments

In this chapter, we have pointed to the fact that the mental health of Asian American children and adolescents has not been extensively examined. However, the available evidence suggests that significant mental health problems exist—problems that are often masked or hidden from the public. The most important task is to conduct more research on the nature and extent of emotional problems, factors that are associated with maladjustment, and the means to prevent and alleviate such problems. We have tried to point to some of the experiences of Asian American children, such as migration stress, acculturation, and language barriers. These experiences are important to consider in the understanding and evaluation of Asian American children. We have also indicated means by which therapists can culturally intervene with Asian American children. These forms of cultural intervention are important to consider in the attempts to provide effective and credible forms of treatment.

6

Kenji Ima
Jean Nidorf

Characteristics of Southeast Asian Delinquents

Toward an Understanding

S outheast Asian communities are proud of their valedictorians and superachievers but this image feeds into the "model minority" myth, which admires Asians as people to emulate and who do not require special attention in schools. This creates unfortunate consequences. Southeast Asians are given limited attention and may "fall between the cracks." For example, there are students who need English language development, but are passed along from grade to grade without language skills for academic achievement (Ima, 1991a; Strohl, 1994).

There is a general picture of well-being and successful adjustment in Southeast Asian refugees, especially in education (Caplan, Whitmore & Choy, 1989; McNall, Dunnigan & Mortimer, 1994; Rumbaut & Ima, 1988). In spite of this depiction, the transition between cultures is not uniformly smooth. Some refugee youth have encounters with the juvenile justice system. We address the following questions: What are the characteristics of delinquent Southeast Asian youth? What are their histories of delinquency? How do they compare with each other, and delinquent youths from White and other minority communities? What are the implications for schools?

Background

After the immigration reform of 1965, the Chinese American community experienced an increase of crime reflecting the influx of new immigrants, resembling earlier times when newcomers who were dissociated from stable social networks sought out companions who could fulfill their needs for identity and security (Song, Dombrink & Geis, 1992; Toy, 1993). The influx of disassociated individuals created conditions for a rise in Asian delinquency (Sung, 1987). How does this characterization of previous Asian communities, in terms of seeing it as largely a phase in the adjustment of migrants, relate to Southeast Asian communities?

The first-wave Southeast Asian refugee has been here only for a little more than two decades, and for the bulk of the second- and third-wave refugees, it has been less than a decade. Associated with the change has been both social and emotional adjustments reflecting the consequences of a war-torn past (Eppink, 1979; Freeman, 1989; Ima, 1991a; Masuda, Lin & Tazuma, 1979, 1980; Nidorf, 1985). Does this rapidity of change and history of war-related traumas foreshadow different patterns of Asian juvenile delinquency? Are the refugees comparable to the older Chinese, Japanese, and Korean communities, or are we, in fact, seeing entirely different communities and consequently different patterns of delinquency?

Among the Southeast Asian Chinese-speaking refugees, especially those in contact with post-1965 Chinese immigrants from Hong Kong and Taiwan, some refugees find association with the new secret societies attractive, especially those who are having a difficult time developing financially and emotionally secure niches in a new country. The prior existence of this network, rooted in Chinese history, establishes a model for not only the Chinese-speaking refugee but also other refugees. Their pattern of deviancy has been at variance with gang behavior found in the African American and Latino communities. For example, the assumption that gangs are territorial, while true for African American and Latino gangs, was not the case for Asian gangs until recently.

We suspect that a similar response occurs for the refugees as probably occurred for previous Asian immigrants—the search for money and security in a new society whose challenges seem insurmountable through the conventional channels of education and work. The youth, especially those who arrive in their postpuberty years with little schooling and few occupational skills, are vulnerable to delinquency. Added to their economic needs are the inducement of excitement and a sense of belonging, though these are often fleeting considerations (Sung, 1987). Our examination of the Southeast Asian youth rests on the theme that maladjustment to the new society motivates many of those youths to seek deviant solutions.

Southeast Asians in San Diego

When referring to refugees, the terms *Indochinese* or *Southeast Asian refugees* are used in their restricted meaning and include only people coming from Cambodia, Laos, and Vietnam while excluding individuals from Thailand, Malaysia, and other surrounding Southeast Asian countries. The refugees arrived in three waves. As Tran described in her chapter, the first wave came between the fall of Saigon and the onset of the boat people (1975–1979). They were primarily Vietnamese and individuals with higher than average social resources such as educational degrees, professional and managerial occupational experiences, and familiarity with urban life. The second wave or the boat people (1979–1982) began arriving after the Vietnamese communist invasion of Cambodia, which precipitated a flow of refugees from Cambodia, Laos, and Vietnam. From Cambodia came many individuals who were fleeing both the Vietnamese and the Khmer Rouge or the Cambodian communists; the war between Cambodia and Vietnam gave many individuals the chance to flee the "killing fields" of Cambodia. This second wave included not only a wide mixture of ethnic groups including Cambodian, Chinese, Hmong, Lao, and Vietnamese, but also a wide mix of persons from diverse socioeconomic backgrounds, especially including those from more modest backgrounds such as farmers and fishermen. These individuals were not only less likely to be educated and to have fewer transferable job skills but were also less likely to know English. In general they were less prepared for survival in the United States.

The third wave (1982 to the present) were affected by changes in U.S. refugee policies. The U.S. government, in collaboration with the Vietnamese government, established an orderly departure program (ODP), which permitted some Vietnamese nationals the possibility of leaving Vietnam as an immigrant rather than as a refugee. The third wave continues in the diversity of individuals in terms of ethnicity and social class backgrounds on top of the changes in the processes of leaving. Many individuals now accepted for admissions into the United States have even fewer social resources than the earlier waves—including education, work skills, and urban experiences. Many refugees have had children who are now second generation born in the United States and their growing numbers foreshadow changes in the characteristics of Southeast Asian delinquents. Nevertheless, this chapter concentrates on those youth who were born in Southeast Asia.

Refugees often settled in areas with lower housing costs. In those areas conflict erupted between refugees and older residents. One area noted for this problem was East San Diego, an area with high residential turnover of persons from all backgrounds. It has a reputation for having one of San Diego's highest crime rates. In this rapidly changing and unstable area is an wide mix of ethnic groups who not only harbor ill feelings toward each other but also seem willing to be physically and verbally confrontive with each other. Associated with ethnic hostility is the increasing level of criminal activities, the daily sound of gunfire, and increasing numbers of youth who claim gang membership. These observations on settlement patterns are important because of refugee exposure to gang/delinquent cultures and racial discrimination. Clearly, many Southeast Asians entered San Diego neighborhoods characterized by urban poverty, crime, and ethnic hostilities.

Methodology

In reviewing the evaluation of Southeast Asian juveniles who were charged with serious crimes, the repetition of the same stories raised questions about pattern of delinquency, especially as their stories reflected similar stresses such as the traumas of departure and the disruption of traditional family relations (Nidorf, 1985). Questions were raised about the representation of these cases since it could be easily assumed that the courts were sending only the most serious cases for evaluation and counseling.

A prior San Diego study of White and minority delinquents described their numbers, types of crimes committed, charges, and their processing through the court system. None of the individuals were identified as Asian, let alone Southeast Asian, but it was clear that the study did have a representative sample of delinquents and formed benchmarks from which to assess Southeast Asian delinquents. We read files from the San Diego County Probation Department that included all Southeast Asian delinquents who were charged with an offense during a given year. We identified all Southeast Asian delinquents who had files for the years 1984 and 1990. Some files contained extensive observations. These reports were psychosocial descriptions and analyses used by the court to decide the disposition of cases. The reports included sources of data, which include interviews with defendants and others in the defendant's immediate social environment, review of police reports, psychological testing when cultural biases may be minimized, reason for referral, background information/social history, clinical observations including intellectual and emotional functioning (cultural values and beliefs that impinge on understanding the defendant's functioning), defendant's accounts of the events, and conclusions/recommendations.

Thus the files offered an unusually rich data about Southeast Asian delinquents in San Diego County.

Since all of our materials are drawn from one county, we cannot make empirical claims about refugee delinquents in other counties or regions but we believe that the patterns for the San Diego refugee population are parallel with those occurring in other urban areas such as San Jose (see Long, 1996). It should be noted that the data include all Southeast Asians who were in the San Diego juvenile justice system during the selected years. Given the data were extracted from files collected from the mid-1980s up through 1990, they contain time limitations and a record of changes among Southeast Asian delinquents since the collection. The strengths of this data are the totality of San Diego Country court records, a panel design that enables us to capture changes over time, and a comparative design that enables us to make systematic comparisons between the four major Southeast Asian groups—Cambodian, Hmong, Lao, and Vietnamese. Thus the data provides benchmarks in evaluating the phenomenon of Southeast Asian delinquency.

Results

The Tam Bao Case

What are these youths like? The case study of Tam Bao (pseudonym) is presented here to represent the experiences of Southeast Asian delinquents. Tam was a seventeen-year-old Vietnamese refugee who was arrested for a drive-by shooting charge. His companion was an older Vietnamese who not only owned the pistol but was in possession of auto burglary tools, suggesting that he was on the other side of the law. Until his arrest, Tam was living with two older brothers (twenty-three and twenty-nine years old) and their families.

His father was a farmer of modest means and his repeated attempts to escape from Vietnam led to incarceration in a reeducation camp. Tam's older brother decided to escape with Tam when he was eleven years old. At the time of departure neither Tam nor his mother knew about the plan and it was only when the brothers were finally at sea that Tam was told of the flight. His brother explained that Tam would not see his parents again but that they were going to a "more peaceful life." The trip was particularly traumatic for Tam—several people died at sea as a result of a lack of food and water; many ships passed by these stranded boat people; and last, but not least, was the attack of pirates who raped the women and beat and robbed the men. After a year and a half in a Malaysian refugee camp, where Tam felt sad over being separated from his parents, Tam and his brothers were accepted for admission into the United States. They arrived in San Diego two years after leaving Vietnam and were assisted by an uncle who was already a U.S. resident and could provide them housing and employment.

Tam's first school was a local middle school where he did very well, receiving A and B grades, but when he transferred to the adjacent high school his grades plummeted. He found the work there harder and lost the motivation to achieve. According to his older brother he fell in with a group of less desirable peers who had dropped out of school and were either working at unskilled jobs or supporting themselves through illegal means. It should be noted that prior to his current charge of shooting a revolver, he was arrested for petty theft and malicious mischief but in those instances the court handled his charges informally, dismissing him to the supervision of his brothers.

Nevertheless, his brother felt that the lack of parental supervision led Tam back into criminal activities. The brother and other siblings felt they were going through turmoil, grappling with survival and associated problems of adjusting to a new country and cultural values. Additionally, the brother had several new children born in rapid succession, leaving him with little energy left over to supervise Tam. Perhaps more important was his brother's lack of sophistication in supervising an adolescent going through the complex psychosocial crises specific to refugee adolescent development, such as working through an identity formation in the context of culture shock. As with many other unaccompanied minors, the culturally approved disciplinary tactics and authoritarian role assumed by the eldest sibling have lost efficacy in the context of contemporary American teenage life.

Tam loves and respects his oldest brother and has wanted to be obedient; nevertheless, the brother's virtual absence from his life has made him vulnerable to the influences of "big brother" figures on the street who held out the immediate promise of a more exciting lifestyle of fancy cars, clothes, and girls. Unfortunately, these "brothers" were more often involved in Vietnamese crime networks. Though he appeared intelligent and had non-disrupted schooling in Vietnam, and his values appeared supportive to social conventions, including obeying authorities, he is a follower and had selected a support system in conflict with his own values. Tam did not present the personality profile of the hardened, criminally sophisticated Vietnamese youth that one associates with Vietnamese street gangs, but out of loneliness and desperation he has embraced them and their behaviors. Tam's conduct deteriorated as he became truant from school, began to affiliate with peers who were not attending school, and started using drugs. He admitted his guilt in the shooting and wanted to remove himself from peer influences. When asked what he would wish for, Tam wrote in English:

"The only wish is when I get out this place I will go to school and after that I will find a job and work. That is the only wish in life and sometime I feel sadder."

The following data support Tam's case—male, detached from parents, affected by the war's aftermath, involvement with other youth in delinquency, and remorseful over criminal activities. Though Tam's case is representative of many Southeast Asian delinquents, the panel data suggests changes among refugee delinquents toward a profile more like U.S.-born delinquents suggesting a theme of acculturation to the new society.

Profile of Southeast Asian Juvenile Delinquents

Let us now examine the data on Southeast Asian delinquents: (1) their background characteristics (ethnicity, age, and gender), (2) their social adjustment measures (English language proficiency and school adjustment), (3) their family structures, and (4) their peer group/gang involvement.

Background Characteristics

From 1984 to 1990 there was a 243 percent increase in the number of Southeast Asian youth in the juvenile justice system. Though the Vietnamese youth represent the largest proportion, they had a lower percentage increase (152 percent) than Cambodian, Hmong, and Lao youths whose numbers increased over 500 percent. Individually their increases were 514 percent (Cambodian), 575 percent (Hmong) and 630 percent (Lao). The percentage increases were not explainable by increasing overall numbers of Southeast Asian youth but rather by their increasing involvement in the neighborhood youth culture.

Another way to view ethnicity is to look at the changes in the relative proportions of each group over time. The proportion of Vietnamese delinquents dropped from 71 percent to 44 percent while Lao proportions increased from 17 percent to 29 percent. Cambodian and Hmong delinquents also increased proportionately but less than the Lao. What are the implications of these observations? Instead of grouping all Southeast Asians together, these and subsequent observations document variations among Southeast Asians in terms of their involvement with delinquency over time. Initially the Vietnamese were more likely to be involved in crime but the other three groups have caught up and exceeded the Vietnamese delinquency rate. More will be discussed below when we examine peers and gangs.

Southeast Asian refugees charged with serious crimes are older than delinquents from White and other minority groups. The latter two groups begin criminal involvement at an earlier age and continue criminal involvement for a longer period of time. By contrast, refugee youths begin their criminal involvement at older ages and leave criminal activities earlier than nonrefugee delinquents. The delinquent refugee youth increase in numbers as they move from grade school to high school, peaking at the tenth-grade level and then falling off at the eleventh and twelfth grades. The age of first involvement in the juvenile justice system probably reflects a period of initial adjustment among refugee youths who obey laws in their initial period of residency but drift into criminal activities as they learn the ropes of American adolescence and the relatively benign punishments of the juvenile justice system. There is a puzzle regarding age. Gang detail officers report an increase in the number of younger Southeast Asian delinquents, which would seem to contradict the above data. We agree that refugees initially are older when they become involved in delinquency but the longer they live this country the younger they are when they commit delinquent acts. The shift in the age of criminal involvement reflects acculturation to the neighborhood and youth cultures.

Most delinquents are males (South & Messner, 1987), but refugee delinquents are more likely to be males than Whites and other minorities. Furthermore, comparing only juveniles who committed serious offenses, there are significantly fewer refugee females involved than females from White or other minority groups. The lower involvement of refugee females reflects the greater social control their families have over daughters versus sons. Though from 1984 to 1990, the percentage of refugee females increase was only 2 percent, not only does the increase portend future patterns but we anticipated a rise in the seriousness of female involvement as the Southeast Asian youth acculturate to their neighborhoods. In the earlier data set, females were charged with nonviolent crimes such as running away from home or shop lifting. In the later data set, females were charged with possessing stolen property, residential burglary, auto theft, auto burglary, and interference with the police—all charges likely to be connected with male delinquents. No female had prior criminal charges and it is probable that they were being used by male gang members; for example, male gang members give female associates their weapons when they enter a party and once at the party they retrieve their weapons. Though refugee females were less likely to be apprehended as delinquents than females from other groups, recent developments signal a small but increasing involvement of refugee females in more serious criminal violations.

Social Adjustments

Of the 1984 delinquent refugees over half needed translators. Among the serious offenders, even more needed translators. In general, this delinquent population had a poor command of English. Though the precise role of English language fluency remains to be determined, it seems likely, given the need for translators, that English fluency remains a candidate factor in exacerbating conditions that may combine with other pressures toward delinquency. A clue for this interpretation emerges in files where delinquent youths comment about having troubles with school, especially over not understanding the language of instruction. In 1990, of those assessed on their level of English language fluency, only 28 percent needed translators. This is a significant decrease in the proportion requiring translators and this fact is associated with their likelihood of being in the United States twice as long as the earlier cohort. The shift of English language fluency also foreshadows changes in the nature of Southeast Asian delinquency including shifting attitudes toward crime.

Using evidence such as grades and reports on school behavior, we estimated the school adjustment by weighting the numbers and severity of reported difficulties. Approximately 72 percent were having school troubles, despite the generally positive image of refugee youths in schools. Among those charged with serious crimes, 82 percent had poor adjustments. A Vietnamese youth counselor in Orange County, Vy Do (personal communication), estimates that only 40 percent are experiencing school troubles. If this estimate is confirmed with larger and more systematic data files, then our inference that school adjustment is a factor in refugee delinquency will be supported. Surely, this profile of refugee delinquents reveals school adjustment is a primary problem. In the Tam Bao case, school difficulties began in the late middle or junior high school level, which suggests that school troubles may begin at the onset of adolescence or shortly thereafter.

Some suggest that school troubles and delinquency are closely connected among all groups, including Whites and other minorities; however, we suspect that though there may be a general pattern across ethnic groups, the specific meanings and the dynamics of how they are interconnected have important implications. Even within the refugee population, delinquency patterns and school troubles differ between the different groups. Some Vietnamese youth, especially males who are "detached minors," were under great pressure to succeed in schools because of their responsibility to be successful in America so they could help their parents in Vietnam. Thus the psychosocial/psychocultural dynamics for refugee youth are in many ways unique and call for understanding of that uniqueness as a basis for more effective intervention than under the auspices of a generalized assumption that school failure and delinquency are "naturally" linked.

Family

Delinquent refugee youth were more likely to live with both natural parents, less likely to live with single parents, and more likely to live without natural parents than White and other minority delinquents. However, the interpretation of what constitutes "disrupted" home settings varies between groups. For example, American-born persons may perceive single-parent households as normal, whereas refugees view single-parent or household without both parents as disrupted. Over half of delinquent refugees come from such households.

Although many Vietnamese delinquents fell within the category of "unaccompanied" status, a number were living with a widowed or divorced parent, or a surrogate parent (for example, "aunt") at the time of arrest. The living situation that best typified the unaccompanied youth was one where the youth was living with an older sibling (a brother or sister in his/her twenties) who had been officially designated by both the authorities and the family as guardian. This sibling was more than likely working long hours at a relatively menial job and had neither the time nor the experience to provide appropriate guidance or nurturing. The relative absence of emotional support and social control in this familial context created the propensity for the youth to seek an alternative family.

It is sometimes uncertain who the "real" guardian is; a youngster may have been sold to a distant relative or even a stranger for money in exchange for the promise of having the youngster do household chores as a servant, or as becoming an additional welfare source. Thus, a so-called aunt having no blood ties or emotional bond to the youngster may treat him/her in a formal fashion or even in an abusive manner. In a majority of clinical interviews, unaccompanied youths reported being directed by older, more criminally oriented adults, sometimes called "master." These youth, frequently with histories of petty thefts, had fallen prey to their more manipulative elders. Frequently they had been on the fringe of more serious deviants, for a period of time spending more time away from home, and seduced into relationships with adults who held out the promise of a more glamorous life, of material possessions (cars, jewelry, fancy clothing), and girl friends (Long, 1996).

While there were few Lao youths who fit this portrait of the unaccompanied youth since the most of them lived with both parents, nevertheless there was an increase in the number of Lao youths encountering troubles with the law. Most Lao delinquents came from intact families; however, in these homes, parents felt helpless, weak, and ineffectual as disciplinarians. Lao parents reported that their traditional methods of physical discipline were considered unlawful in this country and, as a result, they saw themselves without alternative disciplinary tools. Lao youths might be described as compliant with authority, influenced by peers, often assuming the overt physical characteristics in dress and behavior of deviant youth in neighborhoods and school settings of whichever ethnic group dominates.

Nearly half of serious offenders were unaccompanied—a finding that reinforces the inference that unaccompanied status increases being at risk of delinquency. Although we are cognizant of the possibility that some, perhaps most, unaccompanied youth were not delinquents, and, depending on household situations as well as personal factors, that they were able to successfully adjust, nevertheless, the statistical probability of success for youths who are detached minors was less than that for youths who were accompanied. Naturally, success is also contingent on background human resources as well as adaptive resources in this country. Our data are insufficient to produce a tight statistical comparison between delinquent and nondelinquent youth and their likelihood of unaccompanied status; therefore our conclusion is tentative though it is one that strongly corresponds to case materials. In short, the refugee experience does create difficult adjustment issues, sometimes leading to delinquency.

Peer Groups and Gangs

Refugee youths, especially those involved in serious offenses, were more likely to be associated with peers than were White and other minority serious offenders. This tendency toward collective action is definitely a factor of significant proportion in refugee delinquents.

For the most part, refugee peer groups did not resemble traditional African American and Latino gangs, which are characterized as having territory, names, symbols, special clothing, and permanence. On the contrary, their groups were very fluid, nonterritorial, often without symbols or special names. Nevertheless, though the files do not reveal tendency toward "expressive" crimes, in almost all of the face-to-face interviews, delinquents were preoccupied with saving face or honor and thus would initiate aggressive acts or brandish weapons against those whom they interpret to have humiliated them or toward those whom they perceive to have the potential for degrading them. The initial introduction to aggressive acts occurred in middle or junior high school where the Southeast Asian youth experience physical and verbal abuse from nonrefugee youth and in return respond with physical retaliation. Because many were smaller than nonrefugees, they frequently sought to protect themselves with weapons such as knives and guns. As one youth stated, "we are not as big as the Americans but they know not to mess with us because they know we carry guns."

Associated with peers was the increasing importance of gangs. Refugee youths, especially those involved in serious offenses, were more likely to be associated with gangs than White and other minority serious offenders. This fact corresponds to case materials that revealed a striking likelihood of associating with peers beyond what one expects of other youths. In 1984, 16 percent of refugee delinquents were officially labeled as gang members versus less than 1 percent among whites and 16 percent of other minority delinquents. However by 1990, refugee delinquents officially designated as gang members increased to 37 percent though almost double that percent were suspected of gang affiliation. Though every gang had a mixed membership, crossing Southeast Asian group lines, each was associated predominantly with one ethnic group. There was a striking underrepresentation of Vietnamese youth in gangs—26 percent of Vietnamese delinquents were officially identified as gang members versus the substantially higher percentages among the other three refugee groups (60 percent of the Lao, 57 percent of the Hmong, and 61 percent of the Khmer or Cambodians). This documents a significant difference within Southeast Asian delinquents and suggests the importance of both cultural and social differences among them.

Refugee youth were more likely to have companions when they were charged with a crime—88 percent were in the company of other youths while 62 percent of White and 64 percent of other minority delinquents had companions. What is even more striking is that 48 percent of refugee youth were with three or more companions when charged versus only 14 percent of White and 15 percent of other minority delinquents. These observations document the more collective nature of refugee delinquency and the greater importance of gangs among refugee youth. There was also a shift toward the African American and Latino gang models (using formal gang names, claiming territory, wearing gang markers, and identifying self as a gang member), yet the shift varied by ethnic group. The Vietnamese were less inclined to adopt those gang models than the Hmong, Khmer, and Lao youth, perhaps in large part because they are more likely to follow their more traditional emphasis on secrecy linked to adult criminals. The other three groups were less likely to have supervising adult criminals who provided money and organization linked to secrecy. Instead they were more inclined to adopt the culture of gangs they saw in their neighborhoods. Nevertheless, the overall refugee portrait is one of collective versus individual delinquency.

Criminal Histories

Sixteen percent of refugee delinquents had a prior arrest history at the time of the study's identification of a first arrest by police during the study year. By contrast, White and other minority delinquents were more likely to have had prior records—65 percent of the Whites and 69 percent of other minorities. Thus Southeast Asian refugees were less experienced with crime and the juvenile justice system. In part, their lessor criminal history was explained by their newcomer status, not having the same number of years of residency in the United States and hence less time and opportunity to commit crime. About 28 percent of the refugees were charged with serious offenses, a rate half of that of White and minority delinquents. Furthermore, they were half as likely to be charged with crimes against persons such as assault with a deadly weapon than other minority delinquents. In short refugee youths were for the most part involved in minor crimes, and when they were involved with serious crimes, they were more like White youth in their proclivity to be involved in property crimes rather than crimes against persons. However that has changed to reflect increasing numbers of weapons and personal violence charges. They have been in the process of learning the ropes of committing more serious criminal violations.

Finally, on the whole, refugees were more likely to be viewed as having good attitudes toward authority by the arresting police officer. Thus, when they are caught, they were more likely to act remorseful and to deferentially acknowledge the legitimacy of law enforcement authorities, especially as indicated by their "good attitude" rating by officers. This respect and deference for authority has been decreasing as the youth acculturate to American standards, especially within juvenile incarceration units, where they are learning to defy authority.

Implications and Conclusions

Though the above data are now dated, they do capture the changing trend among Southeast Asian delinquents. As noted above, from 1984 to 1990, the number of Southeast Asian juvenile offenders increased by 243 percent though the general population of Southeast Asians has increased by less than 25 percent in the same years. Compared to African Americans and Latinos, Southeast Asian delinquents were still more likely to commit crimes against property than against persons, more likely to commit crime for financial gain rather than for "kicks." They were likely to be involved in burglary and car theft, frequently for accessories and parts that can be sold to chop shops. While their crimes were more likely to be "instrumental" rather than "expressive," recent developments show an upturn in expressive ones, especially since gang-related homicides reflect not only crimes against persons but also ones that show a display of power. About 40 percent of the reported crimes are now weapons related. This is a change. Tragically, gang-related homicides among Southeast Asians have become all too commonplace. Before 1990, there were no Cambodian gang-related homicides but in that year there were four Cambodian victims of gang-related homicides. Then about a third of all gang-related homicides in San Diego involved Southeast Asian gang members even though they constituted less than 6 percent of all documented gang members in San Diego. Why had this happened? Though the main explanation seems to be one of responding to intimidation and physical abuse by other youths, they have also increasingly adapted the attitudes of other youths in their neighborhoods.

Ironically, Southeast Asian delinquents have become increasingly more like other American minority delinquent youth in terms of violence and gang-related behaviors. The power of the social context is surely striking in the celebration of drugs and violence. "Gang bangers" have become role models for many youth, and memories of the past, of being refugees, of having origins in Southeast Asia, seemed to be increasingly forgotten. Everyday life and survival on the streets of America dominates the preoccupation of these youth. The dynamics of change also reflects the problems of youth juggling conflicting cultures and the struggles to make successful adaptations to this country. The novelty of being newcomers has worn off and indeed the previously identified problem of not knowing the English language has become a secondary issue. Whereas earlier the majority of Southeast Asian delinquents were identified as having troubles with the English language, now, most speak a passable English and even fewer require a translator. Increasingly Southeast Asian youth cross ethnic boundaries as reflected in gangs having members who are Cambodian, Lao, Hmong, and Vietnamese. There are even members from non-Southeast Asian backgrounds such as Korean, African American, and Filipino. In mixed ethnic gangs, English becomes the language of discourse since it is the only common language. The streets of San Diego have fostered yet another group of delinquents and gangsters who seem all too ready to use violence to settle even minor disputes.

The Tam Bao case study represented the profile of Southeast Asian delinquents, from the 1980s—male, detached from parents and weak home support, traumatized by the war and its aftermath, involvement with delinquency in the late junior high school stage, vulnerable to delinquent peer group, relatively minor crime history and remorseful over criminal activities. Into the 1990s, Southeast Asian delinquents, though similar, show marked changes toward more serious criminal involvement. Although their involvement with delinquency for the most part had been on the "light" side as reflected in having fewer prior charges, lower rates of recidivism, less serious histories of crime involvement, more positive attitudes toward authority and rehabilitation and low relative drug use, this pattern is changing toward criminal violations characteristic of American-born delinquents, especially those with gang association. Some might explain this by an acculturation theory whereby refugee youths shed their home values in exchange for the street values found in urban America, but as we have observed, this theory is excessively general and does not take into account the differing backgrounds and circumstances of refugee youths. Surely it involves an acculturation to America's underclass society, especially survival strategies of youth in urbanized areas, but it must also be interpreted based on the youth's cultural and social circumstances.

We are witnessing the affects of neighborhood and social conditions in conjunction with refugee adjustment issues, which shapes delinquency. Background factors associated with delinquency among refugees focus on adjustment issues including acquisition of the English language, acculturation, and the stability and strength of households. The differences between Southeast Asian refugees and East Asians immigrants reflect the refugee experience, including the trauma of departure, timing (age at admission to the United States, length of time in the United States), and access to resources. In particular, the conjunction of the detached status of many refugee youth and survival troubles such as jobs and acculturation creates conditions for the motivation of Southeast Asian refugee youths to seek delinquency as a solution to their emotional and socioeconomic needs. In effect, we are witnessing some Southeast Asian refugee youths who are troubled and delinquent. The overall patterns of troubles resemble prior Asian newcomers as they coped with the problems of adjusting to a new society; but the particulars and the circumstances of their troubles reflect both background factors and social circumstances of the refugee experience that separate them from prior immigrant Asian delinquents.

This study reveals the impact of refugee background on youth who are attempting to make it in America. The journey is not the singular story of Asian Horatio Algers who through their own efforts begin at the bottom of American society and climb to the top by attending MIT to become an engineering professor or going to Stanford to become a physician. Troubled and delinquent Southeast Asian youth reflect in part their special educational needs; they are often at-risk students who are not only underserved in schools but also likely to drop out of school. We believe deviant-prone Southeast Asian youngsters' troubles in school turn out to be a major factor in their delinquency career. School is one of the major institutions that links these youth with our society and so the severing of that link has major consequences on the life chances of these youth and their participation in the criminal world.

What are the implications for educators? Surely educators cannot resolve all of the troubles discussed here but they definitely have a role in not only keeping Southeast Asians in school but also creating hope for a future. Noticing and listening to troubled youths is a first step. Though the above information on Southeast Asian delinquents is ultimately flawed in terms of not capturing the full diversity among those youth, it does point beyond the usual stereotypes of troubled youth. Educators should not only consider the experience of being refugees, but what it means to live in changing/disrupted families and dangerous neighborhoods. The struggles for survival of their families and the changing ideas of how life is to be lived, especially when they conflict between guardian and child, requires a rethinking and retooling that can be assisted by adults who can hear and empathize. Their turning to delinquent peers and accessible adult criminal role models means that there are opportunities for making a difference. Why should we permit the Fagans of the world to have sole access to these youths when others can listen and help them create their own futures in more socially productive ways? We are not proposing new strategies in addressing the needs of these youth but rather recognizing the long-standing wisdom that adults who care and act appropriately have always made a difference. Long (1996), a Vietnamese counselor observes, " I try to save Vietnamese children one by one, and even the 'hopeless cases' like Ban are savable—most of them" (p. 225). The key is entering the relations as a bilateral one whereby the youths themselves have an active role in co-creating their own futures with the help of teachers and counselors. The heart of the matter is noticing, understanding, caring, and doing.

Note

We thank the San Diego County Department of Probation, especially Cecile Steppe and Mary Ramirez, for cooperation in gaining access to files. This report does not purport to represent the opinions of the department nor individual members. Also we thank Eric Branson and David Gauss for assistance in coding data from case files. We also thank Bounhong Khommarath, Thong Thanh Le, and Khom Som for invaluable insights on Southeast Asian juvenile delinquents. This chapter is an extension of a previously published paper titled "Troubled Southeast Asian Refugee Youth: Profile of a Delinquent Population" in Russell Endo, Clara C. Park, and John Nobuya Tsuchida (Eds.), *Current Issues in Asian and Pacific American Education* (El Monte, Calif.: Pacifica Asia Press, 1998).

7

Li-Rong Lilly Cheng

Beyond Multiculturalism

Cultural Translators Make It Happen

> All [cultures] have their own identity, language, systems of nonverbal communication, material culture, history, and *ways of doing things.*
>
> —Hall, 1976, p. 2

The field of multiculturalism has been investigated by numerous scholars (Banks, 1995; Cheng, 1990, 1991; Gollnick & Chinn, 1994; Pang, 1995; Sleeter, 1995; Gay, 1995). The purpose of this chapter is to explore what might not be examined in depth in discussions of multiculturalism, namely, the implicit culture. This chapter involves the reader in understanding the acquisition of multiculturalism. It attempts to explain that the true essence of multiculturalism or, often, of cross-cultural communication, is knowing the underlying guiding principles of the implicit culture. Three main areas of culture, as described by Hall (1976), will be discussed: tradition (ways of doing things), language, and social interaction, including systems of nonverbal communication.

Students and children must understand the implicit culture so that they can become empowered in society. They will need to know how to push society to change so it is more equitable and respects the demographic change and the riches culturally diverse people bring to "the table." Educators must help our students make those important connections and help them develop the critical cross-cultural competences as described in this chapter.

Examples will be presented in each domain in which the explicit expression will be examined from an implicit perspective. Finally, suggestions will be made for enhancing and enriching multicultural literacy. Recent U.S. demographic trends warrant a closer look at population shifts and their implications for cross-cultural communication.

Demography

Significant demographic changes in the United States indicate an urgent need to understand the meaning of diversity and issues accompanying such diversity (Greene, 1991; Minkin, 1995).

- Twenty-two of the twenty-five largest central-city school districts have student populations that are predominantly minority.
- 30 percent of public school students (twelve million) are minority.
- Members of the predominantly White baby boom generation will start reaching retirement age by the year 2010.

If current trends continue:

- By the year 2000, 40 percent of public school students will be minority.
- Hispanics will surpass African Americans as the largest U.S. minority group by the year 2015.
- Immigration will make up half of all population growth by the year 2015.
- By the year 2030, 20 percent of the nation's population will be Hispanic.
- California will have twice as many people in 2040 as it does now. Hispanics will account for almost 50 percent of California's population. Asians will triple their share of the population in just two generations.
- By 2088, minority populations will become the U.S. majority.

Educators need to become knowledgeable about the implications of such diversity. The following sections will discuss the implicit aspects of tradition, language, and social interaction.

Tradition
Ways of Doing Things

All cultures have traditions followed and practiced by large groups of individuals, while others are referred to as "foreigners," thus showing a sense of ethnocentrism. Each group practices and follows certain traditions. Some examples of traditions important in the cultures in the United States are the Superbowl, the Rose Parade, Cinco de Mayo, Quincanera (the fifteenth birthday celebration for a young girl), bar mitzvah and bat mitzvah (a Jewish rite of passage for young men and women), Kwanzaa (an African American holiday), and Thanksgiving dinner. In these cross-cultural encounters the most observable (explicit) tradition is the choice of food and how food is presented. Yet, beyond the explicit, there is the implicit message. The examples below (concerning tea, rice, peanut butter, Buddha jumping over the wall soup, soy sauce, and lettuce), are used to illustrate implicit meanings that may be missed even by those sensitive to multicultural issues. It is important for a visitor to any culture to be sensitive of his/her ethnocentrism as well as aware of the cultural/social rules of the other culture. A person from the United States visiting Korea may find "kimchee" (fermented vegetables) very difficult to swallow; likewise, a person from Korea may find "salad" (raw vegetables) unappetizing. Through the process of welcoming diverse experiences, one may find a deeper respect for all cultures and traditions.

Tea

There are great differences in the cultural significance of tea and how it is served. For example, it can be drunk hot, cool, or icy cold. It can be served with lemon, cream, sugar, or nothing. Some use tea leaves to "predict the future"; some spit out the leaves; some put tea leaves in little bags, which they throw away after making the tea, some place the tea in a strainer. The Japanese have a Tea Ceremony and serve a tiny amount of tea in each cup. In India clay cups are often used to serve tea and are thrown away afterward. The Chinese carry their tea cup (often a glass jar) with them to work and meetings. In Africa, tea leaves are boiled with milk and sugar, so the guest has no choice about how much sugar to add, or whether or not to use milk, and yet cannot refuse to drink the tea without offending the host.

Going to a "tea" means different things to different people at different times. When one is invited to "drink tea" in Canton, it generally means breakfast or brunch in a "dim-sum" restaurant, and it takes place before noon. "Dim-sum" means "a bit of my heart" and consists of a variety of Chinese delicacies served as a light meal. British "high tea" is also a light meal that generally includes meat and is served in the late afternoon. In Africa, tea is served any time of the day or night, especially when unexpected visitors arrive.

During a meeting concerning international affairs, there was an announcement of a Japanese tea ceremony. When asked what a tea ceremony was, a Japanese member gave a thirty-minute description informing the members of the board that the tea ceremony is the highest form of Japanese culture and that they would understand the culture better through participating in this type of ceremony.

Ceremonies and customs often have implicit cultural meaning; the sharing of tea is an important example of cultural transmission.

Where Is the Rice?

A group of American dignitaries was invited to a Chinese banquet in Beijing, China. This is what the Americans found on the English version of their bilingual menu:

Jelly fish cold dish
Bird nest soup
Stir-fried couch
Buddha jumped over the wall in Cantonese style
Eggs of white swan
Sea cucumber with bamboo shots
Buddha's delight
Rape
Whole Fish
Needles
Date cake

Metalinguistic knowledge (higher-level comprehensive linguistic understanding) is used by educated people to comprehend words and phrases using any cues available, including contextual, orthographic, phonological, and semantic. Perhaps an American with metalinguistic skills could detect the spelling errors in the menu and replace "couch" with "conch," "shots" with "shoots," "rape" with "rapeweed," and "needles" with "noodles." This menu, however, illustrates that metalinguistic skills are not sufficient in cross-cultural encounters. Multicultural ability is needed to discover the true meaning.

The social/cultural (implied) meaning of this menu is that the host thinks the guests are important and deserve the very best. The actual dishes served were:

Seafood salad with jelly fish
Chicken soup with parts taken from a special bird nest
Seafood stir-fry with conch slices
Stew, prepared in the Cantonese style, that smells so good that monks will jump over the walls of the monastery to eat the dish

Seafood in the shape of swan's eggs
Seaslugs with sliced bamboo shoots (Sea Cucumber)
Tofu and other vegetables (Buddha's Delight)
Green vegetables (rapeweed)
Steamed fish
Noodles with vegetables
Date cake

For any individual learning to understand the Chinese culture, this ten-course banquet is a true test of cross-cultural competence (Cheng, 1996). After being a guest at several banquets, one member of the group asked "Why isn't there rice with the meal?" The host felt embarrassed and said that rice is not included in a Chinese banquet, since it is considered a very common food and not fit for distinguished foreign visitors. Visitors are often shocked by the large amounts of food offered in a Chinese banquet and generally feel full after the first three or four courses. Likewise, a Chinese visitor to the United States or Mexico may be shocked that there is only one entree during the course of the dinner.

It is possible for a foreigner to attain cultural competence in some countries after living there for many years, particularly if the culture is related to that of one's own country. However, "any Westerner who was raised outside of the Far East and claims he really understands and can communicate with either the Chinese or the Japanese is deluding himself" (Hall, 1976: p. 2).

In open societies, where cultural rules, mores, and traditions are discussed openly, "foreigners" can have access to becoming bicultural more easily than in societies (such as China) where "foreigners" are not expected to enter society completely and are held at a distance from the culture.

Peanut Butter

An American woman adopted several Asian orphans. When they first came to the United States, she bought peanut butter and bread for them, since that is a healthy food that is liked by American children. The children refused to eat it. Concerned, the woman asked a cultural informant what the children might prefer to eat. She was told they would probably enjoy plain rice (without condiments—especially without soy sauce), chicken soup, and cooked vegetables (not raw vegetables). They were very happy with that diet and thrived in their new home. This anecdote demonstrates the lack of sensitivity to food preference and the assumption that foods valued in one culture will be valued by visitors from another culture.

There is a peanut butter test used by Speech-Language Pathologists to test pragmatics. The first assumption of the test is that the child will want to eat crackers and peanut butter. Part of the test includes handing the child a jar of peanut butter with a tight lid. The child is expected to ask the adult to open the jar for him, and this is considered pragmatically appropriate behavior. This test is culturally inappropriate for Asian children for at least two reasons. One is that peanut butter itself may not be appealing, either in appearance or taste, to those not used to it, and so a child might not even *want* peanut butter. The second is that Asian children might have been taught not to ask adults for things, but to wait until the adult helps without being asked. Asian children may anticipate help from adults since the Asian cultures generally are more protective of children and do not stress self-help skills as much as parents in the United States. The strategies suggested for this test might not work with Asian children and hence cannot be used as an indicator of pragmatic disorder.

The Use of Soy Sauce

In the movie *The Joy Luck Club*, a scene was most illustrative of cultural causes for breakdowns in communication. A girl brought her boy friend home for a meal. He asked for soy sauce, and spread it lavishly over the food. Chinese cuisine is known for its flavor; salt, pepper, and soy sauce are generally not used on the dinner table. The indication of a good chef is that the dishes are well prepared and there is no need to add any more flavoring to the dish. When soy sauce was used by this young man, he nonverbally insulted the hostess, causing embarrassment to her and her guests since everyone else knew the importance of not using anything on the food. The boy friend kept praising the food, not realizing that his (explicit) use of soy sauce meant (implicitly) that he was rejecting the mother's efforts to make a special meal.

The hostess considered his words dishonest, as his actions expressed (in her interpretation) his distaste for the food. The girl friend did not expect this to happen. Since these nonverbal actions have significant and implicit cultural meaning, she should have found an excuse for him by saying, "He has too strong a taste for soy sauce," indicating that the dish was perfect and *he* was the problem so that the hostess could "save face."

Lettuce

An American girl was sharing a room in a rooming house with a group of international students. She was surprised to find that some of the girls were cooking lettuce, while she felt it was supposed to be eaten raw. In many countries, vegetables are washed thoroughly and cooked carefully, in order to avoid germs (such as infectious hepatitis) that may be carried in the soil in which the vegetables were grown. Individuals from those countries may feel that eating raw vegetables implies a lack of concern for hygiene and health.

The above section deals with traditions that transcend generational or linguistic boundaries and are often what is observed in cultures after several generations of cultural adaptation. On the other hand, language is often lost after one or two generations.

Language

> Language is not a machine you can break and fix with the right technique, it is a function of the whole person, an expression of culture, desire, need. . . . Inside our language is our history, personal and political.
>
> —Kaplan, 1994: p. 66

Language is the tool for people to say what they mean. Without a full grasp of language, a person has a limited ability to express himself or herself fully. Furthermore, without a full grasp of more than one language, a person may have a limited worldview.

> Ludwig Wittgenstein wisely noted: "The limits of my language mean the limits of my world." Conversely, introductions to new languages shatter these limitations and open up new worlds! (Wawrytko, 1995)

A few scholars have used the genre of "language memoir" to describe the process of learning a second language. Kaplan (1994) put it this way: "The difference, in language memoir, is that it's not yourself you're growing into, but another self, perceived as better, more powerful, safer. The change in language is the emblem of a leap into a new persona" (p. 69). Additionally, when one learns a new language, one not only learns the literal meanings of words and passages, but also goes through a process of quest for culture.

Language is human and is the place where our bodies and minds collide, as Kaplan (1994) wrote:

> A friend who taught me much of what I know about French, a doctor named Micheline Veaux, once told me that speech is the highest and lowest human function, the *endroit charniere* (the hitch post), between the mechanical grunt of the vocal chords and the poetry of cognition.
>
> Language is the place where our bodies and minds collide, where our groundedness in place and time and our capacity for fantasy and invention must come to terms. (p. 64)

Language is explicit when it appears in print or is expressed in words. The implicit cultural meaning of language is often observed in failed attempts to translate and in inappropriate responses, leading to communication breakdowns, which, themselves, may be explicit or implicit. If it is implicit, the breakdown may not be noticed by the second language learner unless there is a cultural informant who is able to explain it.

Language may confirm or deny the life histories and experiences of the people who use it. Unless all languages receive equal respect, resulting in an appreciative and positive (not a problematic and negative) view of second language acquisition, learners will receive implicit and explicit messages about the languages. They will devalue the language considered less prestigious.

One of the key concerns in providing equitable services to children and their families with a different language background is the use of translators/interpreters. The following sections will focus on this area.

The Art of Translation/Interpretation

There are more than three thousand languages spoken in the world. When people come in contact with speakers of a language they have not learned, translation and interpretation become a necessary part of the interaction. What gets translated from one language to another may lead to miscommunication and communication breakdown. At the outset, a differentiation must be made between interpretation and translation. Interpretation is the process of converting an oral message from one language to another; translation is the process of converting a written message from one language to another.

There are a number of barriers to service delivery including linguistic, cultural, financial, and social. The central issue is the language barrier. Service providers need to have an interpreter who can accurately transmit the messages they want to convey so that proper assistance can be provided. An interpreter assists the interviewer in the initial screening process to provide information about the individual's speech and language skills, and also acts as a counselor who furnishes service providers with information about the culture of the students, facilitates communication, and establishes rapport.

The roles of interpreters/translators include assisting the interviewee in comprehending the questions by modifying and explicating what is asked; using cultural knowledge to filter and amend the original information to make it more culturally sensitive; and knowing taboo areas requiring alteration of the question or message to adhere to propriety or convey the implicit meaning.

An interpreter can be a gatekeeper who controls what information passes from the sender to the receiver of the message, who filters, screens, and amends the message to make it professionally, culturally, and linguistically appropriate. The interpreter can also be a barrier who can block certain information or distort the information being transmitted. Misinformation can be accidental, due to human error or lack of competence. Incompetent informants act as though the given message is understood, yet have very little grasp of the true meaning. Misinformation can also be intentional distortion of the message either for malicious reasons, or to show the student in the best light.

There are several levels of interpretation. Linguistic interpretation is the literal interpretation in which the meaning is conveyed. It is the most common level of interpretation and most useful in dealing with documents, and in science and technology. Sociocultural linguistic translation implies that the social and cultural meaning is also infused into the message. This requires a higher form of translation/interpretation and is often missing in intercultural communication, resulting in misunderstandings. It requires experience, metacognitive skills, metalinguistic skills, and training. It also requires the use of professional judgment based on cultural knowledge to provide the best equivalent message. Ultimately, the interpreter is a cultural conduit and must have the knowledge to translate not only the words but also the nuances of the original message into the second language.

An interpreter must be able to detect mixed messages and incongruencies in perceptions; be knowledgeable about issues of ethics and confidentiality; be familiar with the physical setup; be skilled in time management and the management of silences; understand proper social distances; and know attitudes, beliefs, and religious convictions of both cultures. Each of these factors needs to be taken into consideration when working with the interpreter and the student's family. The overall success of the interaction is contingent upon preencounter preparation, sensitivity, empathy, awareness, experience, and training of all service providers who are committed to offering quality service. It is important for individuals providing services to understand the students' needs and, consequently, to provide proper services to meet those needs.

Working Suggestions

In working with an interpreter, it is essential to provide thorough training and adequate information. The following guidelines should be heeded:

1. Check with the family before choosing an individual to interpret. It may be that the family knows the individual and would not feel comfortable divulging personal feelings to him or her.

2. Preplan for an interpreter's services to ensure that the individual understands the specific clinical procedures to be used.
3. Provide extensive training to the interpreter concerning purposes, procedures, and goals. The interpreter should also be taught to avoid the use of gestures, vocal intonation, and other cues that could inadvertently alert the individual to the correct response during the administration of tests.
4. Train the interpreter concerning the confidentiality of all issues addressed during all interactions.
5. Use the same interpreter(s) with a given language minority family rather than one selected at random.
6. Use observation or other nonlinguistic measures as supplements to the translated measures, such as (a) the child's interaction with parents, (b) the child's interaction with peers, and (c) pragmatic analysis.

Those who work with interpreters must provide them with the best possible context for proper interpretation. In giving the family information through an interpreter, for example, the clinician should:

• Speak distinctly and at a normal pace.
• Keep sentences short and simple.
• Provide pauses for the interpreter to organize his/her thoughts for proper translation.
• Avoid excessive use of colloquial terms and idioms because they can be difficult to translate.
• Always check to see if information transmitted is understood.
• Provide context when complex information is transmitted.
• Break long messages into units and present them sequentially.
• Ask if the interpreter needs clarification or elaboration.
• Use abstract words sparingly. Words of feelings, attitudes, and qualities should be avoided as much as possible, since direct translation tends to distort the meaning.
• Use direct messages and do not depend on indirect subtleties.

Interpretation is a dynamic and interactive process. Service providers who work with interpreters need to be trained, and in turn train the interpreters, to maximize the process so that families can benefit from quality, compassion, and empowerment.

Just as the service provider must assist the interpreter and provide essential information, the interpreter must also take responsibility to ensure the process is successful. Most importantly, the interpreter must:

• Be honest about any difficulties that may be encountered.
• Listen carefully in order to translate effectively.

- Pay attention to the speaker's body language, tone of voice, and facial expressions.
- Take notes during the session.
- Never hesitate to use reference materials such as a dictionary.

There exist three basic communication styles that have a direct impact on the interpretation process: nonassertive, aggressive, and assertive. Identifying the type of communicator with whom one is involved in the interpretation/translation process will warrant a much more successful encounter if the idiosyncracies of the distinct communication styles are known. Nonassertive communicators do not express feelings, needs, and ideas. Consequently, they are emotionally dishonest and allow others to choose for them. Aggressive communicators, on the other hand, show emotion; however, they ignore the rights and feelings of others or attempt to dominate the expressions of others. Finally, assertive communicators are emotionally honest, expressing feelings yet also respecting the feelings and ideas of others. The assertive person makes choices and allows others to do the same.

By noting the communicative style characteristic to an individual, the interpreter can most effectively interpret, being sensitive to the emotions expressed or repressed, as the case may be.

Ultimately, a person who is capable of interpreting two languages and cultures is ideal in dealing with cross-cultural issues. For example, when a Chinese speaker says "ni fa fu le," which literally means, "You have gained weight," a skilled interpreter will interpret the remark as "You look healthy," so that the actual cultural communicative intent is transmitted.

Another area of language difficulty is lack of familiarity with language content and use in multiple contexts. The following is an example of specific language and rules used in meetings.

There Is a Motion on the Floor, Who Will Second It?

Attending a meeting of an organization can be stressful for new members, and the special vocabulary involved adds to the demands placed on the person who is new to the English language, new to the United States, and new to the organization holding the meeting. Many terms are used specifically for meetings, and a person who is fluent in English, but who has not attended meetings in the United States, will be confused by the vocabulary taken for granted at meetings.

In general, the minutes of the previous meeting are approved. What are minutes? How would the hypothetical newcomer know that the word *minutes* refers to a written document, and not to something you look for on a watch? There must be a "quorum" present for voting to take place. When there is a proposal, the Chairperson may "call for a motion," and someone must "second the motion." The "motion on the floor" does not indicate any movement of the floor. When voting takes place, the "ayes and nays" are counted and some of the members may "abstain." The newcomer, totally confused by this procedure, may keep quiet, and be counted as "an abstention." The "motion is carried" if the "ayes have it." She was also curious about the result of the vote since she did not know how a "motion" (movement) could be carried.

After the vote had been taken, the newcomer, who still had comments to make about the issue, was told by the chairperson that it was a "fait accompli," and so a "moot point." This comment was totally incomprehensible to her, but it certainly had the intended effect of preventing her from making her comment.

Finally, the meeting was adjourned "sine die," leaving our newcomer confused, but reluctant to ask the meaning of the term in case the answer was incomprehensible. She was left feeling that her English was not really as good as she had thought!

Social Interaction

In the United States, oral language competency and verbal fluency are valued. Barba and Pang (1991) reported that teacher/student target behaviors are an important component of the social organization of schools. Furthermore, Erickson (1984) also discussed the how teachers may misinterpret and fail to understand that the students' observed "inappropriate" behaviors are considered acceptable or may be expected in the home environment. For example, an Asian may look down to show respect, and this may be interpreted by her teacher as a sign of discourtesy.

Discourse Style

Individual discourse styles are influenced by environment, experience, and multiple social interactions. For example, New Yorkers are sometimes thought to be aggressive, leaving no space for others to respond. The conversation partners echo each other at times, overlap speaking, and in general leave no time for response lag (C. Westby, personal communication, December 1995). On the other hand, a Japanese person may nod, giving nonverbal cues that the message was heard, but may not respond verbally. These different styles may lead to further misunderstanding and confusion. What is offensive in nonverbal and verbal messages in one culture may be entertaining and acceptable in another. A person may code-switch between styles depending on context: from formal to informal, from serious to playful.

Sociocultural customs that are prevalent in one culture may be viewed as incomprehensible in another. For example, it is common in the United States for someone to host a "pot luck," or "no-host" party or to ask a guest to "bring your own bottle (BYOB)." These concepts are not easily understood by Asians, who expect that their hosts provide the food and beverages when an invitation is extended. They may not know the sociocultural rules that dictate those functions.

Let's Do Lunch

One of the most intriguing social encounters is called a "no-host party." How can you have a party without a host? What are you supposed to do in a party without a host? I was invited to a "no-host cocktail party." I entered the room and realized that everyone had something to drink, so I went to the line and watched what people did. They ordered their drinks: Bloody Mary, Pink Lady, Martini, Manhattan, Gin and Tonic, Virgin Mary, White Russian, Screwdriver, Grasshopper. Furthermore, they said "on the rocks, with an olive, straight, on the side." By the time I got to the counter, I was totally confused. So I pointed to the orange juice and said, "That."

After getting the drink and paying for it, I searched for a friendly face. Someone looked marginally friendly, so I walked over and said hello. What else could I say? I tried to think of some appropriate social topics. We could talk about the weather or the party. After exchanging a few social conventions, I realized that I had no topic to establish any conversation. I could say, "I like your shoes," or "What a pretty dress!" I knew enough about the culture to know that I could not ask "What size do you wear?" or "How much did you pay for it?" It is difficult to ask "What do you do?" It is inappropriate to ask "How much do you make?"

Sometimes, an Asian phrase is used when someone greets you, thinking that because you appear to be an Asian, you know Japanese or Chinese. When people try to find out where you are from, they may ask "Do you live here?" or "How long have you lived here?" If you say, "I am local," they may look disbelieving and say "I mean, really, where are you *really* from?" showing that they do not think you are one of them. One may comment, "You speak very good English. Where did you learn it?" When your answer is "I was born in this country and have always spoken English," they look puzzled and walk away.

Finally, you find someone that you can talk to and the person says to you "Let's do lunch!" You are so excited to find someone who cares and reach into your purse for your date book only to find out that the person you were talking to is gone. "Let's do lunch" means I have to leave now. "I will call you" means I need to talk to someone else. "Let's talk later" means the topic is boring. "I'll see you later" means goodbye. After repeated misunderstandings, one may give up and simply leave the party.

What is wrong with social encounters? Why is cocktail speech so empty? Why do people not mean what they say? Why is it that Americans ask "How are you?" as a greeting, but don't really want to know how you are? The ritualized response, "Fine," is used even when the person is not at all "fine." Likewise, when someone greets you saying "What's happening?" They don't really want to know what is happening. On the other hand, if Americans ask, "Have you eaten?" they intend to provide food if the answer is "no." When a Chinese-speaking person asks, "Have you eaten?" there is no intention to provide food, although the response may be "I have not."

Faux pas, n'est pas?

Many new Americans have experienced culture shock and committed the so-called cultural faux pas. This is not atypical but rather common. In our professional attempts at improving "accents," we often miss the central point—the acquisition of multicultural literacy, which includes the understanding of peoples, places, times, facts, and many other aspects of a culture and people (Cheng, 1989a; 1993a,b).

Children often experience "difficult discourse" and are puzzled by the "hidden curriculum." These concepts are important for educators since many of us work with adults and children who come from an entirely different cultural, social, educational, and linguistic background.

Many limited-English-proficient (LEP) students continue speaking their native languages at home; they regard English as the school language and encounter difficulty. They may feel shy and are often excluded from socialization and participation due to their lack of familiarity with mainstream culture and language. They often feel alienated and not accepted. Lack of exposure to English ultimately results in difficult discourse. Furthermore, they are challenged by the adjustments they have to make in order to have a smooth acculturation. One way educators can help is to teach the implicit aspects of the school culture so that the students are less likely to be hampered by cultural miscommunications or cultural conflicts. Research on adjustment problems has repeatedly addressed the question of why some refugee and immigrant groups adapt readily to the American way of life, while others do so more slowly.

What we fail to understand is that some students do not know the "hidden curriculum" and do not know the rules (nonverbal as well as verbal) which exist tacitly both in and out of the classroom. Jackson (1968) defined the "hidden curriculum" as "The crowds, the praise, and the power that combine to give a distinctive flavor to classroom life . . . which each student (and teacher) must master if he [sic] is to make his way satisfactorily through the school" (pp. 33–34).

Adaptive Strategies

Spindler & Spindler (1971, 1990) have argued that immigrant groups experience different levels of adaptation related to their degree of cultural conflict. Some reaffirm their native traditions by attempting to revive them, while rejecting the mainstream culture; some combine selected aspects of one culture with those of the other. Others withdraw and reject both conflicting cultures, remaining noncommittal toward both. Those embracing both mainstream and home cultures require cultural and linguistic code switching to function within them.

Educators need to understand the adaptive strategies of newcomers and focus on school and classroom interactions. Additionally, the issue of the acquisition of multicultural literacy and educational implications of difficult discourse in American academic and home contexts must be discussed. Many LEP children proficient in their home language work rigorously to improve their school language. Through helping them, their parents learn about the school, its curriculum, and its language.

Multicultural Communication

Multicultural communication goes beyond describing and learning the rules and traditions of the other culture; social historical knowledge is essential, and this involves understanding the social knowledge, cognition, and culture of native speakers of the language. Social pragmatic differences can lead to breakdowns in communication. There are multiple challenges that must be understood especially in assisting teachers and other service providers to empower their students and clients to be active citizens in the culture of power.

Challenges beyond semantics include multiple meanings and connotations of words. Challenges beyond phonology include awareness of the importance of subtle differences in pronunciation. Challenges beyond pragmatics include relating to the cognitive styles, cultural patterns, and differences in the concept of time, so that one is able to code switch pragmatically as well as linguistically. Challenges beyond translation include understanding the feelings and cultural imperatives of the interpreter. Nonverbal messages also differ among cultures (Cheng, 1996).

In his book about cultural literacy, Hirsch (1988) included what he thought every American should know. Many English-speaking monolingual children from lower socioeconomic households have not been exposed to common elements of North American culture. Students who recently immigrated to the United States and are learning English also need to be introduced to aspects of mainstream American culture in order to succeed in school. These aspects include, for example, appropriate language to use on the telephone, on the playground, and in the classroom, and the use of humor in peer interactions. Indeed, there is a point beyond which formal education cannot help the non-native to achieve cultural familiarity. If one is not familiar with the old schoolbook use of Dick and Jane characters, then modern-day references such as the movie "Fun with Dick and Jane" (with Jane Fonda and George Segal) or the popular t-shirts imprinted with stick figures of "Dick" will have no meaning.

Those who immigrate to the United States as adults may have even more difficulty than children do in adapting to the new culture. The following suggestions may be useful for all individuals and some are particularly useful for teachers:

- Be an ethnographer: observe interactions and take notes (Trueba, Spindler & Spindler, 1989). Talk to child and adult immigrants, migrants, and refugees and learn about their life histories and do cultural interviews.
- Become familiar with colloquial usage (e.g., Give me a break; Break a leg; coffee break; If it ain't broke, don't fix it!).
- Try to learn the explicit (observable) and implicit (unobservable) aspects of different cultures.
- Find out about cultural ways of life (e.g., time, food), share commonalities and differences (e.g., holidays), and learn about foods (such as sushi, moo-shu pork, tortas, Greek cuisine, Italian cuisine, souffle, lumpia).
- Read books by ethnic authors, for example, Sandra Cisneros (*The House on Mango Street*); Sarah Lawrence Lightfoot (*I've Known Rivers*; *Balm in Gilead*); Amy Tan (*The Joy Luck Club*; *The Kitchen God's Wife*); Anchee Min (*Red Azalea*); Toni Morrison (*Beloved*; *The Bluest Eye*); Alice Walker (*The Color Purple*).

More specifically, in the classroom:

- Speak to students in private and encourage them to speak in class and provide them with positive feedback when they do try to communicate (Clark & Cheng, 1993).
- Find someone in the class who shares a similar cultural background as a source of support to newcomer students.
- Share information about the American culture with students and have students share their cultures with the rest of the class (Trueba, Cheng & Ima, 1993).
- Find out more about the educational experience, cultural assumptions, and personal history of the students (Cheng, 1989b). Students can write autobiographies or make personal timelines.

- Review all data pertaining to the student.
- Conduct interviews with teachers, peers, and family members to gain a better understanding of the student (Zappia, 1989).

Cultural Therapy

Cultural therapy was originally described by George and Louise Spindler (1982) as an encounter with cultural evidence showing individual biases associated with interethnic interaction. In their original study of Roger Harker, an exemplary teacher who was unconscious of his preferential treatment of children who shared his cultural background, the Spindlers showed him

> where and how his perceptions and understanding were skewed and quite out of line with both reality as I [George] perceived it and the realities of classroom life as the children perceived them. At first he was disbelieving and hostile. Eventually he assimilated what was being presented. (Spindler & Spindler, 1982, p. 30)

Teachers function as cultural managers who transmit proper values and protect "common culture." The Spindlers recognize that there are different ways of coping with cultural conflict such as Roger Harker faced in his ethnically diverse classroom. Cultural therapy is viewed as a possible instrument to resolve such conflicts (Trueba, Cheng & Ima, 1993). The following description illustrates the importance of cultural therapy:

Kim, a Korean-speaking boy, used an English expletive in a public school, despite being reprimanded by his teacher. Disciplinary measures did not curtail his behavior. A bilingual Korean-speaking aide was asked to talk to him about this unacceptable behavior. It turned out that he didn't know what it meant, but used it as an attention-getting device; whenever he heard someone say that word, others paid attention to that person. He thought the "discipline" was a way of showing him attention. The manner of the teacher was so calm that Kim, unable to understand the meaning of most of her words, didn't realize it was verbal punishment; he associated hitting or spanking with discipline and did not recognize the severity of the problem.

Conclusion

This chapter explores some of the least discussed areas of multiculturalism and advocates promotion of literacy and multicultural literacy. Multicultural literacy lays the foundation for school and future success. We cannot assume that all students are receiving home literacy support, nor can we assume that the students and parents understand the "hidden curriculum" of the school. Teachers, parents, and students need to welcome the challenges of diverse experiences and appreciate the fact that all need to learn so much about each other. Asian Pacific Americans, European Americans, African Americans, Hispanic Americans, Native Americans, and other groups all deserve a chance to voice their opinions, cherish their experiences, share the power of equity, and ultimately reach their optimal potential socially, politically, educationally, and economically.

Working suggestions for acquiring multicultural literacy are offered.In order to be successful in school, students need to develop Basic Interpersonal Communication Skills (BICS) and Cognitive Academic Linguistic Proficiency (CALP) (Cummins, 1981, 1986). Students need to master the hidden curriculum in order to develop CALP. They need to have "comprehensible input" in classroom interactions (Krashen, 1981). LEP students who find classroom discourse and its oral/written and nonverbal rules incomprehensible may become disengaged (Tran, 1991). Some may be referred to speech-language therapy for assessment due to lack of language output and "inappropriate classroom behavior." Cultural therapy is a method that can be adapted to work with students who feel out of place in the classroom setting.

It is through their own language that linguistically different students will be able to reconstruct their history and culture and that language must be understood via social, political, and ideological relationships to which it points. Teachers need to be cultural translators and interpreters in the school setting to decipher language patterns, traditions, and social interactions that their students bring to the classroom. It is not enough to acknowledge cultural differences and celebrate cultural diversity through activities such as "Black History Month" or "Cinco de Mayo Parade." It is imperative that teachers understand not only the explicit cultures but also the often hidden and implicit meanings beyond language, traditions, and codes of social interactions. It is only through a deeper appreciation and understanding of such implications that teachers can be empowered to be effective transmitters of cultures.

III

Schooling and Asian Pacific American Children

8

Adel Nadeau

The Linda Vista
Elementary Story

Where Diversity Is the Mainstream

This case study of Linda Vista Elementary School in San Diego, California, is presented as an example of how one school transformed itself to better serve the needs of its linguistically diverse student population, many who were Asian Pacific American students. It describes the decisions, processes, and artifacts of this schoolwide reform effort and how a building staff can make effective decisions by applying basic premises about language and learning.

Several components of the reform process are presented. They are as follows: The Decision-Making Process, Instructional Program, Support Systems, Assessment and Accountability, and Conclusions.

Background

Linda Vista School is a large urban school with a satellite campus about one-half mile away from the main campus. The Linda Vista area of San

125

Diego has traditionally been the most culturally diverse in the city and has undergone numerous changes. Through the 1960s and early 1970s the area was home to roughly equal numbers of White, African American, and Hispanic families. In the early 1970s, Southeast Asian refugees moved to the area in substantial numbers and displaced many established families. At one time, almost 70 percent of Linda Vista's enrollment was Southeast Asian. Recently, the number of Latino families moving into the area has risen. At the time of this writing the school's enrollment was 44 percent Asian, 40 percent Hispanic, 6 percent African American, and 10 percent White. More than 95 percent of its students received free or reduced-price lunch, making the school eligible for schoolwide Chapter I (now Title I) funding. At least 77 percent of the students were non- or limited-English proficient.

Linda Vista's diverse student body presented a unique challenge to the staff. Five major languages—Hmong, Vietnamese, Lao, Spanish, and English were represented as well as several other language groups with small numbers of students. Students from newly arrived immigrant or refugee families, and often with no previous exposure to formal education, arrive at the school's doorstep on a regular basis. Thus, the staff was presented with an extraordinary opportunity to tailor a program to its distinctive student body.

Decision-Making Process

The Linda Vista staff began its restructuring process before the school district had officially launched its initiative. The new principal arrived at Linda Vista in the summer of 1987. She found students performed substantially below average, were assigned to classes without regard to their English language proficiency, and spent what seemed to be more time out of class in supplementary language or basic skills instruction than they spent in class. This situation created an immediate need for change. The following winter the staff at Linda Vista brainstormed and formulated a strategic plan. They began implementation of the plan in the fall of 1988. Considering the poor situation that existed at the school, this rapid planning and implementation of a schoolwide restructuring process is a testament to the potential of any staff to reinvent itself and pursue a vision given a systematic decision-making process.

Rather than imposing solutions, the new principal called a faculty meeting to present data on conditions within the school. She charged the faculty with developing strategies to improve working conditions and student performance. For six months the faculty examined its beliefs about the student population, bilingual instruction, developmental education, and many other issues. They then began to meet in small groups to develop a list of need statements for the school. From these needs emerged a vision, goals, and ultimately, a dramatically different program.

According to most of the staff, this process proved to be extremely difficult, but when the staff was asked to look at the most critical factors to the success of the restructuring process, most point to the same factors: (a) the open process, in which all parties could express their thoughts without fear of repercussions or ridicule; (b) the involvement of all school staff, including instructional aides, cafeteria personnel, and custodial staff, (c) The leadership of the principal, and (d) support from the assistant superintendent under whose jurisdiction Linda Vista falls.

The staff at Linda Vista was composed of approximately forty certificated and sixty classified staff. Only two Asian American teachers, one Hmong and one Vietnamese, were on staff; however, there were several Asian American instructional aides and a Hmong community aide. At the beginning of the restructuring process the rich cultural and linguistic resource of the Asian staff was not being utilized to any substantive degree. Thus, the importance of the open process and the involvement of all school staff in that process cannot be overemphasized in Linda Vista's restructuring story. While the open staff meetings allowed the most resistant individuals to challenge the restructuring process, they also allowed the supporters of the change to hear, respond to, and allay the fears of the more moderate resisters. In short, the openness expanded the constituency supporting reform, thereby giving the movement greater credibility. Moreover, the process placed the Asian staff and community members at the forefront of the school's reform effort, compelling people long accustomed to following administrative dictates to step forward and assume leadership roles. The presence of respected leaders within the ranks of both certified and classified staff and parents also contributed to the staying power of the school's restructuring.

As stated above, the process of self-analysis and change began by the spring of the year. A great risk was taken in asking staff members who were demoralized and who were not accustomed to working together to come up with a comprehensive change. At the first meeting when the staff was presented with hard data relative to the achievement of students, degree of classroom interruptions and pullout instruction, teachers were asked to generate some needs statements. The initial needs statements charted by the staff were:

1. More appropriate instructional\language proficiency groupings for each student;
2. Less pullout instruction during morning hours.

3. More integrated learning experiences.
4. Greater equity of services to all students.
5. Less labeling of special needs students.
6. A more unified staff.
7. Better use of space.

It may appear that the above needs statements are simple and perfunctory; yet, these simple statements provided the springboard for the next critical step. The staff was asked to break into groups and brainstorm a plan to meet those criteria. They were also encouraged to think creatively and not be tied down with traditional ideas. From January to June, the committees formed around these issues met on an ongoing basis and formulated a total school plan for implementation in September. The same staff that had previously been plagued by serious morale and communications problems were now able to generate the teamwork necessary to bring about massive change.

Two of the significant contributing factors to this positive turnaround were: the regularly changing committee membership that allowed group dynamics to shift and new leadership to emerge, and the constant reiteration throughout the committee work that decisions were to be arrived at through consensus. As a result of the changing group dynamics new leaders emerged; for example, many Asian staff who were previously relegated roles that offered little opportunity for impact on the decision-making process, were given more and more ownership of the plan as they realized their ideas would not be squelched. This required that the principal constantly redefine consensus and make it clear that all staff should be involved, not just those that were willing to work harder or had more dominant personalities. This set the precedent for the schoolwide governance structure that ultimately emerged in which most of the school community, became active members.

What Was Learned from the Linda Vista Experience?

From the decision-making process the Linda Vista school community found that school restructuring appears to be most successful if

- it is a pervasive, systemic change—it affects each student in the school
- the reform process revolutionizes the school and does not change only one aspect at a time
- it is based on a site-based management system that requires all staff to participate
- decisions for change are student oriented

- the empowering of staff is for a team effort and not merely for individual efforts
- the process for change includes nontraditional approaches
- it provides active support and leadership by the site administrator

The Instructional Program

Mission Statement

Linda Vista's mission was to promote academic excellence through shared decision making, increased teacher/staff/parent leadership, and high expectations for all students. The staff believed that each student could learn and that the staff had the responsibility to ensure the best educational program possible. Each child should be academically challenged and engaged for the entire school day.

Vision

The vision for the restructuring process at Linda Vista included the following challenges:

1. meeting the diverse academic needs of each student through appropriate placement and a nongraded curriculum
2. providing appropriate language placement and, an integrated experience
3. providing student access to all programs
4. assessing student progress through individual, authentic assessment techniques
5. involving the parents and the community at large through the *outreach* program
6. strengthening the effectiveness of the shared decision-making process

Evolution of the Program

Through careful deliberation, the staff ensured that the vision guide their decision making, although two principles played the most prominent role—first more appropriate groupings for each student, and second, greater equity of services to all students. In some ways, these two principles were contradictory. Grouping students by their needs or language proficiency and tailoring instruction to those needs necessarily deprives some students of certain opportunities available to other students. Therefore, ways to balance both of these priorities were developed in Linda Vista's program.

Several umbrella provisions were stipulated by the staff during the initial findings. This "umbrella" provided a systemic process by which every child was positively affected for the major part of his or her school day. In other words, supplementary instruction was not the key factor in supporting underachieving or special needs students. In a school like Linda Vista the underachieving population was the majority.

Because of the needs of the entire school population, the staff made a critical decision to move away from a deficit perspective to one that has high expectations for all students and required the same standards for all. In order to achieve this, the total school program was organized to include: (1) a nongraded curriculum for the entire school, (2) the development of an early childhood program for all prekindergarten, kindergarten, and some age six students and special education students housed at the annex site; (3) class size to be reduced for all classrooms; (4) substantial weekly preparation time to be provided for each teacher; (5) a reallocation of resources in order to implement the program.

Under the preceding umbrella then, the specific plan developed for the school addressed all of the foregoing criteria. Students were grouped in nongraded classrooms within approximately four multiage levels—early childhood, primary, middle, and upper. Given the importance of primary language development and the limited resources available in the Southeast Asian languages, some difficult decisions had to be made about how to offer the best possible primary language program.

The decision was to offer a sheltered English program to Southeast Asian youngsters. Consequently, there would be a focus on English language development for Hmong, Vietnamese, and Lao students, yet by reorganizing the limited bilingual human resources available in those languages, some primary language opportunities were also possible. It was decided that one major content area could be offered in each of the primary languages. That subject was to be social studies. Because of the lack of appropriate literacy materials in the Asian languages, the decision was made to use social studies as a vehicle of oral instruction in which rich concepts and vocabulary could be taught through the primary language. It would provide an opportunity to design the curriculum to not only ensure that students received the required content, but also the rich cultural content represented in the school.

The school had reallocated resources to hire a Hmong teacher, who at that time was probably the only certified Hmong teacher in the state. A Vietnamese teacher was also part of the staff along with a cadre of bilingual instructional aides. These individuals were assigned as primary language staff outside of the regular classroom. At prescribed times during the day, students were regrouped for primary language instruction in Hmong, Lao, and Vietnamese. Math support through the primary language was provided in the regular classroom by this same cadre of staff.

Within each age grouping indicated—early childhood, primary, middle, and upper—students in the sheltered English program were grouped homogeneously by English language proficiency in up to six proficiency levels: Entry level, Sheltered A, Sheltered B, Transition A, Transition B, Nonsheltered, and Bilingual Spanish.

The Southeast Asian youngsters were taught in their sheltered English situation by the regular monolingual staff trained to offer sheltered instruction. For all instruction offered to limited English proficient (LEP) students, staffing, classroom organization, and instruction were arranged so that languages were kept separated and enriched. Teachers used the language of instruction exclusively. This is not to say that students could not use whichever language they were comfortable with, but with consistent teacher models they soon came to respect and use the language of instruction. Language in this configuration, is given the necessary time and intensity to develop thoroughly.

Reflected in the levels of English language proficiency, students were offered a level of entry, sheltered, or transition instruction unique to their needs. Language arts and math were taught during the morning block of time in a sheltered format in which all content appropriate to the age and development of the student was provided as required by the district. (The primary language social studies time was offered in the morning as well.) The sheltered content was communicated to students through strategies that make the concepts comprehensible. Visual, oral, and hands-on activities were used as vehicles to transmit rich content. This approach engages the student in the learning of language through oral and written material filled with science, social studies, and math content. Each level of language proficiency becomes increasingly more difficult and was carefully assessed until the student outcomes began approximating the fluency of a native English speaker.

To ensure that high expectations were maintained, an important element embedded in the program was fluidity of student movement. It was noteworthy that in this process of change, time was not spent in the initial stages of planning and implementation bringing in experts and studying research about high expectations. Keeping efforts focused within the group was necessary, of course, as the grassroots effort took hold. More importantly, the elements that would ensure success were embedded in the ongoing process of change in the organization and instruction. Thus, planning for students to be able to move up the levels of English language proficiency when ready, was one of the most important decisions in terms of raising expectations.

Students were expected to move from level to level as soon as they had met the criteria—not necessarily at the end of the semester or year (see assessment section). A LEP review team similar to a consultation or child study was incorporated into the process in order to enable the process of student movement. Individual student referrals and biannual reviews were conducted to place or move students through the levels. During these reviews, student performance was assessed through the school's standards and the individual portfolio.

In order to meet the criteria for providing students with an integrated experience, the students were heterogeneously grouped during the afternoon. They were integrated by cultural, linguistic groups, and by gender. A departmentalized program was offered in which students were rotated for ten-day blocks for two subjects per blocks. Teachers selected the subject of their choice and taught only that subject for the year. As an example, a student received science and music for ten days and then rotated to physical education and art. The cycle repeated itself four times a year.

One of the complaints often expressed by elementary school teachers was that there was not enough time to cover the entire curriculum. Consequently, subjects usually taught in the afternoon—such as Science, PE, Art, and Music—did not receive adequate emphasis. It is important to note that in the above program not only are all of these taught intensively (required minutes as well), but subjects were added. As an example, during the afternoon rotation, all students received the counseling program, technology, geography, and social development. These were offered as subjects and not as supplemental or remedial programs. A key factor of the vision was to provide equity of services and to decrease or even eliminate the labeling of students. This occurred in the afternoon when all students participated regardless of special needs. There were no remedial pull-out classes, and computer literacy and services such as the counseling program, often reserved for crises intervention were provided to all students. Because the morning instruction provided for the needs of all students there was no need for remedial classes that usually prevent students from participating in many activities.

The afternoon program at Linda Vista school was an interdisciplinary, hands-on one that integrated writing, literature, and math into the curriculum. It was enthusiastically endorsed by the students. The fact that little boredom was seen was evidence of their enthusiasm. Students experienced a wide variety of activities and teaching styles, and most teachers knew most of the students in the school (Table 8.1).

Academic Enhancement?

A critical practice in any reform effort is organizational flexibility. An exemplary innovation may fail if there has not been an effort to make provisions for flexibility of staffing, student grouping, and movement. At Linda Vista, the vision dictated how resources both financial and human, would be allocated to meet the goals set out by the staff.

In the reallocation of resources, several part-time morning teaching posts were allocated to reduce class size as well as to provide special programs that otherwise would not have been possible within the district staffing formula. Consequently, a nontraditional design was implemented for the special education students in the Resource Specialist program and other students who did not qualify for special education, but were older and at risk. This program was called Academic Enhancement. The resource specialist was teamed with a teacher during the morning hours. They were provided the assistance of two instructional aides and also an hour and a half of additional teacher's time, thus providing five adults for approximately thirty-eight to forty students. Two adjacent classrooms were utilized so that a highly intensive and individualized program was possible. The students were integrated with all other students in the afternoon program. This schedule allowed for an intensive morning program of core subjects while at the same time giving these students the opportunity to participate fully in the afternoon rotation as well as all programs available in the school.

The reduction in class size decision was one that was made not to provide equality across classes, but to provide for the needs of students. In a fashion similar to the case of the Special Education program, other classes were also maintained at a much lower level than most For example, the entry level classes for non-English speaking students was kept small in order to provide an intensive program that would accelerate their progress. Entry level classes were designed to accomodate the needs of many Asian as well as Hispanic students who often arrived from other countries as older students, but with little or no schooling.

Decisions to Support and Enhance the Vision

Throughout the restructuring process, the staff at Linda Vista continued to find ways to better meet the needs of students. The upper-level staff reorganized their math instruction to reflect a concept-based program that allowed students at all levels of math proficiency to experience a broad range of math concepts. Each of nine classrooms was a concept station. Students rotated through these concepts every ten days to three weeks. Concepts ranged from basic math to geometry (number sense, numeration, whole number operations, whole number computations, measurement, statistics, probability patterns, fractions, decimals, and spatial sense), so that even though a student might be having difficulty with basic math, he would still experience other concepts. Students were assessed early in the year and after each rotation. A nondeficit perspective was used. While the population of Asian Pacific students was substantially non-English speak-

TABLE 8.1
Linda Vista Elementary School Primary Afternoon Schedule:
Three-Week Rotation Plan—Fall Semester

Group	Period	Week 1–3	Week 4–6	Week 7–9	Week 10–12	Week 13–15	Week 16–1
A1	2	Fine Arts	Music	PE	Sci/Garden	Music	PE
	3		Geo/Curr	Growth		Geo/Curr	Math
A2	2	Sci/Garden	Geo/Curr	PE	Sci/Garden	Music	PE
	3		Music	Math		Geo/Curr	Growth
B1	2	Sci/Garden	Geo/Curr	Growth	Fine Arts	Geo/Curr	Math
	3		Music	PE		Music	PE
B2	2	Sci/Garden	Geo/Curr	Math	Fine Arts	Geo/Curr	Math
	3		Music	PE		Music	PE
C1	2	Music	PE	Fine Arts	Music	PE	Sci/Garden
	3	Geo/Curr	Growth		Geo/Curr	Math	
C2	2	Music	PE	Fine Arts	Music	PE	Sci/Garden
	3	Geo/Curr	Math		Geo/Curr	Growth	
D1	2	Geo/Curr	Math	Sci/Garden	Geo/Curr	Growth	Fine Arts
	3	Music	PE		Music	PE	
D2	2	Geo/Curr	Math	Sci/Garden	Geo/Curr	Growth	Fine Arts
	3	Music	PE		Music	PE	

(continued on next page)

TABLE 8.1 (*continued*)
Linda Vista Elementary School Primary Afternoon Schedule:
Three-Week Rotation Plan—Fall Semester

Group	Period	Week 1-3	Week 4-6	Week 7-9	Week 10-12	Week 13-15	Week 16-1
E1	2	PE	Fine Arts	Music	PE	Sci/Garden	Music
	3	Growth		Geo/Curr	Growth		Geo/Curr
E2	2	PE	Fine Arts	Music	PE	Sci/Garden	Music
	3	Math		Geo/Curr	Growth		Geo/Curr
F1	2	Growth	Sci/Growth	Geo/Curr	Math	Fine Arts	Geo/Curr
	3	PE		Music	PE		Music
F2	2	Math	Sci/Garden	Geo/Curr	Growth	Fine Arts	Geo/Curr
	3	PE		Music	PE		Music

ing struggling with economic deprivation and often arriving with little educational background, the curriculum was designed around the needs of the students and with clear and high expectations and offering a rigorous content.

Other examples of ongoing improvement were the study skills and reading recovery programs. In order to help students keep their active day organized, a highly successful study skills program was implemented. Standard binders and dividers were provided each student with communication pages to parents for homework and classwork. This helped both students and parents focus on day-to-day work and was especially important in helping highly traditional families, connected to a very nontraditional program, keep focused on the clear expectations for all students.

The Reading Recovery program is an early intervention process for first-grade youngsters that has proven highly successful throughout the country. If native English speaking or Asian students entering the transition phase of the English program were still experiencing difficulty with reading, the Reading Recovery program provided a safety net that caught students before they failed.

Supplemental and Noninstructional Programs

Parent and Community Outreach

The staff at Linda Vista had to make a concerted effort to change their thinking about how to involve families and the community at large. One of the largest groups represented at Linda Vista, to use one example, is the Hmong group. Although committed to education, the Hmong culture is a highly traditional one and parents believe teaching is the responsibility of the professionals. Therefore, the staff had to assess their beliefs and understandings about the Southeast Asian cultures. They came to understand the very dramatic differences among these cultures and the importance of earning the trust of each community. Many had suffered greatly and had given up their homeland for a new and extremely different society. If we were to win their trust, their perspective had to become our perspective.

It was decided that the parent and community program would be called "Outreach." A commitment was made to reach out to the families on their terms and to approach this process as a developmental one. The point at which parents are part of the decision-making structure of the school would be arrived at over time and by first establishing trust.

A cadre of community aides who spoke the languages of the community were already employed at the school. However, they were basically involved in crises intervention. The Outreach Committee, as it came to be known, planned a totally different role for these aides. They would reach out to families through monthly home visits. These home visits were tied to a specific agenda and to various groups of students. For example, during the first month of school all the new families were visited to orient them with the school. At another time of the year, all of the at-risk students were visited with an agenda of providing ideas for parents about homework, discipline, and organizing time. The community aides were trusted members of the community, including clan leaders, so they were able to discuss concerns with families in their native language.

A second aspect of the family involvement program was the education program. An assessment was completed early in the year to find out what the parents felt their educational needs were in order to be effective. This needs assessment was a regular part of the initial workshops so that parents were able to give input about their needs in a comfortable situation explained in their language by someone they trusted. In the beginning stages of the restructuring process, family members were often able to express needs only in cryptic terms—for example, discipline, math, or reading. As time progressed and parents realized that we would carry out what they had requested, and as they learned new skills themselves, the requests became much more detailed. For example, as the staff brought in extensive information about gang activity and prevention through the utilization of community law enforcement agencies, parents began feeling more and more secure in expressing their fears about gangs and in asking for information about how to assist their children to seek other avenues for support groups. The staff, through the assistance of Asian community leaders worked hard to find agencies like UPAC (The Union of Pan-Asian Communities) that identified police officers, counselors, and other individuals who were Asian Pacific Americans themselves.

Several workshops throughout the year were planned based on the needs assessment. The Outreach Committee planned the agenda, often bringing in experts to help with particular lesson plans; the community aides or teachers who spoke the languages of the parents, however, delivered the instruction. Each workshop was conducted simultaneously in separate rooms in five languages. Understanding and communication were primary. The opportunity for families to exchange ideas and learn collaborative practices was as important as the content. Also, it was understood that, if we were to reach out to parents, transportation and child care must be provided, and the staff, both certificated and classified, worked diligently to ensure that this support was provided to parents.

Over the years a rich variety of workshops were offered. Parents became accustomed to and comfortable with hands-on type of activities and interactive sessions. Family math and reading, interactive science, and student-taught computer literacy were but a few of the offerings families experienced. If a video could have captured sessions with parents in the fall of 1987 and compared it to workshops in 1993 the difference depicted would be dramatic. In the earlier scenario, parents sat quietly, women separated from the men, and any attempt to ask them to collaborate with each other was met with stony silence. By 1993, the scene was one of mothers and fathers sitting with their child conducting scientific experiments and enthusiastically asking for assistance from the classroom teachers. In another scene families were crowded around multimedia computer stations learning from their children about their projects, but also talking to each other about the progress the school had made.

As we developed a cohesive school community, many alternative means of support were provided to families. Health care and social services were coordinated by staff members so that students and their families had access to necessary services, information, and support. Community agencies gradually became part of the school family and were integral to the parent education program, lending their services on a regular basis. Where a closed environment existed before, an open and accessible one became the mode.

At this point in time, parents now felt the school was theirs. They served as volunteers, guest speakers, and translators. It became a tradition at the school to have cultural New Year celebrations planned jointly by community members and staff, and the celebrations became an integral part of the curriculum. Stations were set up, particularly at the annex site, in which parents and other community members assisted with each instructional station. Parents often came into classrooms and discussed with students their oral traditions, legends, and stories.

As parents became active members of the school-site council and Outreach Committee, their input was always requested during the planning, implementation, and evaluation stages of the change process. For example, during the first year of piloting the new Growth Record as the progress reporting tool, every parent's comment about the Growth Record was recorded during parent conferences. These comments served as the foundation for revisions.

Once the families of Linda Vista school became an integral part of the school community, the web of inclusion extended to the community at large. In fact a multifaceted partnership grew from the school's commitment to involve its community in the education process. As the community recognized the openness and success of this school, many agencies approached the staff with proposals for collaboration. At the time of this writing, Linda vista enjoyed partnerships with eight agencies: The San Diego Police Department Western Division, The San Diego County Office of Education, Francis Parker, a nearby private school, the local YMCA, Linda Vista

McDonald's restaurant, the Price Club, the Fashion Valley local shopping mall, and the University of San Diego.

The partners provided many valuable services to the students. For example, Price Club, a large corporation with many locations in the greater San Diego area, donated seed fertilizer, equipment, and fencing for the school's one-acre garden, where students cared for the garden as part of their science classwork. A few years into the process the local YMCA approached the Linda Vista staff and proposed that the school use their facility with students and even offered the help of their instructors. A major obstacle was transportation of the students to the YMCA. The local McDonald's restaurant heard of the plan and wrote a grant to the McDonald's corporation to fund the purchase of buses. The grant was funded and has resulted in an extensive physical education program for the students. Four days a week, physical education classes from the school were bused to the YMCA where they participated in gymnastics, swimming, and soccer classes. Beyond the physical education program, the staff of the YMCA have become part of the Linda Vista family. They are often on campus at lunch time or after school interacting with students. Many times these individuals act as big brothers and sisters to students after school or on weekends.

During a reception for the outgoing principal of Linda Vista school, the following story was told by the executive director of the YMCA to exemplify what he felt the partnership had accomplished for himself and his staff. A Hmong child had some difficulty during the swimming lessons. The parents refused to let the child return to the class until a ceremony was completed over the pool. As the executive director tells it, he would never have agreed to such an event before the partnership with Linda Vista, but after learning and understanding about the cultures represented at the school, he realized that by reaching out to these parents it would do much to solidify the relationship with the community. Thus, the ceremony was conducted and the child was returned to swimming class. A great deal was achieved by this simple act of acceptance.

The County Office of Education, another community partner, offered tutors from among its many employees. Video productions and printing of many school items were but a few of the opportunities that have resulted from this partnership. The San Diego Police Department collaborated with the school in providing ongoing education for students and parents about gang and substance abuse prevention. The partnership resulted in a greater trust for law enforcement in the community since many of the sessions with police officers offered opportunities for dialogue between the community and the officers. The inherent message here was that such partnerships go beyond the specific materials and activities provided to the school. They encourage trust, develop cultural understanding, and open lies of communication.

Social Development Programs

The underpinnings of a positive school culture included a great many activities beyond actual classroom instruction. Recognition activities, schoolwide discipline plans, conflict resolution, and counseling programs provided the glue that bound people together. A major foundation for social development was a comprehensive, schoolwide discipline policy that was clearly articulated to students, staff, and parents. At Linda Vista, a great emphasis was placed on recognizing students' individual achievements. These achievements were celebrated at monthly assemblies where the students received a variety of awards. A school bulletin board featured the awards and the student's photos. The Asian parents responded to these recognition programs with enthusiasm, but the process was gradual. It took special invitations and many phone calls for the parents to trust that they were essential to the programs. In, fact it was part of the ceremony to recognize each parent as their child received the award. In time, parents brought grandparents, uncles, aunts, brothers, and sisters. After a few years, the ceremonies began to include cultural programs, usually timed around a particular celebration such as the Lao New Year.

Recognition activities such as the "Caught You Being Good" program and other rewards offered through the counseling center, were implemented to focus on positive behaviors. In addition, many students were trained in the method and language of conflict resolution. As conflict managers, students assisted one another, especially on the playground during recess. In all of these and the above recognition activities, great care was taken to ensure that all students had opportunities to participate throughout the school year. If a Hmong student, for example, had poor attendance due a family need to care for younger siblings, the community aides worked in a caring manner with the family to assist in finding alternatives so that the child improved her attendance and could subsequently be rewarded. Alternative avenues for success were consistently being sought so that all students had opportunities for recognition.

Assessment and Accountability

Any substantial, systemic school change must include an internal mechanism of assessment and accountability from its inception. At the very heart of the restructuring process is a foundation of student assessments embedded in the curriculum and involving the learner. It is an individual assessment, yet systematically linked to provide instructional continuity and ongoing information about students for parents, teachers, and for school accountability. Thus, the continuous progress of students becomes inextricably linked to the school's overall performance and the performance of the school professionals.

At the beginning of the restructuring planning process at Linda Vista, discussions regarding assessment and accountability were consistently being raised. In the meantime, the school's assessment committee began exploring alternative means of assessment. A natural outcome of this thinking was the establishment of schoolwide standards reflective of the California frameworks but incorporating Linda Vista's six levels of English language proficiency. This process alone took two full years to accomplish. The process of rethinking the concept of student assessment usually takes the extremes. At one extreme is standardization such as norm-referenced test results, grades, and the like, that give a number, rank, or letter representing the student's performance compared to other students, locally or nationally. At the other extreme is an individual teacher-developed student portfolio in which the teacher makes individual, subjective judgments about student progress.

A schoolwide, alternative assessment process such as portfolio assessment, lies somewhere between the above two extremes. It assesses the actual work of students, work that is in process and reflects high-order thinking. However, the school standardizes expectations based on its own needs and population of students, thus ensuring continuity and accountability. These standards should be designed within the framework of the larger organization—that is, district and state expectations.

Educators and policy makers often assume that Asian Pacific students who enter school speaking a language other than English arrive with little or no English, and only at beginning levels of schooling. The reality is that they enter at all ages, from across all socioeconomic levels, with varying educational backgrounds, and with linguistic capacities ranging from monolingual to varying degrees of bilingualism. There are many factors to consider and this creates a dilemma regarding how to place students and how to monitor and assess student progress. To meet this challenge a multifaceted approach that distinguishes second-language proficiency from educational ability is essential.

Consequently, the decision to incorporate portfolio assessment at Linda Vista for language arts was a recognition that this multifaceted approach was necessary. At the beginning, the staff began maintaining portfolios for individual students, although not systematically. This was part of the learning process. The next step was to design rubrics for oral language, reading, and writing, then to make decisions as to the specific types of work to be included, the students' involvement in those choices, and at what times during the year. Portfolios were recognized as a form of assessment that has the capacity to maintain a consistent perspective of first- and second-language development and focuses on what the student can do rather than on what they are not yet able to do. Portfolios for Asian students developing a second language take into account the unique developmental path for students in their second language as well as their educational backgrounds. Portfolios can also contribute greatly to understanding and monitoring students' second-language oral proficiency. Oral language development in the second language is a process that has traditionally been measured as discrete points along a scale of vocabulary, grammar, and syntax; however, proficiency in oral language represents a complex constellation of skills. Audio, video, and observational techniques among others, are methods that can result in substantive evidence of progress in second-language acquisition, These assessments are embedded in the day-to-day curriculum of the classroom and can measure natural language ability, confidence, and nuances of language use (Table 8.2).

A few years after it's initiation of the school reform process, Linda Vista School was fortunate to receive a sizable grant from the RJR Nabisco foundation under the Next Century School project. Through this grant, the staff decided to enhance the assessment process by an extensive technology component, which provided for individual electronic portfolios. Teacher computer stations were established at each of the two school campuses with ongoing certificate and classified staff training. The system allowed all types of student work to be stored—oral, graphic, and written. Original work could be electronically scanned directly from a photograph or lifted from a video or audio tape. Each child's portfolio was maintained on the system with the specific rubrics to be entered by the teacher. The individual portfolio was then available to be accessed by the teacher or other staff for ongoing assessment, parent conferences, and schoolwide assessment analysis.

The collaborative decision-making process established at this school led to the next logical step in the assessment process. The staff realized that the current district student progress report was not aligned with a performance-based assessment process. Consequently, the "Growth Record" was developed, which reflected the students' learning growth as measured on the rubrics (Table 8.3). A hard copy of the student's portfolio was attached and parents were informed about the standards the student had met. Again, this reporting allowed the staff to focus on the achievement of child rather than on the deficits. It helped connect both students and their parents much more intimately to the assessment process, but the decision to go forward with the new Growth Record was not made without parent approval. A testament to the level of trust that had been established between staff and the Asian parents to this point was the fact that these highly traditional parents approved the piloting of such a nontraditional form of progress reporting.

The staff assured the community that during the pilot year a survey would be completed requesting detailed opinions regarding the Growth Record. Much effort was taken in conducting the survey. At each conference

TABLE 8.2
Informal Reading Checklist
Early Childhood/Primary/Entry Level

Name _____ Teacher _____ Year _____

	October	March	June
Developing book Sense and Language			
Shows interest in books			
• chooses books independently			
• listens when being read to			
Holds book right side up			
Turns pages from front to back			
Distinguishes between pictures and words			
Identifies parts of a book (front, title, back)			
Early Reading Development			
Memorizes repeat parts of modeled or familiar stories and			
Predictable test			
See evidence of sequencing when acting out or retelling story			
Can read picture			
Verbalizes previous experience to make sense of a book			
Can follow text from left to right			
Participates in shared reading			
Can identify characters			
Uses reference materials			
Evidence of making meaning of text (Example: pictures, act it out)			
Story map			

(continued on next page)

TABLE 8.2 *(continued)*
Informal Reading Checklist
Early Childhood/Primary/Entry Level

	October	March	June
Developing Reading Strategies			
Uses cueing strategies			
• context/meaning cues (semantics) (Example: uses pictures)			
• word structure (syntactic) (Example: reads house for home)			
• visual cues (grapho-phonic) (Example: uses phonic rules)			
Self-corrects miscues			
Can predict outcomes			
Cultural literacy is reflected in knowledge of literary genre			
• fiction, nonfiction			
• folktale			
• myth			
• poetry			
• biography			
Evidence of making meaning of text			

(X) indicates consistent behavior

period during that school year, parents were asked a series of questions about the new reporting tool. As in all parent conferences at Linda Vista, translators were always available, to translate not only the information about the child's progress but the surveys as well. Doing the survey in the context of the actual parent conference period was no casual decision. The parents were able to connect the new progress report to their own child's work. This intimate connection gave the staff data they would not otherwise have received. The Asian parents made such remarks as, "I really know how my child is doing—I see it in his work"; or, "Before, the number she used to get on her report card didn't seem to mean anything, now I can see how much progress she has made." Another parent expressed, "I can see that all my

TABLE 8.3
Upper-Level Rubrics Listings

ORAL LANGUAGE

1. *Silent / Emergent Listener-Speaker*
   - does not yet respond verbally
   - minimal evidence of listening/speaking skills; expresses ideas using gestures and simple words, and is developing vocabulary

2. *Limited Listener-Speaker*
   - expresses ideas using simple words and phrases
   - limited participation in class activities and group settings

3. *Developing Listener-Speaker*
   - experiences speaker, usually attentive
   - occasionally takes part in class activities
   - makes relevant responses
   - expresses ideas with command of the language

4. *Capable Listener-Speaker*
   - confident, effective, attentive
   - actively takes part in class activities
   - makes relevant responses
   - expresses ideas with command of the language

5. *Exceptional Listener-Speaker*
   - confident, effective, attentive
   - actively takes part in class activities consistently in a leadership role

READING

1. *Emergent Reader*
   - enjoys being read to
   - participates in shared reading
   - memorizes and repeats oral language but does not connect to print
   - knows some letters and is gaining awareness that letters have sounds
   - understands "book sense"
   - uses picture cues and "reads" from memory incorporating left to right knowledge
   - beginning to make predictions
   - ability to use prior knowledge

(continued on next page)

children in the different classrooms are being judged by the same standard."

The staff at Linda Vista went on to conduct the same process with math standards, rubrics, tasks, and reporting. This time, the process was much easier but no less significant in informing instruction in mathemat-

TABLE 8.3 *(continued)*
Upper-Level Rubrics Listings

READING *(continued)*

2. *Less Experienced Reader*
   - has limited experience as a reader
   - chooses to read very easy and familiar texts
   - has difficulty with any unfamiliar material, yet is usually able to read own writing with ease
   - needs a great deal of support with reading in all content areas
   - is overly dependent on any one strategy when reading aloud
   - rarely chooses to read for pleasure

3. *Experienced Writer*
   - self motivated and confident writer who uses a wide range of techniques to engage the reader
   - collection of work demonstrates:
     - clear organization
     - use descriptive words
     - complete, varied sentences
     - selection of vocabulary appropriate for the writing
     - beginning to make revisions
     - few errors in conventions and spelling

4. *Exceptionally Experienced Writer*
   - enthusiastic and reflective writer who enjoys pursuing his/her own writing interests independently
   - uses a wide range of techniques to engage the reader
   - writing is fully developed and may show originality, liveliness, excitement, humor, or suspense
   - collection of work demonstrates:
     - definite organizational plan
     - use descriptive words
     - clear sentence sense and variety
     - control over vocabulary choice and arrangement
     - willingness to make revisions
     - few errors in conventions and spelling

---

ics. The cycle of improvement was now imbedded at the school, so that decisions about assessment practices, aligned with instruction, resulted in improved student learning.

School Accountability

One of the most dramatic decisions of the Linda Vista experience resulted from the realization that it was not enough to have created a new assessment system aligned with instruction. It was necessary to design a reporting system that could extrapolate data on a schoolwide basis. Indicators of student success, parent and staff satisfaction, school climate, and community engagement had to be designed. The first major challenge was to formulate an evaluation design that would incorporate both the district required norm-referenced data as well as the performance-based results.

The school's reporting portfolio included the ASAT (Abbreviated Stanford Achievement) results that were consistently mixed. The staff came to realize that even though reality dictated that this data had to be reported, it did not reflect the true progress of students. Alongside these results were reported the dramatic advancement of students in literacy on the performance level rubrics. Portfolios reflected major growth in writing and oral language development that a norm-referenced instrument could not possibly have demonstrated for English language learners. The accompanying staff approved exemplars of student work or anchors, provided greater inter-rater reliability to support the rubric ratings.

It was not until more recently that the staff developed reading strategy check lists and student observation records so that data related to the progress of students in reading could be analyzed. Hundreds of students consistently moved up the standards-based language proficiency levels described earlier.

The school's accountability portfolio also provided indicators of attendance as well as parent and staff satisfaction. Linda Vista's attendance rates were consistently one of the highest in the district. All staff, both certificated and classified, were asked to complete a survey each year. Involvement in the decision-making process, communication flow, and the entire restructuring endeavor were areas on which the respondents indicated a range of 75 percent to 87 percent agreement, with consistent increases in satisfaction over time.

Parents were asked, in their various native languages, about their satisfaction with the school in terms of how they were valued, the instructional changes, whether they felt diversity was valued, and their feelings in general about the parent outreach programs. Over time, responses increased from 80 percent to 88 percent positive agreement with the school's programs and their role as parents in the education of their children. It was apparent after six to seven years of the restructuring process that parents had become partners with the school in the education of their children. From an attitude of hands off, to one of involvement in parent meetings, the decision making of the school, homework, attendance, progress reporting, and a variety of other activities, the school became a focal point for the Asian community. These practices were finally institutionalized.

The assessment\accountability process at Linda Vista school reflected an action research mode. All answers were not embedded in single pieces of data. Indicators were multifaceted and existed within a living, dynamic process. The accountability path was one that was created first and foremost by the community it served—in this case by both staff and community. It included a feedback and reporting system that provided ongoing information about student progress as well as other important indices. Finally, and most importantly, the accountability system tightly aligned the instruction, curriculum, and assessment together and was then linked closely to staff and parent accountability.

Conclusion

The Linda Vista community did not purport to reach ultimate solutions, rather they challenged themselves to find new ways of addressing needs and to be accountable for change. This was a school where the visitor who entered quickly recognized the vitality of the climate. Students were engaged in learning throughout the day, even at the end, when it was time to go home. Learning was student centered and reflected a high value of the diversity. A visitor (of which there have been thousands), saw parents on campus regularly and felt treated with genuine respect and affection.

The staff and parents at Linda Vista appreciated the accolades they received from others outside the community for their endeavors, and they have received much recognition. The school has been named a California Distinguished School, A Next Century School and an Apple Classroom of Tomorrow. Linda Vista Elementary was recognized in *Time* and *Redbook* magazines and was the focus of several research studies. One study, conducted by the Southwest Regional Lab of the U.S. Department of Education, resulted in Linda Vista's program being named an exemplary program for limited-English speaking students.

This case study serves as a unique example of the decision-making processes brought together by one staff with a strong commitment to serve its very diverse student population at a high level of expectation for their performance, and with a keen awareness that the parents and the community at large must be intimately involved. We offer Linda Vista's story to you as a challenge and a vision. It was an ordinary neighborhood school with a formidable task. It was transformed over time through a process of careful planning, intense dialogue, and commitment to children. The main message to administrators and teachers is to not only understand the variety of distinct Asian Pacific cultures but to incorporate them into the day-to-day life of the school through curriculum, parent education, and assessment. However, all of this takes place over time and must be accomplished by reaching out to the community on their terms and gradually reaching a level of collaboration and mutual accountability.

Note

Portions of this chapter are included in *Restructuring Schools for Linguistic Diversity*, pp. 271–90 (New York: Teachers College Press, 1997).

Addison Watanabe

Asian American and Pacific Islander American Families with Disabilities

A Current View

As a young child in elementary school, I often heard, "Do your best,
work hard and you will be rewarded! Do not shame us."
As an adolescent in junior high school, I often heard, "Do your best,
work hard and you will be rewarded! Do not shame us."
As a young adult I high school, I often heard, "Do your best,
work hard and you will be rewarded! Do not shame us."
As an adult in college, I often heard, "Do your best, work hard and
you will be rewarded! Do not shame us."
Now as an adult with over twenty years of formal education and in a
professional position,
I still often hear, "Do your best, work hard and you will be rewarded!
Do not shame us."
I sit and wonder at times, what I would have been like had I not heard,
"Do your best, work hard and you will be rewarded! Do not shame us."

—Addison Watanabe

M any individuals of the general public in the United States have
assumed that Asian Pacific Americans are a homogeneous
group. They have, through the help of mass media, grouped
Asian Pacific Americans as a group physically and culturally distinguish-
able from other racial and ethnic minority groups. The assumption made

by the general public has little validity although it is often said that one cannot "tell them apart." Asian Pacific Americans are made up of physically and culturally diverse groups with different languages, customs, and values. The category of Asian American and Pacific Islander American includes at least thirty-two distinct cultural or ethnic groups (Wong, 1980). Asian Pacific Americans have cultural roots from Japan, China, Korea, India, Samoa, Tonga, Fiji, the Mariana Islands, the Marshall Islands, the Philippines, Vietnam, and other Pacific Rim countries. The only common link that these Asian Pacific Americans (APA) have is the fact that all may have, in one time or another, in the past or through their ancestors, bathed, swam, or touched the waters of the Pacific Ocean.

Individuals with Disabilities

Individuals with disabilities are not a homogenous group of individuals with the same identifying characteristics or similar educational needs. The U.S. Department of Education Office of Special Education and Rehabilitative Services has identified specific disabilities as those disabilities that may interfere with an individual's ability to learn and progress in the current educational system. The disability categories include visual impairments, hearing impairments, multiple disabilities (deaf-blindness), autism, orthopedically impaired, other health impaired, speech impaired, mental retardation, specific learning disabilites, and serious emotional disturbances.

The attitudes held by many in the general populace is that "a disability is a disability." This is quite evident when a sighted person encounters a visually impaired individual. In many instances, the sighted person will tend to speak a little louder to the visually impaired individual, which results in an unusual interchange. Often the visually impaired person will remark to the sighted person, "I'm blind not deaf. I have normal hearing, I just can't see!"

Since the passage of Public Law 94–142, the Education for All Handicapped Children Act of 1975, a systemic awareness of the need to provide appropriate educational and related services to child and youth has become evident. There has been a steady growth in the percentages in the numbers of students being served in special education programs nationwide. From the period of 1976 through 1993, the increase in the numbers of children and youth being served in special education programs has increased approximately 139 percent (U.S. Bureau of the Census, 1972, 1983, 1994). Table 9.1 shows the change in the numbers of students being served in special education programs, while Table 9.2 indicates a breakdown of students being served in four special education programs for the 1992–93 school year (U.S. Bureau of Census, 1993, 1994). By examining the numbers, it

TABLE 9.1

Students Served under Part B and Chapter 1 (SOP)

Number and Percentage Change

School Years 1976–77 through 1992–93[a]

School Year	Change in Total Number Served from Previous Year (%)	Total Served	Part B[c]	Chapter 1 (SOP)
1976–77	—	3,708,588	3,484,756	223,832
1977–78	1.8	3,777,286	3,554,554	222,732
1978–79	3.8	3,919,073	3,693,593	225,480
1979–80	3.0	4,036,219	3,802,475	233,744
1980–81	3.5	4,177,689	3,933,981	243,708
1981–82	1.3	4,233,282	3,990,346	242,936
1982–83	1.5	4,298,327	4,052,595	245,732
1983–84	1.0	4,341,399	4,094,108	247,291
1984–85[b]	0.5	4,363,031	4,113,312	249,719
1985–86	0.2	4,370,244	4,121,104	249,140
1986–87	1.2	4,421,601	4,166,692	254,909
1987–88	1.4	4,485,702	4,226,504	259,198
1988–89	1.8	4,568,063	4,305,690	262,373
1989–90	2.4	4,675,619	4,411,681	263,938
1990–91	2.8	4,807,441	4,547,368	260,073
1991–92	3.7	4,986,075	4,714,119	271,956
1992–93	3.7	5,170,242	4,893,865	276,377

a. From 1988–89 to the present, these numbers include children three through twenty-one years of age counted under Part B and children from birth to age twenty-one counted under Chapter 1 (SOP). Prior to 1988–89, children from birth through age twenty were served under Chapter 1 (SOP). The totals do not include infants and toddlers from birth through age two served under Part H who were not served under the Chapter 1 (SOP) program.

b. Beginning in 1984–85, the number of children with disabilities reported for the most recent year reflects revisions to state data received by the Office of Special Education Programs between the July 1 grant award date and October 1. Updates received from states for previous years are included, so totals may not match those reported in previous annual reports to Congress. Before 1984–85, reports provided data as of the grant award date.

c. Although states must serve all eligible children with disabilities, funds are provided only for up to 12 percent of the state's total school population. This is commonly referred to as "the 12 percent cap."

Source: U.S. Department of Education, Office of Special Education Programs, Data Analysis System (DANS).

TABLE 9.2
Disability of Students Age Six through Twenty-one
Served under Part B and Chapter 1 (SOP)
Number and Percentage
School Year 1992–1993

Disability	Part B		Chapter 1 (SOP)		Total	
	Number	Percent[a]	Number	Percent[a]	Number	Percent[a]
Specific learning disabilities	2,333,571	52.4	35,814	19.7	2,369,385	51.1
Speech or language impairments	990,718	22.2	9,436	5.2	1,000,154	21.6
Mental retardation	484,871	10.9	48,844	26.9	533,715	11.5
Serious emotional disturbance	368,545	8.3	34,123	18.8	402,668	8.7
Other	274,412	6.1	53,340	29.3	327,752	6.9
All disabilities	4,452,117	100.0	181,557	100.0	4,633,674	100.0

a. Percentages sum within columns.

Source: U.S. Department of Education, Office of Special Education Programs, Data Analysis System (DANS).

TABLE 9.3
Percentage of Growth of Students Served in
Special Education Programs from 1980 through 1992

	Learning Disabilities	Speech Impairment	Mental Retardation	Emotional Disturbance	Other
1980	31.9	29.6	21.7	8.2	8.6
1985	42.4	26.1	16.1	8.6	6.8
1986	43.1	26.1	15.3	8.7	6.8
1987	43.6	25.8	15.0	8.7	6.9
1988	47.0	23.2	14.6	9.1	6.1
1989	47.8	23.1	13.8	8.9	6.4
1990	48.6	23.1	13.0	9.0	6.3
1991	49.3	22.8	12.4	9.0	6.5
1992	50.1	22.3	12.0	8.9	6.7

Source: U.S. Department of Education, Office of Special Education Programs, Data Analysis System (DANS).

can be seen that approximatley 93 percent of all students in special education programs receive services under the categories of specific learning disabilities, speech or language impairments, mental retardation, and serious
emotional disturbances. Table 9.3 shows the growth of each of these areas
over a twelve-year period. This information was compiled by the Office of
Special Education Programs (1994) in its annual report to Congress.

Asian/Pacific Islander American
Children with Disabilities
Limited Identification

This heightened awareness to provide services to all individuals with disabilities has not applied to Asian Pacific American children and youth (Ishii-
Jordan, 1994), resulting in the underrepresentation of this group of children
in many special education programs. It is possible that services have not
been provided to APA children and youth because of the perceptions held by
the general public with respect to the myth of Asian Americans as being the
"Model Minority." Table 9.4 shows the percentages of Asian Pacific Americans enrolled in special education programs (Office of Civil Rights, 1990). By
examining the figues, it is easily deduced that APA students are underrepresented in special education programs. This is by no means a phenomena

TABLE 9.4
Percentages of Asians and Pacific Islanders
Enrolled in Selected Categories of Exceptionality

Category	1978 %	1980 %	1982 %	1984 %	1986 %	1988 %
Educable mentally retarded	0.34	0.50	9.46	0.91	0.90	1.03
Trainable mentally retarded	0.94	1.36	1.62	2.29	2.10	2.14
Seriously emotionally disturbed	0.44	0.43	0.48	0.64	0.60	0.75
Specific learning disabled	0.78	1.01	1.21	1.49	1.40	1.34
Speech impaired	1.31	1.62	1.69	2.14	2.10	2.00
Gifted/Talented	**3.37**	**4.35**	**4.72**	**6.78**	**6.70**	**6.20**
Asians/Pacific Islanders as a Percentage of Total School Enrollment	1.42	2.24	2.56	3.65	3.60	3.76

From State and National Summaries of Reported Data from the Department of
Education, Office of Civil Rights, 1988 Elementary and Secondary School Civil
Rights Survey.

Bold type indicates overrepresentation.

confined to the United States. Tomlinson (1989) noted that in schools in London, Asian students were underrepresented in schools for the emotionally and behaviorally disordered, the autistic, the language impaired, and individuals who had moderate learning difficulties. Brosnan (1983) conducted an examination of special education programs in California and also found that Asian Pacific American children and youth were underrepresented in programs for individuals with learning disabilities.

A Current Problem

The educational and economic achievements of a small segment of certain Asian Pacific American groups have provided the impetus for the attachment of the Model Minority label to the group as a whole. Researchers and scholars have shown that the Asian Pacific Americans are also beset with the numerous social and economic problems which are common to all ethnic and cultural groups found in the United States (Sue, 1981; Pang, 1995, Chan, 1992a).

The data indicate that there are some "real issues" occuring within the Asian Pacific American community with regard to serving children and youth with disabilities. Many would remark that it should not be a concern because, afterall, this shows that Asian Pacific Americans are doing "just fine" in the U.S. educational system. By adopting this stance, the myth of the Model Minority is reinforced. If the notion is that abilities and disabilities are normally distributed, then it could be concluded that the data presented by the U.S. Department of Education may be invalid. The premise of a normal distribution assumes that, within each group examined, there would be individuals in both ends of the spectrum, with the majority of the individuals falling within an "average" range. It is important to examine what might be possible agents in causing underrepresentation of Asian Pacific Americans in special education programs.

Impact of a Child with a Disability

Before discussing what issues may be involved in the underreporting, underidentification, and underserving of the Asian Pacific American child and youth with disabilities, it is important to understand the impact a child with a disability has on the family.

When a family is initially confronted with a child with a disability, be it initially at birth or at a later stage in the child's lifetime, a profound impact is felt by members of the family. The family experiences many feelings and reactions. Initially, when an infant is born with a disability, parents' usual reaction is a type of depression, which is often exhibited in the form of mourning or grief. Mothers tend to mourn for a longer period of time before they recover from the initial shock (D'Arcy, 1968). In Asian Pacific American families, these feelings may be more hidden because, culturally, some people believe disabilities are an indication of personal or family failures. In addition, many Asian Pacific American families have little knowledge of or are uncomfortable with disabilities.

Family members also exhibit reactions of shock, uncertainty, disappointment, anger, frustration, guilt, denial, fear, withdrawal, and rejection (Blacher, 1984; Bristor, 1984; Gargiulo, 1985; Rose, 1987). Roos (1975) elaborates on more specific ecological variables that contribute to the feelings expressed by parents. These include the loss of self-esteem, shame, ambivalence, depression, self-sacrifice, and defensiveness.

These factors, variables, and their impact on the family may create a family crisis of considerable magnitude. This will then involve the family in a sequential process of emotional and psychological development associated with the presence in the family of a child with a disability. Gargiulo (1985) has suggested that parental responses may be separated into three stages: primary phase, secondary phase, and a tertiary phase. Gargiulo characterizes the primay phase as one in which the parent undergoes the emotions of shock, denial, and grief. During this phase, parental emotions are also accompanied by the effects of depression. The secondary phase is marked by ambivalence, possibly accompanied by feelings of guilt, anger, shame, and embarassment. The tertiary phase commences with bargaining, followed by adaptation and reorganization, and ending with the feelings of acceptance and adjustment.

Professionals working with parents of children and youth with disabilities accept these as stages parents must go through. Professionals also realize that culture plays an important role in how quickly parents move through these various stages when confronted with a child who has been identified as having a disability. It is important to understand some of the views held by Asian Pacific Americans with repect to families, as well as how family members relate to an individual with disabilities. Anderson (1989) noted that the initial behaviors of family members to newborns may differ from culture to culture and that behavior that may appear to be ambivalent or uncaring by one group may be the socially approved behavior for that specific cultural group. Anderson also stated that "Potential cultural variations in the relationships of family members . . . must be kept in mind to avoid misunderstandings or faulty judgements" (p. 172).

Cultural Orientations Affecting
Family Views on Disabilities

While it is important to note that Asian cultures are diverse and varied, there are some similar constructs that guide the social structure of the family and the families' interactions in the larger social construct of their respective communities. The values are complex combinations of various belief systems. The following describes possible value conflicts or misunderstandings about disabilites.

Many of the familial systems have been strongly dominated by influences arising from the beliefs and attitudes of the Confucian, Taoist, and Buddhist teachings (Chan, 1992a; Ishii-Jordan, 1994; Leung, 1988), Judeo-Christian ethics (Agbayani-Siewert & Revilla, 1995; Chan, 1992b; Min, 1995b), animism, and Brahmanism (Chan, 1992a), or a combination of various elements from these different religious teachings (Chan, 1992a; 1992b). Through generations and centuries, lifestyles, family practices, and behaviors have changed and been modified, but much of the traditonal values, belief systems, and practices have been maintained through these ancient religious and philosophical underpinings.

Representative examples of how the family system of values and beliefs shapes and guides the individual are presented. The two values and beliefs presented are related to individuals with Japanese and Filipino ancestral roots. One system is highly influenced by the teachings and philosophies of Confucianism, Daoism, Buddhism, and forms of animism (Japanese), while the Filipino system is influenced heavily by the Judeo-Christian religious teachings with some underpinings of animism.

In Japanese society, the family and not the individual is the basic unit for which socialization and the maintenance of social control rests. The family assumes control of its members and is held accountable for the actions of individual members (Miyamoto, 1984; Nakane, 1970; Reischauer, 1981). The important, overriding ethical basis of the cultural values are social relationships, through which the values are manifested and incorporated in the individual's conduct through the family. Miyamoto (1984) stated that:

> Ethics for the Japanese is a practical social code applied to the regulation of daily social behavior . . . regulating the relationships of men. . . . Duty, or the conception of the social responsibility, is . . . the dynamic focus of the Japanese ethical system. . . . It is the ethical system of collective obligations . . . which give the Japanese family a type of solidaity hardly conceived in the Western mind. (pp. 5–6)

Nishi (1995) compiled information on the preferred values of Japanese Americans and provided examples for each of the value areas. Nishi characterized the values: (1) collectivity/individual; (2) earned by established criteria/aleatory; (3) formal/spontaneous, (4) law/grace; and (5) public/internal.

Collectivity/Individual. With respect to the rank ordering of social objects, the more inclusive collectivities are ranked higher than the less inclusive collectivites. In the rank-ordering scheme, the private individual is ranked the lowest of importance. Lower-ranking objects (private individuals) are expected to subsume their own interest to the notion of enhancing the more inclusive group. The needs of the larger entity are noted to be more important than the needs of the one. Programs/activites which will benefit all of the family collectively are more acceptable than a specific program/activity for an individual.

Earned by established criteria/Aleatory. With regard to status achievement, emphasis is placed on the training and performance of skills by an individual (group) in a status role which earns status recognition and self-respect. Aleatory or chance factors that place a person in a role of authority or status diminish the legitimacy of the role occupied by the individual. This is evident in the perceptions and actions associated with "work hard, study hard and you will gain respect and stature" ideals held by many individuals of Japanese ancestry. These principles are a constant echo in many American families of Japanese descent.

Formal/Spontaneous. Within interunit relationships, there is a preference for formality (correctness) to be exhibited by the Japanese American family. Spontaneous behaviors are not viewed as being acceptable. Family units instruct members to exhibit acceptable interpersonal skills. These skills are guided and demonstrated based on the circumstances surrounding the interactions. There are rules of conduct, the selective acknowledgment of inappropriate feelings and misconduct of other individuals, and the empathetic alertness to the verbal and nonverbal cues given by others.

Law/Grace. There is an emphasis on the moral requisites of behavior rather than the voluntary expression of compassion, gratitude, and other types of behaviors associated with grace. Families place the burden of guilt on a child if that child fails to carry out an obligation expected of him. The rules of obligation weigh heavily on each member of the family unit. The idea of *giri* (reciprocity) is associated with the moral requisites of behavior. Giri is inherent in the value structure of the Japanese.

Public/Internal. The Japanese society has developed a high sensitivity to public regard, as well as control of private feelings for expression in appropriate situations and ways. Child rearing by many Japanese Americans has been built on shaming, ridiculing, and admonishing the child so as not to damage the family name through nonconformity to societal expectations. A high degree of sensitivity to the approval of others is manifested and is often accompanied by the potential for experiencing guilt.

The Filipino family system is also ruled by a system of values that reflect a similar pattern to those expressed by Nishi. Agbayani-Siewert and Revilla (1995) indicated that the Filipino family structure is built on the ideals of cooperation and provides both a supportive and protective secure system members can depend on for a sense of belonging and help. The value of smooth interpersonal relationships are held in high regard by the members of the Filipino family structure. Outward displays that may lead to confrontive behavior are not promoted but passive nonconfrontational exhibitions are encouraged.

As in the case with the Japanese, Filipinos are also bound by a value system that stresses cooperation over individualism (Bulato, 1981; Tagaki & Ishisaka, 1982). The Filipino family places a high value on loyalty to, dependence on, and solidarity of the family and extended family. The needs, wants, and desires of the individual must be sacrificed to ensure that the needs, wants, and desires of the family are obtained. The "for the good of the family" belief outweighs the "for the good of the individual" concerns (Agbayani-Siewert & Revilla, 1995; Chan, 1992b). The smooth interpersonal relationships permeate and guide the daily routine of the Filipino family. This type of relationship has been described as the way to get along with others without creating any visible signs of open conflict. The smooth interpersonal relationships serve to bind the family together and are maintained by four means: reciprocal obligation (*utang ng loob*), shame (*hiya*), going along with the main group (*Pakikisama*), and the protection of self-esteem (*amor propio*).

Reciprocal obligations (Utang ng loob). Utang ng loob is the function that maintains the binding relationships within and between family groups. The underlying principle dictates that when a favor or some service has been received, this favor or service must be returned (Almirol, 1982). Inasmuch as the reciprocal obligations are generally conducted through the exchange of services, it is very difficult to know when or if a debt has been paid in full (Agbayni-Siewert & Revilla, 1995). This value is also very prevalent in the Japanese value system, and has been previously mentioned as giri. The failure of a Filipino individual to participate in utang ng loob, brings feelings of guilt that may affect the individual's psychological well-being (Duff & Arthur, 1980). Reciprocal obligations are forms of social control that assure the Filipino family member of help and protection (Gochenour, 1990).

Shame (Hiya). When an individual fails to meet an intended goal or has performed an act that results in either familial or community disaproval, hiya or shame is the result (Almirol, 1982). The intensity with which an individual conforms to the social structure of the family or community is controlled by the desire to avoid hiya. The function of hiya is to maintain the importance of the group over the individual. The concept of "face," or the preoccupation with how one appears in the eyes of others, is a strong agent that serves to strengthen the power of hiya in the individual (Chan, 1992b).

Going along with the main group (Pakikisama). The strength of the Pakikisama attitude may force an individual to contradict his or her own desires and intentions. The following of Pakikisama insures that good feelings are maintained and that cooperation is practiced by all (Agbayni-Siewert & Revilla, 1995; Chan, 1992b). Individuals will sacrifice their needs in order to maintain the good feelings of cooperation.

Self-esteem (Amor Proprio). Related to the function of shame (hiya) is the attitude of amor proprio (self-esteem). When an individual is criticized, the function of amor proprio may require the person to adopt an aggressive stance in order to protect him/herself. But because of the attitude of hiya, in many instances the aggressive behaviors are repressed, thereby protecting the individual against the shaming of others (Agbayni-Siewert & Revilla, 1995). It is essential that an individual behave in ways so that all of the "faces" and amor proprio of concerned individuals are not threatened (Gochenour, 1990).

Harry (1994) noted that due to the collectivist orientation held by some ethnic and cultural groups, the needs of the individual are subordinated to the needs of the family, as a group, or even the community. This is quite evident in the Japanese and Filipino family system orientations presented. Harry went on to posit that the collectivist orientation held by some cultural groups "represents a central point of departure between modern Western society and most traditional minority cultures" (p. 153). Harry further indicated that the professionals working with various diverse cultural groups need to understand the differences between the collectivist orientation and the individualistic orientation. Only when professionals understand these orientations can progress be made and working relationships be developed between individuals/groups of contrasting orientations.

These two examples of how a series of set values and beliefs guides and controls an individual to conform to the social norms of the large group to which he/she belongs have an impact on how an individual may relate to a different group's values and belief systems. A system of values and beliefs with respect to the identification and education of individuals with disabilities is one such system.

Yao (1987) noted that the term *learning disability* is unheard of in Asia. She reported that most parents and teachers do not think that it should be a concern for education. This belief was reiterated to this author when a group of special educators from China were asked about programs for students with learning disabilities and behaviors disorders. They replied that they did not have any students with those problems and that there were programs for the sensory impaired, severely cognitivly impaired, and for individuals with orthopedic disabilities. On a recent visit to the Pacific, this author also had conversations with individuals from Japan, Korea, and China. As in the previous statements, they also remarked that they knew there were programs for individuals with the more visible disabilities, but that they had no knowledge of programs for students with mild learning and behavior difficulties.

As Chan (1986), Lim-Yee (1983), and Morrow (1987), have indicated, the values of "pride and shame" directly impact the Asian American's family relationship with a child or youth with a disability. However, Bui (1997) presented a contrasting viewpoint. Bui found that Vietnamese parents did not experience as many difficulties in accepting their children with disabilities as other Asian and Pacific Islander families. She indicated that the Vietnamese parents in her study did not feel that they were directly responsible for their child's disability, or that the disabling condition was the result of poor parenting. Bui further reported that most of the parents believed that their children's disabilities were primarily related to medical factors or due to human error at the hospital or birthing center. Bui also indicated that these parents tended to rely on the medical causation factors, which allowed for hope in finding possible cures for their child's disabling conditions.

Bui also found that the ideas of "pride and shame" as related to work by Chan (1986), Lim-Yee (1983), and Morrow (1987), did not apply to the participant sample of her study. She stated that the parents presented views indicating that they had absolved themselves of the feelings of guilt and shame. Bui went on to state that the Vietnamese parents interviewed did not present the common perception that they felt shame and embarrassment toward their disabled children, but rather that they treated their children with love and affection. It was also noted that the parents expressed feelings of sadness and anger at the disabling condition afflicting their children. The sadness and anger were accompanied by feelings of pride with respect to the accomplishments of their disabled children in the educational setting, as well as in the familial organization.

What Can You Do?

The professional can assist individuals to break down the cultural values and views that may hinder the acquisition and development of educational, social, and medical services for individuals with disabilities from Asian American and Pacific Islander families.

Based on the information presented, it is clearly evident that there are a variety of interventions and activities that can be accomplished. First, professionals in the field of special education can be made aware of the cultural views and orientations held by the Asian and Pacific Islander cultures with respect to family relationships and their views on disabilities. Training sessions can be developed, offered, and taken.

Second, parent information sessions can be developed to assist the parents in understanding disabilities and what can be provided to assist a child or youth with a disability. These workshops should not be referred to as "Parent Training Workshops" but, instead, as workshops that give parents "tips on how to help your child do better in school." It is important to stress that this would be in perfect harmony with the views held by Asian and Pacific Islander American parents—families will accept assistance if activities and services will help the "whole" family or community. These parent information and training sesssions should be conducted in the parent's first language, materials prepared in the parents' first language, as well as having the jargon associated with educational, medical, and social services translated into common terms in the parents' first language. This empowers the parents with respect to the rights afforded to their disabled children. Parents need to become empowered to "fight for their child." Bui (1997) found that the majority of the Vietnamese families were legal immigrants to the United States and were happy just to be here—they felt lucky to be here and did not want to appear greedy by asking for services for their children (Bui, 1997).

Third, educational and other service providers must develop programs and adopt attitudes designed to build trust with Asian and Pacific Islander families. Without trust, it is very dificult for individuals outside the cultural group/unit to assist the family/group in making changes in their orientations for relating to the needs of individuals with disabilities. The service providers can invite, welcome, and encourage parents to become involved in their children's educational programs. Bui (1997) makes these recommendations also, as she found that Vietnamese parents believe that the educational, medical, and social service personnel are professional and will ensure that the best services will be provided. Bui states that parents' confidence in schools is a cultural behavior transplanted from respect for the educational system in Vietnam. Bui and others make the point that lack of parent participation should not be viewed as a lack of interest in their children's education; minimal parent participation implies confidence in the ability of school personnel.

While these three suggestions may appear commonplace, they are sorely needed. Without effective activites and active particiapation by all parties involved, the needs of Asian and Pacific Islander children and youth will not be met. When we close our eyes or have our vision clouded because of distorted perceptions, we will truly fail to help or to hear the silent voices of Asian and Pacific Islander American children and youth with disabilities. Empowering individuals and families is the key.

10

Fred Cordova

The Legacy

Creating a Knowledge Base on Filipino Americans

The Filipino presence continues to remain in the background within the society at large. In fact, the history of Filipinos in the United States did not exist for many mainstream historians. How many Americans even know Filipino Americans exist? They are often mistaken for Japanese, Chinese, Hawaiian, Hispanic, or other non-Whites. If Americans are unaware that the Philippines was an American colony, might they not also be unaware of the contributions of Filipino Americans in American labor, sports, religion, literature, performing arts, entertainment, community and family life, and other American socioeconomic life pursuits? Examine the disparity of books and other printed, graphic, film, and audio-visual materials on Filipino American and Philippine subjects in public institutions—as an example your own campus library—while noting such meager materials as being outdated and stereotypical in detailing Filipino Americans and Filipinos.

The Filipino American story is an important one for all Americans because it is part of American history. For young Filipino Americans, the

165

contributions form a foundation of greater understanding of their ethnic and cultural identities. For other students, the knowledge broadens their understanding of how the United States is a nation of diverse peoples with a rich legacy.

To enable teachers and other service providers to understand the cultural, social, and historical contributions of Filipino Americans, the Filipino American Historical Society (FAHNS) was established to conduct research and provide a repository for gathered materials. FAHNS is an important voice in the community and the nation. The organization is dedicated to bringing the voice of Filipino Americans to the attention of all Americans because they believe Filipino Americans have a long historical legacy that should be celebrated. The purpose of this chapter is to provide teachers with information about Filipino American contributions that can be integrated into the educational curriculum.

Historical Information
Filipino American Roots

The voice of past and present Filipino Americans often goes unheard. They are the invisible Asian (Cordova, 1983). Teachers can present information about Filipino Americans in the curriculum to affirm their presence in the U.S. community. Teachers can explain to all students that the traditional values of Filipino Americans originated from an archipelago in Southeast Asia which strings like a pearl necklace of 7,107 islands, no two of which are alike. Filipinos are predominantly of Malay stock and look like Indonesians, other Southeast Asians, as well as some Pacific Islanders. Today Filipinos number some sixty-two million people who speak eighty-seven different languages and dialects. Their ancestral land is the Philippines. However, in searching for Filipino American cultural identity, teachers must leave those islands and cross the Pacific, the "Ocean of Dreams," and examine their experiences in the United States.

Students should know that Filipino Americans have a long historical legacy in the United States that began two hundred years before the Declaration of Independence was signed. Filipino American history begins when Pedro de Unamuno led an expedition from Spain to California and brought Luzon Indian explorers, the first Filipinos, to Morro Bay on October 18, 1587. The explorers included Unamuno, twelve soldiers, a priest, and a number of Luzon Indians. During their survey, two Luzon Indians, because of their color, were sent ahead as scouts to make contact with the local Indians. Contact was made but led to bloodshed, and one of the Filipinos lost his life in the skirmish (Crouchett, 1982; Wagner, 1923; Craig & Benitez, 1916). There are additional recorded accounts of other landings and the presence of other Filipinos in California between the sixteenth and nineteenth centuries (Crouchett, 1982; "Vanished Camp of Tulitos Is Forgotten by Historians," 1989).

Most teachers do not know that Filipinos have been permanent settlers in what is now known as the United States since 1763. Espina (1988) has shown that Filipinos have lived along the bayous and marshes of southeastern Louisiana as early as 1763. As a librarian Espina undertook extensive oral histories and, along with old records and vintage documents, she brought together a rich source about Filipino life in eighteenth-century Louisiana (Cordova, 1983). These immigrants originally were ship hands on Spanish galleons who jumped ship because of harsh treatment from their brutal Spanish masters. They escaped into the bayous and marshes of Louisiana and built their villages on stilts. Filipino crew members founded the first of seven eighteenth-century villages in Louisiana and fished for their livelihood. These strong men married Native American and African American women from the area and established the first Asian American communities (Cordova, 1983).

Filipinos have had a great impact on our nation's development (Cordova, 1983). For example, Antonio Miranda was one of forty-six founders of Pueblo de Nuestra Senora Reina de los Angeles—Los Angeles—in 1781. In 1788 a Filipino, one of the captain's servants on the British ship, *Iphigenia Nubiana*, spoke the language of the indigenous Nootka Indians in what is now the Canadian Province of British Columbia and the northwestern portion of the state of Washington. Filipino immigrants also were active in the Battle of New Orleans against the British, joining the efforts of Jean Lafitte, the smuggler. Filipinos also were crew members in the 1850s of whaling ships wintering on Alaska's Arctic coast at Point Hope and lived among Inupiat Eskimos (Cordova, 1983).

By 1930 the U.S. Census reported 45,200 Filipinos in the continental United States and, of these, 30,000 lived in California. Many Pinoys worked in agriculture and many resided in the San Joaquin Valley. They could also be found in Sacramento, Salinas, Imperial Valley, and Borrego Springs harvesting crops like asparagus, tomatoes, lettuce, and grapes. Most worked under contracts of piecemeal labor, which called for at least a ten-hour day and twenty-six-day month. There were many hardships.

One of the most important legacies the Filipino American community has provided the nation is a commitment to unionism. In 1911 Pinoy unionism was born with the Filipino Federation of Labor in Hawaii. Later following in this tradition, Antonio Gallego Rodrigo, only twenty-three years old, helped found the Cannery Workers' and Farm Laborers' Union local 18257 (CWFLU) in Seattle on June 19, 1933 (Cordova, 1983). The CWFLU was the first Pinoy-dominated Alaska cannery union. He served as one of the first treasurers and secretaries of the organization.

In 1965 Larry Itliong coordinated a successful grape strike in Coachella Valley, east of Los Angeles. He then brought his Agricultural Workers Organizing Committee, affiliated with the American Federation of Labor-Congress of Industrial Organizations, to Delano, California. When the growers refused to agree, Itliong's Agricultural Workers Organizing Committee struck on September 8, 1965. Later his group merged with Cesar Chavez's National Farm Workers Association, which had a large Mexican American membership. The Pinoy and Mexican American unions merged in 1967 and became known as the United Farm Workers Organizing Committee and this later became known as United Farm Workers of America.

The year 1988 marked the 225th anniversary of the permanent settlement of Filipinos in the continental United States in Louisiana. The Philippines and the United States have shared a common heritage since 1763. The ties that bind the Philippines and America have been strengthened by more than 230 years of Philippine immigration and American birthrates, the period of U.S. colonization beginning in 1898, the tragedy of World War II, and more than four centuries of mutually nurtured Western traditions and values. Filipino Americans today constitute the largest ethnic group among Asian/Pacific Americans, with more than two million in the nation. The Philippines has been second only to Mexico in the total number of immigrants entering the U.S. annually since 1965. The U.S. Report of the Commissioner of Immigration and Naturalization Service showed immigration figures with fluctuating averages from 35,000 to 45,000 Filipino entries every year in the United States. (Appendix A provides a short chronology of Filipino American history.)

Teachers can use Filipino American history as the basis for issues-centered lessons. This approach to education fosters examination, discussion, and resolution to public issues in the context of a multicultural society (Pang & Park, 1992). Some questions that could be used to focus class discussions are:

- How would you describe the historical experiences of Filipino Americans?
- What role did Filipinos have in the development of unionism and the labor movement in Alaska and California?
- What role has the state and federal government played in the rights of Filipino immigrants?

Filipino Americans Who Have Contributed to U.S. Society

Through the sweat and pains of hard work, contributions by Pinoys are innumerable. First-generation Filipino Americans labored in fields, orchards, plantations, canneries, kitchens, hotels, ships and shipyards, the bandstand, the boxing ring, and other places of hard, common labor to give to those who followed, a legacy of a viable Pinoy community. Filipino Americans built communities, distinguished themselves in the U.S. Army and Navy, and contributed words like *yo-yo* and *boondocks* to the U.S. culture. Contrary to popular and published opinions, these pioneering Pinoy men and women did not all come to America to become menial laborers. Most came for education, adventure, and a better life.

There are many Filipino American role models who can be found in American society. Appendix B lists many in a variety of occupations. Filipinos should be proud of the contributions they have made to American society. Carlos Bulosan, the great Filipino American poet-novelist, wrote before he died in 1956 in Seattle: "In spite of everything that has happened to me in America, I am not sorry that I was born a Filipino. . . . I am proud that I am a Filipino. I used to be angry, to question myself. But now I am proud."

Filipino Americans have had and continue to have an enormous impact on American society. Appendix B provides educators a broad listing of individuals who have made contributions to American society. The list includes historians, lawyers, actors, scientists, painters, writers, entertainers, sports figures, musicians, educators, and politicians.

Conclusions

A common stereotype is that all Filipinos in the United States are Philippine-born immigrants, sojourners, exiles, or expatriates. Filipino American diversity in America mirrors the rich variation of the Philippines itself. Within Pinoy communities there is a diversity based on regionalism, dialect, age, mixed parentage, generations, educational attainment, and economic pursuits, as well as varied cultural, political, philosophical, and religious thoughts.

Filipino Americans are a diverse people. They are immigrants, the Philippine-born first generation who include "old-timers," U.S. permanent residents since the 1920s, and "newcomers," whose ranks burgeoned since the 1965 Amendment to the Immigration Nationality Act. They are also the much overlooked American-born Pinoys, who range from babies to great-grandparents down to the tenth generation hidden in communities such as New Orleans. American-born Filipino Americans are of mixed parentage, White Pinoy, American Indian Pinoy, Mexican Pinoy, Puerto Rican Pinoy, Latino Pinoy, African American Pinoy, Chinese Pinoy, Japanese Pinoy, Korean Pinoy, Asian Pinoy, Hawaiian Pinoy, Chamorro Pinoy, Pacific Islander Pinoy.

Filipino Americans are one of the fastest-growing populations in the United States. They have created a rich legacy for all Americans, a legacy of courage, hope, and hard work. Teachers can share with their students that the Filipinos were the first Asians to settle in what is now the continental United States in 1763, thirteen years before the Declaration of Independence. Filipino Americans have and continue to contribute to the growth and development of our nation. For example, Eduardo San Juan was the conceptual designer for the lunar rover used on several of the Apollo space missions. Evelyn Mandac became an opera singer whose beautiful soprano voice filled many concert halls. And Ben Menor was the first Filipino American to serve on a State Supreme Court. He became a State Supreme Court Justice in Hawaii and also served in the Hawaii State Senate. Students need to know that Filipino Americans are an important community in our nation of many nations. The voice of Filipino Americans must be heard in schools throughout the United States. Their legacy is an American legacy.

Appendix A

Fred Cordova

Filipino American History
Historical Benchmarks

1587: Two Luzon Indian explorers, the first Filipinos, were members of Pedro de Unamuno's expedition that landed on Morro Bay, California (October 18).

1763: Filipino sailors on Spanish galleons jumped ship because of harsh treatment from their brutal Spanish masters. They built villages on stilts. Crew members founded the first of seven eighteenth-century villages in Louisiana and fished for their livelihood.

1784: The funeral of Antonio Miranda, a gunsmith credited to be among the founders of the Pueblo de Nuestra Senora de los Angeles, now L.A., was held in San Buenaventura Mission (May 26).

1781: Antonio Miranda was one of forty-six founders of Pueblo de Nuestra Senora Reina de los Angeles, Los Angeles.

1788: A Filipino who was a captain's servant on the British ship, *Iphigenia Nubiana*, spoke with the indigenous Nootka Indians in what became the Canadian Province of British Columbia.

1815: Filipinos from Louisiana's Barataria Bay joined smuggler Jean Lafitte to battle the British in the Battle of New Orleans.

1898: Sixteen warriors were displayed in the Omaha exposition (June 1–October 31).

1901: Five musicians performed in the Buffalo, New York, exposition (May 1–November1).

1903: 103 pensionados became the first Filipino students in American universities and campuses (November).

1906: Fifteen sakadas walked off the Doric gangplank into Hawaiian plantations (December 20).

1911: Pinoy unionism was born with the Filipino Federation of Labor in Hawaii.

1917: Approximately 25,000 Filipinos served in the U.S. military during World War I.

1927: White sport hunters menaced Filipinos in Toppenish, Washington, to begin the first anti-Filipino violence in the United States (November 17).

1928: A bellhop, Pedro Flores, playing with a toy on the end of a string, was spotted by Donald Duncan, who built a multi-million-dollar yo-yo empire.

1930: 25,000 Filipinos served in the U.S. Navy, while 4,200 Alaskeros worked in the salmon canneries.

1933: Claiming he was Malay and not Asian, Salvador Roldan won his case in the Los Angeles Superior Court and caused California to revise its antimiscegenation laws forbidding marriages between White women, Asians, and Malays.

1939: Ted Navarro introduced airbrush retouching in color photography.

1948: Vicki Manalo Draves, in the London Olympics, became the first American woman to win two gold medals in diving.

1954: Peter Aduja was elected to Hawaii's Legislature.

1957: One-armed Marcelino Monasterial won the twenty-fourth World Table Tennis Championships.

1961: Alfonso Sorio exhibited at the Whitney Museum of American Art in New York City.

1965: In the middle of their grape strike in Delano, California, Larry Itliong and his Agricultural Workers Organizing Committee were asked if they could be joined in the strike by the fledgling National Farm Workers Association, headed by Chicano Cesar Chavez (September 16).

1968: Eugene Resos designed the pilot seat for the Boeing 747 jumbo jet.

1969: Roman Gabriel of the Los Angeles Rams was named All Pro in the National Football League. (He went on to coach the Raleigh Durhams of the new World League of American Football.)

1969: On the moon roamed the lunar rover, conceptually designed by Eduardo San Juan (July 16).

1974: Benjamin Bumanglag Menor was named Supreme Court Justice in Hawaii and Thelma Garcia Buchholdt was elected to Alaska's House of Representatives in the State Legislature.

1979: Tai Babilonia won the world's doubles skating championship in Vienna.

1981: Joe Dela Cruz of the Quinault Indian Nation in Washington state was elected president of the American Congress of Indians.

1991: Lynda Barry's play, "The Good Times Are Killing Me," opened on Broadway (April 18).

Appendix B

Fred Cordova

Famous Filipino Americans

Literature

ARUEGO, JOSE: Children's author and illustrator
BACHO, PETER: Novelist
BARROGA, JEANNE: Playwright
BRAINARD, CECILIA MANGUERRA: Novelist, essayist
BULOSAN, CARLOS: Novelist, poet, short-story writer
GONZALEZ: Novelist N V M
HAGEDORN, JESSICA TARAHATA: National Book Award nominee
PENARANDA, OSCAR: Writer
RAMOS, TERESITA: Tagalog scholar
SANTOS, BIENVENIDO, N.: Novelist, poet, short-story writer
VILLA, JOSE GARCIA: Short-story writer

Entertainment, Television, and Movies

AQUINO, RUBEN: Walt Disney animator, *The Lion King*
BUMATAI, ANDY: Standup comic
CASTILLO, STEPHANIE: Award-winning filmmaker and former *Honolulu Star-Bulletin* reporter
DACASCOS, MARK: Martial arts movie actor
ESCLAMADO, ALEX: Newspaper publisher
FRIEDMAN, FRITZ: Columbia TriStar's Home Video division vice president of worldwide publicity
HARU, SUMI SEVILLA: Actress, producer, writer, director, television host
LACUESTA, LLOYD: Oakland television bureau chief
LAGAPA, DEBRA: Telecommunications services legal specialist
LUNA, BARBARA: Actress

MANDAC, EVELYN: World-class opera soprano
NATORI, JOSIE CRUZ: Fashion executive and designer
PEEPLES, NIA: Dancer and television late-night boogie queen
PHILLIPS, LOU DIAMOND: Actor
RESPICIO, FAUSTINO: Television-radio producer/director
REYES JR., ERNIE: Television actor and martial arts expert
SCHNEIDER, ROB: Television and movie comedian of *Saturday Night Live*
TOMIMBANG, EMME: Honolulu television news anchor
TOMITA, TAMLYN: Actress, named one of "fifty most beautiful people in the world" for 1991
VEGA, JOSE DE: "Chino" in the Broadway stage musical and Academy Award-winning movie, *West Side Story*
WILLIAMS, MARSHA GARCES: Movie producer
YUCHENGCO, MONA LISA: Magazine publisher

Sports

ALUNAN, SERGIO (SKIP): Wheelchair Athletic Association 1982, national gold medalist
BABILONIA, TAI: World champion ice skater
CLARK, ANTHONY: Super heavyweight power-lifting world record-holder
DAGAMPAT, DEBBIE DOBBINS: Fitness model
DRAVES, VICKI MANALO: U.S. Olympic two-time diving gold medalist
GABRIEL, ROMAN: All-Pro American Football League
GARCIA, CEFERINO: World middleweight boxing champion
JONES, KEITH D.: World super-heavyweight arm-wrestling champion
MARINO, DADO: World flyweight boxing champion
MASAKAYAN, LIZ: World-class beach and indoor volleyball player and 1988 U.S. Olympian
PACYGA, JEANNA: World powerlifting champion
PADUA, RUDY: Karate's National Black Belt League 1991 North American overall champion
PUNSALAN, ELIZABETH: 1994 U.S. Olympic ice dancer
RADOVAN, JOSE: Yo-yo artist
REYES SR., ERNIE: Three-time national tae kwan do champion and black belt Hall of Famer
RIVERA, RON: National Football League linebacker for the Chicago Bears
SATO, ERIC: U.S. Olympic volleyball 1988 gold medalist and 1992 bronze medalist
SATO, GARY: U.S. Olympic volleyball gold medal-winning assistant coach
SATO, LIANE: U.S. Olympic volleyball 1992 bronze medalist
SIPIN, JOHN: National League second baseman with the St. Louis Cardinals and the San Diego Padres

TOWNSEND, RAYMOND: National Basketball Association guard of the Golden
State Warriors

VILLA, PANCHO: World flyweight boxing champion

Folk Arts

ACADEMIA, ELEANOR: World-class multifaceted pop artist and ethnomusicologist

ALEJANDRO, REYNALDO: Cookbook and folkdance author

Fine Arts

BARREDO, MANIYA: Atlanta Ballet principal ballerina

BARRY, LYNDA: Cartoonist

HOSTALLERO, GARY: Mixed-media master painter

IGARTA, V. C.: Painter

INOSANTO, DAN: Martial arts master

JACKSON, KRISTIN: Modern-dance choreographer

LABRADOR, VICENTE: Woodworker

LAGUNDIMAO JR., CLEMENTE: Design awardee

LAIGO, VAL: Painter muralist

OCAMPO, MANUEL: Master painter

OSSORIO, ALFONSO: Whitney Museum of American Art exhibitor

TATAD, ROBERT: Broadway tehater dancer

UBUNGEN, PEARL: Dancer, choreographer

VERA, FEDERICO DE: San Francisco art collector

VILLA, CARLOS: Painter

Music

BALTAZAR, GABRIEL (GABE): Reds Jazz saxaphone artist

CARRERE, TIA: Actress-singer, named one of "fifty most beautiful people in
the world" for 1992

ENRIQUEZ, BOBBY: Jazz pianist

GOMEZ, VINCE: String bassist

HAMMETT, KIRK: 1992 Grammy Award-winning heavy metal band Metal-
lica's guitarist

KALANDUYAN, DANILO: Philippine gong master

KIM, PRIMO: Jazz artist

MONTANO, MIKE: Las Vegas musical director

NUNEZ, FLIP: Jazz pianist

PAULO, MICHAEL: Jazz saxaphonist

PRINCE (NELSON): Rock superstar

TRIMILLOS, RICARDO: Ethnomusicologist

Education

APILADO, MYRON: University of Washington vice president for minority affairs

BANOS, DOMINGO LOS: Hawaii eduator and 1960 Thailand Olympic basketball coach

CRUZ JR., JOE: Ohio State University engineering dean

DANGARAN, RONALD: 1985–90 Merced City School District superintendent

GIL, LIBIA: Chula Vista City School District superintendent

HERNANDEZ, PROSPERO: Academic publisher

RODIS, RODEL: San Francisco Community College Board trustee 1989–90

Business

CLEMENTE, LILIA CALDERON: Global money manager

HALEY, MABILANGAN: Director of the Export-Import Bank of the United States; former special assistant to President Bill clinton and associate director of presidential personnel in the Clinton Administration

PASION, MERLYN: Resin products patent holder

REYES, JOSE FORMOSO: Nantucket Lightship basket maker

ROXAS, SIXTO K.: American Express International Banking vice chair

SUGUITAN, ARTHUR: Corporate executive in business administration, financial planning and management, systems analysis, capital projects, and human resources

Medicine

BALAGOT, REUBEI: Anesthetist

CARLOTA, LUPO: Acupuncturist and National Football League's New York Giants team physician

CHUA, THOMAS: Laser surgeon

DULAO, FLORENCE RICE DUL: Hospital personnel management and human resource develoment authority

GARCIA, JORGE: Heart surgeon

LACSINA, EMMANUEL: Washington's Pierce County medical examiner

MEDIOLA, ROLANDO: Laser surgeon

NICODEMUS, HONORATO F.: President Reagan's anesthesiologist

NISPEROS, MICHAEL: Oakland "drug czar"

Science

BACDAYAN, ALBERT: Anthropologist, Philippinologist

BANATAOS, DIOSDADO (DADO): Semiconductor chip designer

BANTUG, EFREN L.: Antitoxic safety equipment inventor

BOLIMA, STERLING: Wilderness preservation advocate
CABEZAS, AMADO: Quantiative analyst
DEGRACIA, RONALD: Microtunneling equipment cost analyst
DIOKNO, ANANIAS: Urologist researcher
DIZON, JOSEPH A.: Radioactive gases in underground nuclear detonations, tool designer
ESTOQUE, MARIANO: Meteorologist
FONTANILLA, JAMES E.: U.S. Department of Energy nuclear chemist, testing
JUAN, ED SAN: Lunar Rover conceptual designer
LIM, PACIFICO: Data processing author
LUGAY, JOAQUIN: General Foods biochemist
OLIVERA, BALDOMERO: Leading conotoxin researcher
PATENA, JAIME: Mechanical, structural, electronic design draftsman
ROOT, MARIA PRIMITIVA PAZ: San Francisco Public Utilities Commission president, psychologist, author
SANTOS, BENJAMIN: Designer of the 1961 Buick Riviera body and 1971 Bay Area Rapid Transit System
TALAUGON, MARGIE: Children's carseat pillow inventor

Military

BUGARIN, TEME: Uss Saginaw commander, U.S. navy captain
BULOSAN, CARLOS: Author, writer, poet
DIANGSON, WILLIAM: Brigadier general of the California Army National Guard
LATOSA, RENE: Combat escrima developer
PAZ, WILLIAM M.: U.S. Navy, deputy assistant secretary in President Jimmy Carter's Administration

History

CORDOVA, DOROTHY LAIGO: Oral historian/researcher
CORDOVA, FREDERICK: Historian, journalist, Smithsonian Fellow
ESPINA, MARINA ESTRELLA: Researcher, historian

Politics

CAYETA, NOBEN: Hawaii, governor
CORPUZ, RAY: Tacoma, Washington, city manager
CRUZ, JOE DELA: Quinault Indian Nation chairman, past president of the National Congress of American Indians
ESPALDON, ERNESTO M.: Guam, three-term senator
JAMERO, PETER M.: Washington State, King County, and San Francisco City/County department head

KIHANO, DANIEL: Hawaii, speaker of the House of Representatives

LAIGO, AL: Union City, California, postmaster

LEON, RON DE: San Francisco Parks and Recreation superintendent

LEWIS, LOIDA NICOLAS: Chairwoman and chief executive, TLC Beatrice International

LIDDELL, GENE CANQUE: Lacey, Washington, former mayor

MAPUA, RENE: Nerw York City, deputy financial director under Mayor Giuliani

MASTERS, NORA: City of Seattle, Washington, auditor

MENDOZA, DAVID: National Campaign for Freedom of Expression, executive director

OCHOA, GLORIA MEGINO: Santa Barbara County Board of Supervisors

SANTOS, BOB: Community activist, U.S. Department of Housing and Urban Development Secretary's Representative in Region X

SIBONGA, DOLORES ESTIGOY: 1976–1991 Seattle City councilwoman

TLIONG, LARRY: Labor organizer

VELORIA, VELMA: Washington State representative

ZAPANTA, ALBERT: U.S. Department of Interior, assistant secretary, in President Jimmy Carter's Administration

Law

BUCHHOLDT, THELMA GARCIA: Alaska, former legislator

CANTIL, TANI: Sacramento, municipal court judge

ESPINOSA, NOEMI: Patent lawyer

FELIPE, JOE SAN: California State Department of Corporations, supervisory counsel

LIM, LILLIAN: San Diego, municipal court judge

MARSHALL JR., THURGOOD: Director of legislative affairs in the office of Vice President Al Gore

MENOR, BENJAMIN: Hawaii, supreme court justice

PECHETTE, JEAN MARIE REYES: High-technology litigation expert

QUIDACHAY, RONALD: San Francisco, municipal court judge

QUON, LILLIAN: San Diego, municipal court judge

RAMIL, MARIO: Hawaii, supreme court justice

RECANA, MEL (RED): Los Angeles, municipal court judge

VALDERRAMA, DAVID: Maryland Legislature House of Delegates

Special Honors

BETH BRYNES, ERICA: Los Angeles' Queen of the 105th Rose Parade

CALUGAS, JOSE: Medal of Honor winner

CANDA, JEMY: Arabian show horse exhibitor

CASTRO, HONEY: 1985 Miss Washington finalist and Miss America third runner-up

RUNAS, ROY: National elementary school chess champion

SANDOVAL, CEASAR: 1980 U.S. Bartenders Guild grand champion

Special Organizations

MONCADO, HILARIO: Fraternal organization founder

NATIVIDAD, IRENE: National Women's Political Caucus chair

SUYAT, STANLEY D.: Peace Corps associate director of management

11

Li-Rong Lilly Cheng

Language Assessment and Instructional Strategies for Limited English Proficient Asian and Pacific Islander American Children

The future will be much brighter if we enhance our educational efforts by teaching respect for each other's dignity and humanity, and we work to make our differences our strength.

—Castro, 1994

Inadequate Identification of Students for Special Services

Numerous reports have documented the inadequacies of U.S. schools in meeting the needs of culturally and linguistically diverse students (Olsen, 1988). There are at least 2.2 million limited English proficient (LEP) students in the schools (University of California, 1994). While the number of LEP students has increased over the past twenty years, support for bilingual education for LEP students with special needs has decreased. Schools often have difficulty in appropriately identifying and serving LEP children (U.S. Department of Education, 1995). Records of past evaluations are sometimes unreliable. Some children are too apprehensive or shy to answer questions or to participate in taking standardized tests. Furthermore, there has been an escalating concern in education to identify assessment measures and instructional strategies that will be conducive to student success (Cheng, 1995). Although educators have been aware of the possible biases and inadequacies of intelligence and language tests in the identification process, the more pressing and central issue is educational intervention for children with different social, linguistic, and cultural backgrounds (Leung, this volume), and the second issue is student, teacher, and parent empowerment (Cheng and Chang, 1995).

The purpose of this chapter is to review research on culturally affirming assessment and instructional practices for Asian Pacific Island (API) American students. The philosophical guidelines regarding the education of such a diverse population and, more specifically, the at-risk children among this population will be addressed. Furthermore, it will analyze the needs in service delivery and provide possible solutions. Case studies are presented to provide a more cohesive and comprehensive understanding of the challenges children, teachers, and parents face. Research needs are presented, and the research will be used to provide strategies to improve our current practice in identification, assessment, intervention and instruction and program development for API students.

Preassessment Considerations

Immigration Patterns

East Asia, Southeast Asia, and South Asia are the main areas of origin of recent immigrants to the United States. These areas encompass the People's Republic of China, India, Japan, South Korea, Taiwan, Hong Kong and Singapore, North Korea, Kampuchea, Pakistan and Bangladesh, Vietnam, and the Philippines (*Asian Pacific Horizons*, 1994). When they settle in the continental United States, the API populations concentrate mostly on the east and west coasts.

Stages of Acculturation

Immigrants go through stages in their adaptation to their new country. Different immigrants stop at various stages, and those who proceed through stages beyond rejection of the mainstream culture vary from one stage to another day to day, with frequent "regressions" to earlier stages. The optimal stage, for the individual's self-esteem and personal fulfillment, is biculturalism. However, education in the mainstream schools often leads to compensatory adaptation (rejection, or at least avoidance, of any identification with their native culture), especially for children who immigrate at a very young age (Trueba, Cheng & Ima, 1993).

Diversity Issues

Understanding intergroup and intragroup diversity is the key to education success.

Intergroup Differences

Not only do API immigrant/refugee groups come from diverse regions of Asia and the Pacific Islands, they speak different national language(s)/dialects, practice different religions and folk beliefs, and have diverse personal, educational, social, and cultural experiences.

A good example of intergroup differences exists between Asians and Southeast Asians. Unlike most other Asians who have immigrated to the United States, the Southeast Asians came as refugees, who may require assistance and often are traumatized. Recent immigrants from Taiwan have a very different experience, as many immigrate to the United States with entrepreneurial experience and wealth.

Intragroup Differences

In general, refugees share common experiences and backgrounds, including physical and/or emotional trauma, war, and the loss of family members. They do not speak English as their first, or even second, language. Although most did not learn English in their native countries, many did learn some English prior to their arrival in the United States. However, differences such as different languages and religions and intragroup differences such as socioeconomic status and educational background make refugees from the same area very different from each other. Some refugees are preliterate in their home language and may have had little or no schooling (Te, 1995), while some came with high levels of academic training. Many recent refugees from Eastern Europe are highly educated. There are also intergenerational and intragenerational differences, including the difference between the FOBs (fresh off the boat—considered an ethnic slur by some) and the ABCs (American-born Chinese). We are cognizant of the dangers of overgeneralizing to all newcomer groups and are alerted to the cultural diversity within the larger newcomer pool (Ima & Kheo, 1995).

La Costa: Questions about Overrepresentation and Underrepresentation of LEP Population in Special Education

In 1993, in La Costa District, 62.9 percent of the students enrolled in special education were Hispanic, 21.6 percent were Asian, 13 percent White, 2.31 percent Black, and 0.2 percent Native American. The overall district population were 40.4 percent Hispanic, 46.4 percent Asian, 12 percent White, 1.15 percent Black, and 0.12 percent Native American. A comparison of the two data indicated an overrepresentation of Hispanic and underrepresentation of the Asian student population in special services (Dung, Viernes & Mudd, 1994). On the other hand, there is an underrepresentation of API LEP students in gifted and talented programs. (Cheng, Ima & Labovitz, 1994).

Inadequate Education in the Past

LEP students may have experienced fragmented schooling and missed opportunities for learning (Chang, Lai & Shimizu, 1995). Educators can focus on creating optimal language learning opportunities for these children (Cheng, 1994; Figueroa, 1989). Children as well as their families need to be encouraged to embrace their new culture while maintaining their native cultures so that equilibrium and personal identity can be maintained. They need to have maintenance of cultural and linguistic identity while moving into the mainstream.

Basic English Skills vs. Academic English Skills

LEP students often demonstrate minimum level Basic Interpersonal Communication Skills (BICS) but less competency in Cognitive Academic Linguistic Proficiency (CALP) (Cummins, 1981), due to lack of exposure to printed texts and home literacy support (Chang and Lai, 1992). Since major differences exist between competencies required by BICS and CALP, there may be students whose use of English is satisfactory in social situations but who continue to lag behind in academic English.

The placement of children in English as a Second Language (ESL) classes may be questionable. In California, for example, students who fall below the thirty-sixth percentile in the California Test of Basic Skills (CTBS) reading comprehension and math application are classified as LEP (Dung, Viernes & Mudd, 1994). Once they score higher than the thirty-sixth percentile on both language comprehension and math application, they are reclassified as fluent English proficient (FEP). Timely assessment of students' FEP status may not always be available, and those who remain classified LEP may miss out on the more complex learning that takes place in mainstream classes.

Factors Contributing to Language Learning Disabilities

Language learning disability (LLD) encompasses a heterogeneous group of individuals with various types of mild to severe language disabilities (Lyon, Gray, Kavanaugh & Krasnegor, 1993; National Joint Committee on Learning Disabilities, 1994; Wallach & Butler, 1994). The phenomenon of language learning disabilities is complex, and its causes are controversial (Chang, Lai & Shimizu, 1995). Briefly stated, LLD can be associated with any individual who has low to average or above average intelligence and has specific discrepancies between the estimated intellectual ability and achievement in one or more of the following areas: oral expression, listening comprehension, written expression, basic reading skills, or reading comprehension (Federal Register, 1977).

Some of the main factors that put a child at risk for language learning disabilities are:

• disrupted schooling
• disrupted family support system
• experience of trauma
• long stays at refugee camps
• poor health
• lack of prior schooling
• lack of supervision at home
• lack of participation in extracurricular activities
• lack of information about health services
• lack of guidance and counseling for life goals (Trueba, Cheng & Ima, 1993)
• parents' lack of awareness of their rights or needs (Chang, Lai & Shimizu, 1995)
• low socioeconomic status

Some LEP children have been referred for speech language therapy by their classroom teachers because they showed slow English acquisition, poor oral expression, or lack of comprehension of school discourse (Cheng, 1994). Recent research indicated that limited English proficient (LEP) students are very likely to experience inadequate cognitive and language learning environments in school. According to Goldenberg (1991), LEP children are limited in their opportunities to produce complex language, and Ramirez, Yuen, and Ramey (1991) point out that LEP students have few opportunities to engage in complex learning.

Assessment

The goal of language diagnosis is to determine a child's communicative competence. Ethnographic techniques for the collection of data make it more likely that a truly representative sample of the child's communicative repertoire will be sampled. The diagnostician must determine the cultural, linguistic, and experiential factors affecting the child (Cheng, 1993). Using alternative assessment strategies, assumptions are not based on any single source, and the family is involved throughout. It is important to provide time and space for family members to interact with the examiner and for the examiner to share concerns about the student, soliciting feedback from the family (Cheng, 1993).

The examiner must adjust styles of communication and interaction where appropriate, and must not judge the family's values, which may not be easily comprehensible (Cheng, 1995). Teachers and service providers should differentiate between language learning errors and language disorders; identify cultural issues that impact teacher perceptions; understand the effect of second-language acquisition on student achievement; and consider the educational environment.

Differentiating Differences in Language Learning from Language Disorders

When a student with slow English acquisition, poor oral expression, or lack of comprehension of school discourse is referred for diagnosis, teachers and other professionals face the problem of ascertaining the source of the difficulties (Cheng, 1994). Is the etiology linguistic, sociocultural, traumatic, neurophysiological, or perhaps a combination of these factors? When a student seems withdrawn or unresponsive, how will the teacher be able to determine whether the child is suffering from posttraumatic stress, depression, a language learning disability, or all of the above?

Because educators have difficulty identifying the source of students' problems, a large number of LEP students either remain in regular classrooms or are referred to special education programs, which may not have the preparation to deal with the child's linguistic and cultural background. The following critical questions must be asked in working with the LEP population:

- How should one interpret individual response, given cultural differences between teacher and student?
- How should one talk to parents and involve them in decisions?
- What language should be used in assessment?
- How does one determine whether or not a student should be placed in a special education program?
- If the educator determines a student belongs in a special education program, how should the parents be told?
- What language should be used in intervention?

The diagnosis of language delay must change to accommodate diversity among students. In order to differentiate between intrinsic language learning difficulties and problems due to difficulties entering the mainstream culture, diagnosticians need to recognize cultural forces affecting students' lives (Cheng, 1990a).

The following may serve as guidelines to help teachers detect if the student might have a language disorder (Cheng, 1991):

- paucity of vocabulary development in both languages over time
- continued delay in both languages over time in concepts, structures, and functions
- clues from medical history
- presence of other disabling conditions
- unintelligible speech/distortions
- dysfluency and voice disorders
- oral motor difficulties
- unevenness in performing in different languages areas
- short and choppy sentences
- communication difficulties in the home

Foster-Cohen (1994) provided a valuable teacher's guide about first language acquisition:

- Use milestone charts with caution because of individual variations.
- Children will only learn what they have had a chance to learn.
- Social variation in a child's experience with language at home versus school is extremely important.
- The teacher has an important role in teaching language structures and pragmatics.
- Children's ability to think and talk about language metalinguistically develops fairly slowly and lags behind their ability to use the linguistic skills in question.
- Do not let your instincts about children's language development be overridden by unnecessary concern for the correct theoretical approach.

Diagnostic Practices

The traditional approach for diagnosis and the preferred focus for diagnosis are presented here.

Traditional Focus	*Preferred Focus*
Assessment personnel unfamiliar with LEP populations	Assessment personnel familiar with language and culture of LEP student to be assessed
Family/health information gathered in English	Family/health information gathered in home language, using home culture's norms

Traditional Focus	*Preferred Focus*
Testing in English	Testing in English and home language
Formal assessment	Formal assessment adapted and informal assessment
Use of standardized procedures	Documentation of adaptations/translations
Norms based on U.S. population	Norms used only when appropriate
Testing adapted, but usual scoring	Adaptations noted; norms not used
Reevaluations use a standard test battery	Reevaluations consider student's unique needs; progress monitored closely

(Ortiz, Garcia, & Wilkinson, 1988)

Recommended Procedure

The following are general guidelines for diagnosis, often referred to as the RIOT procedure (Leung, 1995):

Review all pertinent documents and background information:
    school records
    reports
    medical records
    teacher's comments
    social and family background
    previous therapy or testing results

Interview teachers, peers, family members, and other informants:
    questionnaires available from multiple sources (Cheng, 1990a, 1991; Erickson & Omark, 1980; Langdon, 1992; Westby, 1990)

Observe student in multiple contexts with a variety of people:
    interactions at school both in the classroom and outside
    interactions at home
    interactions in the community
        Check:
        comprehension of verbal input
        verbal output and language expression
        language preference and dominance
        overall cognitive function
        peer interaction
        family dynamics

Test both school language and home language:
    use informal assessment
    obtain language samples in both languages

select instruments for assessment battery
adapt formal testing procedure
use alternative scoring
use dynamic assessment
use portfolio

Identifying Cultural Issues That Affect Perceptions

Many LEP students who find school affairs—including communication with teachers, administrators, peers, and staff—incomprehensible, threatening, and foreign, go home to non-English speaking environments where home language television programs, newspapers, books, and magazines are available. Lack of practice in English can lead to disenfranchisement and school failure; thus intensive English language training is crucial for students at risk.

Nonverbal cues such as eye contact, physical contact, and body language are embedded in sociocultural contexts. Cultures may vary the amount of information that is explicitly transmitted through verbal channels as opposed to information that is transmitted through the context of the situation, the physical cues present, and the person's body and facial language. Scollon and Scollon (1995) described nonverbal communication in the following domains: kinesics (the movement of our bodies); proxemics (the use of space), and the concept of time. Edward Hall (1969) also observed the importance of nonverbal communication. Some cultures reflect high-context orientation, and participants closely gauge nonverbal interactions (Hall, 1976). In Asian cultures more meaningful information is conveyed in the physical context or internalized in the person who receives the information than in the verbally transmitted part of the message. Asian verbal interaction is considered circular rather than linear (Kaplan, 1966), setting it apart from expectations held by the American mainstream educational system. For example, a paper may not have a topic sentence or central theme; many different thoughts or opinions may be presented without any concluding statement, leading readers in a circular manner and offering no conclusion. In general, mainstream cultural patterns pertain to minimal context orientation and convey information in a precise, linear, and straightforward manner (Cheng, 1993). Educators should be prepared for differing degrees of context orientation among culturally and linguistically diverse students.

Teachers and clinicians must investigate home cultures and recognize the legitimacy of minimal eye contact and infrequent physical contact among some LEP students (Cheng, 1989). For example, there are major differences between American and Chinese modes of school and home interactions. Cheng (1991) explains that American teachers expect students to be interactive, creative, and participatory, while Asian parents, in general, have trained their children to be quiet and obedient. Bishop (1988) reported that Vietnamese bilingual children were using English along with home-culture discourse rules, simultaneously engaging two different codes, one linguistic and one pragmatic. Since many Asian American children feel ambivalent and confused about class participation, we must recognize the conflicting messages they are receiving from teachers and parents.

Understanding the Effect of Second-Language Acquisition

Immigrants experience cultural discontinuities, and individuals and groups react differently. Research indicates that responses and reactions to cultural discontinuities need to be considered in the historical, sociological, and political contexts of immigrant communities (Suarez-Orozco, 1989; Trueba, Jacobs & Kirton, 1990). The adjustment of immigrants and refugees depends largely on their ability to recognize differences and to cope with drastic changes (Trueba, Cheng & Ima, 1993). Children do not all learn language at the same speed; some are less self-conscious and more confident than others and have an easier time acquiring a second language. Krashen (1981, 1982) discussed the concept of affective filter in language acquisition, referring to a language learner's subconscious attitude toward the second language, including motivation, self-confidence, and anxiety. The lower the anxiety and the higher the motivation, the faster language learning proceeds.

Consideration of the Educational Environment

Many education researchers proposed that students bring diverse learning styles into the classroom and advocated instructional conversations as a way to manage learning diversity (Garcia, 1991; Tharp & Gallimore, 1991). Some students study alone, others in groups; some study in quiet environments, others in the midst of distractions. Teachers and practitioners should recognize the diverse learning styles used by students and understand the mismatches of styles that may occur. For example, the teachers want students to work in groups, but some API children may be better able to work alone.

Limited English proficient (LEP) students are very likely to experience inadequate cognitive and language learning environments in school. According to Goldenberg (1991), LEP children are limited in their opportunities to produce language, especially more complex language. As the U.S. population becomes increasingly diverse in age, ethnicity, culture, language, and social and economic status, the challenges of managing diversity will place more demands on educators and service providers.

Instructional Strategies

Coelho (1995) has the following advice for teachers:

- Many students do not share the cultural and linguistic experiences that the curriculum planners have taken for granted.
- All teachers must identify, explain, and provide opportunities for students to practice using the cultural and linguistic parts that are relevant in the context of "whole" language environment of the classroom.

Futhermore, Coelho provided the following areas for enhancing language teaching:

- vocabulary: subject specific and context defined
- figurative language and metaphor
- Latinate vocabulary: roots and affixes
- syntax and morphology: passive voice, abbreviated relatives, verb tenses, plural marker, subjunctive mood, etc.
- patterns of thinking and the use of discourse markers: sequence, spatial relationships, comparison and contrast, cause and effect, etc.

Many researchers have assessed the needs of LEP students (Chang, Lai & Shimizu 1995; Cheng & Chang, 1995; Dung, Viernes & Mudd, 1994). Some recommendations for intervention with Asian Pacific Island LEP students include access to multiple learning sites, individualized lessons, providing cultural experiences, helping children understand the hidden curriculum, systematic support for development of the home language and English, and providing relevant educational experiences (bilingual education or sheltered English).

Access to Multiple Learning Environments
Inside and Outside of School

A limited knowledge base and limited understanding of their world tend to be associated with LEP+LLD children. Their inability to process language as efficiently as their peers and their limited access to public libraries (selecting books that emphasize the richness of our diverse history and experiences), museums (Chinese Historical Museum; the Holocust Museum; the African American Museum), parks (Chicano Park), and theaters often contributes to their lack of information presented in most of the school curriculum. Teachers and other service providers need to inform API LEP+LLD students' parents about the value of prior experience and provide access to field trips to various communities and hands-on activities such as learning the Pow-Wow Dance. Through an integrated curriculum approach, experiences from the home environment can be connected to academic experience.

Individualized Lessons

Lessons should be tailored to the student's level and language-learning ability, and teaching styles matched to the learning styles of diverse students. Language learning progresses in natural stages; beginners should receive gradual introduction to vocabulary and be expected to participate verbally as little or as much as they wish. Overcorrection of errors should be avoided, as it causes inhibition.

Helping Students Understand the Hidden Curriculum

The rules that exist in schools, which are tacitly understood by students who grew up in the mainstream culture, make up the "hidden curriculum." For example, sometimes students must raise their hands and be recognized in order to answer a question, but certain questions require students to simply call out the answer without being recognized. Although the teacher does not explicitly state this, children who have been in the mainstream school since Kindergarten generally know which question requires which degree of formality.

LEP students from diverse cultural and social backgrounds must attain and master cross-cultural competence in all areas of life, especially in education (Cheng, 1990b). LEP students must develop both linguistic and cultural code-switching strategies to succeed within American schools. Often even second- and third-generation immigrants, who have no problem with linguistic code switching, still share their parents' and grandparents' values and participant structures (Kitano & Daniels, 1988; Mura, 1991), and may have some difficulty with cultural code-switching strategies. Yet they consider themselves thoroughly American and experience frustration when others ask them questions such as, Where did you learn English? Where are you from? How did your become so fluent in English? assuming that they are "foreigners" (Mura, 1991; Takaki, 1989).

Academic success in a cross-cultural environment requires not only literacy but also "comprehensible input." Students must learn nonverbal communication cues and codes. Classroom discourse dictated by oral/written and nonverbal rules, as well as hidden curriculum, may be incomprehensible to LEP students (Krashen, 1981), who may violate these rules without realizing it. Teachers can model and explain classroom rules and examine the relationship between language and culture. They can invite an open dialogue with students, engaging them in a discussion of classroom culture, which gives students motivation to participate more in the class.

Systematic Support for Development of the Home Language and English

The child's home language (the most familiar language) is the best tool for learning. Fluency in one language becomes the basis for learning other languages. Those who have learned concepts in one language are able to use those concepts in other languages. Once a child has understood a body of knowledge, labeling the information and remembering it in one language, it is necessary to learn the labels for the knowledge in another language, and then the concepts already learned can be used. Once the skill of reading is learned, one can use that same metalinguistic skill as a tool to learn to read another language. Bilingual education is, therefore, the ideal for LEP children who can learn concepts in their home language while learning English as a second (school) language.

Providing Relevant Educational Experiences

Bilingual education may not be practicable when one of the following conditions is present.

• Teachers who speak the child's home language are not available, or are in short supply.
• There are numerous home languages used by children in one classroom.
• There are children, born in the United States, but brought up using another language, who have not had the opportunity to learn basic concepts in English.
• There are immigrant children with a strong academic background in their home language who need to attach English labels to concepts they already know.
• There are immigrant children who have intermediate English fluency for interpersonal communication but not academic English.

Under these circumstances, sheltered English classrooms may be the best way to give students comprehensible input.

Sheltered English is an approach used to make academic instruction in English understandable to LEP students: "It is a step-by-step process that communicates meaning in subject area while students acquire additional English usage and vocabulary" (Gonzales, 1994: p. 1). Using visuals, props, and body language to make meaning clear, English is taught for fluency, and content of subjects is made understandable. Both language and concepts are introduced in sheltered classrooms. The language used in subjects such as history, math, and science is taught. Study skills such as note taking, outlining, and organizing the information are explicitly explained in English, giving learners methods to acquire the language and organizing skills to benefit from English-only instruction. The teacher makes language clear and provides the opportunity for students to experience the content and language of subjects, also guiding students to understand thought patterns, inferences, and logic used by English speakers.

One method used in sheltered classes involves facilitating students helping each other to learn, using grouping and periodic regrouping. Cooperative learning, working in pairs, and joint projects are used to increase communicative competence. "Within sheltered instruction, it is important to make language demands on students by creating appropriate social settings and interactions. The teacher should guide, support, monitor, encourage and facilitate learning, not control it" (Gonzales, 1994: p. 30). The students are given frequent, timely, performance-based feedback that supports improved performance.

Sheltered English is often the best solution to the problems of too many languages and too few bilingual teachers. It may be the only alternative to "sink or swim" in English-only classrooms for many LEP students.

Multicultural Literacy

Multicultural and social literacy are necessary across the educational continuum. Some of the demands that need to be addressed in staff training (Banks, 1990; Banks, Cortes, Gay, Garcia & Ochoa, 1976; Cheng, 1993, 1994; Figueroa, 1989; Figueroa, Ruiz & Baca, 1988) are:

- matching teaching styles to the learning styles of diverse students
- infusing curriculum with information about the bilingual and multicultural population
- adopting alternative assessment strategies
- adjusting styles of communication and interaction when appropriate
- evaluating and monitoring teaching/intervention effectiveness with diverse students
- giving students with special needs frequent, timely, performance-based feedback that supports improved performance

Conclusion

As we approach an increasingly multiracial and multiethnic twenty-first century, educators continue to play an important role in educating our diverse students. There is a need for the systematic study of the educational institutions' culture, self-perceptions, and operations. Educators and policy makers can benefit the diverse groups by viewing society as multicultural, rather than trying to fit students into the dominant culture.

Another research need concerns social, language, and literacy issues among the bilingual/multicultural population from sociological, linguistic, psychological, educational, and anthropological perspectives (Cazden, John & Hymes, 1972; Cheng, 1990a, 1994; Trueba, 1987). Multidisciplinary and collaborative research will increase our understanding regarding a wide range of issues relating to how students learn English, maintain home language and culture, socialize in diverse contexts, survive in schools, fare in the job market, and in general, acculturate into American society (Cheng, 1987, 1990b, 1995; Trueba, Guthrie & Au, 1981; Trueba, Cheng & Ima, 1993).

The collective wisdom of multidisciplinary researchers can lay a foundation for understanding the interactions among language, thought, achievement, learning, teaching, and acculturation.

12

Grace Fung

Meeting the Instructional Needs of Chinese American and Asian English Language Development and At-Risk Students

S chools often use labels to identify students who differ from the mainstream as slow learners, learning disabled, culturally deprived, limited English proficient, or at risk. Who are these children? Many are children of diverse language and ethnic backgrounds, children from low socioeconomic home environments, and children who speak English as a second language. The goal of this chapter is to examine the instructional needs of Chinese and other Asian students who are culturally and linguistically diverse and through this discussion move educators from limiting labels to educational strategies that work in the classroom. The five purposes of the chapter are:

1. discuss the importance of addressing the Chinese and other Asian culturally and linguistically diverse (CLD) children's instructional need
2. present a theoretical framework for empowering learners of English as a second language

3. explain the need for and the benefit of using native language arts for classroom instruction
4. highlight the Chinese linguistic structures as they are employed in native (both Mandarin and Cantonese) children's literature
5. explore the instructional strategies for increasing Chinese and other Asian CLD children's cognitive academic language proficiency

It was not until recently that educators began to take a closer look at the language needs and problems of Chinese and Asian CLD students. After several decades (from 1965 to 1990), due to changes in the immigration and naturalization laws, the numbers of Chinese and Asian immigrants have increased dramatically in the past decade (Fung Pih, 1993). Today there are approximately 3,859,000 Asians nationwide whose home languages are other than English (*New York Times*, 1993). Schools and society are facing tremendous challenges to meet the needs of the diverse Asian Pacific American students, so that the new immigrants will, like their predecessors, become contributing members of the larger society. For this reason this chapter is specifically pertinent to newly arrived Asian immigrant children.

Empowering Learners of English as Second Language

Virtually all students who have historically fallen outside of the mainstream in American schools are at risk for poor treatment in a system that is only beginning to adapt to their needs. Little attention has been paid to analyzing relationships between characteristics of the learning environment itself and aspects of school failure. While a number of CLD students may have personal characteristics that contribute to a lack of academic progress (e.g., a genuine disability or an unstable home life), they may also be at risk because characteristics of the school setting are detrimental to the learning process. In fact, the inability or perhaps unwillingness of educators to distinguish between internal and external factors in the learning problems of CLD students may be the major contributor to their school failure.

Who Are Asian Americans?

The term *Asian American* covers a variety of national, cultural, and religious ancestries. Asian Americans represent numerous subgroups, however the four major groups are East Asian, such as Chinese, Japanese, and Korean; Pacific Island, such as Hawaiian, Chamorro, and Samoan; Southeast Asian, such as Thai and Vietnamese; and South Asian, such as Indian and Pakistani (Pang, 1995). Although there are similarities among the various subgroups, they have different origin, ecological adaptations, and histories. In additions to these between-group differences, diversity exists within national groups and individuals. Individual differences are found in reasons for migration, related hopes and expectations, and reception by the dominant culture. Some immigrants are refugees from countries torn apart by war, others from the middle class of stable countries.

Many children, struggling with a new language and culture, drop out of school. Not all Asian children are superior students, a fallacy and misleading stereotype that masks individuality and conceals real problems. If Asian students are viewed as instant successes, there is less justification for assisting those who may need help. The result may be neglect, isolation, delinquency, and inadequate preparation for the job market among those students.

For many Asian children, the challenge of cultural assimilation in schools contradicts their own cultural system and also undermines their sense of well-being and self-confidence (Trueba, Cheng & Ima, 1993). Many Asian families' attitudes and beliefs about education stem from Confucianism, a doctrine that emphasizes the malleability of human behavior. In some Asian societies, individual potential is deemphasized, great importance is placed on the role of effort and diligence toward the group outcome. Given such different cultural perspectives, Chinese and Asian CLD children of immigrant families often bring a different set of attitudes and aspirations to the classroom. They may be more willing to accept the notion that achievement depends on diligence and not on intelligence, that they need to work hard in school in order to "learn" well and thus become "outstanding students"—a desirable honor to be considered at home and in the community. The ethnic identity of Asian children is often based on their collective grouping. In contrast, American schooling emphasizes independence, individualism, and competition (see Leung's chapter for discussion of the cultural conflict with these values). However, this kind of value system and belief in the importance of education, at times, can inevitably bring about greater demand and pressure on youngsters, especially when they are making slow or less progress in a new environment.

Dominant and Dominated Group Dynamics

Cummins (1986) in his theoretical framework proposed a model for empowering students of diverse backgrounds. He stressed the importance of both social and political factors when planning for language minority students. Cummins argued that within the societal context there is a dominant group or mainstream group and dominated or subordinated groups. Within the school context, Cummins believed that schools must break away from traditional practices, which have focused on mainstream educational issues, and take action in the following areas: incorporate the cultural and linguistic backgrounds of subordinate group students; encourage community participation; review and revise pedagogy; and reevaluate assessment procedures and strategies.

The first area, incorporation of students' language and culture, deals with the degree to which school programs address students' language and culture similarities and differences. Cummins suggested that students of diverse backgrounds will achieve at higher academic levels when schools recognize and build upon strengths in a student's home language and reinforce the student's cultural identity.

The second area emphasizes the collaboration between school and community. Contrary to the common belief that parents from dominated groups are often uncaring and unconcerned, in reality, most parents of culturally diverse students have high aspirations for their children and want to be involved in promoting their academic progress (Fillmore, 1990). It is feasible to involve nearly all the parents in educational activities (such as listening to their children read), even when the parents are nonliterate and largely non-English speaking (Chang & Fung, 1996).

The third area is pedagogy or instruction. In contrast to a pattern of classroom interaction that promotes instructional dependence, teaching that empowers will aim to liberate students from being passive learners. Teaching should enhance students' own initiatives in exploring and generating new knowledge.

The fourth area in the framework is assessment. Cummins distinguished between legitimized (traditional) assessment and advocacy-oriented (proposed) assessment. Cummins argued that diagnosis and placement were influenced frequently by bureaucratic procedures and funding requirements rather than students' academic performance in the classroom; therefore, the label of being diagnosed as academically handicapped is essentially arbitrary. In order to delegitimize the traditional function of psychological assessment in disabling culturally diverse students, educators must critically scrutinize the societal and educational context within which the child has developed (Cazden, 1985).

As educators and advocators for Chinese and other Asian immigrant students, a question we must ask ourselves is What have we done for our students in terms of pursuing and maintaining the equal opportunity and access for them to learn, both in schools and communities, as compared to their counterparts.

Bilingual Instruction and the Development of Cognitive Ability

In an important study, Tucker (1990) found cognitive and social correlates in additive bilinguality. After many years of field observations and studies, he proposed a language education model for bilingual children that maximizes the integration of native language and majority language in school curriculum. This model, as Tucker pointed out, seems to hold great promise for building and sustaining valuable natural language resources within the United States, which at this time are either allowed to decay or are never sufficiently developed. In addition, there is an abundance of research findings to support the positive correlation between bilingualisim and cognitive flexibility (Diaz, 1985; Hakuta, 1987). That is, the more balanced the bilinguality of the children, the more cognitively flexible and creative they are. Youngsters with a high degree of bilingual proficiency exhibited enhanced flexibility, creativity, and divergent problem-solving abilities compared to their monolingual counterparts.

For Chinese and other Asian bilingual language learners, like most other second language learners, their ultimate academic goals are to develop the ability to use English, in both oral and written forms, and to effectively use their language in their personal and school tasks. Students need to communicate effectively in English and use this language to learn school content. An effective and well-balanced bilingual educational program will enable students to achieve these goals. Researchers have demonstrated that well-balanced bilinguals with strong biliteracy and bicultural skills can enjoy not only academic but professional and lifelong success as well (Hakuta, 1986; Tseng, 1983). In exemplary bilingual educational programs, as Fillmore (1990) pointed out, the level of the curricular content offered to the students is consistent with the level of the curriculum for all other students. English is used in these programs so that students master English, however English does not displace the ethnic language as a means of carrying out the instructional discourse of school. Indeed, the importance of developing native literacy was also evidenced by Hudelson (1990). In her extensive classroom experiences working with bilingual/second language learners, she documented ways that children acquire a second language by building on the knowledge and skills of their home languages. Hudelson also gave examples of the ways in which using a language other than English contributes both to children's progress with English and to their academic development.

Elements of an Effective Bilingual Instructional Program

A sound bilingual educational program for Chinese and other Asian bilingual students must meet the following criteria:

- Dual language input should be provided through communicatively sensitive language instruction and subject-matter presentation.
- Communicative arts of the target languages should be integrated within the total content curriculum.

- Ample opportunity and demand for language output must be allowed. A child should be required to utilize both the home language and the second language productively and receptively.
- The bilingual pedagogue and personnel should be well prepared and committed to making the program work.
- Sensitivity to the reality of the cultural differences should be incorporated into the classroom. Effective bilingual teachers are willing to make adjustments in classroom interactions to provide classroom experiences that are more congruent with varied home patterns. Both the teachers and students realize that these adjustments work both ways.
- The value and the level of the curricular content offered to the bilingual/second language students is consistent with the level of the curriculum for all other students. The program is well articulated across classes at a given level, as well as between levels.
- Appropriate use of a student's native language and culture must be a part of classroom instruction.

Developing Native Literacy
Conceptual Issues

Using First Languages
Bridges to Second Language Acquisition

Snow (1990), in her review of research on the instruction of ESL students, concluded that ESL students should first learn to read in their native language, instead of being asked to learn to read in a second language they do not know well. In another study on innercity Chinese immigrant students who resided either in San Francisco or New York City and whose home languages include several Chinese dialects, Chang and Fung (1994) found that a majority of students who resided in New York City used their native language at home. When asked, Which language do you prefer to use? the answers were, unanimously, "Chinese (of dialects)." Although some children also expressed that they like spelling and reading (English subjects). When asked why, some children replied, "It is easy" or "I like my teacher, she makes it easy, and she reads stories to us. It's fun." In these situations, the teachers were fully bilingual and developed strong bilingual student-teacher rapport, which enhanced learning.

Having a strong native language literacy component in the bilingual education program will strengthen children's ability to fully understand the purpose of reading and writing and the various ways one can achieve communication. When teachers use the home language that children speak fluently, children learn how language can be used to make sense of their experience. For example, after studying the story about "Yeh-Shen: A Cinderella Story from China," in Mandarin, Mrs. Ho had this discourse with her student, Ling, an eight-year-old, Mandarin- and Foochowese-speaking girl who recently emigrated to this country from Foochow, China:

MRS. HO: Who was Yeh-Shen's friend?
LING: The fish.
MRS. HO: How did they become friends?
LING: She had nobody she could talk to, so she talked to the fish. She was happy that the fish listened to her. So they became friends.
MRS. HO: How did they get along?
LING: Yeh-Shen saved her food for the fish. When she walked along the river, the fish followed her.

Ling was able to follow the details in the story because she learned the language arts skills in her native language first. Ling understood the story's complicated plot. Mrs. Ho, a competent Chinese bilingual teacher, then introduced the story in English. This activity provided Ling with an opportunity to build on her English reading skills through her Chinese literacy skills. Figure 12.1 is an example of how the elements of the story Yeh-Shen were explained to Ling.

Learning to read is more easily accomplished in a language the child speaks fluently, because the reader is able to use the cueing systems found in language and then predict the meaning of written language. Research reveals that language and literacy instruction in the native language gives students advantages that help them to become literate in English. Lanauze and Snow (1989) found that children who were the better writers in Spanish were also better writers in English. Their writing ability in first language gave them an edge when they transferred to the second language.

This language acquisition process, on one hand, helped youngsters deal with ethnic and personal identities and, on the other hand, facilitated student mastery of English reading, writing, and other content areas. They learned, for example, that they could use journals to reveal personal feelings or opinions. After reading "Grandfather Tang's Story," students wrote both in Chinese and English in their journals and designs using Tangrams, seven geometric shapes.

Topics depicted in "Yeh-Shen" and other culturally relevant stories can be expanded into thematic study of different genre. For instance, the familiar European fairy tale "The Little Glass Slipper," which Charles Perrault first published in 1697, is comparable to the Chinese version of Cinderella "Yeh-Shen," which was written around the seventh century of the Tang dynasty in China. A Hmong version of the story of Cinderella, "Jouanah," which took place in the remote mountains of Southeast Asia, delineated the

FIGURE 12.1
Story Structure of "Yeh-Shen"

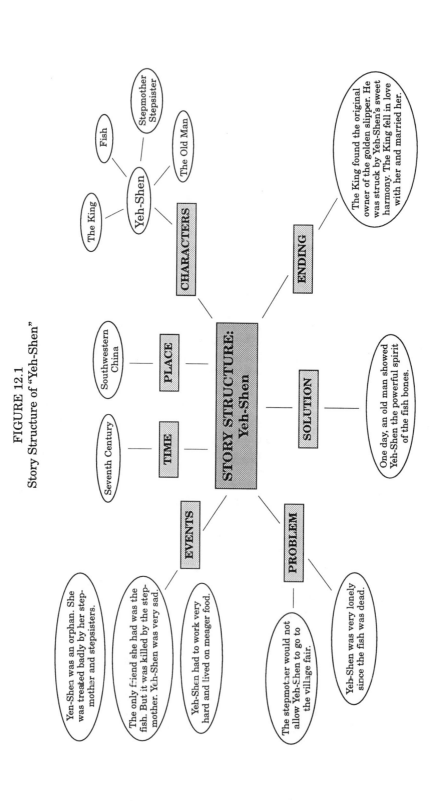

rites and rituals of ancient mountain culture. A thematic study unit will help students and the teacher to discover that there are at least forty additional versions of Cinderella from around the world. Through the theme, various cultures, beliefs, and values are compared, contrasted, and connected. It is easier for CLD children to comprehend the story through concepts with which they are already familiar. This process of concept building through native language arts (NLA) helps children organize information in specific ways that are relevant to real-life situations while they are learning to read and write in both languages. The rationale is to introduce the conceptual understanding of universality of people and cultures so that children can understand one another better early on, even with conceivably different backgrounds, while they are acquiring a second language.

Psycholinguistic Considerations for Chinese CLD Students

Given an information processing task such as decoding phonetic symbols or putting Chinese characters in sequential order by sounds can pose tremendous challenges for Chinese academically at-risk children. These tasks require step-by-step (successive simultaneous sequential) information processing skills, which for many children is often a great demand (Fung Pih, 1984; Kirby, Das & Jarman, 1975; Luria, 1966). In the study Fung Pih (1984) conducted on school children who had learning and reading disabilities, she found that children who were identified as having difficulties in reading often had problems with simultaneous sequential processing skills. This effect will make graphic-phonemic tasks, such as putting letters and sounds together in English or identifying Chinese characters by phonetic symbols, extremely challenging and difficult. The phenomenon, in part, explains why the majority of reading disability cases are diagnosed at around second or third grades, when phonics instruction is an essential part of school curriculum in this country. A language program that emphasizes comprehension skills and focuses on semantic structures would be more academically effective and appropriate for these children than a reading program built solely on conventional reading skills such as decoding or word recognition skills. Chinese linguistic structures rely heavily on both oral language skills (for sentence pattern) and visual-perceptual skills (for configuration of the character). When teachers conduct a decoding lesson, they should try to tap children's strength of auditory discrimination as well as the visual-spatial ability acquired when learning Chinese characters. This technique, along with encouraging youngsters to tell or retell a story, could help them develop a better understanding of the letter/sound relationship in English, which in turn strengthens reading comprehension and spelling.

Social-Cultural Identity

When educators capitalize on student native language abilities, the instruction not only enhances children's cognitive consequences and linguistics skills, but also fosters positive cultural identity, which will lead to higher levels of academic achievement.

Chinese and Asian Pacific American literature provide children with rich resources of their cultural backgrounds and heritage. Well-written native literature can reinforce positive portrayals, unambiguous illustrations, strong and resilient characterization, accurate historical accounts, and culturally pluralistic themes (Pang, Colvin, Tran & Barba, 1992). Asian children's literature can provide youngsters both intangible input, in terms of children's confidence as readers and writers, and tangible feedback, in terms of strategies children use in dealing with ESL literacy (Hudelson, 1990). Once children see themselves as readers and writers in their native language, their self-esteem will rise as they learn a second language. Children gradually become willing and often eager to take risks reading and writing in a new language. The official recognition of the value of the home language and home culture, as portrayed in literature can contribute greatly to increase the sense of self-worth and self-esteem in children.

Once children appreciate their heritage and their abilities, teachers may encourage them to write about their feelings and reflections in simple writing assignments or through journal writing. When teachers understand their students, they may encourage students individually or collectively. The purpose of this exercise is two-fold: first, to boost children's self-confidence and identity, and second, to increase their leadership ability. Only when children are positively self-assured and unconditionally supported by adults will they be willing to speak up with confidence and be more readily prepared to initiate tasks on their own. The more knowledge they have about their own people, culture, and heritage, the more they will be able to speak for and defend themselves and others.

A Pedagogic Framework
Using Chinese and Asian American Children's Literature for Classroom Instruction

Linguistic Differences

Languages such as English and Chinese, which seem to have vast linguistic differences, do have elements teachers can build on. In the Chinese language, each separate character has its own meaning, which can stand for one or more English words, for example, 恐 (fear), 龍 (dragon). When two or several characters are put together, the result is a new meaning that may be different from the meanings of the two characters separately—for example, 恐龍 (dinosaur). This means that the written form of the Chinese language can be either semantically and/or phonologically based. Several characters, *zhi* (字) put together, make a semantic unit, *chi* (詞). Combinations of *zhi*, the characters, and *chi*, the semantic unit of characters, make comprehensive units of a sentence, *ju* (句). The combination of these meaningful speech segments, the *zhi*, *chi*, and *ju*, in turn, generate passages. In addition, Chinese, as a language, relies heavily on oral forms and idiomatic expressions, for example, 走著瞧 ("play by ear"); (" Eat, drink, play, and pleasure alone are undesirable habits"). Chinese language places great emphasis on oral forms and expressions. There is plenty of evidence in various literary genre, including poetry and stories, to document cogent, quit wit and the use of metaphor. The use of these forms not only adds to the embellishment of the language, it is also an essential part of the language and literature. To be able to write productively in Chinese, one must first acquire a wealth of oral literacy.

There is a considerable number of similarities as well as linguistic differences between the two languages. Chinese bilingual teachers need to demonstrate that children can and should use their knowledge of native language arts and vice versa. They can encourage children to make predictions about dependent structure within the context of the story, and generate meaning rather than relying only on the identification of each character/word. Occasional use of mixed language and code switching for beginning second language learners is a developmental phenomenon. Code switching is a commonly observed type of verbal interaction in bilinguals that involves shifting from one grammatical system to another. For example, a Cantonese-English bilingual child might begin an utterance in English and end in Cantonese, "I put on a red 衫 (shirt)." This kind of verbal behavior may occur within one utterance, as is the case with the previous example, or it may occur across several utterances. That is, the individual might begin an utterance in one language, complete a sentence or two in that language, and then shift to the other language. "It has been a very cold winter. 春天什麼時候才到？ (When will Spring come)?" In these cases, teachers should not be overly concerned with correcting children's mistakes (mixing the language). Instead, teachers must allow children the flexibility of learning the second language through exploring, experimenting, and discovering with their peers. Peer coaching can be effective and fun. Children may take turns playing the "little teacher" in mini lessons. These activities provide children opportunities to see commonly made mistakes, which they may not otherwise notice. In peer coaching, a more able student can serve as an excellent role model for other students. These strategies have been proven to be useful in helping children make easier transitions from one language to another.

Children's awareness of books and print may reflect their concepts of the Chinese writing system. So far, we have discussed linguistic considerations for both Mandarin and Cantonese-speaking Chinese students. The principles apply to other major Chinese dialects as well. In dealing with additional Asian languages, a good rule of thumb would be to consider children's native linguistic abilities. When in doubt, consult with experts and/or the children themselves, making sure to encourage students to use their native literacy. Psycholinguists believe there are reading and writing universals that occur in all cultures. Given the fact that Chinese and Asian CLD children have linguistic structures and speech patterns very different from English, teachers should be encouraged to provide enough comprehensive input, such as prediction of dependent structures or depicting main ideas, through illustrations and other cues (e.g., visual or audio), and tap into the available facility of natural language from children's whole environment. By doing so, CLD children will eventually become more proficient and independent readers in effective and interesting ways.

Planning the Literature Session for Chinese and Other Asian CLD Students

Many of the Asian CLD children are immigrants. Some of them are at the initial stage of adjusting to the new environment and new culture. Others are in the process of assimilation. In either case, a curriculum that emphasizes establishing routines and maintaining records of CLD children's progress is essential. A planned literature-based program (see Table 12.1) is an excellent example of this type of instruction. The following components are recommended to allow CLD children to develop their literacy:

- select books to read
- work independently
- read with a partner, or a small group
- use a response journal
- set up and use a reading log
- work on a special activity
- sign up for a conference with the teacher
- practice a needed skill
- use the audio-visual equipment

In order to provide adequate amounts of comprehensive input for CLD children, teachers should organize the instructional material in a predictable manner and provide time for:

TABLE 12.1

A Literature-Based Curriculum for

Culturally and Linguistically Diverse (CLD) Students

Children or Teachers	Instruction	Specific Activities	Time Frame
Children	Read aloud	• share prior knowledge about story topic • make predictions about text • share a literacy experience • broaden understandings of story structure and genre • read with teacher • talk about their reactions to what was read	15–20 minutes
Teachers		• share knowledge of author's background • share reasons for selecting books • read children's literature • discuss story structure (beginning, middle and end) • ask children to share their responses to what was read • model how to respond in a journal	
Children	Respond to literature	• write in journals daily to respond to literature and other experiences • write about characters and spell as best they can • punctuate as best as they can • ask an adult or a more able peer to write down the story • work on retelling activity • talk with peers about books	15–20 minutes
Teachers		• actively move from group to group listening to children • encourage children to reflect on their literacy experiences • provide strategies for solving character writing or spelling problems • provide strategies for making and practicing expressive Chinese phrases	

(Continued on next page)

TABLE 12.1 *(continued)*
A Literature-Based Curriculum for
Culturally and Linguistically Diverse (CLD) Students

Children or Teachers	*Instruction*	*Specific Activities*	*Time Frame*
Children	Share	• read journal • read excerpts from books • share a reading strategy • retell a favorite part • display follow-up activities (e.g., pantomime, dramatic version, art work)	15–20 minutes
Teachers		• manage sharing session by pre-selecting presenters • extend children's understanding • express delight in children's discoveries	
Children	Independent reading	• select their own literature • read independently, or read with a peer • discuss in a group their reactions to books	30 minutes
Teachers		• confer with readers • facilitate children's reading • discover children as readers • provide strategies that help readers tackle print	

Source: Board of Education, City of New York, 1994.

• reading aloud or teacher-guided reading
• independent, paired, or cooperative reading
• responding to literature, journal time, retelling activities
• sharing

It is best to allow CLD, and children who need more time, to break a task into smaller units so students have more opportunities to master the activity.

Infusing Native Language Arts into the Curriculum
The Integrated Curriculum Approach

One of the most important thrusts in curricular implementation, as Ogbu (1992) pointed out, is to value what children bring to school—their communities' cultural models and social realities, what their communities use or do not use in seeking enhancement for their children's education.

When teachers integrate native language arts into instruction, they provide children with the opportunity to make connections among concepts, topics, and subject areas. Curriculum integration can take many forms—from the connecting of two subject areas to the ultimate nesting of the entire curriculum in or with interdisciplinary themes.

An interdisciplinary theme gives children an opportunity to study topics in depth, explore concepts, and have experiences that extend through all academic areas. Children working in learning centers or corners with theme-related tasks have an opportunity to explore problems and use hands-on materials to develop a broad understanding of concepts. Content becomes more meaningful because it is grounded in experience. As children work on themes together in centers, they make choices as they develop their talents and interests. Using Asian and Asian American children's literature as the base for the thematic studies offers Chinese and Asian second language learners an excellent opportunity to develop a fuller self-identity, while increasing cognitive and academic language proficiency (CALP). An interdisciplinary example using the story "Yeh-Shen" can be found in Figure 12.2. For most of the children of CLD background this approach allows them to:

- develop self-esteem
- appreciate their linguistic and cultural identity
- explore their own background, language, and culture, as well as those of their peers
- understand the importance of family and community as valued resources
- develop a full range of literacy skills

Developing Theme Plans

Developing theme plans can be a challenging and time-consuming project. To make the task more interesting and less time consuming, theme plans may be created with a partner or a small group. Teams work together to select theme areas and brainstorm components of their plans. Individual members develop specific theme plans. After completion, these plans are distributed to all group members to be kept on file until needed. Teachers are important facilitators in this process.

Based on field experiences working with teachers in developing their own curriculum for the CLD students, the following steps (Board of Education of the City of New York, 1994) were designed to implement interdisciplinary and thematic instructional units (see Figure 12.3).

FIGURE 12.2

An Interdisciplinary Approach to Chinese Native Literature

CHINESE NATIVE LITERATURE: "Yeh-Shen"

Oral Language
- Retell the Story
- Literacy Conference
- Oral Report
- Small Group Report
- Discussion

Teacher Read Alouds
- Yeh-Shen
- The Milky Way
- The Empty Pot
- The Seven Chinese Brothers
- The Artist and the Architect

Social Studies
- Guangzhou on a Map
- Compare Land System
- China and the United States
- The Seven Chinese Brothers
- Government Structure

Science
- Constellation
- August Moon Festival
- Dragon Festival
- Fortune Cookie (writing sentence for messages)
- Potsticker (dumpling) for a balanced meal
- Folk Dance: The Bai an Yee People

Math
- Tangrams
- Word Problems that Relate to the Stories

Music
- "The Little Glass Slipper"— (灰姑娘) a Musical
- Adaptation of Rhythms from Other Children's Play
- Pantomime

Art
- Chinese Brush Painting
- After Visiting a Chinese Gallery: Draw Different Scenes from the Story of "Yeh-Shen"
- Make Puppets

Written Language
- Reconstruct the Story into a play: Yeh-Shen
- "My House in China"
- "How I Remember My Teacher in China"—reader response
- Write a Report About Cinderella Stories Around the World

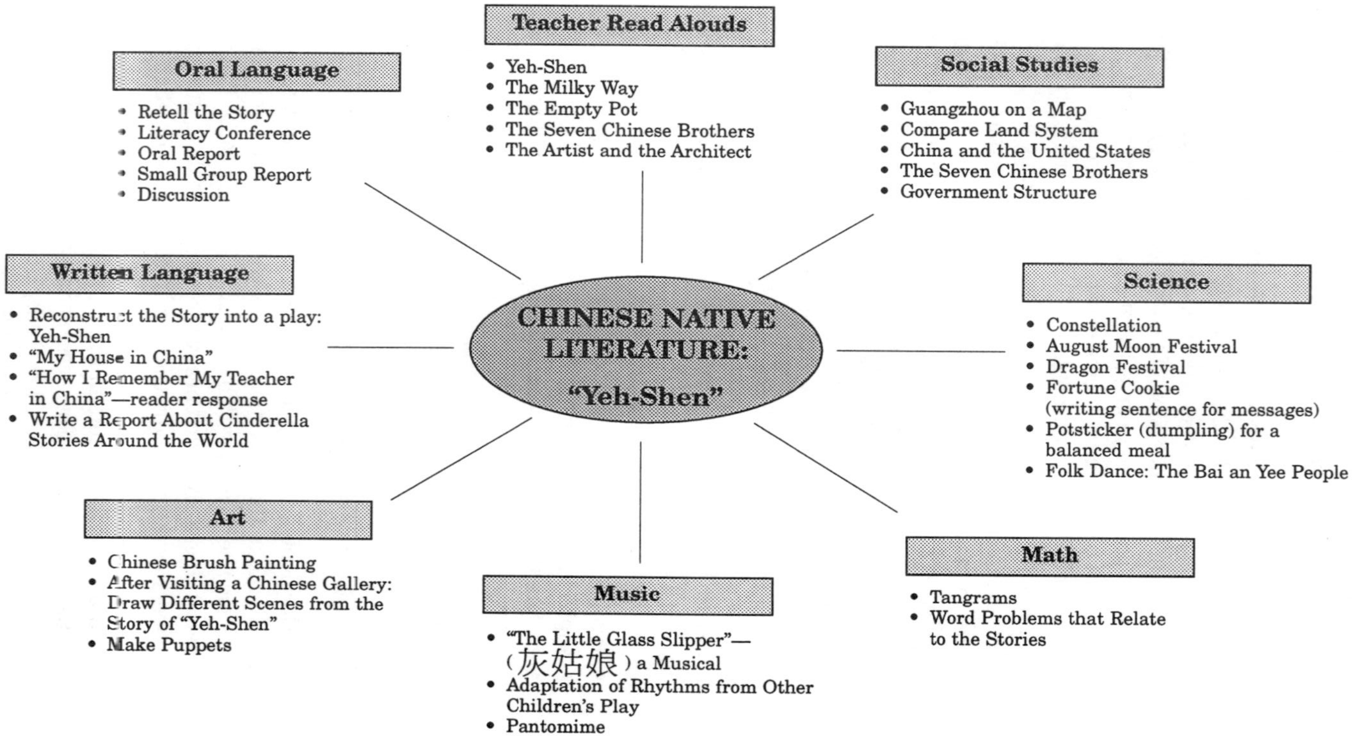

FIGURE 12.3

Interdisciplinary and Thematic Instructional Units for Use with CLD Students

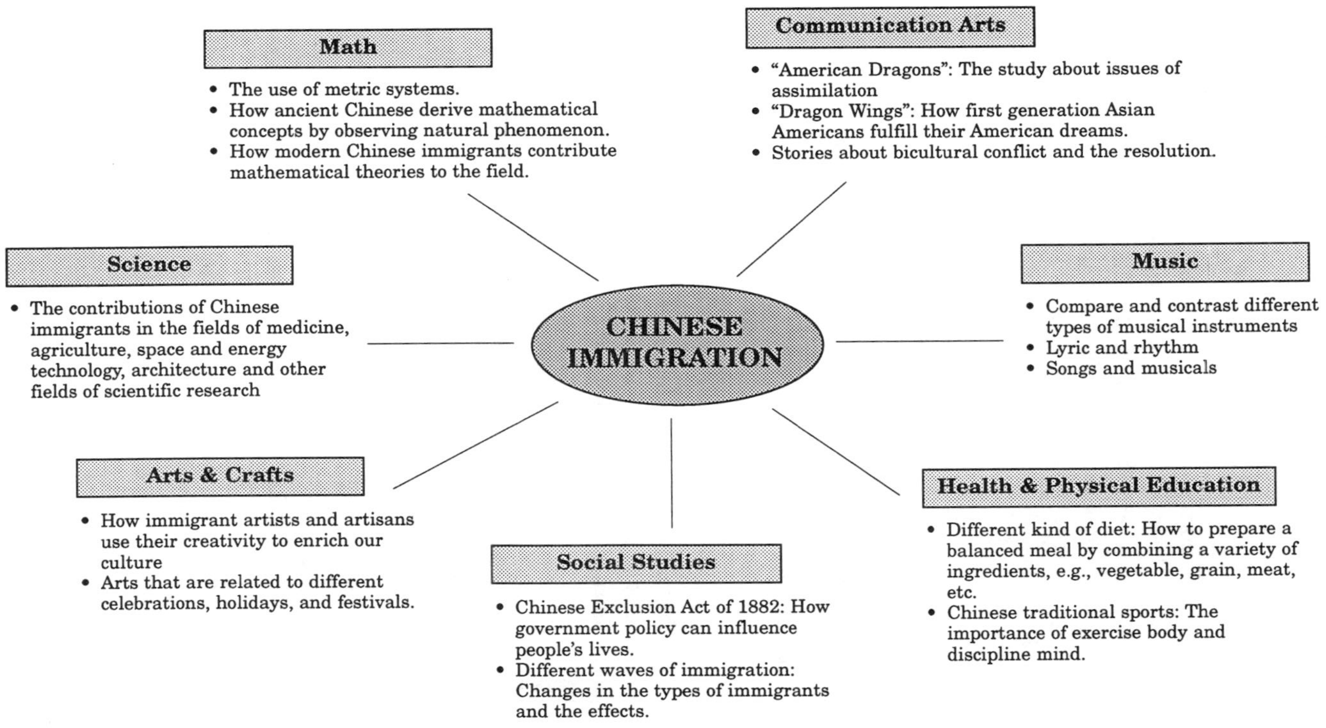

Communication Arts

- "American Dragons": The study about issues of assimilation
- "Dragon Wings": How first generation Asian Americans fulfill their American dreams.
- Stories about bicultural conflict and the resolution.

Music

- Compare and contrast different types of musical instruments
- Lyric and rhythm
- Songs and musicals

Math

- The use of metric systems.
- How ancient Chinese derive mathematical concepts by observing natural phenomenon.
- How modern Chinese immigrants contribute mathematical theories to the field.

CHINESE IMMIGRATION

Science

- The contributions of Chinese immigrants in the fields of medicine, agriculture, space and energy technology, architecture and other fields of scientific research

Health & Physical Education

- Different kind of diet: How to prepare a balanced meal by combining a variety of ingredients, e.g., vegetable, grain, meat, etc.
- Chinese traditional sports: The importance of exercise body and discipline mind.

Social Studies

- Chinese Exclusion Act of 1882: How government policy can influence people's lives.
- Different waves of immigration: Changes in the types of immigrants and the effects.

Arts & Crafts

- How immigrant artists and artisans use their creativity to enrich our culture
- Arts that are related to different celebrations, holidays, and festivals.

Theme: Chinese Immigration

Name _____ Date _____

Step 1: Objective

Decide on the purpose for studying this theme. The reason may come directly from the children, based on a concern, or it may relate to an area prescribed by the school's curriculum. In either case, teachers should use an opening activity that allows children to validate their previous experience in the area and to encourage students to identify what they might investigate. The following K-W-L (know-want-learn) approach, provides a guide:

Step 2: Getting Ready

A. What do I know about Chinese immigration?
B. What do I want to find out about Chinese Immigration?
C. How I can find the information?
D. What have I learned?

Step 3: Identifying the Resources

Locate the materials that relate to this topic—for example, books, tape, magazines, and places to visit. Also tap the expertise of parents, resource people, other community members, and appropriate social service agencies.

Step 4: Time Required

Time frame can be flexible. Depending on children's interests, the unit can be expanded or shorten.

Step 5: Planning for a Variety of Integrated Curriculum Areas

For example, use the video "The Great Wall," which portrays a family who emigrated to the United States from Beijing. The film gives children a closer look at sociopolitical and sociolinguistic adjustments a family made to live functionally in a new country. Attention should be paid to the theme's learning objectives as well as to the individual curriculum areas. Remember to focus on development of curriculum-related skills and concepts.

Step 6: Fun to Learn

Make learning exciting and fun by bringing various resources to the children. Keep energy and enthusiasm high. Involve children in learning experiences outside the classroom. These kinds of activities may include field trips, scientific investigations, conducting interviews, and participating in volunteer activities.

Step 7: Performance-Based Assessment

Use work collected over a period of time to evaluate each child's growth and development. The work can be collected in portfolios, which may consist of folders or large envelopes; other kinds of containers may be used for large or three-dimensional products.

In summary, when incorporating the thematic units into the implementation of the interdisciplinary curriculum, teachers of Chinese Asian second language learners or CLD students will identify the following characteristics:

- integrate instructional plans around areas of study and interest;
- identify clear concepts, attitudes, skills, and abilities in the unit;
- allow for rich interactions between children and adults;
- focus on activating children's prior knowledge and home experiences; and
- utilize performance and outcome-based assessment activities.

Working with Academically Challenged Chinese and Asian CLD Children

Guiding Principles

The current focus on individual ability is based on the evidence that productive persons are those who cultivate various modes of intelligence. There is no single quality of mind that should be labeled "intelligence." Accumulated scientific research demonstrates that human beings evolved to carry out many forms of thinking. A person might be stronger or weaker in one form of thinking, this does not necessarily carry over to other forms of thought. Society has given preference to linguistic and logic-mathematical abilities. According to Gardner (1983), equal significance must be accorded to musical, spatial, bodily kinesthetic, interpersonal, and intrapersonal intelligence.

When working with academically challenged Asian CLD youngsters, educators must keep in mind that *all children can learn*. The challenge lies in determining how much, how fast, and how effectively each individual child can learn. The teacher, as a role model, conveys the message to children that, regardless of outward appearances or abilities, they are valuable human beings to be treated with dignity and respect. The following list will aid teachers in planning and assessing developmentally appropriate materials and activities for CLD children with special needs (Board of Education of the City of New York, 1994):

1. *Direct Experience.* During the first phase the introduction of new concepts begins with the physical manipulation of real objects in the child's immediate environment (such as tables, chairs, books, etc.) Using oral language, children describe their explorations with the materials.
2. *Concrete Materials.* The second phase involves varied interactions with manipulatives (flannel board pieces, games, puppets, etc.) concurrently with the use of oral language. Children are encouraged to retell stories using manipulatives .
3. *Two-Dimensional Materials.* The third phase uses photographs, films, and filmstrips to further reinforce the concept being learned. Children are encouraged to described the process verbally.
4. *Abstract Material.* The fourth phase utilizes only abstract symbols (characters, words) to illustrate the language process. This can include picture/character or word cards, games, or storybook. Children use oral language to describe the activity.
5. *Extending Concepts.* During the fifth phase, the children can be provided with many opportunities to apply the newly learned concepts in a variety of contexts, using oral language concurrently (sentences, stories, games, wipe-off cards, sequencing story events on sentence strips, etc.).

An example:

Child's Name:
Activity: Story Time—Teacher reads to Cha "Grandfather Tang's Story"

Developmental Stage of Learning Preferred by Child

1. *Direct Experience:* Cha visits real fox at zoo.
2. *Concrete Materials:* Cha arranges tangram pieces.
3. *Representational Materials:* Cha arranges tangram pieces in "fox."
4. *Abstract Material:* Cha matches character/word card to "fox."
5. *Extending Concepts:* Cha expands 3 and 4; makes a picture story about fox; writes characters/words and sentences about fox; retells the story.

Teaching Strategies

Chinese and Asian CLD children with special needs will generally prefer, and benefit from, many reality-based experiences that are reinforced through the use of concrete manipulatives. With the teacher's help, children will begin to use oral language to describe experiences and later move along to more abstract activities. Moderate code switching during this period might best be overlooked. The following flow chart presents a schematic view of some teaching strategies (Board of Education of the City of New York, 1994):

Proceed Developmentally

- Be realistic and flexible in your expectations of the child's development.
- Think in terms of the child's chronological age.
- Use task analysis to present activities. Task may by broken down into component parts and taught in step-by-step sequence.
- Make sure that activities are a challenge but are not frustrating.

Be Sequential

- Start with what the child can do: move from the known, simple, and easy to the more difficult and complex.
- Build complexity very gradually.
- Plan activities based on the following progression: from concrete experiences (object/motor/oral language) to representational experiences (pictures) to symbolic experiences (verbal and written symbols).

Use Multisensory Approaches

- Provide a variety of activities and materials (e.g., paints, manipulative materials, creative dramatics, music, blocks, movement, cooking, listening to stories).

Be Flexible

- Provide adequate time for the child to complete tasks and participate in group activities.
- Allow the child to engage in an activity that he/she has greater confidence with.
- Allow individual rates and styles of learning.

Be Repetitive

- Allow the child to repeat an activity several times.
- Present a variety of activities to let the child practice a skill.
- Repeat instructions when necessary.

Be Concrete

- Accompany oral directions with hand gestures, body movement, objects, or pictures.
- Provide a wide variety of physical activities
- Use modeling and imitation: The child looks and listens as the teacher performs the task or desired behavior, which the child then imitates.

Be Specific

- Provide a clear structure for each activity:
  - Let the child know the sequence of the activity.
  - Give clear cues for the child to recognize when the activity begins and when it ends.

Be Positive

- Develop and nurture a positive attitude in the child: "I can do." "I can learn."
- Address the child by name.
- Recognize and praise small efforts.
- Reinforce responses that come close to achieving the desired behavior.
- Verbalize what the child is doing right.
- During an activity, maintain eye contact periodically to keep the child's attention on the task.

Be "Firm Yet Fair"

- Explain to the child the reasons behind decisions you make.
- Set limits appropriate to the developmental needs of the child.

Be Precise

- Use clear language. Avoid mixed-language instruction.
- Give precise directions (e.g., "Read the story silently, then you may discuss it with your peer").

Have Fun

- Allow the child to learn through exploring, experimenting, and discovering.
- Provide many opportunities for peer modeling; the child observes and then assists another child in completing a task.
- Plan activities that encourage the child to use learned skills in a meaningful way and natural context (e.g., the child participates in cooking experiences to reinforce an increasing ability to follow directions).
- Be sensitive to children's learning styles. Some children may prefer group over individual learning situations.

Summary

This chapter described how to use children's native language and literature as major components in designing interventions for Chinese and Asian second language learners and culturally and linguistically diverse students who are not proficient in English. Central to this intervention is the concept of maximizing children's strength and minimizing their weaknesses. In spite of all labels (e.g., L.D., LEP, CLD, at risk, etc.), to empower the second language learners who are of Chinese and Asian origins, educators and interventionists need to learn about the students' cultural background and its impact on learning styles. Teachers are encouraged to use this knowledge to organize their classrooms and programs.

13

Kenji Ima

Educating Asian Newcomer Secondary Students

Four Case Studies of Schools

This is a descriptive study of Asian newcomer students, educators, and parents in a school district seeking school reform, especially in the development of site-based management. District administrators have been aggressive in seeking change. Observation and assessment of how well this district provides education for newcomer Asian students must be seen in light of districts with increasing enrollments of non-English speaking immigrant and refugee students. Educators face great challenges in addressing the needs of a complex, growing population differentiated by language, culture, level of schooling, and life experiences.

Newcomer students have become an increasingly larger share of students enrolled in the district. Over a third of all district students are either foreign born or have parents who are foreign born. More than a quarter of all students are limited English proficient while another 10 percent are fluent English proficient and have a home language other than English. About 18 percent of enrolled students are Asian and Pacific Islanders and the majority of these students come from immigrant or refugee homes where a language other than English is the dominant language. This is a study of four schools and their attempts to educate these newcomers. The descriptive materials were derived from observations of and interviews with educators and students. The cases give educators materials for thinking about ways to improve schooling for Asian and other newcomer students.

Both educators and students face heroic challenges in achieving educational success. Truly they are all testing the limits of the American Dream, which promotes the notion that all individuals will be given equal opportunity to be successful. The reality has been unequal access for Asian newcomer students (First & Carrera, 1988; Olsen, 1988; Sather, 1996), but there remain hopes that the level of inequality will be reduced (Olsen, 1994). Three schools are located in lower-income neighborhoods and one is located in a middle-income area. The lower-income areas are the first points of residential entry of immigrants and refugees while the middle-income area is a second point of entry for families who can afford next higher level housing. There are also socioeconomic differences between the families of students in those two different areas corresponding to housing costs; they differ by income, education of parents, occupation, fluency in the English language, and the number of years of U.S. residency. Three schools are large comprehensive secondary schools and the fourth is a small specialty school for students who have had troubles in other schools. This is an exploration in search of an understanding of how schools facilitate or interfere with the success of Asian immigrant and refugee students.

Washington High School
Coping with Newcomers

Washington is a school with a small but growing number of newcomer students. The school was designed to educate students who were rejected by other secondary schools because they are delinquents, drug abusers, pregnant minors, or on suspension. Like other specialty schools, this school was initially designed for native-born, monolingual English speakers. Latinos and African American students are overrepresented, while Whites, Filipinos, Asians, and Southeast Asians are underrepresented when compared to districtwide student statistics.

Many students attending Washington are lacking units, which means they are as much as a year to two years behind classmates from their home schools. Some students attend Washington because of the nursery program where their children are taken care of while they attend classes. In other cases, principals from other high schools encourage troubled students to attend Washington. Some principals do not want at-risk students dropping out of their school, since every dropout will count against the site administrator in site evaluations. The school's philosophy differs from general comprehensive high schools. Washington's teachers have attitudes more akin to elementary school educators where the emphasis is on process and the individual's personal development. By contrast, the comprehensive school philosophy is to teach content matter rather than survival skills.

Washington teachers consider their strength to be personalized instruction, which is made possible by the staffing of 32 teachers for 450 on-site students and 400 once-a-week students. This translates into a one-to-twenty teacher/student ratio with often fewer than twenty students per class. The teachers claim the main advantage for students is the higher level of individual contacts. They feel individualized attention overrides their lack of skills in addressing second language acquisition and literacy.

Teaching Understandings
Cultural and Linguistic Issues

Teachers readily admit their ignorance regarding the cultures and languages of newcomer students, especially Asians and Pacific Islanders. They are particularly concerned with their lack of knowledge of Southeast Asians who number twenty-six students, which is a sharp increase from the previous year. The school lacks appropriate bilingual materials and personnel. Teachers are having difficulty dealing with the home languages of Asian students. Though most Asian students speak English, teachers seem to lack knowledge about the level of their students' English competence. While there are four Spanish speaking aides, several bilingual teachers, and one bilingual counselor, there is not a single staff member who speaks a language of Southeast Asian newcomers. The staff members are not organized to deal with non-English speakers except on a crisis basis.

Teachers struggle to find strategies that work with newcomer Asian students, particularly those who speak English poorly. They are by necessity practicing a policy of submersion, given their lack of resources and preparation in dealing with limited English proficient (LEP) students. Submersion refers to the use of English as the language of instruction with little consideration given to the student's primary language. This pattern of "backing into" a submersion policy is commonplace at schools having relatively small numbers of any single non-native English speaking group. In contrast, with increases in the number of Spanish speaking students, the school responded with a limited bilingual program relying on aides. The school does not have an official bilingual program but has assigned several teachers to use Spanish in math and foreign language classes.

Given the teachers' lack of training in second language acquisition, they make mistakes in assessing the language skills of newcomer students. They begin with an implicit assumption that students are native English speakers. One teacher mentioned that he has a sheltered English class and has found no difficulty teaching students the English language. He commented on their ability to pick up American idioms. However another teacher stated that many Southeast Asian American students demonstrate below grade level reading comprehension skills. One English teacher mentioned that to cover required class materials, it takes more time than is available because newcomer students do not have the foundation in English. Some teachers, upon hearing students' poor oral English language performance, assume incorrectly that their reading and writing skills are also low. In most instances, however, these students are more proficient in speaking English than reading or writing it. Moreover, there is general ignorance of how to assess the language competence and needs of newcomers.

Cultural Conflicts in the Classroom

When discussing differences in learning styles and expectations, Washington teachers view the Southeast Asian immigrant student as more responsive to teacher authority—an observation also made at other schools. The teachers claim that more "Americanized" newcomer students cause more problems. Though some newcomer students are viewed as uncooperative, overall, they are seen as more compliant than other students. Teachers feel the need to be specific and directive with newcomer students, but this directive style of instruction contradicts their philosophy of helping students make choices. They prefer to teach students about options and reasons for those options and the consequences of having made choices. This approach doesn't work as well with students who are looking for more authoritative direction. According to one teacher "they seem to want to be told what to do," which is clearly an attitude that is at variance with the school culture.

Moreover, the cultural gap between teachers and newcomer students is rooted in the philosophy of the teachers. Teachers believe that their role is to help students learn how to think rather than to fill them with information. While teachers emphasize content to fulfill district requirements, they are clearly more interested in the affective aspects of learning with a central focus on personal development. Newcomer students have yet to be acculturated to the American cultural traditions of individuality that underlie this philosophy and so they find themselves at a cultural distance from teachers and other students. While some newcomer students have begun to speak in the new vocabulary of personal development, most are uncomfortable with the orientation. Nevertheless, regardless of how unfamiliar the cultures, teachers from this school were the most open toward understanding how best to serve these students.

Additionally, individualized instruction is based on a contract system, which in turn is based on reading competence. Many newcomer students do not have the cultural or academic knowledge to manage these contracts. At some schools, newcomer students are placed in "newcomer" programs that teach the basics to incoming students so they will have a common understanding of the school culture.

The Challenge of Providing Effective Counseling

Washington's school counselors have also been concerned with their lack of familiarity with Southeast Asian American students. They observe that newcomer student obstacles may include dysfunctional home lives. Yet, counselors have trouble knowing how to approach students. For example, a high school counselor was unsure of the age of a Vietnamese student who had been absent from school and arrested for burglary. According to his school counselor, this student was nineteen years old instead of his listed age of sixteen years. His older age placed him "out of step" with the younger students whom he considered to have minor problems compared to his own. He lived with four brothers while his parents remained in Vietnam. He did not care about school and apparently only attended so he could continue receiving Aid to Families with Dependent Children (AFDC) funding. He told his counselor that he and his brothers stayed up late at night drinking and smoking and therefore he had trouble waking up for school. Although the student did not feel right going to school or receiving welfare money, he did not feel he had other options. This case of unaccompanied minors is commonplace among Vietnamese delinquents (Nidorf, 1985). However, counselors are often unaware of the dynamics of maladjustment found among unaccompanied Vietnamese minors and the strategies that work well with such students (Long, 1996). Their response, as well as that of other staff of this school, has been an openness to admitting their ignorance and expressing a desire to learn.

Summary

In conclusion, Washington was designed for monolingual English speaking populations and based on a philosophy of personal development. Thus, it is underprepared for these newcomers who need to gain competence linguistically and culturally—lacking bilingual staff, bilingual materials, trained monolingual staff to deal with cultural and linguistic differences and an understanding of the unique needs of newcomer students. And last, contrary to the Asian "model minority" image, many of these students are alienated from the schools. Many came with a positive attitude toward school but because of the mismatch of teachers and curriculum with their educational needs in previous schools, they reacted negatively to schools and teachers. This alienation was associated with truancy and sometimes even delinquency as they attempted to sort out their existence on the edge between home country memories and the realities of American streets. Nevertheless in spite of the school's poor initial response to Asian language minority students, we can see in their work with Spanish speaking students a willingness to make adaptations. In time this school shows promise that educators will find solutions for Asian newcomers. They have the desire to serve these newcomer students but lack the understanding and skills to deliver appropriate educational services.

Jackson High School
For Middle Class and Eurocentric Students Only

Jackson teachers pride themselves in teaching in a distinctly middle-class area and in providing among the better offerings of college oriented courses. Many are mentor teachers, a status given to the more highly qualified teachers of the district. While approximately half of the students are White, there is a full range of other groups including African Americans, Cambodians, Chinese, Filipinos, Hmong, Japanese, Lao, Latinos, and Vietnamese.

Teachers at Jackson represent a variety of views about culturally diverse students. Some teachers resent dealing with students who do not adhere to Eurocentric, middle-class views and behaviors. During an inservice training for faculty, they were found to be defensive about the low reading performance of Asian Pacific American students. The session focused on the characteristics of Asian American students and their needs. Some teachers responded with hostility to a discussion of the problem of language development and the negative occupational consequences of "blocked mobility" or the "glass ceiling" facing Asian newcomer students. One teacher felt outsiders did not understand the teachers' viewpoint. She wanted the presentation to leave her with good feelings. Another mentioned the need to build up the teachers' self-esteem. The following comments give a flavor of their attitudes: "It's always our fault that the child doesn't succeed." "It's all on our shoulders!" "We have a lot of students from dysfunctional families." "The Vietnamese are from dysfunctional families who expect too much from their children—they can't all expect to have straight A averages." These comments reflect a defensiveness and a desire to reverse the blame for failure on students and their families. The teachers feel imposed upon in having to deal with home problems students bring to school. The principal reinforced this view by suggesting that teachers should not be expected to act as counselors for students' home problems.

Eurocentric Orientation

Faculty resentment must be seen in a broader context of demographic change that demands teachers to deal with cultural differences when they entered the profession expecting to teach White middle-class students. Many conflicts stem from the teachers' inability, or perhaps unwillingness, to deal with cultural and linguistic diversity. A former teacher from Jackson characterized social class as a key underlying foundation for the school. "The school treats everybody well as long as they respond to middle-class demands regardless of race." Additionally, Eurocentric behavior and culture seem to be the only acceptable characteristics of students, which results in friction between teachers and Asian Pacific American students.

Cultural Conflicts between Home and School

Newcomer students are generally competent in the English language and are compliant with teacher authority. They seem eager to please their teachers. However, the ongoing conflict between school culture and home culture is an issue that is not adequately addressed. The conflict for students includes being raised by "authoritarian" parents whose attitudes and behaviors differ from teachers. In one case, a student receiving a B+ grade contemplated suicide rather than face his father. According to one teacher, there are frequent instances of attempted suicides among Asian students reflecting cultural conflicts between child and parent. Asian students are not just imagining cultural conflict—it is their reality.

One central office administrator suggested that the district's secondary schools have been run as personal fiefdoms by principals and that those schools in the largely White areas have been resistant to the implications of the changing student population, primarily because they continue to receive a majority of White students. They accept students of color, but only on their terms, without recognition that these students may have different learning styles and needs. A tragic postscript to the complaints of Asian students regarding conflicts between home and school cultures is the suicide of an Asian student. He was despondent over his inability to deal simultaneously with the demands of his father and living in a society that preached values of self-determination.

Teacher Resentment

Teachers and staff at schools such as Jackson have resented the presence of human relations teams, which are responsible for sensitizing staff to racially and culturally different communities. The staff resents being told that they are racist. They feel "picked on" by the teams. Few admit to having racist feelings and most claim they are not racist. They want practical suggestions and assistance in dealing with minority students. Teachers at Jackson resent having fewer dollars per student than schools with larger enrollments of African American and Latino students. They question the feasibility of bussing students and wish that more of the integration money could be used to assist in direct teaching service.

The School's View of English Language Development Programs

In light of their feelings about multiculturalism and newcomer students, how have they responded to bilingual students? This site has both LEP (Limited English Proficient) and FEP (Fluent English Proficient) students. Some Asian language aides have been hired and they provide a crucial link with staff that they would not otherwise have, especially with Vietnamese, Chinese, and Filipino students. There are no teachers who also have that ability. Presently, among a staff of over one hundred teachers, there is only one Asian teacher. Perhaps the most serious deficit is the lack of trained bilingual or second language staff. In many instances, LEP students are left to fend for themselves, similar to the sink-or-swim bilingual policy of years past.

The school's response to LEP student needs is to offer ESL (English as Second Language) classes, but few teachers, if any, apart from ESL teachers, are trained to deal with bilingual students. In one instance, a teacher said LEP students were placed in his class without any prior notification, while he had no formal training nor even discussions with inservice or experienced teachers on how to deal with bilingual students. The teacher noted that in class, LEP students seem to "fumble around," relying on other students to help them through the day, if they are fortunate enough to have other students who understand them.

Jackson administrators are not strongly supportive of bilingual education. Though there are no primary language bilingual classes at this school, administrators and other teachers do not understand the ESL teachers' needs. According to site English teachers, ESL classes are far from adequate. Jackson offers only the minimum number of ESL courses and even at that level the principal objects because he wants all students to be in regular classes. He feels that European immigrants succeeded in the U.S. without special classes and believes that current newcomers should also be able to learn in the same manner. One teacher said, "There is a feeling that we are coddling newcomer students in ESL classes."

There are over two hundred students in ESL classes and the program has been expanded to three teachers. The reading program does not include sheltered approaches because they have little funding for these students. Knowing that other schools have the funds for special programs, these teachers feel deprived and resent them for getting the "gravy" while they struggle with slimmer budgets.

Jackson is a middle-class school with a faculty that is indifferent to the cultural and linguistic differences between themselves and their Asian newcomer students. The overriding attitude toward implicit cultural challenges of newcomers is that teachers are upholders of high academic standards and that the business of any high school is to prepare students to pass the SAT and other measures of content level competence. The school produces its share of high performing students as measured by the high number of college scholarship awards received by its students and their high college admission rates. Usually, newcomer students accept the teachers' views and struggle privately with how to effectively juxtapose Old and New World values. For the English learner, it is a sink-or-swim world—one ruled illegal by the *Lau v. Nichols* Supreme Court decision, which formed the basis of bilingual education policy. Without central office pressure and with the lack of trained bilingual teachers, the school ignores the legal statutes on bilingualism. However, given the middle-class backgrounds of many newcomer students, they are prepared to accept whatever a teacher will demand, and hope they will do well enough to be admitted to a high status university. As in other middle- and upper middle-class schools, newcomer students are likely to have educated parents, intact families, and literacy in their primary language if they entered U.S. schools midway in their K–12 schooling career. Indeed, these students are largely middle class and are willing to accept a Eurocentric education whatever the personal costs.

Parent Participation

The principal has cultivated relations with White parents who form the core of the school's parent participants. The principal claims Asian parents are not active nor as concerned about what happens in school. He sees them mostly as passive. In their home countries, Asian parents believed that teachers knew what was best for their children. Their role was to ensure that children were compliant with school demands. When Asian parents attempt to make changes for their children, these changes must also be accepted by White, native-born parents who themselves share the Eurocentric view of school personnel. At Jackson, Asian parents have not been successful in having their voices heard and respected.

Summary

In summary, schools such as Jackson have yet to address the changing composition of students. The traditional response to culturally and linguistically different students has been the Americanization policy of teaching them the English language while suppressing their home language and traditional cultures, and of infusing them with American cultural norms and values. At the turn of the century, schools responded similarly to European immigrants with the attitude of cleansing them of their un-American ways, or in the not too distant past, the attempted acculturation of Mexican children through the suppression of the Spanish language (Olsen, 1990). Teachers at Jackson face newcomers who are willing to accommodate to their preconceptions of what is good and desirable, but teachers themselves seem unwilling to learn from students and truly create a bilateral educational process that addresses the linguistic and cultural gaps the students are not capable of bridging alone.

Cleveland
Politics of Schooling Change

Cleveland has a long history with newcomer students and it illustrates the variable nature of primary language instruction reflecting the politics of school response. During the 1980s, about a quarter of all students were Latino and another quarter were Southeast Asian. In the 1990s, both the Latino and Southeast Asian percentages increased to a third each of the school population. Growth occurred not only in the ethnic proportion of these two groups, but more significant was the growth of English learners who now constitute a majority of the students.

The Need for Southeast Asian Teachers

Despite the overall growth in the Asian LEP population, the school abandoned its Southeast Asian language based classes for ESL students during the mid-eighties. Those classes were reinstated more recently. In a meeting with the principal that led to this decision, Southeast Asian parents argued their case for hiring teachers who could speak their languages. In conjunction with this request and subsequent activities of Asian advocates, the principal hired Southeast Asian teachers over the objections of teachers. These Southeast Asian teachers were assigned to math and social studies classes where they used native languages. However, the text materials were written in English, and their primary languages were used to explain concepts when students were unable to understand the materials. Additionally, they provided an after-school tutoring and guidance program. According to the principal, these teachers helped considerably the at-risk refugee English learners who were becoming increasingly truant and defiant of school authority. With these changes, students were less likely to be suspended or truant. Counselors reported that students were having fewer discipline problems and more parents were coming to the school as a result of having new bilingual teachers.

The Impact of the New Principal

The principal replaced an administrator who had been at the site for many years and developed a close relationship with teachers. The new principal brought a different outlook given his experience with bilingual and bicultural education. Cleveland's English speaking teachers objected to the transfer of a monolingual English speaking teacher to another school, which was made necessary when Southeast Asian teachers were hired. Several ESL teachers also complained about the falling enrollment in their ESL classes. The teachers believed students should be taught in the English language and also that the new primary language classes would only hold those students back. The Southeast Asian students were not of a single mind on the changes. Some felt that they were being held back by not being exposed to more English language practice. On the other hand, some welcomed these classes because they felt they are no longer "drowning." Nevertheless, all of these students felt more comfortable with the Southeast Asian staff as role models.

Curiously, one of three Southeast Asian teachers was not well received by some students because his teaching style reflects American pedagogical ideas such as experiential and cooperative learning techniques. Many students prefer the more traditional Asian pedagogy of hearing lectures and memorizing for tests. These views vary among the students, who are at different stages of acculturation to American ways. Since the hiring of the three teachers, not only has there been a drop in suspensions of Southeast Asian students, but those teachers have picked up counseling duties and have given students guidance even into the after-school hours with a special tutoring program.

Increase in Neighborhood Violence

In recent years, the school has seen an increase in youth violence and gang membership. School police officers report a 100 percent increase in the use of firearms during the past several years and some even refer to the area as a "war zone," where every weekend residents report gunshots. In adjacent areas, the police have difficulty closing drug houses since every block is reported to have one or two such drug outlets and as soon as one is closed down another one opens. Increasing numbers of Latinos and Southeast Asians have been charged with criminal acts and their presence in the area is more visible, marked by gang graffiti. According to school police, the growth of gangs has been in response to the violence directed against new-comers.

The neighborhood violence has affected Cleveland with frequent phys-ical conflicts between ethnic groups on campus. The neighborhood has also become home to increasing numbers of poor people. As a consequence, the feeder elementary schools have been "exploding at the seams"—schools built for fourteen hundred students have enrollments of over a thousand students, and two nearby elementary schools have approximately fourteen hundred students each. The majority of these students come from homes having incomes below the poverty level and many are on welfare. This depiction of poverty is confirmed by the majority of area students eligible for free school lunches. The increasing student numbers and the impover-ishment of the area has resulted in an increasing number of at-risk-of-fail-ure students at Cleveland. This neighborhood condition feeds into the pressure to create a school atmosphere that neutralizes tensions emanat-ing from those very same neighborhoods.

Summary

Southeast Asian parents have commented on the changes in the atti-tudes of their youths away from traditional attitudes toward "American" attitudes embodied by native-born peers. A combination of the so-called Americanization of the newcomer youth and the atmosphere of racial and neighborhood violence works against the educational successes of new-comer youth. It is in this context that the active involvement of Southeast Asian parents at Cleveland is notable. In a nearby elementary school a new program combining the forces of the school district, the community college district, the department of social services, and the parks and recreation department have embarked on a community development plan that increases parent involvement in schools. This development parallels a spe-cial outside program to educate parents on their role as 30s supporters of their children's' schooling success. The directors of both programs are work-ing toward increasing the involvement of parents in school decision mak-ing, a move consistent with the school board's policy of increasing parental involvement in school governance. Indeed, this is part of the earlier men-tioned school restructuring policy of the district.

Parents seem to agree that the deterioration of the community—as seen in the weakened fabric of families, churches, and neighborhoods—signals a need to revitalize it through increasing participation in local institutions such as Cleveland High School. The Mayor's commission on neighborhood improvements characterizes the area as a "code blue zone,H a medical term for emergency need. Nevertheless, some teachers express fears that parents may meddle too much. The ambivalence over involving parents in their children's' education persists in the face of the increasing demands to educate students who seem even less prepared to succeed than students of a generation past. Nevertheless, the conjunction of active parents and a principal who was willing to respond to parents, overriding teacher objections, lay the groundwork for change to create a school more attuned to bridging the linguistic and cultural gaps between home and school.

McKinley
Keeping Order

The central theme at McKinley is "keeping order" as reflected in the preoccupation of the staff with keeping students under control. This impression is illustrated by my research notes regarding the atmosphere: "I arrived at 2:15 P.M., approximately fifteen minutes before the end of the V school day. There were security officers in front and police officers on the street. The vice principal walked toward me with a two-way radio. I also noticed other adults carrying two-way radios. Additionally, while attempting to talk with a student on the other side of a fence, I realized I couldn't enter the school grounds without going through the office. This was indeed a security conscious campus."

On another day, during lunch period, adult supervisors had loudspeakers and used them whenever they observed disorderly conduct. Two male students were pushing each other when a supervisor yelled at the top of his lungs for them to stop. This startled a visitor, but to the supervisor it was just a minor routine for he resumed talking with the visitor in his normal voice as if the incident had not occurred.

One parent also related how she was upset over the yelling she observed during her school volunteer work. Eventually, she found herself yelling in the same manner as if it were an ordinary occurrence. She said, "It's surprising how quickly you get used to it." Her son attended McKinley last year and transferred to another school this year. He told his mother that he wasted time going to McKinley because too much time was spent keeping order. Some classrooms are so disorderly that little learning takes place—for example, students walk around and talk with each without permission while lessons are being given. Toward the end of class, one teacher with disorderly students "blew up" and yelled at them.

The Neighboring Community and School Population

McKinley is located in a low-income neighborhood that once had a predominance of small single-family dwellings, but in recent decades it has become dominated by multifamily rental units. It is a part of the city that has cheaper rent and, hence, is the point of first residency for many newcomers, particularly immigrants and refugees. The area is known for its variety of foreign-born newcomers as reflected in the numerous foreign restaurants.

In the previous year, the student enrollment increased 14 percent to nearly two thousand students. Other district middle schools have seven hundred students, which is considered by many administrators to be the ideal size; therefore, this is a large enrollment. Additionally, there is an increasing number of poorer families in the area. Asian students are approximately a quarter of the student body and the majority of those are Vietnamese with smaller numbers of Cambodian, Hmong, and Lao students. An ESL teacher observed: "Students come from all over the world—Lao, Hmong, Vietnamese, Mexican, Guatemalan, Russian, Ethiopian, and Afghanistan." Not only are many residents newcomers but many have low incomes, including native-born Whites, African Americans, and Latinos. The turnover rate of the area is approximately 127 percent each year—meaning in the school for every 100 seats there are 227 students who have sat in those seats.

Keeping Order
A Central Goal

Teachers at McKinley agree that keeping order is a priority issue. One teacher said: "At this school, with diversity and constant conflict between kids, you've got be especially aggressive to defuse negative energies. In my class, I establish rules and apply them consistently. Many teachers are hesitant to respond to bad behaviors and confuse behavior, culture, and race. They don't want to be seen as racist and therefore ignore misbehaviors that should be directly addressed. However, in this troubled area with racial and cultural diversity, you have to establish some common grounds that are acceptable to all students. I must establish classroom order, for to do otherwise is to accept disorder and classroom conflict. Without order how can you teach?"

The theme of keeping order is illustrated in a meeting between Vietnamese parents with McKinley's administrators. Parents were concerned because Vietnamese girls were being assaulted and threatened. The school seemed to be slow in responding to the incidents. The principal prefaced his remarks about violence with the note that middle school children are naturally active and troublesome. He also mentioned that Asian youths tend to be smaller, hence more likely to be victims. He referred to a series of incidents in which a group of Latino girls and two White girls assaulted Vietnamese females. He reported that they were suspended and had conferences with parents and counselors.

In response to troublesome students, McKinley has had teachers give advisory lessons addressing "picking on other youths," held several school assemblies addressing this issue, and increased efforts to contact parents regarding student assaults. The school staff has communicated with African American, Hispanic, and Asian parents on this issue. According to the principal, the fighting is caused by less than 1 percent of the students and the other 99 percent are cooperative and nonconfrontive. He sees a need for constant monitoring and has identified six to ten students for special intervention. Additionally, the head counselor has developed an "adopt a student" project in which fifty staff members have "adopted" at-risk students.

According to school security officers, area violence has encouraged Southeast Asians to join gangs for protection. The evidence for this claim is found on local streets, which are filled with the graffiti of an Asian gang and the presence of Asian students who show gang affiliation such as wearing gang tattoos. City police officers report that "Oriental" youth have developed a reputation for being "gang bangers" and as a consequence Latino and African American youths have backed off from physically intimidating them, especially those with gang affiliations.

The neighborhood violence spills over into McKinley, creating the perception among newcomer students that school is a dangerous place. The complaint of racial name calling and physical violence is a constant theme in this lower-income area. The issue of intergroup violence and conflict varies in intensity from site to site. However, it is more likely to be present in lower-income area schools. According to one teacher, the resulting preoccupation with keeping order undermines student attention to academic matters, reducing time on task and causing diversions away from academic study.

Summary

Since the above observations, revisitations to the school indicated a reduction in overt disruptive behaviors among students, both on the school grounds and in classrooms. Nevertheless, this does not deny the reality of the above observations on the continuing pressures to deal with disorder. In fact, they retain the emphasis on keeping order while instituting further order measures implementing an assertive discipline policy, hiring a consultant to help teachers with classroom management techniques, keeping students in class for two consecutive periods rather than having them transfer between classes at every hour, eliminating teachers who had management problems, and instituting a year-round schedule, which results in shorter terms and more frequent relief from routine. Nevertheless, the program at McKinley has yet to address more aggressively the programmatic needs of linguistic and cultural minorities. They have yet to address more fully the question, Is there education beyond order?

Analysis and Implications

Though outsiders tend to view education holistically, a dose examination of four schools reveals situational factors reflecting the uniqueness of each school and the consequences on the quality of education. In short, not all schools are alike. Nevertheless they face the common problem of how to address the educational needs of a changing school population, such as the growing numbers of Asian newcomers. What do they need? How do the linguistic and cultural differences define need? How do they create a staff that is informed, trained, and willing? What are the implications for curriculum materials? Has the school designed an assessment that addresses the linguistic and cultural issues and how closely does the school monitor the progress of students? If students experience cultural and social conflicts, what is the responsibility of schools to address those conflicts? These are similar to questions raised in district reports, which identified the following management problems—coordinating central office bilingual policies with school implementation, providing adequate staffing (such as having trained bilingual and ESL teachers), having adequate teaching materials (such as having texts that fit existing curriculums and in the appropriate languages), and monitoring and assessing programs and individual students.

Washington, which is experiencing an influx of refugee students, is backing into a submersion strategy, not knowing how they should respond to Asian Pacific American students. They face practical problems of budget constraints, ignorance of teaching strategies for language minority students, and preoccupation with their pedagogical philosophy, which differs from the cultures of these students. Nevertheless, the saving grace of Washington's small staff is their willingness to deal with the above problems without being defensive.

Jackson approaches newcomer students with a traditional emphasis on academic excellence, which assumes students will enter college. Jackson avoids developing strategies that address the increasing numbers of culturally and linguistically different students. They have put up a wall against multicultural views, and espouse the secondary school mentality that teaching is about content above process. Their response to a diverse student population lacks sensitivity of different cultures of newcomers, leaving them unresponsive to students who are struggling with conflicts between home and school cultures.

At Cleveland, the administrator has been receptive to requests from newcomer parents who have been active in requesting school changes. Cleveland is sensitive to the growth and needs of Southeast Asian newcomer students. The ebbs and flows of their bilingual services reflect a changing political context. This site has had a history of having bilingual students. Initially, it offered primary language classes but it moved away from such offerings, given the inclination of staff to move toward an English as a second language approach. The politics of the school, including parent demands and a new principal, reversed the earlier decision to remove primary language offerings.

McKinley, like Cleveland, resides in a low-income and troubled neighborhood where the first priority is to create an environment that neutralizes conflicts between ethnic groups. Both have successfully addressed those conflicts by creating order, but Cleveland went to the next step of creating programs that more aggressively address the linguistic and cultural differences between staff and students. Both an active parent community and responsive administrators seem to be critical ingredients in making schools responsive to newcomers.

Overall, organizational inertia is a problem that results in a resistance to change, including rejecting bilingual programs, not hiring bilingual personnel, not upgrading ESL teachers, not supporting the acquisition and development of primary language materials, not monitoring and assessing the progress of language minority students, and not dealing with the unique problems facing newcomer students including their counseling needs. There is a long-standing conflict of interests between existing staff and newcomer students. That conflict is embodied in the response of two major interest groups, administrators and teachers, whose attachment to the status quo or past schooling practices creates a barrier for making changes that accommodate Asian newcomers. Educators seem loath to make changes and complain about having too many demands placed on them and feeling they are on society's front lines for solving the seeming deterioration of family and society.

Thus, staff and administrators need to be persuaded and supported to make changes they have not yet made. There are few if any incentives for meeting the different needs of newcomer students. Resistance to change is supported by the mismatch between staff and newcomer students based on linguistic, racial, social class, culture, and experiential differences. This is particularly true at the secondary level. By contrast, elementary level teachers are more responsive to the growing newcomer population, given their training as teachers of the individual rather than as v' experts of content level. Washington's smaller size and the staff's philosophical commitment to the progress of individual students were factors that addressed these barriers. On the other hand, the other three schools were less committed to change, though Cleveland's principal was bold enough to go against the resistance of teachers. Surely the lesson of parent participation at Cleveland supports the role they have in making changes.

Bilingually trained educators are more attuned to the needs of these students but they are exceptions. Generally, the unspoken understanding is that English is the common language and that accommodation to other languages is made only under pressure, particularly evident at Jackson. Perhaps it is fair to say that most teachers do not have an overt ideological antibilingual or antinewcomer view. Unless their jobs are threatened, they are likely to be indifferent as to whether or not a school offers more primary language courses or increases ESL offerings. Administrators attempt to avoid confrontation by waiting until teachers retire or transfer to another school so they can hire teachers who may be more amenable to teaching newcomers. To some extent, the influx of new teachers and the retirement of old teachers creates an opportunity to overcome organizational inertia. Whether or not this will significantly allow for necessary changes remains to be seen. Nevertheless, with staff turnover and administrators who are attuned to the needs of newcomer students, change seems possible. Finally, there remain questions on whether school reform policies will be significant in persuading and supporting teachers to become advocates for newcomer students.

Why do some newcomer students fail while others succeed, given what educators do? What changes will increase success? Though most educators would agree that school policies condition the outcomes, we are aware of the complexities involved in assigning weight to which factor for what outcome. For example, the debate over the use of primary language is mired in other considerations such as teacher quality, classroom size, and other contextual factors. Nevertheless, it is necessary to consider how newcomer students' backgrounds affect their schooling. Why are some newcomer students successful? I suspect the successes of many newcomer students are the result of their individual efforts in spite of ill-matched teachers and materials (Caplan, Choy & Whitmore 1992; Gibson, 1991; McNall, Dunnigan & Mortimer, 1994, Rumbaut & Ima, 1988). Many successful students simply accept the given situation and find ways to get around the many barriers. These would be called "model minority" students such as the many successful Asian students at Jackson (Sue & Okazaki, 1990). Unfortunately, there are far too many newcomer students who are discouraged by unresponsive schools. Even among Asian newcomers at Jackson who are seen as successful, there remain questions about their nonacademic experience, such as learning to live with cultural conflicts. For the less successful and the more successful Asian newcomer students, we believe that improvement in schools would make a difference.

The lesson I learned from looking at four schools is that change is possible but it requires persuading and supporting teachers to be genuine educators who not only transmit knowledge to students but also as learners themselves who can be better equipped to cross the linguistic, cultural, and social barriers. Surely Washington teachers represent the willingness, but in part it is a structural issue of size that affects the sense of collective purpose required for change. This calls for a renewal of commitment from teachers but also stronger systemwide support for upgrading teacher training/inservice, teacher recruitment from newcomer communities, recirculation of teachers within the district to change from being wedded to outdated mind sets as.sociated with mental and emotional premature retirements, direct involvement in curriculum upgrading especially in the language arts, restructuring of teacher-student relations from content toward process and counseling, recognition and rewards for teacher successes, and a more frequent monitoring and assessment of the progress of these students. And last, but surely not least, is the surprising importance of Asian newcomer parents and guardians such as those at Cleveland. It is clear they love their children and want the best for them. This was evident also at Jackson and Mckinley. Their role ought not only to challenge teacher and administrator vested interests but also they should be coparticipants in improving their children's chances to be successful. They can be invited to help teachers learn more about newcomers themselves and become genuine partners in the education of their children.

In short, Asian newcomers can be offered more equitable educational opportunities. They will find their American Dream if educators are willing to learn from students and are rewarded by their schools for the success of their students. Surely these newcomers are testing our ability and resolve to affirm the American Dream.

Note

The names and descriptions of schools and individuals have been altered and in some cases composite portraits were drawn; nevertheless an attempt was made to preserve the essence of the portraits. This chapter reflects real schools and individuals and thus are genuine case materials that can be used in thinking about and making changes.

IV

Recommendations

14

Peter Nien-chu Kiang

"We Could Shape It"

Organizing for Asian Pacific American Student Empowerment

With the doubling of the Asian Pacific American school-age population during the 1990s, the unmet needs of Asian Pacific Americans are escalating dramatically in schools throughout the country. In most settings, teachers, counselors, and administrators do not share the ethnic, linguistic, and racial backgrounds of their Asian Pacific American students. Constrained by limited resources, an increasingly hostile, anti-immigrant climate, and their own stereotypical assumptions, educators have been unable to respond effectively to the full range of academic, social, and personal challenges that face growing numbers of Asian Pacific American students (Cheng & Ima, 1993; Kiang & Lee, 1993; Kitano & Chinn, 1986; Morrow, 1989; Tran, 1992; Trueba et al., 1993).

This chapter examines how Asian Pacific American high school students struggle to gain social support, cultural affirmation, and political empowerment. Four distinct case studies are highlighted: City South High School—an urban neighborhood (nonelite) public school; City Academy High School—an urban public examination (elite) school; Westlake High

School—a wealthy, public, suburban school; and the Conference/Coalition for Asian Pacific American Youth (CAPAY)—a project of students and youth supported by university and community resources outside of school.

Based on participant observation and extensive interviews with Asian Pacific American students in each setting, these cases offer opportunities to listen, as Nieto and others urge, to the voices and views of both urban immigrant/refugee students and suburban immigrant and American-born students in a variety of institutional contexts (Nieto, 1994; Phelan, Davidson & Cao, 1992; Poplin & Weeres, 1992).

The first three cases illustrate ways through which students in specific school settings analyze and respond to critical issues that affect them, including racial harassment, the need for bilingual/bicultural support services, and stereotypes in the curriculum. Students' commitments to organize and make positive changes in each case, however, are not shared by most adults in their schools, and ultimately go unfulfilled. The fourth case focuses on students from a variety of schools who become the core of a collaborative, community-based effort to organize a regional conference for Asian Pacific American youth. In contrast to the three school-based cases, students with strong adult support in the final case succeed in establishing an ongoing student/youth network following their landmark conference, and in the process, empower and transform themselves. By sharing lessons from both the failures and successes of students' organizing efforts, this chapter suggests how educators, parents, and community members can support their efforts more effectively.

Confronting Racial Harassment
Who Cares

I'm not going to walk home with tears running down my brown cheeks like the old days. . . . I would stand up for myself because, if I don't, who will? Nobody stood up for me when I was spat at, kicked at, or cussed out just for being Cambodian.

—Pho, 1993: p. 14

Issues of racial harassment affect Asian Pacific American students severely, as documented by the U.S. Commission on Civil Rights (1992) and other studies of school climate (First & Willshire Carrera, 1988; Pompa, 1994; Sing & Lee, 1994). The Commission's landmark report states: "The pervasive anti-Asian climate and the frequent acts of bigotry and violence in our schools not only inflict hidden injuries and lasting damage, but also create barriers to the educational attainment of the Asian American student victims" (97–98).

Confirming the Commission's national findings, Michele Ott (1994) found, based on a survey of 266 Asian Pacific American students from a variety of urban and suburban school districts in New England, that:

- 54 percent of the respondents had been called names or harassed and 24 percent had been physically attacked in school.
- Nine out of ten had heard of or witnessed an Asian Pacific American student being harassed and six out of ten had heard of or witnessed one being physically attacked.
- 69 percent had never reported any incident to a teacher.
- 25 percent felt that teachers would not care and 30 percent believed that teachers would not do anything, even if incidents were reported.
- Of those students who had experienced harassment, one out of three had considered dropping out of school.

Ott's regional findings are further validated by ethnographic profiles of individual schools (Kiang, Nguyen & Sheehan, 1995; Kiang & Kaplan, 1994; Kagiwada, 1989). Though not the case in every school, similar dynamics are explored in the following first example.

Case #1
City Academy High School

The City Academy is an urban school serving about fifteen hundred students in grades seven to twelve. The student population is approximately 19 percent Asian, 41 percent White, 33 percent Black, and 7 percent Latino. The school is one of the city's three elite, public "examination" high schools for which admissions are based on results from standardized tests administered by the school district during students' sixth grade. Four out of the school's seventy-one teachers are Asian Pacific American. There are no Asian Pacific American administrators. The headmaster is a Hispanic female. The curriculum is traditional with an emphasis on "classics," although students have opportunities to participate in educational and cultural activities sponsored by various cultural clubs after school.

Racial climate became a focus of the school's attention following a fight in the cafeteria started by a White male student who called Jenny,[1] a Chinese American female, "a fucking gook." After Jenny reported the incident, the school's headmaster scheduled a disciplinary hearing for the White male student, as required by district policy.

An ad-hoc group of Asian Pacific American students, including leaders of the school's Chinese and Asian student clubs, quickly formed after the incident to demand that those responsible for racial harassment be severely punished. They also called for a more diverse curriculum and schoolwide training in prejudice awareness and conflict resolution. To press their concerns, many of the school's Asian Pacific American students agreed to walk out of school en masse the next day when the disciplinary hearing was scheduled to take place. A modest multiethnic coalition also formed in solidarity.

The school administration responded immediately by threatening to suspend any student who walked out of school. Not wanting to jeopardize their academic standing, students agreed to cancel the walkout, and in its place, to meet with the administration as a group. Following the meeting, the school's headmaster expressed surprise at how marginalized the Asian Pacific American students felt from the larger school community. She asserted, "The kids have always worked together. We pride ourselves on having a nurturing atmosphere" (Tong, 1992: p. 19).

Student views, however, contrasted sharply. Angela, a Chinese American senior, recalled: "An Asian girl, Lisa, was having a hard time with some white boys who kept telling her to give up her seat to them. Two teachers came over to see what the trouble was and ended up telling Lisa just to give her seat over to the boys!"

While describing examples of specific incidents among peers, many students also criticized school officials for denying that racism was a problem. Sunthon, a Lao American senior, stated, "it's totally swept under the rug, it's never discussed. It's a taboo subject and it goes completely unmentioned." Angela agreed, "the teachers did not seem to want to talk about what happened."

Asian Pacific American students were not alone in these views. Bill, a white male sophomore observed, "the topic of racism is not really ever discussed in classrooms, but Asians get the most mistreatment as far as racism goes." Tonisha, an African American senior, added, "I've been in the school for six years and this is actually the first incident I ever remember being discussed."

The school's elite reputation figured prominently in staff and student discourse about racial conflict. Many were reluctant to report incidents because of not wanting to damage the school's public image. Jenny explained, "they try to create the impression that this kind of stuff doesn't happen at our school because we are an exam school." However, students also expressed disappointment, if not bitterness, with the lack of support they received from the school's faculty and administration. Sunthon explained:

> The school clearly had a choice between supporting its students or looking good. . . . We approached them and they immediately tried to say, "Oh, there's no such thing here," covering it all up. . . . The whole point of going to [the headmaster] was to set a precedent, to let the student body know. But she did nothing; no letters, nothing over the intercom, nothing in the student newspaper. . . . She has so much power and she has done nothing.

Kim, a Black sophomore, agreed, "teachers don't want to talk about it, but we still bring it up. It's dying down and [the headmaster] wants it that way. We like her and she likes us but when we go to her, she's too busy or she's in a meeting. Sometimes we think she's trying to save her own butt."

Recognizing the importance of having faculty who care, and especially having Asian Pacific American teachers as mentors, Angela explained:

> Having younger teachers on the faculty is very important. Younger teach-
> ers have an easier time relating to students, they can understand what
> students are going through a lot better. . . . I can think of only one teacher,
> Mr. Siu who is Chinese, who really gets involved with his students.

However, students' disappointment also extended to some adults who were themselves Asian Pacific Americans. Kim recalled:

> Even the [deputy] superintendent came. He's Asian and they [the Asian
> students] thought that he would side with them but he did not. He just
> kept putting them down. Whenever they thought they brought up a good
> point, he'd just put them down. He was really angry about the flyer which
> said "Asian American Student Rally."

Through these experiences, Asian Pacific American students learned some hard lessons in how dynamics of race, culture, class, and power affect relationships in a school community. Although they had articulated a thoughtful, comprehensive set of proposals for school improvement that addressed such areas as school climate, the curriculum, faculty/staff hiring, student activities, and disciplinary policies, only one recommendation for a schoolwide diversity awareness orientation was adopted by the administration. Even then, students had to do the leg-work of identifying trainers and community resources to make it happen.

In the end, Jenny, the sixteen-year-old "victim," expressed her biggest disappointment with the school's disciplinary decision after the hearing. She recalled:

> I resented the fact that she [the headmaster] seemed to be defending the
> boy by trying to make me understand that he was under a lot of pressure.
> That really has nothing to do with the kinds of things he said to me. . . .
> The boy ended up only being suspended for the rest of the day immedi-
> ately after the hearing. He basically got to have a half day and I have
> been told that he cannot be retried in the hopes that he might receive
> some harsher punishment. That is it.

Despite her frustration, though, Jenny voiced no regrets for her own actions, noting that "after the incident, a lot of students spoke to me about how similar incidents have happened to them. . . . Maybe the younger students will realize how important it is to come forward if this kind of stuff happens."

Developing Asian Student Organizations
Creating New Space in School

When students at City Academy initially responded to the racial slur against Jenny, their first line of support came from the school's two Asian student organizations. Organizations have taken the form of both pan-Asian and specific nationality clubs (Filipino or Korean for example) as well as broader multicultural clubs and international or ESL student associations. The impact of these groups individually and institutionally, however, has been uneven, depending in large part on how adults in particular schools and communities have chosen to relate to them, as the following case illustrates.

Case #2
City South High School

> The [Vietnamese Student] Association is going to provide opportunities for the "torn leaves" to help the "more torn leaves."[2]

City South High School (CSHS) is a nonselective urban high school with a student body that is 12 percent Asian, 24 percent Latino, 27 percent White, and 37 percent Black. Of the adults in the school, there are no Asian administrators, counselors, or regular education teachers. Khmer and Vietnamese bilingual teachers and paraprofessionals are the only Asian Pacific American staff inside the building.

Asian Pacific American students at CSHS, even more so than their peers at City Academy, vividly described examples of racial harassment, including name calling and physical assault. One Vietnamese student sighed, "I feel like I get stepped on everyday in that school." Like City Academy, however, the school's principal asserted, "we have not had confrontations, we have not had tensions" (Ellemont and Gorov, 1993: p. 1).

Through interviews conducted for a larger study with fifteen Vietnamese students ranging from tenth through twelfth grade, every student recounted examples of witnessing or experiencing harassment as part of their daily lives. While one said, "the White kid always messing with the Asian," another noted, "I experience problems with Black more than any other," and still others described conflicts with Hispanic and Haitian students.

In three years' time, the number of Vietnamese students at City South High School tripled from thirty to more than one hundred. Most were newly arrived immigrants. School officials never discussed the implications of this dramatic demographic change within the school community, however. Many non-Asian students, therefore, disregarded the Vietnamese students' ethnic, linguistic, and cultural identities as Vietnamese and, instead, assigned them a racial identity under the label of "Chinese" and "Chinks."

Confusion surrounding the Vietnamese students' presence was evident in the experiences of almost every student interviewed. Thuy, a junior, recalled: "When we pass by them they give you some kind of like a dirty look. . . . They say, 'Look at that Chinese girl,' and then they call like, 'Chinks, go back to where you belong.'"

Whether because of personal experience, observation, or advice from friends and siblings, Vietnamese students at CSHS crafted individual survival strategies to get through school—typically by choosing to be quiet in class, rushing through the hallways in groups, confining themselves to particular tables in the cafeteria, and avoiding certain areas like the bathrooms where they expected racial conflict. Ky, a twelfth grader, explained: "I try to keep myself very very careful, you know. I think about where I'm going before I'm going there. . . . My eye open . . . so I can get out of some situation quickly as I can."

However, a few students—those who had lived in the United States longer than five years and who were more proficient in English—asserted themselves as equal members of the school community. This challenged the school's social dynamics according to Kieu, another senior:

> I see other Asian students . . . after the class change they just go straight to the class or they walk in a whole group. . . . [But] Ky and I or even Thuy, it seems like we speak more English, and we walk like [we're] a part of the school. . . . That's why the problems started . . . they want to be power in the school. . . . When I walk in school I feel like I'm equal to anybody else. And I guess that what they not wanted.

In this context, with the escalating needs of Vietnamese students going unrecognized at City South, Thuy, Ky, and Kieu decided to launch a Vietnamese club for the school. Thuy's idea for the club grew out of her middle school experience in another state:

> They have all kind of ESL, bilingual programs for Asian kids [at the middle school] . . . and they have this club called the ESL club . . . and all Asian kids can join the club and the teachers, the ESL teacher, she do a lot of activity with us . . . then I went to City South. I saw a lot of

Vietnamese kids, right, they don't speak English at all, but the school didn't do anything for them. It's like either they learn or they don't. . . . So I felt kind of bad, and I start talk to my teacher. . . . I complain to her. And I say that they should have an ESL program or something you know. Or at least a Vietnamese club that we could help those students.

Ky voiced similar sentiments, "I just miss the old school back in Vietnam, so I want to try to recall some of those memories. We wanted to form a club so we can all get together."

Assisted by a Vietnamese tutor from a local university, a Cambodian bilingual teacher, and one English teacher, the group attracted roughly thirty students to its first meeting. Ky and Kieu delivered the welcoming speech:

None of us wants, ten to twenty years later when we travel half our lives, to not have any nice memory about our first steps into life at our student age. The Vietnamese Student Association is going to be the first means to help us to build those memories. . . . Of course, the Vietnamese Student Association (VSA) is not going to be a place only for fun. But it is also the place for studying. . . . We will have occasions to improve and exchange our experiences as students and the initial difficulties when trying to adapt into new schools and a new society. We can share the good poems, the good novels and songs in order to help keep the national culture in our hearts. This is also a good way that we can prove to the foreigners that even though we have to take their culture daily, we are not going to forget to improve our national culture.[3]

Participants in the first meeting discussed their hopes for the club to provide academic and ESL tutoring, advising about cultural expectations in U.S. society, and ways to share Vietnamese language and culture. After three well-attended meetings, however, the club had still not gained any backing from the school itself, particularly in terms of having an approved time and place to meet. While some teachers were willing to help when asked, others criticized the new club for encouraging segregation. Thuy observed, "They [school personnel] are not so happy about [the club] . . . it's so hard up here to do those things."

The club also faced internal conflicts, reflecting gender dynamics and differences in acculturation. Thuy recalled: "At every meeting when I open my mouth, he [Ky] always jump in and say let him handle it. . . . The guy try to be the head, you know. They don't want any young lady or woman to take their place. So every thing I say, he always jump in and cut me off. So that's a problem."

These gender conflicts reflected important issues for the students to work through. Ky asserted, "most of the girls I know who've been here more than two years, they always act that way. They're bolder, aggressive," Thuy countered: "A lot of Vietnamese kids go to school, whatever the people say, they just sit there. They sit there and be quiet. . . . I say no! I'm not gonna sit there and be quiet. I won't. I won't be quiet."

Without bilingual/bicultural faculty or staff in the school, no one helped the students to analyze their points of view or guided their actions. As a result, students were unable, individually or collectively, to sustain their organizing initiative and overcome the lack of formal, institutional support never received from the school's administration.

Interestingly, students found no guidance at home either. None had told their parents about either their interests in the club or their problems with racial harassment at school. A junior noted, "They don't know what happened, and they feel okay because they don't know everything. My mother and father don't speak English." Ky described the relationships between Vietnamese students and their parents in these terms:

> Our parents not involved enough in our schools. One of the things is English barrier. They try and protect themselves inside their house . . . and sometime they too busy with their work, trying to earn a living, trying to survive in this society. So they try so hard they just forget about us. . . . I don't blame at all. They try so, make a living so hard.

Though very conscious of the sacrifices and hardships their parents endured in order to provide a better life for their families, most students did not describe close relationships with their parents. While challenging Vietnamese students' silence in school, Thuy sighed that her parents viewed her as "too Americanized" at home. Kieu also felt discouraged that her parents did not understand the difficulties she faced at school. She revealed to them some of the more dramatic incidents of racism that she experienced only after they criticized her for receiving mediocre grades. Kieu explained, "I go home and struggle. When I go outside, outside I struggle."

Without space or sanction, the Vietnamese Student Association dissolved after two months and was not reactivated during the following year. Ironically, instead of embracing Vietnamese students' leadership and resourcefulness in responding to a growing need within the school, some adults at City South labelled students' efforts to organize themselves and support their newcomer peers as separatist and divisive. This dominant response by adults was both powerful and chilling. Similar dynamics play out in the next case, which focuses on choices and priorities for the curriculum.

Confronting the Curriculum
Anything Goes

"Rich man cannot buy Chinese honor."
"I'll make it five thousand."
"Chinese honor sold."

—dialogue from the musical,
Anything Goes[4]

In the previous two cases, urban Asian Pacific American students organized to improve their school environment by challenging racial harassment and addressing their own needs for academic, social, and cultural support. Adults, in large part, failed to respond meaningfully to the issues raised by students in each example. Though focusing their efforts primarily on peer relations, the students in those cases acknowledged and linked their concerns to issues of curriculum development and the need for faculty to foster diversity awareness.

Sunthon at City Academy, for example, stated explicitly, "we should have a diversified curriculum, a multicultural curriculum to teach that people without white skin are not outsiders." Ky from City South High School further asserted, "talk about this [racial conflict] to kids . . . start from kindergarten, first grade, second grade . . . teach them to live together, to tolerate people, respect people." In the next case, Asian Pacific American students directly confront the curricular choices and priorities of their teachers.

Case #3
Westlake Suburban High School

Westlake High School serves roughly eight hundred students in a wealthy, predominantly White, suburban town. Asian Pacific Americans comprise only 2 percent of the high school student body. There is one teacher of color (African American) and no Asian Pacific American teachers, administrators, or counselors in the building.

As a highpoint of the spring school calendar, faculty in Westlake's Drama Department select a play or musical for the student Drama Club to perform publically. Choosing the play represents a major curricular decision for the school, with significant implications for faculty time and student learning, especially if the play includes controversial content, as in the case of Cole Porter's musical, *Anything Goes*.

Written in the 1930s, *Anything Goes* includes two characters named "Ching" and "Ling" who are portrayed as subservient gamblers in need of Christian conversion and described in the script as "two Chinamen"

(Bolton et al., 1977: p. 67). They and other characters speak pidgin English like "so soree no sow wild oats in China, sowee wild rice" (p. 103) and imitation Chinese nonsense syllables such as "Confucius say, Wa ho ding so le tow" (p. 106).

Concerned about the high profile and legitimacy that the musical would lend to racial stereotypes, Asian Pacific American students challenged the play's demeaning references to Chinese men and women as well as to Chinese language and music. With no active Asian student club in the school, the Diversity Club, which included students of many backgrounds who were committed to promoting multicultural awareness, took the lead.

After analyzing the script and developing what they considered to be reasonable demands for changes, members of the club led by Cara, a Chinese American senior, prepared a leaflet outlining their concerns, and distributed it in faculty mailboxes, albeit without approval. School administrators, however, removed the leaflet before most faculty saw it, and criticized the students for "not following procedures."

Students' demands included, "No Pidgin English," "No Fake Asian Languages," "Change the Names of Ching and Ling," and "Cut Out the Word *Chinamen*." Referring to the school's student handbook, they stated, "If this racist behavior (slurs) is not tolerated in the school halls, it should not be tolerated on stage for a public school play."

As tension about the musical and the Diversity Club's unmet demands intensified, club members agreed to meet directly with the Drama Department students and faculty to voice their differences. The meeting, however, only escalated the conflict further. Anita, a Chinese immigrant senior described the reaction of the Drama Club students as: "Why are the Asians making a big fuss? It's just a play." Wendy, a Chinese immigrant junior, similarly recalled: "We were going through the play point by point, and there were lines specifically that Cara was going over, and people were asking what's wrong with that? She was trying to explain it and they wouldn't understand."

Asian Pacific American students were especially critical of the Drama Department Chair who defended his selection of *Anything Goes* based on the entertainment value of its music/dance numbers. Cara challenged him in the meeting, explaining that the play was offensive rather than entertaining for many Asian Pacific Americans. Radha, an Indian immigrant junior, described the Chair's reaction: "He didn't handle it right because then he went bitching to his students . . . obviously he didn't want to hear what Cara was saying, and then his students became hostile and they were after us, too." Wendy added, "He didn't handle the situation discreetly . . . maybe he was angry or maybe he was worried," to which Anita replied, "He might have been insulted because she [Cara] criticized his choice as a teacher and then he was embarrassed so he had to cover it up or something."

The Drama Department chair, who was also the director of the play, rebutted students' demands by accusing them of advocating censorship. From that point on, the students never recovered from being on the defensive. Discussion among both students and faculty shifted to protecting First Amendment rights and artistic license rather than recognizing diversity and making responsible educational choices.

At a faculty meeting called to discuss the controversy, many teachers voiced support for the Drama Department chair's position. Anita recalled, "There were [only] a couple of teachers who spoke on our behalf at the faculty meeting, but they didn't follow through, so nothing came of that."

In a letter to an Asian Pacific American parent who had expressed concern about the play, the principal articulated the school's official view:

> While cancelling the play would have been an option, I felt that it would be more educationally sound for the students and teachers to engage in dialogue about the concerns and feelings that they had about both the negative stereotyping in the play and the dangers of censorship in an educational community.

The show did go on. However, as a concession to the students, a statement on the inside back cover of the program booklet for the musical acknowledged that some in the school community had found the play racist and offensive. The statement also explained that the English and Social Studies departments had facilitated class discussions about Asian American stereotypes in order to understand the sociohistorical context of the play.

Yet, when asked how thorough or systematic these discussions had been, Anita replied, "it did not happen. They were going to talk about it in English and History, and then they didn't." Students saw that only a couple of teachers actually tried, and that their own knowledge of the content was so limited, that the discussions seemed counterproductive. Wendy recalled:

> One of our English teachers brought up the play and basically the whole class was arguing like why are these Asians so upset. . . . This other girl, she was Black, she understood, but the other people were basically like, "I don't care, it's just a play, it's just for fun" . . . I felt like the whole class was against the Asians, and I just felt hurt by it . . . after class I just started crying, and then my English teacher came over to me and said, "I'm sorry you had to go through this." . . . She tried to do something, you know. She said maybe we can discuss it after the play but then she never went through with it.

Like the first two cases, Westlake students were clearly disappointed in the lack of support they received from adults in the school. But unlike the first two cases where students' working-class, immigrant parents typically knew little about and did not participate directly in their children's school experiences, Westlake High Asian Pacific American parents, though also immigrants, tended to intervene more directly in their children's school lives, perhaps due to their own highly educated professional backgrounds.

Yet, parent intervention did not mean support for student activism. If anything, the Westlake High parents played a major role in consciously limiting how intensively the students were able to advocate for their demands. Cara, for example, revealed in writing:

> Just about everyone is upset, frustrated and fed up. Anita had a big fight with her parents last night because they want her to concentrate on school. My parents are concerned with the scholarship issue. It's a bummer but my Dad is the one who's gonna pay my college tuition. . . . We really do not have support from other parents/kids.

Indeed, Cara's parents were counting on her winning a major scholarship to a local university, but this depended on receiving outstanding recommendations from her teachers and the principal. Not wanting to risk those relationships, Cara's father halted her activism. He stated in a phone conversation at the time, "I don't think Cara should be involved in this any longer. Living in this country, I've learned you have to look out for number one."

Also in sharp contrast to City Academy and City South, no student at Westlake described experiences of direct physical harassment. As a much smaller minority population [2 percent compared to 19 percent at City Academy and 12 percent at City South], Asian Pacific American students' sense of their struggle at Westlake seemed more diffused and less urgent.

Anita analyzed the dynamics this way: "I don't think a lot of people realized that they're Asian. They're kind of separated here. There's no like Asian unity. Like a lot of my friends from other cities, there's so many Asians there, and it's kinda cool 'cause they hang out and stuff . . . but there's no sense of Asian unity here at all." Radha echoed, "Most Asians here are passive, and I'm passive, too, so people don't really know each other and they don't make an effort to get together and have an Asian club."

Radha also pointed to the dominant black-and-white paradigm of race relations as a barrier preventing Asian Pacific American issues from being addressed in meaningful ways at the school. She explained:

> I went to a racism workshop like a week ago, and I was like, cool, let's talk about racism, so I went in and they were just talking about black and white

problems and I was like, wait a second, there are Asian problems, you know. And they were like, oh yeah, and then they discussed it like for a minute.

Based on their direct experiences, Asian Pacific American students found their issues, concerns, and perhaps even their presence, to be marginal at Westlake High. In questioning the judgment of a senior faculty member and forcing a schoolwide examination of bias in one aspect of the curriculum, their efforts were quickly undermined both by adults, who labelled their intent as censorship, and by non-Asian peers, who viewed them as "over-sensitive." Wendy recalled: "It's like the day we were having that discussion in my English class, and everyone was focusing on me, like looking at me saying, 'Don't you think you shouldn't censor stuff?' They were looking straight at me like 'what's the problem?'"

Although the Drama Club made some minor changes to the production in order to appease the Asian Pacific American students, the basic flaws remained. By the time the performances took place, the Asian Pacific American students had long given up their demands. Some had followed their parents' wishes to disengage from the controversy, while others simply could not envision ways to overcome their marginalized minority position. An Asian Pacific American community leader, invited by some students to attend the performance, offered powerful testimony that confirmed the depth of students' disempowerment within this wealthy, suburban school: "I never felt so silenced in my life. It was like a sea of white, the whole auditorium, with everyone cheering and clapping, being really proud of their kids. But what about our kids? It's like we weren't even there."

In looking back at the chain of events leading to the performance, Anita, Radha, and Wendy placed some of the responsibility on their own Asian Pacific American community for having allowed others to define their image. But they also criticized inaction by the school administration, using language almost identical to students at City South and City Academy. Wendy stated: "She is the principal, so I think she should care about what her students are concerned with. I mean, if they have any concerns, she should do something about it." Anita added, "I think she just wants to sweep it under the rug, which she did." Radha agreed, "Again, just like other incidents that Westlake has swept under the rug and never dealt with at all."

Cara, whose initial outrage had compelled her to challenge Westlake's faculty and curriculum, concluded, perhaps wisely: "Other racial stuff is *bound* to occur in Westlake, believe me. Next time it will go further. We'll achieve more. I guess we all have to learn to be patient."

Although her tempered assessment of Westlake seems realistic, Cara needs to know that active intervention and dramatic change are possible if resources and support are consciously mobilized. This is the story of the following final case.

Organizing for Empowerment
We Could Shape It

> We believe that youth united by a common purpose can make a dif-
> ference. We aim to establish a forum for free dialogue and for pos-
> itive change in our communities. Our initiatives are diverse and
> include avenues to abolish stereotypes, to educate ourselves and
> others about Asian Pacific America, to celebrate our heritage, and
> to improve race relations.
>
> —mission statement for the Coalition
> for Asian Pacific American Youth[5]

The previous three cases illustrate some of the substantial struggles waged
in different settings by Asian Pacific American high school students to
organize and empower themselves. Without support from adults either at
school or at home, these cases clearly do not represent victories or success
stories. One might conclude, in fact, that while the desires for youth
empowerment may be ardent—which in and of itself should be cause for
respect and celebration—nevertheless, the prospects appear discourag-
ingly slim.

In contrast, the final case focuses on the experiences of a core group of
students who organized a landmark, regional conference for Asian Pacific
American youth from which emerged an ongoing Asian Pacific American
regional youth network.

Case #4
Conference / Coalition for
Asian Pacific American Youth

When an ad-hoc group of adults and youth first gathered to discuss
how community resources could support Asian Pacific American students
confronting the issue of racial harassment in school, no one imagined that
a few months later, nearly seven hundred young people from more than
fifty high schools would attend a Conference for Asian Pacific American
Youth (CAPAY). The ad-hoc group convened initially because such little
support seemed to be coming from home or school.

Following a series of open-ended, initial meetings, a core group of fifteen students—primarily seniors from various high schools in the region—
agreed to work with each other in planning a conference that would gather
Asian Pacific American youth together, and provide opportunities for gaining awareness, sharing experiences, and raising voices in unity. Adults
affiliated with a range of community groups, local universities, and state
agencies agreed, in turn, to pool resources to support the youths' organiz-

ing efforts. Although most of the core group of young people had never met or worked with each other before, they quickly immersed themselves in a collective process to make CAPAY happen—working as interns every day during the summer and every Sunday throughout the fall.

Organizing the conference brought together many students who had been active in their own schools, often as the only Asians in multicultural clubs or schoolwide leadership bodies. After the first meeting, Samantha, a senior from an urban, predominantly Black and Hispanic community, admitted, "I was like shocked because in my school as far as Asians, I'm the one who does everything." Lisa, a senior from an affluent, predominantly White suburban town, recalled, "It was the first time in my life that I had been in a room with people who feel the same way I do. I'm so used to being like the only Asian speaking about Asian issues." Lauren, a Chinese immigrant senior from an urban school, added, "I'm always like the only Asian, but when I started working on this, it's like I can have friends that share the same interest, who have these common goals to work on."

For some, this experience was both thrilling and threatening—directly challenging and, at the same time, affirming their racial, cultural, and social identities. Amy, a Korean American senior from a suburban school, revealed:

> When I first walked in, I swear I just wanted to turn around and walk right out, I was so intimidated. I've never really been in a room with so many Asian students in my age group. I was like, what am I doing here? And then I started coming to the meetings and I got more involved in it, and I was like, oh my god, you know this is really cool! Asians are cool! [Laughs]

In addition to their urban/suburban and public/private differences in school and socioeconomic status, core group members' ethnicities included Lao, Vietnamese, Pakistani, Korean, Japanese, Chinese, Filipino, Vietnamese Chinese, Indian, Taiwanese, and Khmer. Sharing each others' backgrounds while working together on a common goal generated unforgettable learning. Chia Chia, a Taiwanese immigrant, exclaimed:

> I learned a lot from the others. They broke all my stereotypes. Like Pakistani women having no rights, but then I met Attia. I never heard of Cambodia, Laos, etc, and I never thought they were Asians. But then I met Sarouem and Chan and Vira and Chantala. I've always thought Japanese believe they are the best and they don't care about other Asians. But Isamu showed me that he cares in a lot of ways. Many people broke my stereotypes and I'm glad.

In the midst of this diversity, Ivan, a working-class Chinese senior from a suburban school, noted the affection and mutual commitments that emerged among the group: "It feels like a family and we're very close and somehow we have a lot of differences but we are very open to each other. I don't see that often in other activities." Lauren also emphasized the community-building aspect of the process, especially appreciating "the friendship that we have all built or gained through organizing."

Vira, a Lao senior from an urban school, added:

> The first meeting was so exciting! You had a roomful of Asian American youths talking about some of the things that concerned them. Just so many different types of people, and it really impacted me. There was a real sense of—this is for us, you know? And we could make it into whatever we wanted. We could shape it, we could develop it, and I think that was really powerful.

Others like Chantala, a Lao freshwoman in college, gained a similar sense of power and purpose from the conference planning process. She recalled realizing, "instead of everything that's happening to us, it's how we are affecting the outcome." In contrast to the discouragement and disempowerment of students in the previous three cases, the structure, resources, and praxis developed for CAPAY all served to respect, support, and enable those who participated. The difference is striking and fundamental.

Planning for the conference plenary sessions and workshops introduced the organizers to a wealth of community resources and to older generations of activists with whom they could relate. Topics ranged from gangs and media stereotypes to interracial dating and parent-youth relations to civil rights strategies and curriculum reform. Michele, a Filipina college student, noted, "Before, if I got an idea in my head, I would be like too bad I can't do it. But all of us know the outlets to go now, we have connections we can make."

The core youth spoke in moving terms about the significance of working with the adult advisors. Amy commented, "at school, there are no Asian teachers or faculty members, and it's awesome seeing like cool Asian adults . . . it's a really good influence." Ivan agreed:

> In my entire school, there are no Asian teachers that are full-time. And it's a really negative aspect that I never really thought of until I started coming to CAPAY and then finding adults who are great leaders and who are also very good role models. And that makes such a difference because when I was younger, I didn't really have any Asian American role models, and it was so bad . . . that really limited my options when I was younger, and that's why I was such an inactive kid.

The process and impact of the conference transformed those who organized it. Chantala exclaimed, "it's given me a much clearer sense of what I want to accomplish in life. Michele added, "now I can look at the future as being something I can help try to mold, and not just think that everything is not going to change. I have a brighter outlook." Amy rejoiced: "I've become really proud of who I am and where I come from, and I know that I've become stronger. I'm no longer that silent anymore. . . . I have really found myself."

Lisa similarly reflected: "CAPAY taught me how powerful the Asian Community could be and how powerful I as an Asian American woman could be. I became 'empowered'—full of hope and optimism. It boosted me and made me see the need to be more active. It instilled confidence, and gave me a voice.

Originally expecting 250 participants, the organizers had to change the date and location of the conference when over six hundred students preregistered. Although many conference participants complained in the workshops and plenary sessions about "apathy" among their Asian Pacific peers, the overwhelming response to CAPAY ironically indicated just the opposite.

Noting this irony, members of the core group analyzed student disinterest or apathy in light of their own evolution in becoming active. Lisa explained, "it's not because they don't want to know, but because they haven't been taught to know what they should know, and they haven't been given the chance to do something about it, to be empowered." With the CAPAY conference providing that first chance for many, Michele observed, "the more people get used to forums like a conference, the more they will feel that they can speak up some place."

Although most core members had already been active in their own schools prior to CAPAY, their work on the conference greatly advanced their own leadership skills. Attia, a Pakistani American junior and elected student government head from a suburban school, reflected:

> Organization and leadership—I discovered new ways to think about these qualities. All of us were trying to accomplish the same goal, but in such different ways. We had a lot of conflicting ideas, yet we were good friends. I learned how to be more open and democratic. . . . It really is a process— brainstorming, working with people, putting it on paper, trying it out, implementing it, seeing what happens—that's something really cool that I learned. . . . This was the first big event that I had a real impact on. It's so easy to say, "oh, things will never change," so easy to let all this energy inside me become negative energy. But it's a lot more fun trying to solve things. You can always make things better.

Five months after the historic first conference, sixty youths gathered to reinvent "CAPAY" as an ongoing Coalition for Asian Pacific American

Youth. Governed by a steering committee and general membership consisting entirely of youth and supported by an adult advisory group and the Asian American Studies program of a local public university, CAPAY continues to serve as a unique vehicle for networking, skill building, and leadership training among immigrant and American-born Asian Pacific youth of many nationalities from urban and suburban backgrounds and both public and private schools. While sponsoring a major annual conference as well as retreats, a quarterly newsletter, a summer learn-and-serve program, and many other activities, CAPAY is working toward long-term institutionalization within the Asian Pacific American community.[6]

As CAPAY continues to evolve, it not only provides a valuable voice for youth, it actively enables individual young people to take on larger leadership roles in the various Asian Pacific American communities. Several community organizations, for example, have invited CAPAY members to serve as speakers, to evaluate programs and services from a youth perspective, and even to become board members. CAPAY has also advanced the visions and prospects of a multiracial youth movement. While CAPAY members have participated in many multiracial youth conferences and rallies, some Latino students have discussed how to develop their own youth network, using CAPAY as an organizational model.[7]

Conclusions

The voices and experiences shared in this chapter point to several significant lessons. In both urban and suburban schools, Asian Pacific American youth are actively seeking positive change while, at the same time, they face indifference, misunderstanding, and active opposition from adults as well as peers. Although Asian Pacific American students in urban settings seem to confront more frequent and blatant examples of racial violence, suburban students' degree of disempowerment also seems severe.

Particular incidents or issues such as the harassment of Jenny at City Academy or selection of the *Anything Goes* musical at Westlake lead some Asian Pacific American students to plan rallies and assemblies, to draft petitions and public statements, and to form new organizations or activate existing ones in order to affect their situations in school. Through their organizing efforts, they seek to transform their schools into places "where we can talk" and "build those nice memories."

If asked, students also articulate connections between the specific instances and a more general critique of their schools' learning environments. They point to gaps in the curriculum, for example, in the areas of Asian American Studies, multicultural awareness, and conflict resolution, that reflect and reinforce the problems they experience. From their perspectives, "the discussion is just not happening" and "the school didn't do anything" to enable students or other members of the school community to understand, respect, and support each other. Even well-meaning teachers lack training in these critical areas, and fail to "follow through" on their commitments.

As a result, students' hopes and demands for positive change in their schools go largely ignored or rejected. Yet, despite their frustrations, they feel their efforts are still important, if only to "help the more torn leaves" and set an example that encourages younger students "to come forward" so that "next time it will go further."

While denouncing administrators and teachers who ignore racial issues in order to protect their schools' images, students longingly wish for youth-centered, Asian Pacific American adult mentors and role models with whom they can identify. When provided with opportunities to collaborate with community-based Asian Pacific American adult activists, young people identify much more directly with the possibilities of making positive change for themselves, their schools, and their communities. They also quickly recognize the absence of comparable individuals within their schools and, in most cases, within their families.

Harassment, exclusion, and marginalization contrast sharply with the oft-repeated dreams of immigrant and refugee families to come to this country for the sake of the children. Yet, parents do not offer significant support for students' organizing efforts in school. In urban settings, the students' immigrant and working-class parents have little direct involvement with their children's lives in school because of economic, linguistic, and cultural barriers that prevent their participation. In suburban settings, immigrant parents with professional-class backgrounds may be more knowledgeable and comfortable in dealing with school matters, but they discourage and restrict their children's organizing activities, particularly if such activism leads to confrontations with school personnel.

The voices of Asian Pacific American students in this chapter deserve and demand recognition. However, far greater communication and coordination are needed between the youth and their families, schools, and communities. Over the long term, Asian Pacific American parents, themselves, need multilingual and multicultural leadership training and organizing in order to better understand their children's experiences and to gain greater accountability from schools, service agencies, and local governments.

Given the profound absence of family and school-based interventions to ensure Asian Pacific American children's daily physical and emotional integrity in school, community interventions like CAPAY are urgently needed. As an alternative to gangs, the CAPAY model not only affirms the efforts of young people, but provides them with relevant resources, skills, and an environment within which to transform themselves individually and collectively. The continuing programmatic success and personal impact of CAPAY suggest a greater need for Asian Pacific American communities to develop methods and structures to enable youth leadership more systematically.

But if schools are to become authentic sites of learning, support, and growth for Asian Pacific American students, then organizing projects like CAPAY will need much broader development and direct connection to schools themselves, perhaps along the lines of Vira's vision:

> What I really want to see is the impact on schools.... If Asian Americans aren't respected in the student body and if they are constantly being excluded or overlooked in discussions concerning race, how are they going to see themselves? That's part of forging their identity. They won't see themselves as being powerful, they won't see themselves being adaptive. They'll see themselves as being really insignificant and hopeless . . . we can use CAPAY as a way of legitimizing some of the concerns we have, like having more Asian American faculty and administrators.... If the school is serious about its Asian American students, they're going to listen to what CAPAY has to say.

CAPAY, and organizing projects like it, create rich resources not only for advocacy, but also for continuing research on both the process and outcomes of Asian Pacific American youth empowerment. These potential long-term contributions, like those of the young people themselves, seem limitless.

Notes

This study was completed with funding support from the Research Fellows Program of the Institute for Asian American Studies at the University of Massachusetts Boston, and with research assistance from UMass Boston students Chin-Lan Chen, Marty Cosgrove, Paul Davis, Jenny Kaplan, Carol Ann Neff, and Arlene Reidinger. Case #2 is adapted from a larger study conducted with Jenny Kaplan. I am especially grateful to the Coalition for Asian Pacific American Youth (CAPAY) and the many high school students who have shared their voices and visions with me.

1. With the exception of the CAPAY case study, the names of schools and individual informants cited in this chapter are pseudonyms.

2. Translation of unpublished speech delivered to the Vietnamese Student Association, 8 May 1992. "Torn leaves" refers to being Vietnamese refugees.

3. Translation of unpublished speech delivered to the Vietnamese Student Association, 8 May 1992.

4. See G. Bolton, P. G. Wodehouse, H. Lindsay, and R. Crouse (1977), *Anything Goes* (New York: Tams-Witmark Music Library, 1977, 103).

5. Drafted by Ivan Chan and ratified by CAPAY on 14 May 1994.

6. CAPAY's second conference took place in March 1995, and once again attracted 700+ youth from 60+ schools and communities. The conference also added separate sessions and a resource room for adult teachers and parents who accompanied the youth as chaperones.

7. Although CAPAY offers one powerful example, gangs represent an alternative model of Asian Pacific American youth organizing. Asian youth gangs have proliferated in recent years, reflecting a variety of factors, including limited job opportunities, fragmented family support systems, and academic as well as social alienation due to linguistic and cultural barriers in school. However, not unlike CAPAY, many gangs at the local level have formed explicitly to defend against racial harassment in school or in the neighborhood. According to a twenty-one year-old former Cambodian gang member, "Racism has shaped my life, my experience ever since the first day I set foot in this country. . . . In the gang, I watch your back, you watch my back. We look out for each other" (Kiang, 1994: pp. 141–42). For many youth, neither their parents nor their teachers have offered the requisite support and multicultural understanding needed to deal with the realities of racism in school and on the streets. For further discussion, see Ima and Nidorf's chapter on gang involvement (this volume).

15

Valerie Ooka Pang

Educating the
Whole Child

Implications for Teachers

No where is my name
Hard to keep and not easy to tame
Unlike others I have no road, no ends
No light load but heavy burdens
Going over the endless oceans

—Jocelyn Vo, in *Small Kid Time in Hawaii*
(Chock, 1981: p. 129)

A Dark Music

Music is in everyones mind
But unless the song is sung
It remains dark music

—Paul Imai, in *Small Kid Time in Hawaii*
(Chock, 1981: p. 152)

The goal of this chapter is to present teachers and other service providers with critical concepts about culture so that they can make deeper connections with the three million Asian Pacific American students in schools today (Ong & Hee, 1993). Asian Pacific American (APA) students are often overlooked or misunderstood in schools. Many teachers, social workers, police officers, and other community members do not feel pressured to attend to their needs, leaving many students feeling invisible and neglected.

The two poems at the beginning of this chapter represent the feelings of many Asian Pacific American children; the young poets speak about how they are not heard or understood. Like the saying, "Children should be seen and not heard," many Asian Pacific American students are seen and never heard. It happens in the classrooms of the most well-meaning teachers and in the classrooms where teachers have little interest in their students.

What Do Teachers Need to Know about Asian Pacific American Children to Be Effective?

This chapter will attempt to address aspects of this question. However, the question is somewhat ambiguous because Asian Pacific Americans represent many ethnic communities. In addition, Asian Pacific Americans make up the fastest-growing minority group in the United States (Ong & Hee, 1993; Cheng, 1995; Trueba, Cheng & Ima, 1993). These numbers represent an increase of 145 percent from 1980 to 1990. Ong and Hee estimate that the Asian Pacific American population in 2020 will be twenty million and this will include over six million young people under the age of twenty-five.

The growth in population has been, in part, due to the large increase in immigration from Asian countries since 1965 when the Hart-Cellar Act eliminated the national origins quota system (Hodgkinson & Obarakpor, 1994). In 1965, only 16,000 Asians were allowed to immigrate to the United States, while in 1989 more than 250,000 Asians entered this country (Hodgkinson & Obarakpor, 1994).

The diversity of the group is overwhelming and though there are general patterns within the Asian Pacific American community, teachers must consider how large within-group differences and individual variations impact the classroom. In light of these differences, the chapter provides general information about community tendencies. In addition, it is critical for teachers to understand that each child creates her/his own path through life.

Educating the Whole Child

Many teachers have tunnel vision when viewing Asian Pacific American students (Pang, 1995a). As authors (Chun & Sue, Kiang, Watanabe, Young) in this book have pointed out, professionals tend to see APA children as well adjusted, model students who present few problems. Like many stereotypes, this perception needs to be carefully examined. Teachers may be aware that some students should be placed in English language development programs. However, the students' other needs may not be readily apparent. It is easier to identify problems of language proficiency than to assess issues of cultural conflict, low self esteem, social interaction skills, and mental health.

Thus, teachers must attend to the whole child. Education should be a life-giving pedagogy (Rivera & Poplin, 1995). This is crucial for Asian Pacific American students because teachers and parents tend to be satisfied when these students do well in math and science though they may have serious needs in other content and developmental areas.

To assist teachers in understanding how to look at the whole child, Shavelson, Huber, and Stanton (1976) identified a model of the developing self-concept. Figure 15.1 shows the model. The researchers defined the self-concept as "a person's perception of himself [herself]. These perceptions are formed through his [her] experiences with his [her] environment . . . and are influenced especially by environmental reinforcements and significant others" (Shavelson, Huber & Stanton, 1976: p. 411). A person's perceptions of him/herself influence the way the person acts, thinks, and evaluates him/herself.

Based on a large body of research on self-concept, Shavelson, Huber, and Stanton (1976) developed the self-concept construct with seven features. The construct is organized, multifaceted, hierarchical, stable, developmental, evaluative, and differentiable. Their model divides the general self-concept into two subareas: academic and nonacademic. The academic self-concept includes the subareas of English, History, Math, and Science. The nonacademic self-concept includes the social (peers and significant others), the emotional (particular emotional states), and the physical (physical ability and physical appearance).

How can this construct help teachers and parents to better understand Asian Pacific American students? First, using the model, educators can examine mediating factors that impact the developing self-concept of young APAs. Those factors may include ethnic identity, cultural/family background (values, behaviors, beliefs, traditions, attitudes, and language), socioeconomic status in society, levels of cultural assimilation, cultural conflict, and historical experiences (i.e., war trauma, internment of Japanese Americans, labor movement). Children develop in a sociocultural context and these elements may be important in shaping how they view themselves.

Next, the model directs educators to look at the growth of the whole child. Though teachers and many APA parents focus on academic growth, they need to consider the entire spectrum of the developing self. In addition to intellectual growth, teachers and parents can assist students in their emotional, social, and physical development. Students may acquire more effective social and communication skills as they learn to become

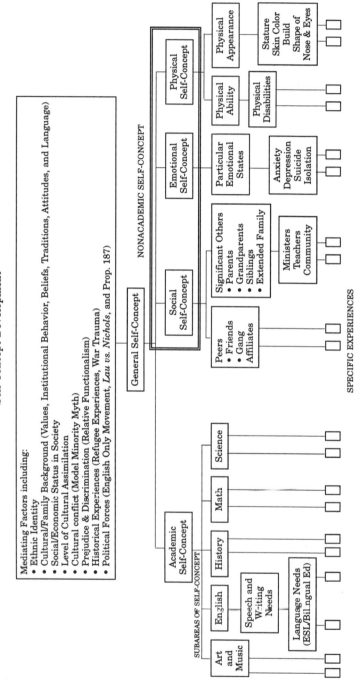

FIGURE 15.1
Self-Concept Development

Mediating Factors including:
- Ethnic Identity
- Cultural/Family Background (Values, Institutional Behavior, Beliefs, Traditions, Attitudes, and Language)
- Social/Economic Status in Society
- Level of Cultural Assimilation
- Cultural conflict (Model Minority Myth)
- Prejudice & Discrimination (Relative Functionalism)
- Historical Experiences (Refugee Experiences, War Trauma)
- Political Forces (English Only Movement, *Lau vs. Nichols*, and Prop. 187)

General Self-Concept

NONACADEMIC SELF-CONCEPT

Physical Self-Concept
- Physical Appearance
  - Stature
  - Skin Color
  - Build
  - Shape of Nose & Eyes
- Physical Ability
  - Physical Disabilities

Emotional Self-Concept
- Particular Emotional States
  - Anxiety
  - Depression
  - Suicide
  - Isolation

Social Self-Concept
- Significant Others
  - Parents
  - Grandparents
  - Siblings
  - Extended Family
  - Ministers
  - Teachers
  - Community
- Peers
  - Friends
  - Gang Affiliates

Academic Self-Concept

SUBAREAS OF SELF-CONCEPT

- Art and Music
- English
  - Speech and Writing Needs
  - Language Needs (ESL/Bilingual Ed)
- History
- Math
- Science

SPECIFIC EXPERIENCES

Adaptation from Shavelson et al. (1976) by Valerie Pang.

independent and well-adjusted adults. Students are also extremely sensitive to physical traits and characteristics as they move from childhood to adolescence. All of these aspects of self impact the emotional self.

Since many teachers and parents channel APA students toward math and science careers in engineering, biology, medicine, and computer science, they may not have opportunities to investigate other interests. For example, students who may have interests in the arts, creative writing, ethnic studies, history, journalism, politics, and other fields may not be encouraged or supported to explore a wider magnitude of subjects.

To encourage the development of a well-rounded person, APA students need school programs that nourish participation in many kinds of activities. For example, parents may believe that physical education is a frivolous waste of valuable class time. Yet, teachers may use this time to introduce the concept of physical, intellectual, and mental health being interrelated.

The model also focuses attention on how significant others impact the sense of self. Significant others such as parents, teachers, siblings, and peers can have a great impact on APA children. For some, criticism from significant others may be seen as an indication that they have failed. Educators need to be sensitive to this and create a nurturing atmosphere rather than a critical one. Teachers should consider not only the academic self-concepts of students, but also their social, emotional, and physical self-concepts. As Sue and Chun and Ima and Nidorf have written in their chapters, some APA students have serious mental health issues whether dealing with gang affiliations, cultural conflicts, or identity formation.

Mental Health Needs

The Self-Concept of APA Children

Many teachers and parents are unaware of the continuing mental health needs of APA students. Asian Pacific American children are visibly different from mainstream children and this can have a powerful effect on their fragile and developing self-image.

While teachers may feel their APA students feel good about themselves, there is evidence that APA students may not feel as positive about themselves as other children. Tidwell (1980) found Asian Pacific American youth to show a disturbing pattern of lower levels of self-esteem in comparison to Caucasian and African American youngsters. Another study reported Vietnamese American students to score lowest on overall self-concept in relation to other Asian Americans, Caucasian, African American, and Mexican American students (Oanh & Michael, 1977). Monzon (1984) found Filipino American college students to show lower levels of general self-esteem than their Caucasian peers. Similarly, Korean American and Chinese American students were not as positive about their physical self-image as African American or Caucasian students (Chang, 1975; Fox & Jordan, 1973). In another study of the self-concept of Japanese American students in the fourth through sixth grades, lower physical self-concept scores were masked by high academic self-image scores, when general self-concept scores were reported (Pang, Mizokawa, Morishima & Olstad, 1985).

Ethnic identification and racial prejudice are powerful elements of American society. Since the United States is a race-conscious nation, Asian Pacific American students are often pressured to fit into the mainstream while not being accepted because of racial appearance, language, accent, or other cultural differences. In some cases students turn racist attitudes aimed at Asians inward toward themselves. Lee (1996) found that some Korean American high school students were ashamed of their ethnic background. From extensive interviews she wrote:

> They made fun of themselves and other Asian Americans, as if to say that they would make fun of themselves before anyone else could. They referred to themselves as "chinks" and to the Korean activities as "chink" activities. When I asked them why they did this, they laughted and said they thought it was "funny" or "no big deal." (Lee, 1996: p. 28)

These findings may be surprising to educators who believe that Asian Pacific Americans are well-adjusted, confident students. Such studies point to the need for schools to take steps to assist Asian Pacific American students in developing more positive perceptions of themselves.

Achievement Anxiety

Many Asian Pacific American students may feel achievement anxiety. Since there are high expectations of them, they may feel threatened, resulting in anxiety. When this is coupled with strong cultural values to perform and the racism they must cope with in school, APA students may feel great pressure to achieve.

Many highly motivated students are also anxious. Their motivation to succeed may be in response to needing the approval of their parents and teachers. Through high academic grades, students can avoid conflicts with or criticism from their parents (Pang, 1991). Research by Pang (1991) indicated that parental support can be a double-edged sword. Pang found that the parental support felt by middle school students of Chinese, Filipino, Korean, and East Indian heritage were predictive of mathematics grades.

However, these students were also more test anxious than their Caucasian counterparts because of their desire to please their parents. The side effect of high parental expectations and need for approval may be test and achievement anxiety.

In her interviews with students, Pang (1991) found APA youth to have internalized their parents values to do well. When asked where the desire to do well in school came from, students said they did not know. However, when Pang interviewed parents, they were extremely verbal about how they wanted their children to earn As. Pang believed that the quest for parental approval by doing well in school was internalized, though children seem to be unaware of the socialization process.

Pang (1991) also found that though APA students felt more parental pressure, they also felt more parental support than their European American peers. Pang hypothesized that the support felt by Asian Pacific American children helps them to diffuse, to an extent, the pressure of high parental academic expectations and the need to please their parents. Parents and teachers need to understand how important their encouragement is to the ability of APA youth in keeping a healthy perspective about achievement.

Communication Anxiety

Asian Pacific American students, generally, have indicated that they would like to be able to express themselves more effectively. Though Ramist and Arbeiter (1986) found 73 percent to rate themselves high on mathematics ability, only 56 percent rated themselves highly on oral expression. Asian Pacific American students seem to have "communication anxiety"—a fear of writing and speaking. As a result, APA youth often feel more comfortable in fields like mathematics, chemistry, and computer science—areas that deal mainly with abstract objective ideas. Though students may need to explain how they found their answers, most are explained in logical terms using mathematical symbols. In contrast, fields like English, creative writing, and speech demand that students express their personal feelings and ideas. These ideas are not necessarily tied to an objective field or abstract line of reasoning.

Communication anxiety may appear when Asian Pacific American students must risk more of themselves by sharing ideas that are emotional and personal in content. If Asian Pacific American students come from families where discussion of personal feelings is limited, it may be extremely difficult to place one's beliefs in the open where others can criticize and disagree with them. Since Asians in many families are taught to keep their feelings private (Kitano, 1976; Union of Pan Asian Communities [UPAC], 1980; Cheng, 1995), activities like writing poetry or creating stories may elicit anxiety. In addition, students must have strong self-concepts to be able to share their ideas and emotions publicly. Though students may have positive academic self-concepts, they may not be confident in other areas of life dealing with peers, parents, physical characteristics, and emotional situations (Pang, 1995a).

Adolescent Suicide

Another mental health area of concern is adolescent suicide. Students who are dealing with the pressures from society to assimilate while parents are demanding that they maintain traditional cultural values, may feel severe cultural conflict. APA students may become so overwhelmed that they contemplate suicide. In the article, "You're Not Alone," Irene Tayag, a Filipina, wrote:

> The first time I thought about suicide was when I was about thirteen years of age. I don't even think I knew the word "suicide" existed. All I knew was that I wasn't happy with my life and I didn't want to "be around anymore." To say I wanted to die is a bit harsh because I didn't really want to die. I just wanted to be away from all the pain I felt about my life. It's hard to pinpoint when it all began or why I was in so much pain. I just was, and not being able to explain it only added to my confusion and feelings of helplessness. I felt alone and ashamed that I could feel this way about my life, especially when on the surface it appeared that I had a lot to be thankful for. . . .
>
> Sure, on the surface, I was the "A" student whose life was so put together, but I was scared to let people see my true feelings.
>
> I internalized everything, and the only way I knew how to bring it to the surface was through self-mutilation. It was easier to explain the pain from a cut on my wrist or a few bruises on my knuckles than it was to explain that my heart was broken. (June, 1995: p. 2)

Unfortunately, Irene's thoughts exemplify the frustration, depression, and confusion of many other Filipino American students.

The results of a survey conducted by the Federal Center for Disease Control and Prevention point to the need for more attention to mental health needs of Filipino American students (Lau, 1995). In 1993, a random sample of 1,788 high school students was given a survey in the San Diego Unified School District. More Filipino American girls indicated that they had seriously considered attempting suicide within the past twelve months of the survey than any other group. Table 15.1 provides selected information regarding the findings of this survey. Unfortunately, 45.6 percent of the Filipino American females who filled out the survey had seriously con-

TABLE 15.1
Thoughts of Suicide in High School Students

Percentage of high school students who seriously considered attempting suicide within the twelve months preceding the survey:

	Total % of Specific Group	Male %	Female %
Caucasian	22.7	19.1	26.2
Black	24.9	23.7	25.3
Hispanic	27.5	21.4	33.4
Filipino	37.8	29.4	45.6
Asian	20.1	6.4	24.1

Percentage of high school students who made a plan in the preceding twelve months about how they would attempt suicide:

	Total % of Specific Group	Male %	Female %
Caucasian	19.1	16.5	21.8
Black	25.9	23.1	28.1
Hispanic	20.8	15.8	25.6
Filipino	32.5	25.1	39.2
Asian	18.2	15.7	20.9

Percentage of high school students who actually attempted suicide one or more times in the twelve-month period:

	Total % of Specific Group	Male %	Female %
Caucasian	7.0	5.7	8.3
Black	6.9	6.2	7.7
Hispanic	12.1	6.0	17.8
Filipino	17.8	11.9	23.3
Asian	8.3	6.4	10.2

Adaptation of "Teen and Suicide," Angela Lau, p. A-19, *San Diego Union-Tribune*, Saturday, February 11, 1995.

sidered attempting suicide; this compared with 33.4 percent among Hispanic females, 26.2 percent among Caucasian and 25.3 percent among Black females (Lau, 1995). In addition, 39.2 percent of the Filipino females had made a plan about how they would attempt suicide and 23.3 percent had actually attempted suicide. These numbers were higher than any other group. The Medical Examiner's Office in San Diego reported that six Filipino males under nineteen years of age had committed suicide in the past five years in comparison to one Filipina during the same time period (Lau,

1995). The problem is serious and complicated. Though more females indicate they think about suicide and have attempted suicide, more males have succeeded.

The results of the survey shocked the Filipino American community in San Diego, but for many Filipino counselors the findings reinforced their beliefs. Filipino youth are dealing with cultural conflict and the social pressure to assimilate. Parents are working two or three jobs to provide a middle-class living for their children. They may not be home to direct and guide their children. In addition, many Filipino parents are in the survival mode and may come from the Philippines with the immigrant mentality of scarcity (Villa, 1995). They may believe it is important for them to work as hard as possible because opportunities may not be available in the future.

Parents are only one possible source of conflict; society does not support the development of a healthy identity as a Filipino American. For example, in San Diego County there are 22,347 Filipino students, yet only 180 Filipino American teachers are employed by the many districts in the area. As Flores and Cordova indicated in their chapters, Filipino American students need role models who understand their points of view and personal struggles. Filipino American students often indicate that they feel marginalized in American society (Villa, 1995). One way they feel their lives have been marginalized is in the history books. Filipinos have lived in what is now the continental United States since 1763 (Cordova, 1983), but few Filipinos or others know this fact. Students ask, "How come I don't see myself in the history books? Don't I count? Don't I exist?"

Asian Pacific American students have serious mental health needs and they should not be ignored (Uba, 1994). The research on these students points to the need to hire additional APA teachers and counselors. Students need opportunities to talk with teachers and counselors without having to go into a lengthy discussion of their cultural values. Asian Pacific American teachers and counselors will already understand them. In addition, funding is needed for peer-support groups that allow students to talk with each other. Many students feel they cannot talk with their parents because their actions would bring shame and dishonor to the family (Monzon, 1984; Lau, 1995). Though students may have high grades and the behaviors of high achievers, these behaviors may mask the internal confusion of APA students. In order to educate and care for the whole child, teachers must also know which mental health issues are most pressing for Asian Pacific American youth.

The Model Minority Myth

One of the social factors which has had a major impact on the developing self-concept is the model minority myth. Young has written extensively about this myth in his chapter. The popular press has indicated high levels of scholarship in APA youth, and often labels these students as "whiz kids" ("Whiz Kids," 1987). Unfortunately, this portrayal does not accurately reflect the actual achievement levels found across the many groups that form this community. The Admissions Testing Program of the College Board collected data for five years (1980–1985) on college-bound seniors (Ramist & Arbeiter, 1986) and found data that refute the model minority myth. The 1985 sample included the responses of 42, 637 Asian Pacific American students who represented a broad spectrum of Asian communities. On the Scholastic Aptitude Test in 1985, the Asian Pacific American verbal mean score of 404 was below the national average of 431, but the mathematics mean of 518 was above the national average of 475. Hune and Chan (1997) reported similar results in a College Board study of 1996 APA high school seniors. The APA average score of 496 on the verbal portion of SAT 1, was lower than the national average of 505 and much lower than the average of 526 for White students. Of the 1985 Asian Pacific American high school seniors who indicated that English was not their best language, the SAT verbal median score was a low 272. The median for other Asians, who reported English as being their best language, was 434, still lower than the mean of 449 for Caucasian students. The large number of immigrants who have migrated to the United States since the 1970s, many of whose families have home languages other than English, may account for some of the findings. However, even those Asian students who identified English as their best language did not score as highly as their Caucasian counterparts.

The pattern of higher scores in mathematics and lower scores in language has also been found in grades seven through twelve in the San Diego Unified School District. Using 1989–1990 school district data, Cheng, Ima, and Labovitz (1994) found Anglos to have the highest mean (63.4) on the reading portion of the Comprehensive Test of Basic Skills (CTBS). In comparison, Southeast Asians had a mean of 33.2, Latinos had a mean of 37.5, African Americans had a mean of 39.9, and Pacific Islanders had a mean of 40.2. The same pattern was seen in the language section of the test: Anglos had a mean of 66.9, Southeast Asians had a mean of 48.7, African Americans performed at 46.7, Latinos had a mean of 46.0, and Pacific Islanders had a mean of 52.5. The gap between Southeast Asians, Pacific Islanders, and Anglos was much less on the mathematics portion of the CTBS. Southeast Asians had a mean of 66.8 and Pacific Islanders had a mean of 56.8, while Anglos had a mean of 71.1.

Why Some APA Students Do Well in School

In some schools, there are proportionately more Asian Pacific American students who do well and these numbers seem to validate the model minority myth. Though a comprehensive discussion of the phenomenon would be lengthy, the work of Sue and Okazaki (1990) and Suzuki (1977) helped to explain the achievement of some APA students. Sue and Okazaki hypothesized that the success of many Asian Pacific Americans, especially early generations, can be explained by the concept of relative functionalism. Students identified what is relative or important to others and adopted these behaviors; studying hard, getting good grades, and pleasing teachers lead to success in school and so are functional behaviors. The researchers found Asian Pacific Americans to exceed the graduation rate from college and universities of any other groups, including Caucasians. Sue and Okazaki explained that APA populations stress education and the attainment of bachelors and advanced degrees in order to be successful in life.

In examining the issue of academic success, Sue and Okazaki (1990) noted that though many scholars believe Asian Pacific Americans have higher income levels and therefore more resources to finance schooling, their research disputed this claim. In fact, they found the median incomes of Asian Pacific American parents to be much lower than their Caucasian peers (Sue & Okazaki, 1990: p. 914).

One of the most popular explanations for educational achievement focuses on cultural values (Caudill & De Vos, 1956; Sue & Kitano, 1973; Kitano, 1976; Mordkowitz & Ginsburg, 1987; Sue & Okazaki, 1990). Scholars have hypothesized that the cultural values of Asians toward education, expectations to succeed, high affiliation needs, use of guilt and shame, and family obligations have socialized young Asians to do well in school. These values are compatible with middle-class, mainstream values. Sue and Okazaki (1990) contended that few rigorous studies have been conducted to support this cultural interpretation of success. Research linking parenting styles and cultural values with academic achievement has been sparse.

Sue and Okazaki (1990) did not believe academic achievement could be solely explained by Asian cultural values. Though APA achievements may be, in part, explained by ethnic values, they also hypothesized that the status of Asian Pacific Americans as a minority group has impacted educational attainment. They believed that education is functionally one of the few avenues available to Asians. Social obstacles in society reinforce the importance of education in becoming upwardly mobile.

Looking at the phenomenon somewhat differently, Suzuki (1977) argued that Asian Pacific Americans pursued education because of the discrimination they faced in employment. Suzuki discovered that Asian Pacific Americans could be found in lower-level white-collar positions, and that few have yet to move upward into corporate positions that have greater authority and decision-making responsibility. He also discovered that the higher levels of family income reported in some Asian Pacific

American communities were due to multiple family members working. Suzuki found that the level of educational attainment of many Asian Pacific Americans did not correlate with incomes. In addition, Asian Pacific Americans were frustrated because positions that had more responsibility and higher incomes were not open to them. Suzuki agreed with Sue and Okazaki (1990) that because of historical discrimination and the marginal place Asians found themselves, Asians instilled in their children a strong belief in education and aspirations of white-collar professions. Unfortunately, however, not all APAs do well in society. There are many who live in poverty.

Poverty and the Model Minority Image

The model minority myth points not only to believing that APAs do well in school, but also that they are from middle-class families. The aura of the model minority contains the image that Asian Pacific Americans have secured high-level technical positions and so they have few financial problems. Poverty rates, test scores, and career ceilings demonstrate that this is not a true picture. Many Asian Pacific Americans are wage and salary workers who have difficulties surviving economically. The model minority myth covers over the economic struggles and realities of Asian Pacific Americans.

Poverty is a critical issue in APA communities. Toji and Johnson (1992) reported that in 1980 there were 334,000 Asian Pacific Americans living in poverty. The overall rate of APA poverty of 13 percent is slightly higher than the 12 percent for the general U.S. population, though Cambodian (46.9%), Hawaiian (14.3%), Hmong (65.5%), Indonesian (15.2%), Laotian (67.2%), Samoan (27.5%), and Vietnamese (35.1%) families have much higher levels of poverty than Caucasian families (7%) and some are higher than for Blacks (26.5%). In 1990, 12 percent of Asian Pacific Americans lived in poverty of which 44 percent were children under eighteen years of age, compared with 37 percent of Caucasians under eighteen (U.S. Bureau of the Census, 1992). The poverty rates reflect high levels of unemployment or employment in low-wage jobs. In 1980, the rates of unemployed Southeast Asians was higher than those for Blacks and Latinos (Toji & Johnson, 1992).

Coping with Cultural Bias and the Model Minority Myth

Asian Pacific American students must cope with the stresses of racism and existence of conflicting cultural messages communicated about the model minority myth ("Whiz Kids," 1987; Pang, 1995a). The model minority myth is often accompanied by the belief that Asian Pacific American students are the students who raise the grade curve to the detriment of others. They are not usually the basketball stars or homecoming royalty; they may be seen more as "nerds." It is not always an asset to stand out academically and be considered an "egghead." Some Asian Pacific American children are easy targets because of their physical and linguistic differences. In addition, students who do well must deal with the mixed messages of the model minority image: "We admire your high grades, but you don't really fit into our group because you're different."

The Asian Pacific American students who do not do well must also cope with the model minority myth. There are Asian Pacific American students who are not intellectually gifted and are unable to reach the high academic standards that parents or teachers have set for them (Pang, 1995b). These students may have difficulty dealing with negative feelings of being considered a "loser." It is not unusual for younger siblings to hear comments from parents and teachers about older brothers and sisters such as "Why aren't you getting straight As like your older brother?" The model minority image can be difficult for students who may not be academically inclined, especially when teachers assume that students from Asian Pacific American groups will be top achievers. These students are trying to deal with the powerful process of assimilation, and mixed messages regarding their acceptance into mainstream society can be a heavy burden to carry.

Understanding the Social Context of Students

Social forces continue to shape the experience of APA children. As Chun and Sue discussed in this text, many young people suffer from depression, sometimes brought on by posttraumatic stress disorder. A number of southeast Asian refugee students have been traumatized by their escape from war-torn countries and lengthy stays in refugee camps. Youth may suffer from nightmares, anxiety, and panic attacks. Educators need to understand that their students may show aggression or passive behavior because of posttraumatic stress disorder. Students may become easily angered when other students bump into them or look disapprovingly at them. Nonrefugee students may have little knowledge of the experiences of APA students and, therefore, may not understand why they have difficulty with depression and anger.

Other students have found gangs to fill the void in their lives. Ima and Nidorf reported an increase in gang activity in APA youth. Most are male. Some students do not fit the profile of gang members. A minority of students in gangs dress neatly and do well in school. They may engage in gang activities primarily in the evening when their parents are at work. Other gang members have little family. They may have come to the United States with a sibling and no parent. Though many APA youth have good intentions of working hard in school, they may become more and more involved in serious crimes. Ima and Nidorf found much gang activity was primarily associated with making money by stealing parked cars or burglarizing homes, rather than assaulting people.

Since one of the most important values in APA communities is to respect authorities, arrested young people seem to respond to authority figures. Schools may need to hire community liaisons who can develop culturally based programs like those created by Kiang and Flores described in this book. In these programs, high school students have had the opportunity to find out what it means to be an Asian Pacific American and to become actively involved in society.

What Values Direct Asian Pacific Americans?
Family, Family, Family

In real estate when buying a home, one of the rules of thumb is location, location, location. For many Asian Pacific American children, the most crucial aspect of their lives is family, family, family. Just as in many other communities, the family shapes the child's worldview. In trying to explain the importance of the family, Appendix 1 provides a list of traditional cultural values for various Asian Pacific American communities. These are tendencies and not absolutes. Overgeneralizations can be destructive, and yet when reading through Appendix 1 differences and similarities between groups will become apparent. People from many cultures value family. However, how those values are manifested will vary. Before reviewing the list, a caution must be given: there is no one person who believes in all the values listed for a cultural group. Rather, the values are those of an idealized, traditional person in that particular community.

Sue and Sue's (1973) model of looking at differences in Chinese personality help educators to better understand how Asian Pacific Americans differ within their ethnic groups. Their model looked at three different personalities: (1) the Traditionalist; (2) the Marginal Person; and (3) the Asian American. Depending on many variables like generation, language proficiency, acculturation level, age, social class, gender, and other personal experiences, individuals will fall into one of the three categories. Appendix 1 represents what Sue and Sue called the "traditional Asian." Young described Sue and Sue's model in depth in his chapter and indicated these personalities are also mediated by the maturation level of a child and his/her desire to please parents.

In reviewing Appendix 1, though all the Asian Pacific American groups felt family was the most important social unit, some groups like the

Samoans were oriented toward the extended family more than others like Japanese Americans. The strength of the Samoan community came from the maintenance of the family (Jung, 1993). Samoans felt responsibilities and mutual obligation to relatives beyond their nuclear family. Though other groups felt somewhat obligated to help others, the Samoan community seemed to have more far-reaching obligations. For example, it is not unusual for a Samoan who has no housing to move in with relatives until the person is able to find a place to live.

The view of family in Asian Pacific American communities differs from Western societies. In some American families, parents are heard saying, "I will take care of my son until he is eighteen, but then he will have to support himself." Many Asian American parents and children form a web of relationships where there is mutual obligation to take care of each other. Parents may continue to assist their children with the understanding that their children will care for them when they are elderly. In several communities like the Japanese American community, elderly parents often live with the eldest son. It is the eldest son's responsibility along with his wife and children to care for his parents for the rest of their lives. Sometimes this obligation can be difficult because in modern American society upward mobility may entail moving to a new city. Asian Pacific Americans may feel tremendous guilt when moving away from their parents and siblings.

Since many APA students are sensitive to the community, they may also worry about what others think of them. This can be a negative aspect of Asian values. APA students may have difficulty standing up for what they believe in fear that others may think less of them. In addition, they may also go along with the views of others and not express themselves in hopes of maintaining smooth relationships.

Cultural conflicts can also occur because of changes in gender roles. Though some groups like Filipino Americans are more likely to have equitable gender status, in many APA families the father maintains a strong authoritarian and decision-making role. As more APA women enter the work force, males see an eroding of their patriarchy. This can cause tremendous stress in the family. Gender roles are continually being redefined as family members become more culturally assimilated to mainstream ways. Women may no longer stay home and tend to the family. They may become assertive and work outside the home to develop a career or to bring in additional income to the family.

Asian Pacific American students are living in a period of many changes. Though mainstream culture is a daily aspect in schools, the influence of the mass media has brought mainstream culture into their homes as well. It is a tumultuous time where parents and students are testing the boundaries of cultural assimilation and cultural preservation (Kiang, 1990). It is also difficult for students who are members of cultures that place community needs before personal needs to understand extreme individualism and the value of independence. Teachers must not judge students based on the mainstream sociocultural context, but acknowledge that students are struggling with the needs of their families and their need to feel comfortable within a highly individualistic, aggressive, and capitalistic society.

Recommendations and Educational Implications

In educating the whole child, educators need to examine how culture impacts the comprehensive development of a student. As Shavelson and his colleague's (1976) theoretical framework demonstrates, it is important to look at the total child. Educators need to consider how culture impacts developmental stages, assimilation levels, self-esteem, the physical self, emotional stability, academic growth, clarification of beliefs, literacy and language, and interpersonal skills. Teachers who understand the impact of culture make a "reality check" every day to assess how relevant their curriculum is to the lives of their students (Irvine, 1990; Gay, 1994).

Is What You See What You Think You See?

Asian Pacific American children are often misunderstood because teachers misinterpret their behaviors. APA children may sit quietly, even if they are bored silly, in deference to teachers and their position of authority. When students seem to be shy, quiet, obedient, and do not volunteer to answer in class, teachers may categorize Asian Pacific American students as passive, weak, or uninterested in school. Cheng's chapter provided numerous examples of how the outward behaviors of people can be misinterpreted because observers did not understand the implicit culture.

In reality, many Asian Pacific American students are not shy or quiet. Tran, in her chapter, explained how APA children may feel it is important to show respect to the teacher and maintain harmony in the classroom. In many classrooms, teachers are likely to attend to the needs of disruptive students. APA children can be seen in classrooms raising their hands for help, but not verbally calling out at the same time. Teachers are more apt to give attention to the disruptive or verbally aggressive students. After a few minutes, when APA students see their teachers are dealing with other young people and they do not get their attention, they lower their arms and stop waving. Students then turn to their peers who are sitting close by for help. Some teachers then assume that the APA students who stopped raising their hands, do not need tutoring and so begin to believe that these students are able to answer their own questions. Unfortunately, APA students may be disappointed that the teachers did not spend time with them. However, in honor of their teachers and to maintain harmony in the classroom, students may not confront their teachers on the matter. In other classrooms, children may be operating on cultural modes of behavior of turn taking, which teachers do not see (Au & Jordan, 1981). Once again educators may not understand how values of community and family manifest themselves in the classroom.

The example given above demonstrates cultural differences between what teachers believe and what students think. In anthropology, this is called the difference between "etics," cultural-general concepts, and "emics," cultural specifics (Brislin, 1993). Teachers may misinterpret what is actually happening. For example, the common experience or etic is that children go to school to learn. However, the emics is that children may bring different patterns of behavior to the classroom. In the United States, most children are expected to be vocal in expressing their needs to the teacher. Otherwise, there is an underlying assumption that the teacher will not know what students need if they do not "speak up." Yet many APA children have been taught not to call attention to themselves or to stand out in a group. They are told not to bother the teacher. Rather, they should work to solve their problems, whether they are academic or personal, on their own.

Erickson (1990) explains that local meanings may differ in subgroups. He has carefully outlined how the interpretation of actions in one group may be distinctly different from another group. Looking at within-group differences, teachers may find that the number of generations their family has resided in the United States may add a new dimension to how APA children think and behave. For example, many Japanese American and Chinese American students are third-, fourth-, or even fifth-generation Americans. As the lives of their parents have become bicultural, parents may socialize their children to include more values and behaviors of the mainstream culture. The local meaning (Erickson, 1990) of speaking out has gradually shifted to offspring of many American born Asian Pacific Americans. Those who are third- or fourth-generation American may be more vocal and willing to answer questions in front of the class and demand more attention from teachers, while many first-generation APA students may believe it is respectful not to talk in class and bring attention to themselves.

Communication Skills
Developing Their Voice

Thus, one of the most glaring needs of APA children is verbal skill development. Teachers may find that Asian Pacific American students are unwilling or unable to participate in discussions, especially Socratic and issues-centered debates. When teachers ask students questions, APA students may feel embarrassed to speak up in front of the whole class because they have been taught not to show off. In addition, APA youth may feel it is improper to ask questions of their teacher because this would show the teacher is not doing a good job of explaining.

The importance of verbal communication in schools is a major area where Asian values may come in conflict with mainstream values. In many classrooms where sharing information and discussion are at the heart of the instructional strategies, teachers will need to teach Asian Pacific Americans oral communication skills. First, teachers need to explain that students are expected to share their thoughts, ideas, and knowledge with their classmates. Second, teachers may provide students opportunities to talk in small group settings rather than asking Asian students in front of the entire group. It may take time for students to become comfortable enough to speak to the entire class. Thirdly, teachers can have other more verbal students model expected behaviors by having those students present first. For example, in one elementary classroom, the teacher asks several students to take the "Hot Seat" every week. When children are on the Hot Seat, they provide information about an identified character of a book. Then classmates ask them questions about the character. The teacher found that if she allowed the more verbal students to be in the Hot Seat at the beginning of the month and then less talkative students at the end of the month, the less verbal students were able to participate more effectively.

Teachers also have allowed children to videotape their presentation so that students who are shy or less verbal can practice talking to a large group privately first. Then students can redo their segments without fear of embarrassment. Many times, young people want to be able to talk comfortably with others and in front of large groups. Ramist and Arbeiter (1986) were surprised to find that the APA high school seniors they surveyed indicated a desire for more effective oral skills.

When teachers use a great deal of dialogue in their classrooms, Asian Pacific American students may find difficulty with group discussion. APA students may need more preparation time than other students. They may freeze up when teachers ask them questions, and it may take them more time to gather their thoughts. In addition, teachers may want to let them think about the question asked, go on to other students, and then come back to the student and allow her/him to answer.

If debating is used in the classroom, teachers may need to explain to APA students the importance of assertive behaviors. APA students may find it disrespectful to talk pointedly to another or to argue in a public situation. Teachers should explain the purpose of debate and that aggressive behavior is expected and valued in this context. This can be an extremely difficult experience for APA students who have learned that harmony is important in life and that confrontation is considered rude.

Just as young APA students want to sharpen their verbal skills, they also need to develop their "voice." Schools must not only provide students with effective bilingual education, second-language programs, and creative writing programs, but students must also strive to become more confident in cultivating their own viewpoints and opinions. Since many APA students often exhibit competencies in technical and scientific fields, educators may overlook their lower grades in English, creative writing, or composition where they must take a stand, write to persuade others, or make an analysis of social interactions. Kiang's chapter is a powerful reminder that high school students are dealing with a multitude of social issues and they need opportunities to clarify their positions and take actions.

Parents
Part of the Educational Team

Within the educational process, APA parents are a crucial factor. APA parents may also hold values that are different from mainstream schools. They may need to be encouraged to participate in school activities (Lee, 1995). As Nadeau indicated in her chapter, some parents are fearful of participating in school affairs because of language differences. Young people may have conveyed to their parents that they are embarrassed that their parents cannot speak English well. Parents need to be reassured that their assistance is welcomed. Parents may contribute by providing playground supervision, working in the library, accompanying classes on field trips, and helping with art projects (Lee, 1995). If possible, interpreters can be used to facilitate communications during back-to-school nights and parent teacher conferences. One way that Lee (1995) recommends building bridges with parents who may be reticent is to visit their homes and reach out to them. Another method is to use community representatives to explain school procedures such as immunization requirements, volunteer programs, parent-teacher conferences, and homework policies in various languages.

Not all Asian Pacific American parents have difficulty speaking English. Some parents prefer to have verbal interaction with teachers rather than written notes. In some communities such as Samoan ones, communication is primarily conducted verbally (Jung, 1993). Parents may not respond to a letter or photocopied note from the school. Teachers may not understand that parents are more comfortable talking with them directly. Though it may be difficult for teachers to find the time to call or visit parents, the best way to communicate with them may be in person or on the telephone.

Parents are also an important element in providing special education services to APA children. Watanabe explained how some parents may be extremely reluctant to allow their children to be placed in special education classes. Some parents believe that children with disabilities represent something bad in the parents' past and, therefore, they feel guilt and shame. Yet, it is crucial for parents to work with special educators rather than to ignore the needs of their children. It takes skilled and compassionate educators to develop partnerships with APA parents and children.

Using Literature in the Curriculum
Carefully Chosen Role Models

As the number of Asian Pacific American students steadily climbs, it is increasingly important for educators to use teaching materials that promote sensitive, positive, and accurate portrayals of Asian Pacific Americans (Pang et al., 1992). As this chapter has indicated, APA students are often confronted with biases from peers, teachers, and friends. Literary resources can present protagonists who are empowered people. These role models should not be generalized depictions of politeness, martial arts, and stilted speech. The characters should represent real people whose cultural backgrounds enrich and guide their lives and who illustrate the struggles of individuals with their bicultural identity. Fung, in this book, gives excellent examples of culturally relevant curriculum using children's literature. When instructors use literature with Asian role models, students may feel validated because the teacher's use of Asian perspectives gives legitimacy to their viewpoints. Asian Pacific American literature can expand all students' understanding of complicated social issues by providing new perspectives and demonstrating the value of diverse cultural worldviews. Excellent books and materials with Asian Pacific American protagonists are available (Pang & Evans, 1995). Appendix 2 lists recommended APA literature for children and adults. These books deal with ethnic identification, immigration, civil rights, biculturalism, marginality, family, gender roles, and personal growth. The literature also presents protagonists who struggle not only with life but to better understand themselves and others.

Integrating Historical Information Into the Curriculum
Asian Pacific Americans Fighting Oppression

Educators need to know that Asian Pacific Americans have a long legacy of fighting for civil rights in the United States. Many APAs have fought against oppression in hopes of creating a just society. Though history and social studies textbooks often portray Asian communities as docile and obedient, Chan (1991) and McClain (1994) document the struggle of

Asian Pacific Americans in fighting three kinds of oppression: Race, class, and national origin. Asians have led strikes, brought class action suits, and picketed in hopes of higher wages, better working conditions, property rights, and attaining an education and citizenship.

Teachers can integrate the following information into their social studies, political science, sociology, psychology, history, and economic classes. There are numerous historical figures who are excellent role models for all students; these role models can inspire young people to work for social justice.

Few students and teachers know that Asian Pacific Americans have and continue to fight oppression in society. Though APA history is taught in some classrooms, students are not given the opportunity to look at various events through perspectives other than the majority's. In addition, children often learn a simplified and chronological view of civil rights, racism, ethnocentrism, and assimilation, although these issues are extremely complex and interrelated. For example, a fifth-grade White male student wrote after covering World War II in his social studies text book:

The Japanese

A long time a go a lot of Asians immigrated to the U.S. One of them were the Japanese. They immigrated to California. They produced food and better farms than Americans. Americans, after a period of time were beginning to dislike the Japanese. Then one day Japanese planes flew overhead and bombed Pearl Harbor. Then the U.S.A. decided to move the Japanese to reservations. After the big war they released them. Then there was no prejudice.

The passage is troubling for several reasons. First, the child presents the underlying perception that the Japanese were not U.S. citizens; then, he seems to confuse the Japanese who bombed Pearl Harbor with those who were native-born U.S. citizens. He also believes a lot of Asians migrated to the United States long ago. These are serious misconceptions. In addition, the child also believes that, all of a sudden, there was no prejudice. The passage demonstrates the need for teachers to teach social studies more carefully using an issues-centered approach, so that all students will have the opportunity to sort through complicated beliefs and attitudes that are a part of the study of history (Pang, 1994). Using an issues-centered approach to social studies, teachers can guide students to view history from numerous viewpoints, which will then assist children in clarifying their own knowledge and views.

Some APA children have expressed their unhappiness about the school curriculum with questions, such as: "Where are the Filipinos in history?"

"Why aren't I in the history books?" "Where are the people who look like me?" "Didn't we have a role in U.S. history?" Teachers must immerse themselves in the cultural, historical, and social information of groups represented in their classrooms. If there are Filipino American students in the school, teachers can ask for a workshop on Filipino American history. Teachers will discover that the first permanent Asian Pacific American settlement in the continental United States was founded in 1763 in the Louisiana bayous (Cordova, 1983). Teachers need to know about the historical contributions of all major ethnic groups. Building this knowledge base can begin with studying the history and cultures represented in their classrooms; then, teachers can study additional communities. Integrating APA history can help all students to understand the proud legacy of strength, resistance, and liberation of Asian Pacific Americans.

Filipinos in Louisiana

One of the earliest examples of fighting oppression occurred in 1763. Filipino sailors jumped ship and hid in the bayous of southeastern Louisiana because of cruel treatment from Spanish ship masters. Spanish-speaking Filipinos had been forced to work for the Spanish as crewmen, woodcutters, shipbuilders, and munitions specialists (Cordova, 1983). Filipino pioneers left the ship and established the first permanent Asian Pacific American settlement in the continental United States; they built a village on stilts in the marshes of Louisiana (Cordova, 1983).

Striking Chinese Workers

Chinese immigrants also fought against social oppression. In June of 1867 during the construction of the transcontinental railroad, Chinese workers struck for better working conditions and higher wages. Though their Caucasian peers were earning $30 a month and board, Chinese workers were earning $30 without board, which could amount to approximately one dollar a day (Chan, 1991). Two thousand workers struck demanding $40 a month, a ten-hour work day, and a five-day work week instead of six days, and an end to physical punishment. Unfortunately, the strike only lasted a week, because the railroad owners would not allow food to be delivered to the men and they began to starve. Their efforts represent our legacy of civil rights in the United States.

Philip Vera Cruz and Labor Activism

Filipino Americans have also been leaders in the fight against oppression in the fields. For example Philip Vera Cruz, as a labor activist in California, dedicated his life to securing rights of Filipino workers (Sinnott, 1993). Many Filipinos had migrated to Hawaii to the fields from the early 1900s (Cordova, 1983) and went to the mainland from the 1920s (Takaki, 1989).

In California, Filipinos often worked as stoop laborers harvesting crops like broccoli, cauliflower, melons, and tomatoes in California and Washington. Others found work harvesting cherries, apples, and peaches in Oregon, Montana, Idaho, Wyoming, Utah, and Colorado (Cordova, 1983). Life was difficult in the fields and Vera Cruz fought for higher wages, housing, safety precautions, and health care for workers. He became the vice president of the United Farm Workers union and worked in the struggle for rights with Cesar Chavez.

The Japanese American Redress Movement

During more recent times, Asian Pacific Americans continued the struggle for civil rights. During World War II after the bombing of Pearl Harbor, Japanese Americans were under attack in the United States. Many people feared their Asian neighbors and extreme racism arose from many Americans. Curfews were imposed on Japanese Americans and later President Roosevelt signed Executive Order 9066, which ordered more than 120,000 Japanese immigrants and Japanese Americans who lived on the West Coast to report to ten internment camps.

Some Japanese Americans fought oppression by volunteering for the armed services. Since loyalty was an important value in their lives, they felt it was crucial to demonstrate to the American public that they were 100 percent American. Many Japanese Americans served in the all-Japanese American 442nd Regimental Combat Team, because the armed forces were segregated during that time in U.S. history. This regimental combat team became the most decorated unit during World War II.

Several Japanese Americans fought for their civil rights and the rights of the community in court. The first to challenge the legality of the curfew order during World War II was Minoru Yasui, a Japanese American who had grown up in the Hood River Valley of Oregon (Hatamiya, 1993). He had graduated from law school at the University of Oregon. Yasui felt that it was wrong that the United States would take away his rights as a citizen because of his race. He deliberately challenged the curfew order by walking into a police office at 11:00 in the evening and demanded to be arrested. Yasui felt as an American, he was responsible for changing the laws (Kessler, 1993). He was convicted of violating curfew and sent to jail for nine months.

Other Japanese Americans fought against Executive Order 9066 and their removal from their homes. Fred Korematsu from California and Gordon Hirabayashi in Washington did not report for evacuation and did not follow curfew orders. They, like Yasui, were arrested, convicted, and sent to jail. They took their cases to the Supreme Court in the 1940s and lost. The Supreme Court ruled in the Yasui, Korematsu, and Hirabayashi cases that the actions of the United States were justified due to "military necessity" and "pressing public necessity." However, in 1983 with the assistance of Peter Irons, lawyer and professor at the University of California, San Diego, and Dale Minami, a civil rights lawyer from San Francisco, the three Japanese Americans filed petitions to have their cases reopened (Hatamiya, 1993). Irons and Aiko Herzig-Yoshinaga found that several critical documents from the Department of Justice had been hidden. These documents demonstrated that there was little or no threat of espionage by Japanese Americans who lived on the West Coast (Hatamiya, 1993). In a series of court decisions, Fred Korematsu's conviction was vacated in 1983 and the removal of Hirabayashi from his home was also vacated in 1986. Hirabayashi's appeal regarding curfew was vacated in 1988. Unfortunately, Yasui died before his appeal was completed.

The internment of Japanese Americans is important to all Americans because when the rights of citizens are taken, every citizen is in jeopardy. The following constitutional rights of Japanese Americans were violated during World War II:

Freedom of religion
Freedom of Speech
Freedom of the Press
Right to Assemble
Freedom from unreasonable searches and seizures
Right to an indictment or to be informed of the charges
Right to life, liberty, and property
Right to be confronted with accusatory witnesses
Right to call favorable witnesses
Right to legal counsel
Right to a speedy and public trial
Right to reasonable bail
Freedom from cruel and unusual punishment
Right against involuntary servitude
Right to equal protection under the laws
Right to vote
Right to habeas corpus (to be brought before a court)
(JACL, 1994)

Young Japanese Americans fought for vindication of the Japanese American community as a whole, and more importantly their parents who had been interned, by creating a redress movement. The redress movement was a comprehensive one including a class-action suit, reopening of wartime cases (discussed above), grassroots community activities, and exhibitions (Hatamiya, 1993). The main principle of the movement focused on equal opportunity as a fundamental freedom and claimed that the government was guilty of discrimination. In addition, crimes had been committed and the government was accountable for them. After many attempts at getting legislation passed, and more than forty years after Executive Order 9066 authorized the removal of Japanese Americans to internment camps, President Reagan signed the Civil Liberties Act of 1988, which called for a national apology from the United States government and monetary compensation to survivors. This act is a milestone in U.S. history because it is the first time "the government granted redress to an entire group of citizens for a deprivation of their constitutional rights" (Hatamiya, 1993: p. 191).

Lau v. Nichols: The Foundation for Bilingual Education

Kinney Lau was a student in the San Francisco Unified School district whose first language was Cantonese. His parents and those of twelve other Chinese American students filed a class action suit against Alan Nichols, who was president of the San Francisco Board of Education (Wang, 1976). For many years Chinese American parents had been concerned because they did not feel their children were receiving adequate instruction due to their English language development needs. After much struggle with the district, parents filed the suit asking that schools hire bilingual teachers so their children could learn English.

During the court hearing the San Francisco Unified Schools District did admit that many children needed special instruction, but the district argued that it was not legally obligated to provide for those needs (Wang, 1976). Though the Federal District Court and U.S. Court of Appeals for the Ninth Circuit agreed with the school district, the Chinese American parents took their suit to the U.S. Supreme Court. After four years of litigation in various levels of courts, in 1974 the U.S. Supreme Court in the decision (which is known as *Lau v. Nichols*) unanimously refuted the findings of the lower courts (Wang, 1976). The Supreme Court took the position that in order for children to participate equally in schools, their education must be "meaningful" and "comprehensible" and in order for this to take place bicultural and bilingual education programs were needed. This ruling became the backbone for bilingual programs throughout the United States and reinforced the right of thousands of children, who spoke languages other than English, to access schools.

Teachers and students must have knowledge of the history of Asian Pacific Americans. Their struggle as an American community has contributed to strengthening this nation's democratic values. Asian Pacific Americans have made important contributions to the struggle for human and civil rights.

Conclusion

Asian Pacific American students attend schools that are oriented toward European, middle class, paternalistic, and heterosexual norms. APA children may bring to schools a complex diversity of cultural values, historical experiences, assimilation levels, and cultural traditions that conflict with the worldview presented in schools. Table 15.2 presents a list of general Asian values toward education and provides insights as to how the behavior of Asian Pacific American students may be in direct conflict with school expectations. While much of U.S. culture is based on individualism, many APA children value being a member of a family or community. Therefore, they are likely to seek group acceptance or find identity in being part of a classroom or school. This key cultural value orientation shapes much of the behavior and motivation of APA young people.

Asian Pacific American students are struggling to be heard by teachers and other service providers. Culture is a key dimension of life that has a profound impact on how children feel, think, behave, and view the world. The cultural worldview of students must be considered when creating school programs in order to effectively educate and care for the whole child, including their emotional, academic, social, and physical needs.

In educating the whole child, teachers must understand that although children may bring diverse cultures to the classroom, schools also are powerful cultural institutions of U.S. society. Educators can be important mediators in teaching Asian Pacific American students how to negotiate the cultural tensions and dissonance that arise as they move through the school system.

One of the continual themes that has emerged in research and practice is how the continued impact of prejudice and racial inequalities on APA students' lives at school. Not only do many APA children hold cultural values that may conflict with values in the schools, but they also must deal with a society where people may hold stereotypical views of Asian Pacific Americans, or may discriminate against them because of their cultural, racial, and physical differences. In addition, it is critical that schools, as cultural institutions, eliminate systemic practices that have perpetuated the invisibility of Asian Pacific American students, parents, communities, histories, and cultures. Teachers can be influential catalysts in the process of ridding schools of stereotypical images, ignorance about Asian cultures, and racism—all of which hamper the ability of school personnel to be caring and effective (Pang, 1994).

Asian Pacific American children are an important segment of our youth population. Educating all of our young people must be one of our nation's most important goals. Why? As one Asian Pacific American child told me, "We're more important than adults, because we are the future!"

TABLE 15.2
General Asian Pacific American Values Concerning Education

Asian Pacific American Themes	Educational Implications
Schooling is a formal process.	Teachers are to be respected and not to be treated casually. Teachers are to be treated formally.
Teachers are to be respected and obeyed.	Students may not ask or answer questions out of respect for teachers. Students may believe in rules like "Speak only when spoken to." Students may appear to be passive to teachers.
Teachers are important authorities.	Students may not question the authority or knowledge of teachers because that would be disrespectful even if the student believes the teacher has given incorrect information.
Humility and modesty are important values.	Students may be reluctant to volunteer in class and may not offer new ideas to a class discussion in fear of looking like they are "showing off."
Cooperation is an important virtue. Harmony is valued.	Students may help each other on their homework. In addition, students may feel it is important to help each other on class work and may not understand the concept of cheating. Students may also encourage each other by providing answers.
Schooling is a serious process.	Students are expected to be on task and work hard at their desk. They may not believe it is acceptable to let students walk around the room.
Teachers have "knowledge" and should impart it to students.	Teachers may be expected to lecture much of the time. Students may not have skills to engage in inquiry, discussion, or Socratic methods because the teacher is expected to explain to students what to do. Students may not engage in discussions with teachers because that would be disrespectful.

(continued on next page)

TABLE 15.2 *(continued)*
General Asian Pacific American Values Concerning Education

Asian Pacific American Themes	*Educational Implications*
Parents trust teachers.	Parents may not be active in PTA or other educational groups. Parents may believe they do not know as much as teachers. If students are successful, then parents may not understand the importance of PTA and parent teacher conferences.
Parents believe in developing technical skills in students.	Teachers may believe in developing a well rounded person. However, Parents and students may see the importance of cognitive development in fields like math, science, and English. Parents may believe other subjects like physical education, auto mechanics, and chorus should be included only if there is time. In addition, parents may not understand the emphasis teachers place on self-esteem, creativity, and independence.
Students should be obedient.	Students may be on task and exhibit behaviors of high achieving students. Though they may not understand the lesson, they will not ask teachers for help.
Reading for information is important to provide facts and lessons.	Students may read for facts, but may not have the initial skills to infer, synthesize, and apply information.
Teachers are expected to give students homework.	If teachers do not give students work to be done at home, teachers are not doing "good" job.

Adaptation of "Asian Attitudes toward Education" and "Incongruencies between American Teachers' Expectations and Asian Parents' Expectations," p. 14. In L. L. Cheng, *Assessing Asian Language Performance*. Oceanside, Calif.: Academic Communication Associates, 1991.

Notes

Portions of this chapter are included in *Critical Knowledge for Diverse Teachers and Learners*, pp. 149–88 (Washington, D.C.: American Association of Colleges for Teacher Education, 1997).

The author would like to acknowledge the contributions of Barbara Boone, Lirong Lilly Cheng, Rey Monzon, Andrea Saltzman, Karen Toyohara, and Dario Villa.

Appendix A:
Key Aspects and Cultural Tendencies
of Selected Asian Pacific Americans

Valerie Ooka Pang

A. Cambodian Americans

- People are called Khmer.
- 1975: Refugees flee to the United States and other countries when Pol Pot leads the Khmer Rouge to take over the country and there are massive massacres of the people.
- Khmer languages have roots in Sanskrit and Pali.
- Culture is rooted in several belief systems: Khmer, East Indian, French cultural traditions and the religions of Theravada Buddhism and Brahmanism (Chhim, 1989; Cheng, 1989).

Tendencies in Traditional Cultural Values

- Many are Buddhists (National Clearinghouse, 1984; Union of Pan Asian Communities [UPAC], 1980).
- Most important social unit is the nuclear family, which sometimes includes other generations (Chhim, 1989; Hopkins, 1996; National Clearinghouse, 1984; UPAC, 1980).
- Status in the community is important (Chhim, 1989; UPAC, 1980).
- Filial piety, respect for parents and elders (Chhim, 1989; UPAC, 1980).
- Respect for authority (National Clearinghouse, 1984; UPAC, 1980).
- Authoritarian parenting (Chhim, 1989)
- Khmer husbands often live with wife's family initially after marriage (Cheng, 1989)
- Value intelligence and education (Chhim, 1989; UPAC, 1980).
- Cooperative and not competitive or aggressive (UPAC, 1980).
- Family good is more important than personal needs (Hopkins, 1996; UPAC, 1980).
- Pattern of rank and class, each person has a role (Chhim, 1989).
- Individual merit can place someone in different class (Chhim, 1989).

- Resolution of conflict is through explanations and not negotiation (Chhim, 1989).
- Personal independence is valued, yet must still uphold obligations and role in society (Chhim, 1989).
- Children should be obedient (Chhim, 1989).
- Community rituals are important social and cultural functions of community (Hopkins, 1996).

B. Chamorros

- Guam is a southern island in the Mariana island chain.
- People on Guam became U.S. citizens when the Organic Act of Guam was passed by the U.S. Congress in 1950 (UPAC, 1980).

Tendencies in Traditional Cultural Values

- Extended family is basic social unit (UPAC, 1980).
- Filial piety, respect for elders (UPAC, 1980).
- Presence of children is valued (UPAC, 1980).
- Family pride is strong (UPAC, 1980).
- Traditional gender roles with fathers as heads of households (UPAC, 1980).
- Sensitive to criticism (UPAC, 1980).
- Competition between villages (UPAC, 1980).

C. Chinese Americans

- First Chinese who migrated to the United States from 1820 to 1847 were students who went to Ivy league universities to study.
- The first wave of Chinese laborers came to the United States from the 1850s until 1882, when all Chinese laborers were barred by race to enter the United States.
- The Chinese Exclusion Act of 1882 was the first law, which excluded a group by race, entrance into the United States.
- Diverse groups of people comprise the Chinese American populations and have roots in Taiwan, Hong Kong, Peoples Republic of China, and Vietnam.

Tendencies in Traditional Cultural Values and their Educational Implications

- The extended family is the basic social unit.
- Family pride and family honor (UPAC, 1980; Sue & Sue, 1973).

- Children try to Live up to parent expectations (Sue & Sue, 1973).
- Mothers believe children should be independent later than European American parents (Sue, Sue & Sue, 1983).
- Family harmony (UPAC, 1980).
- Filial piety (UPAC, 1980; Sue & Sue, 1973).
- Traditional families are patriarchal and patrilineal (UPAC, 1980).
- Educational achievement is more important than other types of achievement (Sue & Sue, 1973; UPAC, 1980).
- Strong sense of family responsibility (Sue & Sue, 1973).
- Parents are more restrictive than other parents (Uba, 1994).
- Hard work is important (UPAC, 1980).
- Respect for elders is equated with respect for authority (Sue & Sue, 1973).

D. Filipino Americans

- 1763: First Asian Pacific Americans settlers in Louisiana bayous jumped from Spanish galleons (Cordova, 1983).
- More than 7,000 islands comprise the Philippines, where more than 87 languages are spoken (Cheng, Nakasato & Wallace, 1995; Santos, 1983).
- Most Filipino American students speak English and many can speak a Filipino language like Tagalog or Ilocano.
- Filipinos represent a wide variety of subcultures, due to language, national origins, regions, and values (Cordova, 1983; Cheng, Nakasato & Wallace, 1995; Santos, 1983), therefore great diversity in cultural values.
- In San Diego City Schools, the suicide rates for Filipinas (Filipino American females) were higher than any other ethnic group (Lau, 1995).

Tendencies in Traditional Cultural Values and their Educational Implications

- "Pakikisama": maintain good relationships between family and friends (Monzon, 1984; Sipma-Dysico, 1994; UPAC, 1980)
    1. Strong sense of obligation, return favor
    2. Power of shame or embarrassment
    3. Criticism may injure one's pride, so be careful not to offend others. People may be indirect.
- Social acceptance and a sense of belonging is extremely crucial (Agbayani-Siewert, 1994; UPAC, 1980)
- Personal dignity is important (UPAC, 1980)
- Friendship is protected by loyalty (Agbayani-Siewert, 1994).

- Both women and men play important role in family, egalitarian patterns (Agbayani-Siewert, 1994; UPAC, 1980).
- Family obligations to extended and nuclear family, grandparents may live with son's family (Cheng, Nakasato & Wallace, 1995; Santos, 1983).
- The extended family is the primary social unit (Agbayani-Siewert, 1994).
- Children are expected to respect not challenge parents (Cheng, et al., 1995).
- Children are indebted to parents for giving them life (Agbayani-Siewert, 1994).
- Parents place a great emphasis on academic achievement and college degrees (Cheng et al., 1995; Santos, 1983).
- Grandparents are respected but may not have authority over family members, as is the case in other Asian families (Agbayani-Siewert, 1994).
- Extended family may include fictive relatives brought into the family by friendship or Catholic rituals like baptism or marriage (Agbayani-Siewert, 1994).
- When there is conflict, "go betweens" may be used to mediate tensions and arguments (Agbayani-Siewert, 1994).
- Children often experience conflict when assimilating Western values of independence, individualism, and assertiveness because of conflict with values of harmonious interpersonal relationships, interdependence, and family unity (Agbayani-Siewert, 1994; Cheng et al., 1995; Santos, 1983; Sipma-Dysico, 1994).

E. Japanese Americans

- Most Japanese Americans have long historical roots in the United States, since immigration from Japan was prohibited by the Asian Exclusion Act of 1924. A minimum of immigrants from Asian countries was allowed again with the McCarran-Walter Act in 1952.
- The internment of Japanese Americans by the U.S. government during World War II led to high levels of structural assimilation and intermarriage with non-Asians (Fugita & O'Brien, 1991).
- Though many Japanese Americans are assimilated into U.S. society, many retain strong ethnic ties and sense of community (Fugita & O'Brien, 1991).
- Japanese Americans led a redress movement fighting for the basic rights of all citizens and were successful in the passage of the Civil Liberties Act of 1988 which called for a national apology from the U.S. government for their internment during World War II and provided reparations for survivors.

Tendencies in Traditional Cultural Values and their Educational Implications

- Hierarchy of social status, know one's place (Caudill, 1952; Kitano, 1976).
- Reserved and disciplined behavior favored (Kitano, 1976).
- "Enryo": Modesty is in part why Japanese Americans may not speak out during meetings and explains lack of talking in a group (Kitano, 1976).
- Careful not to shame, embarrass, or make a fool of oneself (Caudill, 1952).
- Children may not ask questions because student does not want to embarrass teacher or trouble the teacher (Kitano, 1976; Pang, 1991).
- Mutual responsibility and dependency in family (Caudill, 1952; Kitano, 1976).
- Filial piety, taking care of and respecting parents (Kitano, 1976).
- Respect for authority (Fenz & Arkoff, 1962; Kitano, 1976).
- Avoid direct confrontation. Parents may suggest rather than demand a specific behavior. For example a parent may say, "Why don't you put away your Nintendo and study?" (Kitano, 1976).
- Compromising is highly approved (Kitano, 1976).
- Answers may be vague rather than definitive. Lack of direct answers (Kitano, 1976).
- Conformity and obedience (Kitano, 1976).
- Hard work and effort is highly valued (Kitano, 1976).
- Priority of group, rather than individual needs. Team player (Kitano, 1976).
- Difficult to make forceful decisions because of dependency (Kitano, 1976).
- High affiliation needs (Fenz and Arkoff, 1962; Kitano, 1976).
- Personal achievement goals are valued (Caudill, 1952).
- Social control through close-knit community. Informal communication through ethnic newspapers, radio stations, and personal conversations (Kitano, 1976).
- Japanese American students may have lower physical self-concept, but feel confident about their academic self-concept (Pang, Mizokawa, Morishima & Olstad, 1985).

F. Korean Americans

- Korean immigrants were first recruited to work in Hawaiian sugar plantations in the 1880s (E. Kim & Yu, 1996).
- Immigration from Korea primarily took place after immigration laws were changed in 1965 (Kim, 1978).

- Many have contributed to the development of an ethnic business district, opening car dealerships, appliance stores, and banks that serve the Korean community (Kim, 1980).
- Korean Christian churches are pivotal community organizations (E. Kim & Yu, 1996).
- Many parents are having difficulty finding higher level positions and so are sometimes underemployed (Kim, 1980).
- About one-fifth of Koreans have the surname of Kim (E. Kim & Yu, 1996).

Tendencies in Traditional Cultural Values and their Educational Implications

- Value hard work (Kim, 1978).
- Have strong belief in the American Dream (Kim, 1980).
- Adapt well to new situations (Kim, 1980).
- Believe in individualism (Kim, 1980).
- Many parents continue to protect cultural traditions and language in youth (Kim, 1980).
- Parents hold high expectations and standards for children (Kim, 1980).
- Parents often monitor academic achievement of children or actively tutor their young people (Kim, 1980).
- Because of parent's difficulty in finding satisfactory positions, parents feel it is important for children to adapt to mainstream society and learn English (Kim, 1980).
- Parents also pressure students to maintain language and cultural traits (Kim, 1980).
- Many children have career aspirations which parallel parent wishes (Kim, 1980).
- Students may not openly talk about their problems to the teacher (Kim, 1980).

G. Samoan Americans

- American Samoa is a chain of six islands in Polynesia (South Pacific) and is a U.S. territory. Most Samoans live on the island of Tutuila (Cheng, Nakasato & Wallace, 1995).
- Immigration mostly in recent times, 1950s to present (UPAC, 1980).
- Samoan students in San Diego County have the lowest grade point averages of any ethnic group (Cheng & Ima, 1989).
- Critical issues facing elder Samoans are health care, financial stability, and language barriers (Ishikawa, 1978).

Tendencies in Traditional Cultural Values
and their Educational Implications

- "Aiga": The Extended family is most important social unit (Igoa, 1995). This can include relatives either through marriage, birth, and or adoption (UPAC, 1980).
- Kinship relationships are often referred to (cousin, son, sister-in-law) (UPAC, 1980).
- Loyalty and service to the family is pervasive (UPAC, 1980). Helping each other is important (housing, employment, childcare, etc.) (UPAC, 1980).
- Strong Interdependence.
- "Matai" or chief has positional status—makes decisions and is responsible for the family (UPAC, 1980).
- The church (various Christian faiths) is important aspect of life (Ishikawa, 1978; UPAC, 1980).
- In some church communities, the group is known by their minister (UPAC, 1980) and the minister/pastor often acts as an important social and religious leader (Igoa, 1995).
- Prestige in the community is important (UPAC, 1980).
- Children defer to elders (UPAC, 1980).
- Some marriages are marked by conflict and violence (UPAC, 1980).
- Older children have a responsibility to care for younger children (Cheng, Nakasato & Wallace, 1995).
- Storytelling is an art in which elders impart cultural information to youth (Igoa, 1995).
- Some Samoan males (ten years and older) may challenge the authority of women.
- A father may be used as a mediator between school personnel and males (Igoa, 1995).
- Music and song are essential elements of Samoan culture (Igoa, 1995).
- If a teacher embarrasses or shames a student, the student will withdraw, become silent, look blankly, and stare without answering (Igoa, 1995).
- Europeans often view Samoan discipline as being rather harsh (Cheng, Nakasato & Wallace, 1995).

H. Vietnamese Ameicans

- April 1975: First wave of immigration, professionals who had ties with the United States and defeated government of South Vietnam; most were Vietnamese and escaped by boat (California State Department of Education, 1982; Te, 1995; Tran, 1998).

- 1978: The second wave began because of conflicts between China and Vietnam, many Laotians and Cambodians sought refuge (California State Department of Education, 1982; Te, 1995; Tran, 1998).
- 1982: The third wave included many Southeast Asian immigrants who wanted to find their U.S. relatives (California State Department of Education, 1982; Te, 1995; Tran, 1998).
- Many families are fragmented; children living in the United States without parents or relatives (UPAC, 1980, Rumbaut & Ima, 1988).
- Younger people may face more cultural conflicts as they create a bicultural identity (Kibria, 1993).

Tendencies in Traditional Cultural Values and their Educational Implications

- Extended family is basic social unit (Kibria, 1993; National Clearinghouse, 1984; Te, 1987; UPAC, 1980).
- Family is more important than the individual (Long, 1996; National Clearinghouse, 1984; Te, 1987; UPAC, 1980).
- Filial piety is an important value (Kibria, 1993; Long, 1996; Te, 1987).
- Maintaining harmony in family highly valued (Rutledge, 1992; Tran, 1998; UPAC, 1980).
- Mutual obligation in the family (Kibria, 1993; Long, 1996; Te, 1987).
- Families are patriarchal and authoritarian (UPAC, 1980).
- Status, social roles, and family position are important (UPAC, 1980).
- Fulfill one's duty to the family (UPAC, 1980; Te, 1987).
- Wife's role is strong in children's education and family status (UPAC, 1980) and may have the same status as fathers in the family (Te, 1987).
- Respect for learning, intelligence, education (California State Department of Education, 1982; UPAC, 1980).
- Teacher holds high status in society (UPAC, 1980; Te, 1987).
- Saving face and family pride is important (UPAC, 1980).
- Feelings, "the heart," is important, so are very sensitive (UPAC, 1980).
- Showing respect to others is one of their overriding values (Te, 1987; Tran, 1998).
- Community as group may not be as unified (UPAC, 1980).
- Personal needs are important and may clash with community needs (UPAC, 1980).
- Person's name Is crucial in one's identity—family, middle, and personal name—friend would use personal name, while formal situations use Mr. or Ms. in front of the personal name. Family names are not used (Te, 1987).
- Discipline and hard work are core values (Rutledge, 1992).

Appendix B:
Selected Asian Pacific American Literature for Children and Adults

Valerie Ooka Pang

Bruchac, J. (Ed.). (1983). *Breaking silence, an anthology of contemporary Asian American poets*. Greenfield, N.Y.: Greenfield Review Press. (high school/adult)

Cha, Dia. (1996). *Dia's story cloth*. New York: Lee & Low Books. (elementary/middle school)

Chin, F. (1988) *The Chinaman Pacific & Frisco R.R. Co*. Minneapolis: Minn.: Coffee House Press. (high school/adult)

Chin, F., Chan, J. P., Inada, L. F., and Wong, S. (1975). *Aiiieeeee!: An anthology of Asian-American writers*. Garden City, N.Y.: Anchor Books. (high school/adult)

Clark, A. N. (1978). *To stand against the wind*. New York: Viking Press. (intermediate grades)

Crew, L. (1989). *Children of the river*. New York: Dell. (middle and high school)

Feeney, S. (1985). *A is for aloha*. Honolulu: University of Hawaii Press. (primary grades)

Garland, S. (1993). *The lotus seed*. San Diego, Calif.: Harcourt Brace Jovanovich. (elementary grades)

Hagedorn, J. (Ed.). (1993). *Charlie Chan is dead: An anthology of contemporary Asian American fiction*. New York: Penquin Books. (high school/adult)

Hamanaka, S. (1990). *The journey: Japanese Americans, racism, and renewal*. New York: Orchard Books. (intermediate grades)

———. (1995). *On the wings of peace: Writers and illustrators speak out for peace, in memory of Hiroshima and Nagasaki*. New York: Clarion Books.

Hongo, G. K., Lau, A., and Inada, L. F. (1978). *The Buddha bandits down highway 99*. Mountain View, Calif.: Buddhahead Press. (high school/adult)

Japanese American Anthology Committee (Ed.). (1980). *Ayumi*. San Francisco: Japanese American Anthology Committee. (high school/adult)

Lee, M. (1992). *Finding my voice.* New York: Houghton Mifflin. (middle and high school)

Lim, S. G., Tsutakawa, M., and Donnelly, M. (Eds.). (1989). *The forbidden stitch: An Asian American women's anthology.* Corvallis, Ore.: Calyx Books. (high school/adult)

Mirikitani, J. (1987). *Shedding silence: Poetry and prose.* Berkeley, Calif.: Celestial Arts. (high school/adult)

Mura, D. (1991). *Turning Japanese memoirs of a Sansei.* New York: Atlantic Monthly Press. (high school/adult)

Namioka, L. (1993). *Yang the youngest and his terrible ear.* New York: Dell. (primary grades, easy reader)

Okada, J. (1976). *No-No Boy.* Seattle: University of Washington Press. (high school/adult)

Say, A. (1988). *A river dream.* New York: Houghton Mifflin. (primary grades)

———. (1993). *Grandfather's journey.* New York: Houghton Mifflin. (primary grades)

———. (1996). *Emma's Rug.* New York: Houghton Mifflin. (primary/intermediate grades)

———. (1997). *Allison.* New York: Houghton Mifflin. (primary/intermediate grades)

Uchida, Y. (1971). *Journey to Topaz.* New York: Charles Scribner's Sons. (intermediate grades)

———. (1972). *Samurai of gold hill.* New York; Charles Scribner's Sons. (intermediate grades)

———. (1978). *Journey home.* New York: Atheneum. (intermediate grades)

———. (1981). *A jar of dreams.* New York: Atheneum. (intermediate grades)

———. (1983). *The best bad thing.* New York: Atheneum. (intermediate grades)

———. (1985). *The happiest ending.* New York: Atheneum. (intermediate grades)

———. (1991). *The invisible thread.* Englewood Cliffs, N.J.: Julian Messner. (middle and high school)

———. (1993). *The bracelet.* New York: Philomel Books. (intermediate grades and middle school)

Wong, J. (1994). *Good luck gold and other poems.* New York: Macmillan. (elementary grades)

Wong, M. (1993). *Growing up Asian American.* New York: William Morrow. (high school/adult)

Yamamoto, H. (1994). *"Seventeen Syllables."* King-Kok Cheung (Ed.). New Brunswick, N.J.: Rutgers University.

Yashima, T. (1958). *Umbrella.* New York: Viking Press. (primary grades)

Yep, L. (1975). *Dragonwings.* New York: Harper and Row. (middle and high school)

———. (1977). *Child of the owl.* New York: Harper and Row. (intermediate grades)

———. (1979). *Sea glass.* New York: Harper and Row. (intermediate grades)

———. (1991). *The lost garden: A memoir.* Englewood Cliffs, N.J.: Julian Messner. (middle and high school)

———. (1991). *The star fisher.* New York: Morrow Books. (intermediate grades)

———. (1993). *American dragons: Twenty-five Asian American voices.* New York: HarperCollins. (intermediate grades, middle, and high school)

Appendix

Valeria Lovelace

Creating Positive
Asian American Images
on *Sesame Street*

Sesame Street is a television program designed to prepare three, four, and five year olds, especially poor and minority children, academically and socially for school. *Sesame Street* first aired in 1969, and today it is seen by over six million children in the United States and in over eighty countries around the world. Since its inception, *Sesame Street* has always modeled racial harmony; however, as a result of rising racial unrest in the United States, we launched a four-year Race Relations Curriculum Initiative in 1989 designed to be more explicit about physical and cultural differences and to encourage friendship, tolerance, and understanding between people of different races and cultures.

Over the course of the four years, twenty-three race relations goals were developed for preschool children. These goals were the result of a collaboration between producers, writers, researchers, animators, filmmakers, *Sesame Street* related project staff, and African American, American Indian, Latinos, Asian American, and White American race relations and cultural experts.

The first year of our Race Relations Initiative focused on African Americans, the second year American Indians, the third year Latinos, and the fourth year Asian Americans. Each year a seminar was held followed by writing, producing, and researching segments addressing the issues raised by each group. Resource guides were created by the Sesame Street Research Department to provide detailed information on each group's history, customs and traditions, foods, and the contributions that each group has made to the arts, sciences, and sports. This was followed by a lecture series that featured speakers, artists, musicians, and community leaders who provided personal stories and cultural information.

This case study will focus on the fourth year of our Race Relations Curriculum Initiative, where *Sesame Street* turned its attention to developing a new sensitivity, awareness, and understanding of the needs of Asian American children and the role that television, especially *Sesame Street* can play in their lives.

The Curriculum Seminar

The starting point for our research was to identify the experts for the curriculum seminar and to identify and the issues that needed to be addressed for the seminar. This involved an extensive literature review and telephone conversations with Asian American scholars from across the country. Using census data and our knowledge of the diversity of Asian Pacific American groups in the United States, Sesame Street Research sought advisors who could present race relations research findings specifically on Asian Indian American, Chinese American, Filipino American, Japanese American, and Korean American cultures.

Our advisors were: Dr. Rohini B. Ramanathan, cofounder of the Indian Children's Culture Workshop; Dr. Kenyon S. Chan, chair and professor of the Asian American Studies Department at California State University; Dr. Li-Rong Lilly Cheng, professor of communicative disorders at San Diego State University; Dr. Rolando A. Santos, professor of social foundations of education at California State University; Dr. Valerie Ooka Pang, professor of teacher education at San Diego State University; Dr. Harry H. L. Kitano, chair of the Japanese American Program and professor of social welfare and sociology at the University of California, Los Angeles; and Grace Lyu-Volkhausen, chair of the Governor's Asian American Advisory Committee in New York.

During the seminar, the advisors stressed the importance of maintaining languages and cultural practices, recognizing that these varied depending on the length of time families had lived in the United States, which ranged from recent arrivals to families who had been Americans for over

150 years. They discussed the need for segments that fostered pride in being Asian Pacific American: who they are, how they look, their names, and the languages they speak. The advisors also stressed the importance of dealing with gender equality and the issues surrounding exclusion and rejection. They discussed the dangers of the model minority myth, which ignores the large groups of Asian Americans who have failed to succeed or who suffer from poverty, unemployment, language barriers, and other problems.

The advisors underlined the fact that while Asian Indian American, Chinese American, Filipino American, Japanese American, and Korean American cultures share many commonalities, Asian American culture is very diverse. Foods, celebrations, holidays, events, and important figures often differ among the various Asian American cultures.

After reviewing the Race Relations Curriculum goals developed in the three previous years, our Asian American advisors helped to create new strategies for dealing with rejection and name calling. The board stressed that Asian American children are often victims of name calling and that it would be helpful if *Sesame Street* could give the children some strategies. We expanded our definition of what an American is to include all skin colors, hair textures, eye shapes, statures, dress, names, accents, and languages. We also developed goals addressing the positive contributions of Asian Indian American, Chinese American, Filipino American, Japanese American, and Korean American cultures and people.

The Lecture Series

In the months following the curriculum seminar, a lecture series was held featuring Asian American speakers, artists, and musicians who provided personal stories and cultural information. A panel discussion was held on the intergenerational experiences of Korean Americans, and a presentation was made providing a historical and personal account of Filipinos in America. In response to one of the advisor's anecdotes about her son taking Taiko drumming lessons during the curriculum seminar, Soh Daiko, a Taiko drumming group was invited to perform and discuss how this Japanese American tradition has evolved. a troupe of Asian Indian American dancers performed traditional dances and explained the meaning of a variety of musical pieces.

During the curriculum seminar, the advisors discussed the importance of showing and encouraging the acceptance of spoken and written Asian languages. They encouraged *Sesame Street* to use accurate drawings of Chinese characters, and to avoid simply drawing something that looks like it might be a Chinese character. In response to their concern, *Sesame Street* conducted a final lecture featuring a Chinese American calligraphy demonstration and lesson.

To date, over thirty muppet, animation, and film segments have been produced addressing Asian Indian American, Chinese American, Filipino American, Japanese American, and Korean American people and cultures. Two of the segments captured the experiences of a girl and boy taking a Chinese calligraphy lesson. These segments were selected as the focus of our formative research study.

Formative Research

The final step in our process was to determine whether the segments that were produced presented positive portrayals of Asian Americans on *Sesame Street*. We designed a study to investigate whether two new films, *Chinese Character: Rain* and *Chinese Character: Tree*, effectively taught and appealed to Chinese American preschool children, as well as African American, Puerto Rican, and White preschool children.

The children were brought into the room to view the segments in small groups of four or five. Upon entering the room, they were introduced to the researchers. Each child was assigned to a researcher to be his/her "partner." In order to establish rapport and not to single out any children, all preschoolers in the daycare centers were given *Sesame Street* stickers by the researchers, who also wore the stickers. All the Chinese American preschoolers were interviewed by Chinese American researchers who spoke English and Cantonese. Likewise, African American children were interviewed by African American researchers, Puerto Rican children preschoolers were interviewed by Puerto Rican researchers who spoke English and Spanish, and White children were interviewed by White researchers. Children went with their partners to play Mr. Potato Head. This warm-up activity allowed the children enough time to feel comfortable and familiar with the researcher. Once the children finished this activity, they were seated again and asked if they were ready to be reporters. The researcher said:

> Today we are going to play a game called "reporter." Do you know what a reporter is? A reporter is someone who sees something and tries to remember as much as he/she can and then tells someone else about it afterwards. To help you be a good reporter, I'm going to give you a reporter's hat (mimes giving each child a hat). Okay, everyone put your hat on and tie it under your chin so that it won't fall off. Now, we are going to be doing other things while you watch television, so when you're finished watching, you can tell us what you saw and what you heard. Is everybody ready to be reporters? Okay!

After the children watched each segment they went with their partners to play the reporter game and answer some questions about what they had just seen.

Segment 1
Chinese Calligraphy—Rain

In this live-action film, a boy is shown having a Chinese calligraphy lesson with his teacher. As he forms the character, his teacher shows him how to position the brush. The boy finishes writing and asks, "Can you guess what it means? It means rain," while the Chinese character animates and we see raindrops falling and a little man walking in the rain with an umbrella. Results included:

- Chinese American, African American, Puerto Rican, and White children watched this segment very attentively.
- When shown three Chinese characters and asked which one said rain, the majority of the Chinese American, African American, Puerto Rican, and White children correctly chose the character rain.
- When asked how they would feel about writing in Chinese, the majority of children responded positively.
- When asked how the boy felt about writing in Chinese, the majority of children responded positively.
- Over half of the Chinese American children knew that the boy was writing in Chinese. This was significantly higher than the less than one-fourth of the African American, Puerto Rican, and White children who knew the boy was writing in Chinese.

Segment 2
Chinese Calligraphy—Tree

In this live-action film, a girl is shown having a Chinese calligraphy lesson with her teacher. As she begins to form the character, her teacher shows her how to position the brush. The girl finishes writing and asks, "Can you guess what it means? It means tree," while the Chinese character animates and we see a tree forming and a bird flying and resting on the branches. Results included:

- Chinese American, African American, Puerto Rican, and White children watched this segment very attentively.
- When shown three Chinese characters and asked which one said tree, the majority of the Chinese American, African American, Puerto Rican, and White children correctly chose the character tree.

- When asked how they would feel about writing in Chinese, the majority of the Chinese American, Puerto Rican, and African American children responded positively. Significantly fewer White children responded that they would feel positive about writing in Chinese.
- When asked how the girl felt about writing in Chinese, the majority of children responded positively.
- Over half of the Chinese American children knew that the girl was writing in Chinese. Less than a third of the African American, Puerto Rican, and White children knew the girl was writing in Chinese.

Children were also asked general questions about themselves and Chinese people:

- When the children were asked how they felt about Chinese people, the majority of Chinese American and African American children responded positively. Puerto Rican and White children were significantly less positive about Chinese people.
- When the children were asked how the Chinese people on TV felt about being Chinese, the majority of Chinese American and African American children responded positively. Less than half the Puerto Rican and White children responded positively.
- When the Chinese children were asked how they felt about being Chinese, the majority responded positively.

Conclusions

From these findings, it is clear that positive Asian American images can be created on *Sesame Street*. After viewing these two segments, Chinese American children felt positive about themselves, Chinese people, and the Chinese people that they saw on television. They also learned the Chinese characters for rain and tree, and felt positive about writing in Chinese.

After viewing these segments, most of the African American, Puerto Rican, and White children learned the Chinese characters for rain and tree and perceived that the children in both segments felt positive about writing in Chinese. However, the majority of African American, Puerto Rican, and White children did not know that the language the boy and girl were writing in was Chinese. Future segments should explicitly label the language as Chinese at least three times. After viewing these segments, the African American and Puerto Rican children felt positive about writing in Chinese. However, while the White children felt positive about being able to write in Chinese after the first segment, they were less positive about being able to write in Chinese after the second segment. And when the children were asked how they felt about Chinese people and how the Chinese people on television felt about being Chinese, the majority of the Chinese American and African American children responded positively, while the majority of the Puerto Rican and White children did not.

Based on these results, it is clear that both Puerto Rican and White children need to see additional Chinese American images and positive presentations of Chinese writing on television. The data also suggest that there is need for all children, regardless of race, to have additional information about Chinese American culture and people.

This is only the beginning research on the Asian American segments that continue to be produced each year. Through Race Relations research we will refine our approaches and develop new ways to encourage understanding, tolerance, and friendship between all people in the United States. The process will continue with additional information from advisors, experts, and of course children being incorporated into the development of new *Sesame Street* segments.

References

Foreword

Kiang, P. N. (1991). About Face: Recognizing Asian and Pacific American Vietnam Veterans in Asian American Studies. *Amerasia 17*(3), 22–40.

Preface

Cordova, F. (1983). *Filipinos: Forgotten Asians*. Dubuque, Iowa: Kendall-Hunt.

Darder, A. (1991). *Culture and power in the classroom*. New York: Bergin & Garvey.

Gay, G. (1993). *At the essence of learning: Multicultural education*. West Lafayette, Ind.: Kappa Delta Pi, p. 152.

Kanter, R. M. (1995). *World class: Thriving locally in the global economy*. New York: Simon & Schuster.

Mirikitani, J. (1983). Breaking Silence. In J. Bruchac (Ed.), *Breaking silence: An anthology of contemporary Asian American poets*. Greenfield Center, NY: Greenfield Review Press.

Ong, P., and Hee, S. (1993). The growth of the Asian Pacific American population: Twenty million in 2020. *The state of Asian Pacific America. A policy report: Policy issues to the year 2020*. Los Angeles: LEAP Asian Pacific American Public Policy Institute; and Asian American Studies Center, University of California, Los Angeles.

Spindler, G., and Spindler, L. (1993). The process of culture and person: Cultural therapy and culturally diverse schools. In P. Phelan and A. L. Davidson (eds.), *Renegotiating cultural diversity in American schools*. Albany: State University of New York Press, pp. 27–51.

1. Who Are Chinese American, Japanese American, and Korean American Children?

Allport, G. (1954). *The nature of prejudice*. Cambridge, Mass.: Addison-Wesley.

Broom, L., and Kitsuse, J. (1973). *The managed casualty: The Japanese American family in World War II*. Berkeley: University of California Press.

Bruner, J. (1990). *Acts of meaning*. Cambridge Mass: Harvard University Press.

Bureau of the Census. (1990). *Asian and Pacific Islander Americans: A profile*. Washington D.C.: U.S. Department of Commerce.

California State Department of Education. (1983). *A handbook for teaching Korean-speaking students*. Sacramento: California State Department of Education, Office of Bilingual Bicultural Education.

Chan, Sucheng (Ed.). (1991). *Asian American: An interpretive history*. Boston: Twayne.

Divoky, D. (1988). The model minority goes to school. *Phi Delta Kappan* (Nov.), 219–22.

Fong, T. (1994). *The first suburban Chinatown: The remaking of Monterey Park, California*. Philadelphia: Temple University Press.

Kim, Bok Lim. (1978). *The Asian-American: Changing patterns, changing needs*. Montclair, N.J.: Association for Korean Christian Scholars in North America.

Kitano, H., and Daniels, R. (1995). *Asian Americans: Emerging minorities*. 2d ed. Englewood Cliffs, N.J.: Prentice Hall.

——— . (1988). *Asian Americans: Emerging minorities*. 2d ed. Englewood Cliffs, N.J.: Prentice Hall.

Kwak, T. H., and Lee, S. H. (Eds.) (1991). *The Korean American community: Present and future*. Korea: Kyungnam University Press.

Lee, C. S. (1975). The United States immigration policy and the settlement of Koreans in America. *Korean Observer 4*, 412–51.

Lee, E. (1982). A social system approach to assessment and treatment for Chinese American families. In M. McGoldrick, J. Pearce, and J. Giordano. *Ethnicity and family therapy*. New York: Guilford.

Lehrer, B. (1988). *The Korean Americans*. New York: Chelsea House.

Nah, Kyung-Hee. (1993). Personal problems and service delivery for Korean immigrants. *Social Work 38*(3), 289–96.

Nakanishi, D. (1994). *Asian American educational experience*. New York: Routledge.

O'Brien D., and Fugita, S. (1991). *The Japanese American experience*. Bloomington: Indiana University Press.

Ogawa, D. (1978). *Kodomo no tami ni (For the sake of the children): The Japanese American experience in Hawaii.* Honolulu: University of Hawaii Press.

Pang, K. C. (1995). Developments in teacher education in Hong Kong: 1997 and beyond. Paper presented at the annual meeting of the American Educational Research Association, San Francisco.

Sue, S., and Okazaki, S. (1990). Asian American educational achievements: A phenomenon in search of an explanation. *American Psychologist 45*(8), 913–20.

Sue, S., and Zane, N. (1985). Academic achievement and socioemotional adjustment among Chinese university students. *Journal of Counseling Psychology 43*(4), 570–79.

Sung, B. L. (1967). *The story of the Chinese in America.* New York: Collier.

Takaki, R. (1989). *Strangers from a different shore: A history of Asian Americans.* Boston: Little, Brown.

Tamura, E. (1991). *Americanization, acculturation, and ethnic identity: The Nisei generation in Hawaii.* Urbana: University of Illinois Press.

Triandis, H. C., Brislin, R., and Hui, C. H. (1988). Cross-cultural training across the individualism-collectivism divide. *International Journal of Intercultural Relations 12*, 269–89.

Trueba, H. T., Cheng, L., and Ima, K. (1993). *Myth or reality: Adaptive strategies of Asian Americans in California.* Washington D.C.: Falmer Press.

Wei, W. (1993). *The Asian American movement.* Philadelphia: Temple University Press.

2. Filipino American Students

Acuna, J., and Doromal, M. L. (1994). *The school achievement of Filipinos: The Philippine educational system.* Quezon City: University of the Philippines Press.

Aguilar, D. (1988). *The feminist challenge.* Manilla: Asian Social Institute.

Aguilar-San Juan, K. (Ed.). (1994). *The state of Asian America: Activism and resistance in 1992.* Boston: South End Press.

Alabado, C. (1996). *Bataan death march, Capas: A tale of Japanese cruelty and American injustice.* San Francisco: Sulu Books.

Anderson, R. N. (1984). *Filipinos in rural Hawaii.* Honolulu: University of Hawaii Press.

Andres, T. (1987). *Understanding Filipino values in sex, love and marriage.* Manila: Our Lady of Manaoag.

Azores, T. (1986–1987). Educational attainment and upward mobility: Prospects for Filipino Americans. *Amerasia Journal 13*(1).

Bello, W. (1992). *People and power in the Pacific: The struggle for the post–cold-war order*. London: Pluto Press.

Cablas, A. (1991). Pilipino Americans and the scholastic aptitude test at the University of Hawaii at Manoa. *Journal of Asian American Studies 33*, 91–106.

Constantino, R. (1973). *The miseducation of the Filipino people*. Quezon City: University of the Philippines Press.

———. (1975). *A history of the Philippines: From the Spanish colonization to the second world war*. New York: Monthly Review Press.

Cordova, F. (1983). *Filipinos: The forgotten Asian Americans*. Seattle, Wash.: Demonstration Project for Asian Americans.

Corpuz, O. D. (1989). *The roots of a Filipino nation*, vols. 1 and 2. Quezon City: Aklahi Foundation.

Davidman, L., and Davidman, P. (1997). *Teaching with a multicultural perspective: A practical guide*. 2d ed. New York: Longman.

Doi, T. (1971). *The anatomy of dependence* (trans. J. Bester). Tokyo: Kodansha International.

Duggins, J. (1995). Ang sabi nina Lolo at Lola project. *Manila Bulletin USA 3*(42). October 18–24, 1995.

Empeno, H. (1976). Anti-miscegenation laws and the Filipino. In J. Quinsaat et al., *Letters in exile: An introductory reader on the history of Pilipinos in America*. Los Angeles: Asian American Studies Center, University of California, Los Angeles.

Fallows, J. (1987). The Philippines: A damaged culture. *Atlantic Monthly* (November).

Fee, M. H. (1910). *A Woman's impressions of the Philippines*, Chicago: A. C. McClurg. Reprinted by GCF Books, Quezon City, 1988.

Flores, P. V. (1994). Filipino students between two expectations. *Journal of the American Association for Philippine Psychology 1*, 1 (Summer).

Fort Point and Presidio Historical Association. (1997). *Pursuing new frontiers: California volunteers in the Spanish-American war and the Philippines, 1898–1903.*

Gage, N. L., and Berliner, D. C. (1991). *Educational Psychology*. Boston: Houghton Mifflin.

Gay, G. (1983). Multiethnic education: Historical development and future prospects. *Phi Delta Kappan 65*, 8 (April), 560–63.

Human Relations Area File. (1955).*The Philippines*. Chicago: University of Chicago Monograph series, vols. 1–4.

Hsia, J., and Hirano-Nakanishi, M. (1995). The demographics of diversity. In D. Nakanishi and T. Y. Nishida (Eds.), *The Asian American educational experience*. New York: Routledge.

Karnow, S. (1989). *In our image: America's empire in the Philippines*. New York: Ballantine Books.

Kurashige, S. (1992). *Forward Motion* 2, 3 (July). Special issue on Asian Americans and Pacific Islanders.

Lasker, B. (1931). *Filipino migration to continental United States and Hawaii*. Chicago: University of Chicago Press.

Manila Bulletin USA. (1995). Filipinos still grapple with "Filipino." September 14–20: 7 (1994). September 22–28: 7.

May, G. A. (1987). The state of Philippine-American Studies. In G. A. May (Ed.), *A past recovered: Essays in Philippine history and historiography*. Quezon City: New Day, pp. 174–89.

———. (1996). The unfathomable other: Historical studies of U.S.-Philippine Relations. In W. Cohen (Ed.), *Pacific passage: The study of American-East Asian relations on the eve of the twenty-first century*. New York: Columbia University Press, pp. 279–312.

McKeachie, W. J. (1961). Motivation, teaching methods, and college learning. In M. R. Jones (Ed.), *Nebraska symposium on motivation, 1961*. Lincoln: University of Nebraska Press.

Miller, S. C. (1982). *Benevolent assimilation: The American conquest of the Philippines, 1899–1903*. New Haven, Conn.: Yale University Press.

———. (1984). The American soldier and the conquest of the Philippines. In S. W. Peter (Ed.), *Reappraising an empire*. Cambridge, Mass.: Harvard University Press.

Pang, V. O. (1994). Why do we need this class? *Kappan* (December), 289–92.

Philippine Commission report. (1901). Washington D.C.: U.S. State Department.

Pike, K. (1954). Emic and Etic standpoints for the description of behavior. In *Language in relation to a unified theory of the structure of human behavior*. Glendale, Calif.: Summer Institute of Linguistics.

San Juan, E., Jr. (1994). The predicament of Filipinos in the United States: Where are you from? When are you going back? In Aguilar-San Juan (Ed.), *The state of Asian America: Activism and resistance in the 1990s*. Boston: South End.

Sharma, M. (1984). Labor migration and class formation among Filipinos in Hawaii, 1906–1956. In L. Cheng and E. Bonachich (Eds.), *Labor immigration under capitalism: Asian workers in the United States before World War II.* Berkeley: University of California Press.

Sibayan, S. (1978). The topology of the Filipino Bilingual. In E. Pascasio (Ed.), *The Filipino bilingual.* Manila: New Day.

Sobredo, J. (1997). Filipino identity formation: Race, ethnicity and community in the United States. *Journal of Filipino American Studies 1*, 1 (Fall)..

Stanley, P. R. (1972). The forgotten Philippines. In E. May and J. Thomson, Jr. (Eds.), *America East West relations: A survey.* Cambridge: Harvard University Press, pp. 291–316.

Tachiki, A., Wong, E., and Odo, F. (Eds.). (1971). *Roots: An Asian American reader.* Los Angeles: Asian American Studies Center, University of California, Los Angeles.

Trueba, H. T. (1989). *Raising silent voices: Educating the linguistic minority for the twenty-first century.* Boston: Heinle and Heinle.

Wong, M. G. (1994). The education of White, Chinese, Filipino and Japanese students. In D. Nakanishi (Ed.), *The Asian American educational experience.* New York: Routledge, pp. 221–34.

Zwick, J. (1992). *Mark Twain's weapons of satire: Anti-imperialist writings on the Philippine American war.* Syracuse Studies on Peace and Conflict Resolution. Syracuse, N.Y.: Syracuse University Press.

3. Behind the Smiles

Chan, S. (1994). *Hmong means free.* Philadelphia: Temple University Press.

Cheng, L. (1987). English communicative competence of language minority children: Assessment and treatment of language "impaired" preschoolers. In H. Trueba (Ed.), *Success or failure? Learning and the language minority student.* New York: Newbury Harper and Row, pp. 49–68.

Chhim, S. (1989). *Introduction to Cambodian culture.* San Diego, Calif.: Multifunctional Resource Center, San Diego State University.

Hall, E. T. (1976). *Beyond culture.* Garden City, N.Y.: Anchor Books.

Huang, L. N. (1989). Southeast Asian refugee children and adolescents. In J. T. Gibbs and L. N. Huang (Eds.), *Children of color.* San Francisco: Jossey-Bass.

Huynh, D. T. (1988). *The Indochinese and their cultures.* San Diego, Calif.: Multifunctional Resource Center, San Diego State University.

————. (1989). *Introduction to Vietnamese culture.* San Diego, Calif.: Multifunctional Resource Center, San Diego State University.

Keiter, J. (1990). In M. L.Kuehn (Ed.), *The Recruitment and retention of minority trainees in university affiliated programs—Asian Americans.* Madison: University of Wisconsin, pp. 18–22.

Kim, Y. K. (1978). How do Asian students communicate and why? In *Transcultural adaptation: Asian students in American classrooms.* Chicago: Bilingual Education Service Center.

Luangpraseut, K. (1989). *Laos culturally speaking.* San Diego, Calif.: Multifunctional Resource Center, San Diego State University.

Nguyen, D. H. (1972). *Some aspects of Vietnamese culture.* Carbondale: Center for Vietnamese Studies, Southern Illinois University.

————. (1966). *Speak Vietnamese.* Rutland, Vt.: Charles E. Tuttle.

Pang, V. O. (1988). About teachers and teaching—ethnic prejudice: Still alive and hurtful. *Harvard Educational Review 58,* 375–79.

————. (1996). Intentional silence and communication in a democratic society: The viewpoint of one Asian American. *The High School Journal 79,* 183–90.

Samovar, L. A. (1981). *Understanding intercultural communication.* Belmont, Calif.: Wadsworth.

Shor, I., and Freire, P. (1987a). What is the "dialogical method" of teaching? *Journal of Education 169,* 11–31.

————. (1987b). *A pedagogy for liberation.* New York: Bergin and Garvey.

Vuong, G. T. (1978). *Getting to know the Vietnamese and their culture.* New York: Frederick Ungar.

Walsh, R. E. (1981). Indochinese refugees: Cultural and linguistic insights. *CATESOL, occasional papers 7,* 67.

4. Becoming American

A formula for success. (1984, April 23). *Newsweek,* 77–78.

Arce, C. (1981). A reconsideration of Chicano culture and identity. *Daedalus 110*(2), 177–92.

Asian Americans: Are they making the grade? (1984, April 2). *U.S. News and World Report,* 41–47.

Cross, W. E. (1971) The Negro to Black conversion experience: Toward a psychology of Black liberation. *Black World 20*(9), 13–27.

————. (1978). The Thomas and Cross models of psychological nigrescence: A literature review. *Journal of Black Psychology 5*(1), 13–31.

————. (1991). *Shades of black: Diversity in African-American identity.* Philadelphia: Temple University Press.

DeVos, G., and Romanucci-Ross, L. (1975). *Ethnicity.* Palo Alto, Calif.: Mayfied.

DuBois, W. E. B. (1903). *The souls of Black folk.* Greenwich, Conn.: Fawcett.

Erickson, E. (1968). *Identity: Youth and crisis.* New York: Norton.

Greeley, A. M. (1971). *Why can't they be like us? American White ethnic groups.* New York: E. P. Dutton.

Helms, J. E. (Ed.). (1990). *Black and White racial identity: Theory, research, and practice.* New York: Greenwood Press.

Hirschman, C., and Wong, M. G. (1986). The extraordinary educational attainment of Asian Americans: A search for historical evidence and explanations. *Social Forces 65*(1), 1–27.

Hurh, W. M. (1977). *Comparative study of Korean immigrants in the United States: A typological approach.* San Francisco: R. and E. Research.

————. (1980). Towards a Korean-American ethnicity: Some theoretical models. *Ethnic and Racial Studies 3*(4), 444–62.

Hurh, W. M., Kim, H. C., and Kim, K. C. (1978). *Assimilation patterns of immigrants in the United States: A case study of Korean immigrants in the Chicago area.* Washington, D.C.: University Press of America.

Isajiw, W. (1974). Definitions of ethnicity. *Ethnicity 1*(2), 111–24.

Kan, S. H., and Liu, W. T. (1986). The educational status of Asian Americans: An update from the 1980 Census. *P/AAMHRC Research Review 5*(3/4), 21–24.

Kim, J. (1981). *The process of Asian American identity development: A study of Japanese American women's perceptions of their struggle to achieve positive identities.* Doctoral dissertation, University of Massachusetts.

Kim, K. C. (1972). *An exploratory study of the Koreans in the United States: A research proposal.* Unpublished manuscript.

Marcia, J. (1980). Identity in adolescence. In J. Adelson (Ed.), *Handbook of adolescent psychology.* New York: Wiley, pp. 159–87.

Mendelberg, H. (1986). Identity conflict in Mexican-American adolescents. *Adolescence 21*(81), 215 22.

Mordkowitz, E. R., and Ginsburg, H. P. (1987). Early academic socialization of successful Asian-American college students. *Quarterly Newsletter of the Laboratory of Comparative Human Cognition 9*, 85–91.

Nakanishi D. T., and Hirano-Nakanishi, M. (Eds.). (1983). The education of Asian and Pacific Americans: Historical perspectives and prescriptions for the future. Phoenix: Oryx Press.

National Education Association. (1987). *Asian and Pacific islander concerns. Report of the study committee.* Washington, D.C.: Author.

Ogbu, J. (1987). Opportunity structure, cultural boundaries, and literacy. In J. Langer (Ed.), *Language, literacy, and culture: Issues of society and schooling.* Norwood, N.J.: Ablex, pp. 149–77.

Ogbu, J. U., and Matute-Bianchi, M. E. (1986). Understanding sociocultural factors: Knowledge, identity, and school adjustment. In *Beyond language: Social and cultural factors in schooling language minority students.* Sacramento, Calif.: Bilingual Education Office, pp. 73–142.

Park, R. E. (1928). Human migration and the marginal man. *American Journal of Sociology 33*(6), 881–93.

———. (1950). *Race and culture.* Glencoe: Free Press.

Peters, H. A. (1988). *A study of southeast Asian youth in Philadelphia: A final report.* Philadelphia: Institute for the Study of Human Issues.

Phinney, J. S. (1989). Stages of ethnic identity development in minority group adolescents. *Journal of Early Adolescence 9*(1–2), 34–49.

Phinney, J. S., and Alipuria, L. L. (1990). Ethnic identity in college students from four ethnic groups. *Journal of Adolescence 13*(2), 171–83.

Rumbaut, R. G., and Ima, K. (1988). *The adaptation of Southwest Asian refugee youth: A comparative study.* Washington, D.C.: U.S. Office of Refugee Resettlement.

Stonequist, E. V. (1935). The problem of the marginal man. *American Journal of Sociology 41*(1), 1–12.

Sue, D. W., and Sue, S. (1972). Counseling Chinese-Americans. *Personnel and Guidance Journal 50*(8), 637–44.

Sue, D. W. (1989). Ethnic identity: The impact of two cultures on the psychological development of Asians in America. In D. Atkinson, G. Morton, and D. W. Sue (Eds.), *Counseling American minorities: A cross-cultural perspective.* Dubuque, Iowa: William C. Brown, pp. 103–15.

Sue, S. (1977). Psychological theory and implications for Asian Americans. *Personnel and Guidance Journal 55*(7), 381–89.

Sue, S., and Okazaki, S. (1990). Asian-American educational achievements: A phenomenon in search of an explanation. *American Psychologist 45*(8), 913–20.

Sue, S., and Padilla, A. (1986). Ethnic minority issues in the United States: Challenges for the educational system. In California State Department of Education (Ed.), *Beyond language: Social and cultural factors in schooling language minority students.* Los Angeles: California State Department of Education, Evaluation, Dissemination, and Assessment Center, pp. 34–72.

Sue, S., and Sue, D. W. (1971). Chinese-American personality and mental health. *Amerasia Journal 1*(2), 36–49.

Tajfel, H. (1978). *The social psychology of minorities.* New York: Minority Rights Group.

Takaki, R. (1989). *Strangers from a different shore: A history of Asian Americans.* Boston: Little Brown.

Tatum, B. D. (1992). Talking about race, learning about racism: The application of racial identity development theory in the classroom. *Harvard Educational Review 62*(1), 1–24.

The new whiz kids. (1987, August 31). *Time Magazine,* 42–51

Thomas, C. (1971). *Boys no more.* Beverly Hills, Calif.: Glencoe Press.

Trueba, H., Cheng, L, and Ima, K. (1993). *Myth or reality: Adaptive strategies of Asian Americans in California.* Washington, D.C.: Falmer Press.

Why Asians are going to the head of the class. (1986, August 3). *New York Times,* 18–32.

Young, R. (July, 1986). [Ethnic-identity of Chinese minors studying in the United States]. *Teacher's Friend 229,* 54–55.

Yuan, D. Y. (1970). Voluntary segregation: A study of New York Chinatown. In M. Kurokawa (Ed.), *Minority Responses.* New York: Random House, pp. 134–44.

5. Mental Health Issues Concerning Asian Pacific American Children

Aldwin, C., and Greenberger, E. (1987). Cultural differences in predictors of depression. *American Journal of Community Psychology 15,* 789–813.

Baker, N. (1982). Substitute care for unaccompanied refugee minors. *Child Welfare 61,* 353–63.

Bourne, P. G. (1975). The Chinese student—acculturation and mental illness. *Psychiatry 38,* 269–77.

Bui, K. T., and Takeuchi, D. T. (1992). Ethnic minority children in the mental health care system. *American Journal of Community Psychology 20,* 403–17.

Chang, L., Morrissey, R. F., and Koplewicz, H. S. (1995). Prevalence of psychiatric symptoms and their relation to adjustment of Chinese-American youth. *Journal of American Academy of Child and Adolescent Psychiatry 34,* 91–99.

Chung, R. C.-Y., and Okazaki, S. (1991). Counseling Americans of Southeast Asian descent: The impact of the refugee experience. In C. Lee and B. Richardson (Eds.), *Multicultural issues in counseling: New approaches to diversity*. Alexandria, Va.: American Association for Counseling and Development, pp. 107–26.

Daly, S., and Carpenter, M. D. (1985). Adjustment of Vietnamese refugee youths: A self-report. *Psychological Reports 56*, 971–76.

Dao, M. (1991). Designing assessment procedures for educationally at-risk Southeast Asian-American students. *Journal of Learning Disabilities 24*, 594–601.

Erickson, E. H. (1980). *Identity and the life cycle*. New York: W.W. Norton.

Gibbs, J. T., and Huang, L. M. (1989). A conceptual framework for assessing and treating minority youth. In J. T. Gibbs and L. N. Huang (Eds.), *Children of color: Psychological interventions with minority children*. San Francisco: Jossey-Bass, pp. 1–29.

Harding, R. K., and Looney, J. G. (1977). Problems of Southeast Asian children in a refugee camp. *American Journal of Psychiatry 134*, 407–11.

Hong, G. K. (1988). A general family practitioner approach for Asian-American mental health services. *Professional Psychology: Research and Practice 19*, 600–605.

Huang, L. M. (1989). Southeast Asian refugee children and adolescents. In J. T. Gibbs and L. N. Huang (Eds.), *Children of color: Psychological interventions with minority children*. San Francisco: Jossey-Bass, pp. 278–321.

———. (1994). An integrative approach to clinical assessment and intervention with Asian-American adolescents. *Journal of Clinical Child Psychology 23*, 21–31.

Huang, L. N., and Ying, Y. W. (1989). Chinese American children and adolescents. In J. T. Gibbs and L. N. Huang (Eds.), *Children of color: Psychological interventions with minority children*. San Francisco: Jossey-Bass, pp. 30–66.

Kim, L. S., and Chun, C-A. (1993). Ethnic differences in psychiatric diagnosis among Asian American adolescents. *Journal of Nervous and Mental Disease 181*, 612–17.

Kim, S. C. (1985). Family Therapy for Asian Americans: A strategic-structural framework. *Psychotherapy 22*, 342–48.

Kim, S. P. (1983). Self-concept, English language acquisition, and school adaptation in recently immigrated Asian children. *Journal of Children in Contemporary Society 15*, 71–79.

Kinzie, J. D. (1981). Evaluation and psychotherapy of Indochinese refugee patients. *American Journal of Psychotherapy 35*, 251–61.

Kinzie, J. D., Sack, W., Angell, R., Clarke, G., and Ben, R. (1989). A three-year follow up of Cambodian young people traumatized as children. *Journal of Academy of Child and Adolescent Psychiatry* 28, 501–04.

Lee, E. (1988). *Ten principles on raising Chinese-American teens*. San Francisco: Chinatown Youth Center.

Mortland, C. A., and Egan, M. G. (1987, May–June). Vietnamese youth in American foster care. *Social Work*, 240–44.

Nagata, D. K. (1989). Japanese American children and adolescents. In J. T. Gibbs and L. N. Huang (Eds.), *Children of color: Psychological interventions with minority children*. San Francisco: Jossey-Bass, pp. 67–113.

Nidorf, J. (1985). Mental health and refugee youths: A model for diagnostic training. In T. Owan (Ed.), *Southeast Asian mental health: Treatment, prevention, services, training, and research*. Washington, D.C.: U.S. Department of Health and Human Services, pp. 391–429.

Onoda, L. (1977). Neurotic-stable tendencies among Japanese American Sanseis and Caucasian students. *Journal of Non-White Concerns 5*, 180–85.

Padilla, A. M. (1986). Acculturation and stress among immigrants and later generation individuals. *Hispanic Journal of Behavioral Sciences 8*, 270–74.

Padilla, A. M., Alvaraz, M., and Lindholm, K. J. (1986). Generational status and personality factors as predictors of stress in students. *Hispanic Journal of Behavioral Sciences 8*, 275–88.

Pang, V. (1991). The relationship of test anxiety and math achievement to parental values in Asian-American and European-American middle-school students. *Journal of Research and Development 24*, 1–10.

Porte, Z., and Torney-Purta, J. (1987). Depression and academic achievement among Indochinese refugee unaccompanied minors in ethnic and nonethnic placements. *American Journal of Orthopsychiatry 57*, 536–47.

Realmuto, G. M., Masten, A., Carole, L. F., Hubbard, J., Groteluschen. A., and Chhun, B. (1992). Adolescent survivors of massive childhood trauma in Cambodia: Life events and current symptoms. *Journal of Traumatic Stress 5*, 589–99.

Rogler, L. H., Cortes, D. E., and Malgady, R. G. (1991). Acculturation and mental health among Hispanics. *American Psychologist 46*, 585–97.

Rogler, L. H., Gurak, D. T., and Cooney, R. S. (1987). The migration experience and mental health: Formulations relevant to Hispanics and other immigrants. In M. Gaviria and J. D. Arana (Eds.), *Health & Behavior: Research Agenda for Hispanics*. Chicago: University of Illinois, pp. 72–84.

Sattler, J. M. (1992). *Assessment of children*. 3d ed. San Diego, Calif.: Author.

Sue, D. W., and Kirk, B. (1972). Psychological characteristics of Chinese American students. *Journal of Counseling Psychology 19*, 471–78.

Sue, S. (1988). *Sociocultural issues in the assessment and classroom teaching of language minority students*, vol. 3. Sacramento, Calif.: Resources in Special Education (RISE).

Sue, S., Fujino, D., Hu, L., Takeuchi, D. T., and Zane, N. (1991). Community mental health services for ethnic minority groups: A test of the culturally responsive hypothesis. *Journal of Consulting and Clinical Psychology 59*, 533–40.

Sue, S., and Morishima, J. (1982). The mental health of Asian Americans. San Francisco: Jossey-Bass.

Sue, S., and Sue, D. W. (1971). Chinese American personality and mental health. *Amerasia Journal 1*, 36–49.

Sue, S., and Zane, N. (1987). The role of culture and cultural techniques in psychotherapy. *American Psychologist 42*, 37–45.

Touliatos, J., and Lindholm, B. (1980). Behavior disturbance of children of native-born and immigrant parents. *Journal of Community Psychology 8*, 28–33.

Uba, L. (1994). *Asian Americans: Personality patterns, identity, and mental health*. New York: Guildford Press.

U.S. Commission on Civil Rights (1992). *Civil rights issues facing Asian Americans in the 1990s*. Washington, D.C: Author.

Yeh, M., Takeuchi, D. T., and Sue, S. (1994). Asian American children treated in the mental health system: A comparison of parallel and mainstream outpatient centers. *Journal of Clinical Child Psychology 23*, 5–12.

6. Characteristics of Southeast Asian Delinquents

Caplan, N., Whitmore, J. K, and Choy, M. (1989). *The boat people and achievement in America: A study of family life, hard work, and cultural values*. Ann Arbor: University of Michigan Press.

Eppink, A. (1979). Socio-psychological problems of migrant children and cultural conflicts. *International Migration Review 17*, 87–119.

Freeman, J. (1989). *Hearts of sorrow: Vietnamese-American lives*. Stanford, Calif.: Stanford University Press.

Ima, K. (1991a). *What do we know about Asian and Pacific islander language minority students? A report to the California Department of Education's Bilingual Education Office*. Sacramento: California Department of Education.

———. (1991b). *A handbook for professionals working with Southeast Asian delinquent and at-risk youth*. San Diego, Calif.: SAY San Diego.

Long, P. (with L. Ricard). (1996). *The dream shattered: Vietnamese gangs in America*. Boston: Northeastern University Press.

Masuda, M., Lin, K., and Tazuma, L. (1979). Adaptational problems of Vietnamese refugees, I: Health and mental health status, *Archives of General Psychiatry 36*, 955–61.

———. (1980). Adaptational problems of Vietnamese refugees, II: Life changes and perceptions of life events. *Archives of General Psychiatry 37*, 447–50.

McNall, M., Dunnigan, T. and Mortimer, J. T. (1994). The educational achievement of the St. Paul Hmong. *Anthropology and Education Quarterly 25*, 44–65.

Nidorf, J. F. (1985). Mental health and refugee youths: A model for diagnostic training. In Tom Owan (Ed.), *Southeast Asian mental health: Treatment, prevention, services, training, and research*. Washington, D.C.: U.S. Department of Health and Human Services.

Pennell, S., and Curtis, C. (1982). *Ethnic minorities in the juvenile justice system*. San Diego, Calif.: San Diego Association of Governments, Criminal Justice Research Unit.

Rumbaut, R., and Ima, K. (1988). The adaptation of Southeast Asian refugee youth: A comparative study. Washington D.C.: Office of Refugee Resettlement.

Sanders, W. B. (1994) *Gangbangs and drive-bys: Grounded culture and juvenile gang violence*. New York: Aldine de Gruyter.

Song, J. H. L. (1988). *No white-feathered crows: Chinese immigrants' and Vietnamese refugees' adaptation to American legal institutions*. Ann Arbor, Mich.: University Microfilms International.

Song, J. H. L., Dombrink, J., and Geis, G. (1992). Lost in the melting pot: Asian youth gangs in the United States. *Gang Journal 1*, 1–12.

South, S. J., and Messner, S. F. (1987). The sex ratio and women's involvement in crime: A cross national analysis. *Sociological Quarterly 28*, 171–88.

Strohl, J. (1994) Achievement tests as predictors of subsequent high school performance for LEP students. *MinneTESOL Journal 12*, 89–116.

Sung, B. L. (1987). *Chinese immigrant children in New York City*. New York: Center for Migration Studies.

Toy, C. (1992). Coming out to play: Reasons to join and participate in Asian gangs. *Gang Journal 1*, 13–29.

———. 1993. A short history of Asian gangs in San Francisco. *Justice Quarterly 9*, 647–65.

7. Beyond Multiculturalism

Banks, J. (1995). Multicultural education: Historical development, dimensions, and practice. In J. A. Banks (Ed.), *Handbook of research on multicultural education*. New York: Macmillan, pp. 3–24.

Barba, R. H., and Pang V. O. (1991). *Teacher targeting behaviors in the multicultural classroom*. Unpublished manuscript.

Cheng, L. (1989a). Service delivery to Asian/Pacific LEP children: A cross-cultural framework. *Topics in Language Disorders 9*(3), 1–14.

———. (1989b). Intervention strategies: A multicultural approach. *Topics in Language Disorders 9*(3), 84–90.

———. (1990). Recognizing diversity: A need for a paradigm shift. *American Behavior Scientist 34*(2), 263–78.

———. (1991). *Assessing Asian language performance: A guide for evaluating LEP students*. Oceanside, Calif.: Academic Communication Associates.

———. (1993a). Difficult discourse: An untold Asian story. In D. N. Ripich and N. A. Creaghead (Eds.), *School discourse problems*, 2d ed. San Diego, Calif.: Singular, pp. 155–70.

———. (1993b). Faculty challenges in the education of foreign-born students. In L. W. Clark (Ed.), *Faculty and student challenges in facing cultural and linguistic diversity*. Springfield, Ill.: Charles C. Thomas.

———. (1996). Beyond bilingualism: Language acquisition and disorders—A global perspective. *Topics in Language Disorders 16*(4), 9–21.

Cisneros, S. (1994). *The house on Mango Street*. New York: Alfred A. Knopf.

Clark, L. W., and Cheng, L. (1993). Faculty challenges in facing diversity. In L. W. Clark (Ed.), *Faculty and student challenges in facing cultural and linguistic diversity*. Springfield, Ill.: Charles C. Thomas.

Cole, L. (1989, February 21). *Health care imperatives: A preview of the twenty-first Century*. Address delivered at the Patricia Roberts Harris Lecture Series, San Diego State University.

Cummins, J. (1981). The role of primary language development in promoting educational success for language minority students. In *Schooling and language minority students: A theoretical framework*. Los Angeles: California State University at Los Angeles Evaluation, Dissemination and Assessment Center.

———. (1986). Empowering minority students: A framework for intervention. *Harvard Education Review 56*, 18–36.

Erickson, F. (1984). What makes school ethnography "ethnographic"? *Anthropology and Education Quarterly 15*(1), 51–66. (Revised and reprinted from its original publication in 1973, *The Council on Anthropology and Education Newsletter 2*, 10–19.)

Gay, G. (1995). Curriculum theory and multicultural education. In J. A. Banks (Ed.), *Handbook of research on multicultural education*. New York: Macmillan, pp. 25–43.

Gollnick, D., and Chinn, P. (1994). *Multicultural education in a pluralistic society*, 4th ed. New York: Macmillan.

Greene, L. E. (1991). Where minorities rule. *Principal 70*(3), 4.

Greisberger, J. (1996, March 29). Comments to Phi Beta Delta Honor Society. Long Beach, Calif.

Hall, E. (1976). *Beyond culture*. Garden City, N.Y.: Doubleday.

Hirsch, E. D. (1988). *Cultural Literacy*. New York: Vintage Books.

Jackson, P. (1968). *Life in classrooms*. New York: Holt, Rinehart, and Winston.

Kaplan, A. Y. (1994). On language memoir. In A. Bammer (Ed.), *Displacements: Cultural identities in question*. Bloomington: Indiana University Press.

Krashen, S. D. (1981). Bilingual education and second language acquisition theory. In California State Department of Education, Office of Bilingual Education (Ed.), *Schooling and language minority students: A theoretical framework*. Los Angeles: California State University, Evaluation, Dissemination and Assessment Center, pp. 51–82.

Lightfoot, S. L. (1994). *I've known rivers: Lives of loss and liberation*. Reading, Mass.: Addison-Wesley.

———. (1988). *Balm in Gilead: Journey of a healer*. Reading, Mass.: Addison-Wesley.

Min, A. (1994). *Red azalea*. New York: Pantheon.

Minkin, B. (1995, November) A more shocking future. *Hemispheres* 47–52.

Morrison, T. (1987). *Beloved: A novel*. New York: Knopf.

Morrison, T. (1970). *The bluest eye*. New York: Washington Square Press.

Pang, V. (1995). Asian Pacific American students: A diverse and complex population. In J. A. Banks (Ed.), *Handbook of research on multicultural education*. New York: Macmillan, pp. 412–26.

Sleeter, C. (1995). An analysis of the critiques of multicultural education. In J. A. Banks (Ed.), *Handbook of research on multicultural education*. New York: Macmillan, pp. 65–80.

Spindler, G., and Spindler, L. (1971). *Dreamers without power: The Menomini Indians*. New York: Holt, Rinehart, and Winston.

———. (1982). Roger Harker and Schonhausen: From the familiar to the strange and back again. In G. Spindler (Ed.), *Doing the ethnography of schooling*. New York: Holt, Rinehart, and Winston, pp. 20–47.

———. (1990). *The American cultural dialogue and its transmission*. London: Falmer Press.

Tan, A. (1989). *The Joy Luck Club*. New York: Putnam's.

———. (1989). *The kitchen god's wife*. New York: Putnam's.

Tran, M. L. (1991). *Hidden curriculum*. Unpublished manuscript, San Diego State University.

Trueba, H., Cheng, L., and Ima, K. (1993). *Myth or reality: Adaptive strategies of Asian Americans in California*. London: Falmer Press.

Trueba, H., Spindler, G., and Spindler, L. (Eds.). (1989). *What do anthropologists have to say about dropouts?* London: Falmer Press.

Walker, A. (1982). *The color purple: A novel*. New York: Harcourt Brace Jovanovich.

Wawrytko, S. A. (1995, Spring). East Asian philosophies (Phil 456): Logic and language. *Asia & Pacific Horizons, SDSU Asian Studies Newsletter 1*:3, p. 5. (Available from Dr. Sandra A. Wawrytko, Asian Studies Program, SDSU, San Diego, Calif. 92182.)

Zappia, I. A. (1989). Identification of gifted Hispanic students: A multidimensional view. In C. J. Maker and S. W. Schiever (Eds.), *Critical issues in gifted education: Defensible programs for cultural and ethnic minorities*. Austin, Tex.: Pro-Ed.

9. Asian American and Pacific Islander American Families with Disabilities

Agbayani-Siewert, P., and Revilla, L. (1995). Filipino Americans. In P.G. Min (Ed.), *Asian Americans: Contemporary trends and issues*. Thousand Oaks, Calif.: Sage.

Almirol, E. B. (1982). Rights and obligations in Filipino American families. *Journal of Comparative Family Studies 13* (3), 291–306.

Anderson, P. P. (1989). Issues in serving culturally diverse families of young children with disabilities. *Early Child Development and Care 80*, 167–88.

Blacher, J. (1984). Sequential stages of parental adjustment to the birth of a child with handicaps: Fact or artifact. *Mental Retardation 22*(2), 55–68.

Bristor, M. W. (1984). The birth of a handicapped child—A holistic model for grieving. *Family Relations 33*, 25–32.

Brosnan, F. L. (1983). Overrepresentation of low socioeconomic minority students
in special education programs in California. *Learning Disability Quarterly 6*,
517–25.

Bui, Y. N. (1997). *Children, disabilites, and education: Vietnamese and Vietnamese
American perceptions*. Unpublished master's field study, San Francisco State
University, San Francisco, Calif.

Bulato, J. (1981). The Manileno mainsprings. In F. Lynch and A. de Guzman (Eds.),
Four readings in Filipino values. Quezon City, Philippines: Ateneo de Manila
University Press.

Chan, S. (1986). Parents of exceptional Asian children. In M. K. Kitano and P. C.
Chinn (Eds.), *Exceptional Asian children and youth*. Washington, D.C.: Council for Exceptional Children.

——— . (1992a). Families with Asian roots. In E. Lynch and M. Hanson (Eds.),
*Developing cross-cultural competence: A guide for working with young children
and their families*. Baltimore, Md.: Brookes.

——— . (1992b). Families with Filipino roots. In E. Lynch and M. Hanson (Eds.),
*Developing cross-cultural competence: A guide for working with young children
and their families*. Baltimore, Md.: Brookes.

D'Arcy, E. (1968). Congenital defects: Mothers' reactions to first information.
British Medical Journal 3, 796–98.

Duff, D., and Arthur, R. J. (1980). Between two worlds: Filipinos in the U.S. Navy.
In S. Sue and N. Wagner (Eds.), *Asian Americans: Psychological perspectives*.
Palo Alto, Calif.: Science and Behavior Books.

Gargiulo, R. M. (1985). *Working with professionals of exceptional children*. Boston:
Houghton-Mifflin.

Gochenour, T. (1990). *Considering Filipinos*. Yarmouth, Me.: Intercultural Press.

Harry, B. (1994). Behavioral disorders in the context of families. In R. L. Peterson
and S. Ishii-Jordan (Eds.), *Multicultural issues in the education of students
with behavioral disorders*. Cambridge, Mass.: Brookline.

Ishii-Jordan, S. (1994). Behavioral disorders in the context of Asian cultures. In
R. L. Peterson and S. Ishii-Jordan (Eds.), *Multicultural issues in the education
of students with behavioral disorders*. Cambridge, Mass.: Brookline.

Leung, E. (1988). Cultural and acculturation commonalities and diversities among
Asian Americans: Identification and programming considerations. In A. Ortiz
and B. Ramirez (Eds.), *Schools and the culturally diverse exceptional student:
Promising practices and future directions*. Reston, Va.: Council for Exceptional
Children.

Lim-Yee, N. (1983). Parental reactions to a special-needs child: Cultural differences and Chinese families. Paper presented at the Annual Convention of the Western Psychological Association, San Francisco, Calif.

Min, P. G. (1995a). An overview of Asian Americans. In P. G. Min (Ed.), Asian Americans: Contemporary trends and issues. Thousand Oaks, Calif.: Sage.

———. (1995b). Korean Americans. In P. G. Min (Ed.), *Asian Americans: Contemporary trends and issues*. Thousand Oaks, Calif.: Sage.

Miyamoto, S. F. (1984). *Social solidarity among the Japanese in Seattle*, 3d ed. Seattle: University of Washington Press.

Morrow, R. D. (1987). Cultural differences—Be aware! *Academic Therapy 23*(2), 143–49.

Murray, J. N. (1980). *Developing assessment programs for the multi-handicapped child*. Springfield, Ill.: Charles C. Thomas.

Nakane, C. (1970). *Japanese society*. Berkeley: University of California Press.

Nishi, S. M. (1995). Japanese Americans. In P. G. Min (Ed.), *Asian Americans: Contemporary trends and issues*. Thousand Oaks, Calif.: Sage.

Office of Civil Rights. (1990). *State and National Summaries of Reported Data: 1988 Elementary and Secondary School Civil Rights Survey*. Washington, D.C.: U.S. Department of Education.

Office of Special Education Programs. (1994). *Sixteenth Annual Report to Congress on the Implementation of the Individuals with Disabilities Education Act*. Washinton, D.C.: U.S. Department of Education.

Pang, V. O. (1995). Asian American students: A diverse population. In J. A. Banks and C. Banks (Eds.), *The handbook of research on multicultural education*. New York: Macmillan, pp. 412–24.

Reischauer, E. O. (1981). *The Japanese*. Cambridge, Mass.: Belknap.

Roos, P. (1975). Parents and families of the mentally retarded. In J. M. Kauffman and J. S. Payne (Eds.), *Mental retardation: Introduction and personal persoectives*. Columbus, Ohio: Merrill.

Rose, H. W. (1987). *Something's wrong with my child*. Springfield, Ill.: Charles C. Thomas.

Sue, D. (1981). Cultural and historical perspectives in counseling Asian Americans. In D. Sue (Ed.), *Counseling the culturally different: Theory and practice*. New York: John Wiley.

Tagaki, C., and Ishisaka, T. (1982). Social work with Asian and Pacific Americans. In. J. Green (Ed.), *Cultural awarenes in the human services*. Englewood Cliffs, N.J.: Prentice Hall.

Tomlinson, S. (1989). Asian pupils and special issues. British *Journal of Special Education 16*(3), 119–22.

U.S. Bureau of the Census. (1972). *U.S. census of population: 1970, subject reports: Japanese, Chinese, and Filipinos in the U.S. (PC[2]-1-C)*. Washington, D.C.: U.S. Government Printing Office.

———. (1983). *1980 census of population, general characteristics, United States summary (PC80-1-B1)*. Washington, D.C.: U.S. Government Printing Office.

———. (1993). *1990 census of population, general characteristics, United States summary (CP-1-1)*. Washington, D.C.: U.S. Government Printing Office.

———. (1994). *Statistical Abstract of the United States—1994: The National Data Book*, 114th ed. Washington, D.C.: U.S. Government Printing Office.

Wong, H. Z. (1980). Asian and Pacific Americans. In L.R. Snowden (Ed.), *Reaching the underserved: Mental health needs of nedglected populations*. Beverley Hills, Calif.: Sage

Yao, E. L. (1987). Asian immigrant students—Unique problems that hamper learning. *NASSP Bulletin*, 82–88.

10. The Legacy

Bulosan, C. (1960). *Sound of falling light: Letters in exile*. D. Feria (Ed.). Quezon City, Philippines: University of the Philippines, p. 18.

Carmichael, J. (1954, November 21). Manilla village: Town of wet stilts and dried shrimp. *Times-Picayune States Roto Magazine 118*, 20.

Cordova, F. (1983). *Filipinos: Forgotten Asian Americans*. Dubuque, Iowa: Kendall-Hunt.

Craig, A., Benitez, C. (1916). *Philippine Progress to 1898*. Manillas: Philippine Education.

Crouchett, L. (1982). *Filipinos in California*. El Cerrito, Calif.: Downey Place.

Espina, M. E. (1974). Filipinos in New Orleans. *Proceedings of Louisiana Academy of Sciences*, 27, 1371, pp. 117–21.

———. (1988). *Filipinos in Louisiana*. New Orleans: A. F. Laborde.

Kane, H. T. (1944). *Deep Delta Country*. Duell, Sloan, and Pearce.

Pang, V. O., and Park, C. D. (1992). Issues centered approaches to multicultural education in the middle grades. *The Social Studies 83*(3), 108–12.

Phelan, J. L. (1959). The Hispanization of the Philippines: Spanish aims and Filipino responses, 1565–1700. Madison: University of Wisconsin Press.

Vanished camp of Tulitos is forgotten by historians. (1989). *Mariposa Museum and History Center*, second quarter, pp. 1–5.

Wagner, H. R. (1923, July). Unamuno's voyage to California in 1587. *Quarterly of the California Historical Society*, p. 143.

11. Language Assessment and Instructional Strategies for Limited English Proficient Asian and Pacific Islander American Children

Asian Pacific Horizons. (1994). Fall Newsletter, vol.1 (no. 1). Center on Asian Studies, San Diego State University, San Diego, Calif.

Banks, J. A. (1990). *Transforming the curriculum.* Conference on diversity. Oakland, Calif.: Teacher Credentialing Commission.

Banks, J. A., Cortes, C. E., Gay, G., Garcia, R., and Ochoa, A. S. (1976). *Curriculum guidelines for multiethnic education.* Washington, D.C., National Council for the Social Studies, 1976.

Bishop, S. (1988). *Identification of language disorders in Vietnamese children.* Unpublished master's thesis. San Diego State University.

Castro, D. (1994, October 13). *Minority Health Professions Education Foundation: A golden opportunity.* Honoree remarks. Second annual awards luncheon, Sacramento, Calif.

Cazden, C. B., John, V., and Hymes, D. (Eds). (1972). *Functions of language in the classroom.* New York: Teachers College Press.

Chang, J. M., and Lai, A. (1992, November 26–29). *LEP Parents as resources: Enhancing language and literacy development of LEP students with learning disabilities.* Luo Di-Sheng Gen. Berkeley: International Conference on Overseas Chinese, University of California.

Chang, J. M., Lai, A., and Shimizu, W. (1995). LEP, LD, poor and missed learning opportunities: A case of innercity Chinese children. In L. Cheng (Ed.), *Integrating Language and Learning for Inclusion.* San Diego, Calif.: Singular, pp. 31–59.

Cheng, L. (1987). English communicative competence of language minority children: Assessment and treatment of language "impaired" preschoolers. In H. Trueba (Ed.), *Success or failure? Learning and the language minority student.* New York: Newbury/Harper and Row, pp. 49–68.

——— . (1989). Intervention strategies: A multicultural approach. *Topics in Language Disorders* 9(3), 84–91.

——— . (1990a) The identification of communicative disorders in Asian-Pacific students. *Journal of Childhood Communication Disorders* 13(1), 113–19.

———. (1990b). Recognizing diversity: A need for a paradigm shift. *American Behavioral Scientist 34*(2), 263–78.

———. (1991). *Assessing Asian language performance: Guide for evaluating LEP students.* Oceanside, Calif.: Academic Communication Associates.

———. (1993). Asian-American cultures. In D. Battle (Ed.), *Communication disorders in multicultural populations.* Boston: Andover Medical, pp. 38–77.

———. (1994). Difficult discourse: An untold Asian story. In D. N. Ripich and N. A. Creaghead (Eds.), *School discourse problems,* 2d ed. San Diego, Calif.: Singular, pp. 155–70.

———. (Ed.). (1995). *Integrating language and learning for inclusion.* San Diego, Calif.: Singular.

Cheng, L., and Chang, J. M. (1995). Asian-Pacific Islander students in need of special education services. In L. Cheng (Ed.), *Integrating language and learning for inclusion.* San Diego, Calif.: Singular, pp. 3–30.

Cheng, L., Ima, K., and Labovitz, G. (1994). Assessment of Asian and Pacific islander students for gifted programs. In S. Garcia (Ed.), *Addressing cultural and linguistic diversity in special education.* Reston, Va.: Council for Exceptional Children, pp. 30–45.

Coelho, E. (1995, February). *Cultural and linguistic challenges: Teaching and learning in a multilingual context.* Paper presented at Teaching from the Heart: Illinois Conference for Teachers of Linguistically and Culturally Diverse Students, Illinois.

Cummins, J. (1981). The role of primary language development in promoting educational success for language minority students. In Office of Bilingual Bicultural Education, California State Department of Education (Ed.), *Schooling and language minority students: A theoretical framework* (pp. 3–49). Los Angeles: Evaluation, Dissemination and Assessment Center, California State University.

Dung, I., Viernes, B., and Mudd, S. (1994). *Identifying language-disordered Asian students: Data and implications.* Poster Session, American Speech, Language and Hearing Association Annual Convention, New Orleans, La.

Erickson, J. G., and Omark, D. R. (1980). Social relationships and communicative interactions of mainstreamed communication handicapped preschool children. *Instructional Science 17,* 285–91.

Federal Register (1977, Thursday, December 29). (65082–65085) Washington, D.C.

Figueroa, R. A. (1989). Psychological testing of linguistic minority students: Knowledge gaps and regulations. *Exceptional Children 56*(2), 145–52.

Figueroa, R. A., Ruiz, N. T., and Baca, L. (1988). *Technical proposals for the OLE model.* Davis: University of California.

Foster-Cohen, S. (1994). *First, second, bilingual, and exceptional language acquisition: A teacher's guide.* Paper presented at the meeting of TESOL, Applied Linguistics Interest Section, Baltimore, Md.

Garcia, E. (1991). *The education of linguistically and culturally diverse students: Effective instructional practices.* Washington, D.C.: National Center for Research for Cultural Diversity and Second Language Learning, Center for Applied Linguistics.

Goldenberg, C. (1991). *Instructional conversations and their classroom application.* Washington, D.C.: National Center for Research on Cultural Diversity and Second Language Learning, Center for Applied Linguistics.

Gonzales, L. N. (1994). *Sheltered instruction handbook.* Carlsbad, Calif.: Gonzales and Gonzales.

Hall, E. T. (1969). *The hidden dimension.* Garden City, N.Y.: Doubleday.

————. (1976). *Beyond culture.* Garden City, N.Y.: Anchor.

Ima, K., and Kheo, P. (1995). "The crying father" and "My father doesn't love me": Selected observations and reflections on Southeast Asians and special education. In L. Cheng (Ed.), *Integrating language and learning for inclusion.* San Diego, Calif.: Singular, pp. 149–77.

Kaplan, R. (1966). Cultural thought patterns in intercultural education. *Language Learning 16,* 1–20.

Kitano, H., and Daniels, R. (1988). *Asian Americans: Emerging minorities.* Englewood Cliffs, N.J.: Prentice-Hall.

Krashen, S. (1981). Bilingual education and second language acquisition theory. In Office of Bilingual Bicultural Education, California State Department of Education (Ed.), *Schooling and language minority students: A theoretical framework.* Los Angeles: Evaluation, Dissemination and Assessment Center, California State University.

Krashen, S. (1982). *Principles and practice in second language acquisition.* Elmsford, N.Y.: Pergamon Press.

Langdon, H. (1992). Language communication and sociocultural patterns in Hispanic families. In Langdon, H. W. with Cheng, L. L. (Eds), *Hispanic children and adults with communication disorders: Assessment and intervention.* Gaithersburg, Md.: Aspen.

Leung, B. (1995, March 17). *Nonbiased assessment.* Presentation at Alliance 2000 Workshop. Monterey, Calif.

Lyon, G. R., Gray, D. B., Kavanaugh, K. F., and Krasnegor, N. A. (Eds.). (1993). *Better understanding learning disabilities: New views from research and their implications for public policy.* Baltimore, Md.: Paul H. Brooks.

Mura, D. (1991). *Becoming Japanese*. New York: Doubleday.

National Joint Committee on Learning Disabilities. (1994). Collective perspectives on issues affecting learning disabilities: Position papers and statements. Austin, Tex.: ProEd.

Olsen, L. (1988). *Crossing the schoolhouse border: Immigrant students and California public schools*. San Francisco, Calif.: California Tomorrow.

Ortiz, A. A., Garcia, S. B., and Wilkinson, C. Y. (1988, August.) *Handicapped Minority Research Institute: Five years in review*. General session presented at the Bilingual Special Education Summer Conference, Austin, Texas.

Ramirez, J., Yuen, S., and Ramey, D. (1991). *Executive summary: Longitudinal study of structured English immersion strategy, early-exit and late-exit transitional bilingual education programs for language-minority children*. San Mateo, Calif.: Aguirre International.

Scollon, R., and Scollon, S. W. (1995). *Intercultural communication: A discourse approach*. Oxford: Blackwell.

Suarez-Orozco, M. M. (1989). *Central American refugees and U.S. high school: A psychological study of motivation and achievement*. Stanford, Calif.: Stanford University Press.

Takaki, R. (1989). *Strangers from a diifferent shore: A history of Asian Americans*. Boston: Little Brown.

Te, H. D. (1995). Understanding Southeast Asian students. In L. Cheng (Ed.), *Integrating language and learning for inclusion*. San Diego, Calif.: Singular, pp. 107–24.

Tharp, R. G., and Gallimore, R. (1991). *The instructional conversation: Teaching and learning in social activity*. Washington, D.C.: National Center for Research on Cultural Diversity and Second Language Learning, Center for Applied Linguistics.

Trueba, H. T. (Ed.). (1987). Success or failure? Learning and the language minority student. New York: Newbury House/Harper and Row.

Trueba, H. T., Cheng, L., and Ima, K. (1993). *Myth or reality: Adaptive strategies of Asian Americans in California*. Washington, D.C.: Falmer Press.

Trueba, H. T., Guthrie, G. P., and Au, K. H. (1981). *Culture and the bilingual classroom: Studies in classroom ethnography*. Rowley, Mass.:Newbury House.

Trueba, H. T., Jacobs, L., and Kirton, E. (1990). *Cultural conflict and adaptation: The case of Hmong children in American society*. London: Falmer Press.

U.S. Department of Education. (1995). Vision paper.

University of California. (1994, October 4). Linguistic Minority Research Institute 4, 2.

Wallach, G., and Butler, K. (1994). *Language learning disability in school-age children*. Baltimore, Md.: Williams and Wilkins.

Westby, C. (1990). Ethnographic interviewing: Asking the right questions to the right people in the right ways. *Journal of Childhood Communication Disorders 13*(1), 101–11.

12. Meeting the Instructional Needs of Chinese American and Asian English Language Development and At-Risk Students

Board of Education of the City of New York. (1994). *Comprehensive Instructional Program*. New York: Board of Education of the City of New York.

Cazden, C. B. (1985, April). The ESL teacher as advocate. Plenary presentation to the TESOL Conference, New York.

Chang, J. I., and Fung, G. S. (1996, June). Literacy support across multiple sites: Experiences of Chinese American LEP children in inner cities. *NABE News 19*, 34–36.

Comprehensive Instructional Program. (1994). New York: Board of Education of City of New York.

Cummins, J. (1986). Empowering minority students: A framework for intervention. *Harvard Educational Review 56*, 18–36.

Diaz, R. M. (1985). Bilingual cognitive development: Addressing three gaps in current research. *Child Development 56*, 1376–78.

Fillmore, L. W. (1990). Latino families and the schools. *California Perspectives VI*, 30–37.

———. (in press). Against our best interest: The attempt to sabotage bilingual education. In J. Crawford (Ed.), *Source book on U.S. English*. Chicago: University of Chicago Press.

Fung, G. S. (1993). In the Multicultural context of our school: The Asian American perspective. *Multicultural Forum 1*, 3–6.

Gardner, H. (1983). *Frames of mind: The theory of multiple intelligence*. New York: Basic.

Hakuta, K. (1986). *Mirror of language: The debate of bilingualism*. New York: Basic.

———. (1987). Degree of bilingualism and cognitive ability in mainland Puerto Rican children. *Child Development 58*, 1372–88.

Hakuta, K., and Suben, J. (1985). Bilingual and cognitive development. In R. B. Kaplan (Ed.), *Annual Review of Applied Linguistics 6*, 35–45.

Heath, S. B. (1982). *Ways with Words*. New York: Cambridge University Press.

Hudelson, S. (1990). Bilingual/ESL learners talking in the English classroom. In S. Hynds, and D. L. Rubin (Eds.), *Perspectives on talk and learning.* Urbana, Ill.: National Council of Teachers of English.

Kirby, J. R., and Das, J. P. (1977). Reading achievement, IQ, and simultaneous-successive processing. *Journal of Educational Psychology 69,* 564–70.

Lanauze, M., and Snow, C. (1989). The relationship between first- and second-language writing skills: Evidence from Puerto Rican elementary school children in the mainland. *Linguistics and Education 4,* 323–38

Luria, A. R. (1966). *Human brain and psychological processes.* New York: Harper and Row.

New York Times. (1993, April 28). For thirty-two million Americans, English is a second language. *New York Times,* p. A 18 L.

Ogbu, J. U. (1992). Understanding cultural diversity and learning. *Educational Researcher 8,* 5–14.

Pang, V. O. (1995). Asian Pacific American children: A diverse and complex population. In J. Banks and C. Banks (Eds.), *Handbook of Research on Multicultural Education.* New York: Macmillan, pp. 412–24.

Pang, V. O., Colvin, C., Tran, M. L., and Barba, R. H. (1992). Beyond chopsticks and dragons: Selecting Asian-American literature for children. *The Reading Teacher 3,* 216–24.

Pih, G. F. (1984). *A comparison of normal and disabled readers in elementary school on intellectual, self-esteem, and anxiety factors.* Unpublished doctoral dissertation, University of Georgia, Athens.

Snow, C. E. (1990). Rationales for native language instruction: Evidence from research. In A. M. Padilla, H. H. Fairchild, and C. M. Valdez (Eds.), *Bilingual education: Issues and strategies.* Newbury Park, Calif.: Sage, pp. 165–89.

Trueba, H. T., and Cheng, L. (1993). *Myth or reality: Adaptive strategies of Asian American in California.* Bristol, Pa.: Falmer Press.

Tseng, O. J. L. (1983). Cognitive processing of various orthographies. In M. C. Chang (Ed.), *Asian and Pacific American perspective in bilingual education.* New York: Teacher College, Columbia University, pp. 73–96.

Tucker, G. R. (1990, March). *Cognitive and Social Correlates and Consequences of Additive Bilinguality.* Paper presented at Georgetown University Round Table on Languages and Linguistics.

13. Educating Asian Newcomer Secondary Students

Ambert, A. M. (1991). The education of language minorities: An overview of findings and a research agenda. In *Bilingual education and English as a second language: A research handbook 1988–1990.* A. M. Ambert (Ed.). New York: Garland.

Caplan, N., Choy, M., and Whitmore, J. K. (1992). Indochinese refugee families and academic achievement. *Scientific American 266*(2), 36–42.

First, J. M., and Carrera, J. W. (1988). *New voices: Immigrant students in U.S. public schools*. Boston: National Coalition of Advocates for Students.

Gibson, M. (1991). Minorities and schooling: Some implications. In *Minority status and schooling: A comparative study of immigrant and involuntary minorities*. M. A. Gibson and J. U. Ogbu (Eds.). New York: Garland.

Ima, K. (1991). *What do we know about Asian and Pacific Islander Language Minority students? A report to the California Department of Education's Bilingual Education Office*. Sacramento: California Department of Education.

———. (1992). *Testing the American dream: A case study of the education of secondary newcomer students*. Research report submitted to the U.S. Department of Education, Washington D.C.

Long, P. (with L. Ricard). (1996). *The dream shattered: Vietnamese gangs in America*. Boston: Northeastern University Press.

McNall, M., Dunnigan, T., and Mortimer, J. T. (1994). The educational achievement of the St. Paul Hmong. *Anthropology and Education Quarterly 25*, 44–65.

Nidorf, J. F. (1985). Mental health and refugee youths: A model for diagnostic training. In T. Owan (Ed.), *Southeast Asian mental health: Treatment, prevention, services, training, and research*. Washington, D.C.: U.S. Department of Health and Human Services.

Olsen, L. (1988). *Crossing the schoolhouse boarder: Immigrant students and the California public schools*. San Francisco: California Tomorrow.

———. (1990). Then and now. In J. Cabello (Ed.), *California perspectives: An anthology from the immigrant students project*. San Francisco: California Tomorrow, pp. 3–11.

———. (1994). *The unfinished journey: Restructuring schools in a diverse society*. San Francisco: California Tomorrow.

Olsen, L., and Mullen, N. (1990). *Embracing diversity: Teachers' voices from California's classrooms*. San Francisco: California Tomorrow.

Rumbaut, R., and Ima, K. (1988). *The adaptation of Southeast Asian refugee youth: A comparative study*. Washington, D.C.: Office of Refugee Resettlement.

Sather, S. (Ed.). (1996). *Revisiting the Lau Decision: Twenty years after* (proceedings of a National Commemorative Symposium, November 3–4, 1994, San Francisco). Oakland, Calif.: Art, Research and Curriculum Associates.

Sue, S., and Okazaki, S. (1990). Asian-American education achievements: A phenomenon in search of an explanation. *American Psychologist 45*, 913–20.

Weisner, T. S., Gallimore, R., and Jordan, C. (1998). Unpackaging cultural effects on classroom learning: Native Hawaiian peer assistance and child-generated activity. *Anthropology and Education Quarterly 19*, 325–53.

14. "We Could Shape It"

Bolton, G., Wodehouse, P. G., Lindsay, H., and Crouse, R. (1977). *Anything Goes*. New York: Tams-Witmark Music Library.

Commission on Civil Rights. (1992). *Civil Rights issues facing Asian Americans in the 1990s*. Washington, D.C.: author.

Cosgrove, M., and Neff, C. A. (1992). unpublished paper. University of Massachusetts Boston.

Ellemont, J., and Gorov, L. (1993). South Boston High to reopen in stages. *Boston Globe*, May 8, 1 & 14.

First, J., and Willshire Carrera, J. (1988). *New Voices: Immigrant Students in U.S. Public Schools*. Boston: National Coalition of Advocates for Students.

Gibson, M. A. (1988). *Accommodation without assimilation: Sikh immigrants in an American high school*. Ithaca, N.Y.: Cornell University Press.

Kagiwada, G. (1989). The Killing of Thong Hy Huynh: Implications of a Rashomon Perspective. In G. Nomura et al. (Eds.), *Frontiers of Asian American studies*. Pullman: Washington State University Press, pp. 253–65.

Kaplan, J. (1992). *Vietnamese American Students at an Urban High School*. Unpublished paper. University of Massachusetts Boston.

Kiang, P. N. (1994). When know-nothings speak English only: analyzing Irish and Cambodian struggles for community development and educational equity. In K. Aguilar-San Juan (Ed.), *The state of Asian America: Activism and resistance in the 1990s*, Boston: South End, pp. 125–45.

Kiang, P. N., and Kaplan, J. (1994). Where do we stand? Views of racial conflict by Vietnamese American high school students in a Black-and-White context. *Urban Review 26(2)*, 95–119.

Kiang, P. N., and Lee, V. W. (1993). Exclusion or contribution: Education K–12 policy. *State of Asian Pacific America*. Los Angeles: LEAP Asian Pacific American Public Policy Institute and UCLA Asian American Studies Center, pp. 25–48.

Kiang, P. N., Nguyen N. L., and Sheehan, R. L. (1995). Don't ignore it: Documenting racial harassment in a fourth grade Vietnamese bilingual classroom. *Equity and Excellence in Education 28(1)*, 31–35.

Kitano, M., and Chinn, P. C. (Eds.). (1986). *Exceptional Asian children and youth*. Council for Exceptional Children.

Morrow, R. D. (1989). Southeast Asian parent involvement: Can it be a reality? *Elementary School Guidance and Counseling 23*(2), 289–97.

Nieto, S. (1994). Lessons from students on creating a chance to dream. *Harvard Educational Review 64*(4), 393–426.

Ott, M. (1994). *The incidence of Anti-Asian violence in high schools*. Honors thesis, Bates College.

Phelan, P., Davidson, A. L., and Cao, H. T. (1992). Speaking up: Students' perspectives on school. *Phi Delta Kappan 73*, 695–704.

Pho, S. T. (1993). No more tears will run down our brown cheeks. *Asian Week*, May 28, 14.

Pompa, D. (1994). *Looking for America: Promising school-based practices for intergroup relations*. Boston: National Coalition of Advocates for Students.

Poplin, M., and Weeres, J. (1992). *Voices from the inside: A report on schooling from inside the classroom*. Institute for Education in Transformation, Claremont Graduate School.

Semons, M. (1991). Ethnicity in the urban high school: A naturalistic study of student experiences. *Urban Review 23*(3), 137–58.

Sing, R., and Lee, V. W. (1994). *Delivering on the promise: Positive practices for immigrant students*. Boston: National Coalition of Advocates for Students.

Tong, B. (1992). Students protest racial incident. *Boston Globe*, November 13, 19.

Tran, M. L. T. (1992). Maximizing Vietnamese parent involvement in schools. *NASSP Bulletin*, 76–79.

Trueba, H. T., Cheng, L. R. L., and Ima, K. (1993). *Myth or reality: Adaptive strategies of Asian Americans in California*. London: Falmer.

15. Educating the Whole Child

Agbayani-Siewert, P. (1994). Filipino American culture and family: Guidelines for practitioners. *Families in Society: Journal of Contemporary Human Services 75*(7), 429–38.

Au, K., and Jordan, C. (1981). Teaching reading to Hawaiian children: Finding a culturally appropriate solution. In H. Trueba, G. P. Guthrie, and K. H. Au (Eds.), *Culture and the bilingual classroom*. Rowley: Newbury House, pp. 139–52.

Banks, J. (1988). *Multiethnic education: Theory and practice*. Boston: Allyn and Bacon.

Brislin, R. (1993). *Understanding culture's influence on behavior*. New York: Harcourt Brace.

California State Department of Education, Office of Bilingual Bicultural Education. (1982). *A handbook for teaching Vietnamese-speaking students*. Los Angeles: Evaluation, Dissemination and Assessment Center, California State University, Los Angeles.

Caudill, W. (1952). Japanese-American personality and acculturation. *Genetic Psychology Monograph 45*, 3–102.

Caudill, W., and DeVos, G. (1956). Achievement, culture, and personality: The case of the Japanese Americans. *American Anthropologist 58*, 1102–26.

Chan, S. (1991). *Asian Americans: An interpretive history*. Boston: Twayne.

Chang, T. (1975). The self-concept of children in ethnic groups: Black American and Korean American. *Elementary School Journal 76*, 52–58.

Cheng. L. L. (1989). Service delivery to Asian/Pacific LEP Children: A cross-cultural framework. *Topics in Language Disorders 93*, 1–14.

——— . (1991). *Assessing Asian language performance: Guidelines for evaluating LEP students*, 2d ed. Oceanside, Calif.: Academic Communication Associates.

——— . (1995). *Integrating language and learning for inclusion: An Asian-Pacific focus*. San Diego, Calif.: Singular.

Cheng, L. L., Ima, K., Labovitz, G. (1994). Assessment of Asian and Pacific islander students for gifted programs. In Shernaz B. Garcia (Ed.), *Addressing cultural and linguistic diversity in special education*. Reston, Va.: Council for Exceptional Children.

Cheng, L. L., Nakasato, J., and Wallace, J. (1995). The Pacific islander population and the challenges they face. In L. L. Cheng (Ed.), Integrating language and learning for inclusion: An Asian-Pacific focus. San Diego, Calif.: Singular.

Chhim, S. (1989). *Introduction to Cambodian Culture*. San Diego, Calif.: Multifunctional Resource Center, San Diego State University.

Chock, E. (Ed). (1981). *Small kid time Hawaii*. Honolulu: Bamboo Ridge.

Cordova, F. (1983). *Filipinos: Forgotten Asian Americans*. Dubuque, Iowa: Kendall/Hunt.

Dornbusch, S., Ritter, P., Leiderman, P. H., Roberts, D., and Fraleigh, M. J. (1987). The relation of parenting style to adolescent school performance. *Child Development 58* (5), 1244–57.

Erickson, F. (1990). *Qualitative Methods*. Volume 2 in the Research in Teaching and Learning Series. American Educational Research Association project. New York: Macmillan.

Fenz, W. D., and Arkoff, A. (1962). Comparative need patterns of five ancestry groups in Hawaii. *Journal of Social Psychology 58*, 67–89.

Fong, R., and Mokuau, N. (1994). Not simply "Asian Americans": Periodical literature review on Asians and Pacific islanders. *Social Work 39*(3), 298–305.

Fox, D., and Jordan, V. (1973). Racial preference and identification of American Chinese, Black and White children. *Genetic Psychology Monographs 88*, 220–86.

Fugita, S., and O'Brien, D. J. (1991). *Japanese American ethnicity: The presence of community*. Seattle: University of Washington Press.

Gay, G. (1994). *At the essence of learning: Multicultural education*. West Lafayette, Ind.: Kappa Delta Pi.

Hatamiya, L. (1993). *Righting a wrong: Japanese Americans and the passage of the Civil Liberties Act of 1988*. Stanford, Calif.: Stanford University Press.

Hodgkinson, H., Obarakpor, A. (1994). *Immigration to America: The Asian experience*. Washington, D.C.: Institute for Educational Leadership, Center for Demographic Policy.

Hopkins, M. C. (1996). *Braving a new world: Cambodian (Khmer) refugees in an American city*. Westport, Conn.: Bergin and Garvey.

Hune, S., and Chan, K. (1997). Special focus: Asian Pacific American demographics and educational trends. In D. Carter and R. Wilson (Eds.), *Minorities in higher education*, vol. 15. Washington, D.C.: American Council on Education.

Igoa, C. (1995). *The inner world of the immigrant child*. New York: St. Martin's Press.

Ima, K., and Rumbaut, R. (1988). *The adaptation of Southeast Asian refugee youth: A comparative study*. Washington, D.C.: U.S. Department of Health and Human Services, Family Support Administration, Office of Refugee Resettlement.

Irvine, J. J. (1990). *Black students and school failure*. New York: Greenwood.

Ishikawa, W. (1978). *The elder Samoan*. San Diego, Calif.: Center on Aging, San Diego State University.

Japanese American Citizens League. (1994). *The Japanese American experience: A lesson in American history*. San Francisco: Japanese American Citizens League.

Jung, S. (1993, May 19–June 1). Samoans: Struggling to keep traditions alive. *International Examiner*, pp. 3, 7, 10.

Kessler, L. (1993). *Stubborn twig: Three gnerations in the life of a Japanese American family*. New York: Random House.

Kiang, P. (1990). *Southeast Asian parent empowerment: The challenge of changing demographics in Lowell, Masssachusetts* (Monograph No. 1). Jamaica Plain: Massachusetts Association for Bilingual Education.

Kibria, Nazli. (1993). *Family tightrope: The changing lives of Vietnamese Americans*. Princeton, N.J.: Princeton University Press.

Kim, B. (1978). *The Asian Americans: Changing patterns, changing needs*. Montclair, N.J.: Association of Korean Christian Scholars in North America.

———. (1980). *The Korean-American child at school and at home*. Washington, D.C.: U.S. Department of Health, Education, and Welfare.

Kim, E., and Yu, E. (1996). *East to America: Korean American life stories*. New York: New Press.

Kitano, H. (1976). *Japanese Americans: The evolution of a subculture*, 2d ed. Englewood Cliffs, N.J.: Prentice-Hall.

Lau, A. (1995, February 11). Filipino girls think suicide at no. 1 rate. *San Diego Union-Tribune*, pp. A-1, A-19.

Lee, F. Y. (1995). Asian parents as partners. *Young Children 50*(3), 4–9.

Lee, S. (1996). *Unraveling the "model minority" stereotype: Listening to Asian American youth*. New York: Teachers College Press.

Long, P. D. P. (1996). *The dream shattered: Vietnamese gangs in America*. Boston: Northeastern University Press.

McClain, C. (1994). *In search of equality: The Chinese struggle against discrimination in nineteenth-century America*. Berkeley: University of California Press.

Monzon, R. (1984). The Effects of the family environment on the academic performance of Pilipino American college students. Masters thesis, San Diego State University.

Mordkowitz, E. R., and Ginsburg, H. P. (1987). Early academic socialization of successful Asian-American college students. *Quarterly Newsletter of the Laboratory of Comparative Human Cognition 9*, 85–91.

National Clearinghouse for Bilingual Education (1984). *Indochinese information packet*. Rosslyn, Va.: Author.

Oanh, N. T., and Michael, W. B. (1977). The predictive validity of each of ten measures of self-concept relative to teachers' ratings of achievement in mathematics and reading of Vietnamese children and those of five other ethnic groups. *Educational and Psychological Measurements 37*, 1005–16.

Ong, P., and Hee, S. (1993). The growth of the Asian Pacific American population: Twenty million in 2020. In *The state of Asian Pacific America. A policy report: Policy issues to the year 2020*. Los Angeles: LEAP Asian Pacific American Public Policy Institute and UCLA Asian American Studies Center.

Pang, V. O. (1991). The relationship of test anxiety and math achievement to parental values in Asian-American and European-American middle school students. *Journal of Research and Development in Education 24*(4), 1–10.

———. (1994). Why do we need this class? Multicultural education for teachers. *Phi Delta Kappan 76*(4), 289–92.

———. (1995a). Asian Pacific American students: A diverse and complex population. In J. A. Banks and C. M. Banks (Eds.), *Handbook of research on multicultural education.* New York: Macmillan, pp. 412–24.

———. (1995b). Caring for the Whole Child: Asian Pacific American Students. Paper presented at the Invitational Symposium, Defining the Knowledge Base for Urban Teacher Education, Emory University, November, 1995.

Pang, V. O., Colvin, C., Tran, M., and Barba, R. (1992). Beyond chopsticks and dragons: Selecting Asian-American literature for children. *Reading Teacher, 46*(3), 216–24.

Pang, V. O., and Evans, R. W. (1995). Caring for Asian Pacific American students in the social studies classroom. *Social Studies and Young Learner 7*(4), 11–14.

Pang, V. O., Mizokawa, D., Morishima, J., and Olstad, R. (1985). Self-concepts of Japanese-American children. *Journal of Cross-Cultural Psychology 16*, 99–109.

Pang, V. O., and Sablan, V. (1998). Teacher efficacy: How do teachers feel about their abilities to teach African American students? In M. Dilwort (Ed.), *Being responsive to cultural differences.* Thousand Oaks, Calif.: Corwin Press, pp. 39–58.

Ramist, L., and Arbeiter, S. (1986). *Profiles: College-bound seniors 1985.* New York: College Entrance Examination Board.

Rivera, J., and Poplin, M. (1995). Multicultural, critical, feminine, and constructive pedagogies seen through the lives of youth: A call for the revisioning of these and beyond: Toward a pedagogy for the next century. In C. E. Sleeter and P. L. McLaren (Eds.), *Multicultural education, critical pedagogy, and the politics of difference.* Albany: State University of New York Press, pp. 221–43.

Rutledge, J. P. (1992). *The Vietnamese experience in America.* Bloomington: Indiana University Press.

Santos, R. (1983). The social and emotional develpoment of Filipino American children. In G. J. Powell (Ed.), *The psychosocial development of minority group children.* New York: Brunner/Mazel, pp. 131–48.

Shavelson, R., Huber, J., and Stanton, G. C. (1976). Self-concept: Validation of construct interpretations. *Review of Educational Research 45*(3), 407–41.

Sinnott, S. 1993. *Extraordinary Asian Pacific Americans.* Chicago: Childrens Press.

Sipma-Dysico, C. (1994). *The Filipino ethnicity in transition: Voices of the 1.5 and second generation children of immigrant Flipinos.* Unpublished master's thesis, San Diego State University, San Diego, California.

Sue, Donald, Sue, David, and Sue, Diane. (1983). Psychological development of Chinese American children. In G. Powell (Ed.), *The psychological development of minority group children*. New York: Bruner/Mazel, pp. 159–66.

Sue, S., and Kitano, H. (1973). Stereotypes as a measure of success. *Journal of Social Issues 29*, 83–98.

Sue, S., and Okazaki, S. (1990). Asian-American educational achievements: A phenomenon in search of an explanation. *American Psychologist 45*(8), 913–20.

Sue, S., and Sue, D. W. (1973). Chinese American personality and mental health. In S. Sue and N. Wagner (Eds.), *Asian-Americans psychological perspectives*. Palo Alto, Calif.: Science and Behavior Books.

Suzuki, B. (1977). Education and the socialization of Asian Americans: A revisionist analysis of the "model minority" thesis. *Amerasia 4*, 23–51.

Takaki, R. (1989). *Strangers from a different shore*. Boston: Little Brown.

Tayag, I. (1995, June). You're not alone. Tinig Ng Kabataan: Voices of youth. *Pilipino Youth Senate Newsletter*, vol 1, National City, Calif.: Filipino Youth Senate, p. 2.

Te, H. D. (1987). *Introduction to Vietnamese Culture*. San Diego, Calif.: Multifunctional Resource Center, San Diego State University.

———. (1995). Understanding Southeast Asian students. In L. L. Cheng (Ed.), *Integrating language and learning for inclusion: An Asian-Pacific focus*. San Diego, Calif.: Singular.

Tidwell, R. (1980). Gifted students' self-images as a function of identification process, race, and sex. *Journal of Pediatric Psychology 5*, 57–69.

Toji, D., and Johnson, J. H. (1992). Asian and Pacific islander American poverty: The working poor and the jobless poor. *Amerasia Journal 18*(1), 83–91.

Trueba, H., Cheng, L., and Ima, K. (1993). *Myth or reality: Adaptive strategies of Asian Americans in California*. Washington, D.C.: Falmer Press.

Uba, L. (1994). *Asian Americans: Personality patterns, identity and mental health*. New York: Guilford Press.

Union of Pan Asian Communities (UPAC). (1980). *Understanding the Pan Asian client: Book II*. San Diego, Calif.: Union of Pan Asian Communities.

U.S. Bureau of the Census. 1992. *Current Population Reports Population Characteristics P20-459*. Washington, D.C.: Government Printing Office.

Villa, D. (1995). Interview in San Diego, Calif.

Wang, L. (1976). *Lau v. Nichols*: History of a struggle for equal and quality education. In E. Gee (Ed.), *Counterpoint*. Los Angeles: Regents of the University of California and the UCLA Asian American Studies Center, pp. 240–59.

Whiz Kids. (1987, August 31). *Time*, pp. 42–51.

About the Contributors

Li-Rong Lilly Cheng is a Professor in the Department of Communicative Disorders at San Diego State University. She is Assistant Dean for the College of Health and Human Services. Named a national Fellow in American Speech and Hearing Association in 1992, Cheng is an international scholar in speech pathology, linguistics, and Bilingual/Multicultural Education. She has authored many books like *Assessing Asian Language Performance* and the text, *Myth or Reality: Adaptive Strategies of Asian Americans in California*, with Enrique Henry Trueba and Kenji Ima. Cheng serves on the editorial boards of *Topics in Language Disorders, Anthropology Education Quarterly* and *Language Speech and Hearing Services in Schools.*

Chi-Ah Chun is a doctoral student in psychology at the University of California at Los Angeles. Her work focuses on the psychological adjustment of Asian Pacific American populations.

Fred Cordova is a founding member and former President of the Filipino American Historical Society. He is also manager of the University of Washington's News and Information Services. As a Smithsonian Fellow, Cordova studied the early presence of Filipino in the United States. His book, *Filipinos: Forgotten Asians* is a foundational piece on Filipino Americans.

Penelope V. Flores is a Professor of Education, College of Education, Department of Secondary Education, San Francisco State University where she is teaching courses in the Teacher Credentialing Program. Her research interests are in the fields of Multicultural Education and Mathematics Education (ethnomathematics emphasis). Her Bachelor of Science in Education degree was from the Philippine Normal University, Manila; her Masters in Science Degree from the University of Pennsylvania, Philadelphia, and her Ph.D. from the University of Chicago. She taught at the Philippine Normal University and the University of the Philippines before immigrating to the United States.

Grace S. Fung is a senior research associate with Metropolitan Center for Urban Education at New York University. She is the project director for "Starting Healthy," a health education curriculum project in collaboration with the National Center for Health Education. Fung received her doctorate from the University of Georgia.

Kenji Ima is a Professor of Sociology at San Diego State University. Ima has authored numerous publications on the plight of emigrants from Southeast Asia. He was an associate editor of the text, *Myth or Reality: Adaptive Strategies of Asian Americans in California*, with Henry Trueba and Lilly Cheng. He specializes in the social adjustments of Southeast Asian refugee youth and has written on their educational achievements and involvements with the juvenile justice system. He also studies the institutional contexts of these youth, including schools and neighborhoods, while searching for ways to reshape public policies.

Peter N. Kiang is an Associate Professor in the Graduate College of Education and American Studies Program at the University of Massachusetts, Boston where he teaches graduate courses in multicultural education and undergraduate courses in Asian American Studies. Kiang's current work focuses on analyzing racial conflict in schools; developing leadership in immigrant and refugee communities; and ensuring access by communities of color to the Information Superhighway. He has received honors from the Massachusetts Teachers Association, the NAACP, the Anti-Defamation League, the Boston Foundation, and the Rainbow Coalition. He holds undergraduate and graduate degrees from Harvard University and is a former Community Fellow in the Department of Urban Studies and Planning at MIT.

Brian P. Leung is an Associate Professor of educational psychology at Loyola Marymount University. He has worked as a school psychologist in urban school districts serving students from many different racial and ethnic backgrounds. His areas of research interest include language acquisition and appropriate assessment issues.

Valeria Lovelace was Vice President for Research at Sesame Street, a division of the Children's Television Workshop. Her work focused upon the impact of media on young children. As Vice President for Research, Lovelace developed a four-year study of race relations at Sesame Street. In her role she directed the infusion of race and cultural issues into children's television. She is now a private consultant on issues of the media in children's programming.

Adel Nadeau was the "Principal in Residence" at the U.S. Department of Education from September 1994–May 1995. Prior to this assignment she led an extensive and successful school-wide reform effort at Linda Vista Elementary School in San Diego, California. Before her work in school administration, she spent many years as a teacher, Title VII director, curriculum consultant, and university professor in the area of linguistic diversity. She has returned to the San Diego Unified School District where she is responsible for the "Humanities Curriculum." She also continues her work as a part-time professor at San Diego State University. She has recently published a book on linguistic diversity with her colleagues, Ofelia Miramontes, and Nancy Commins. The book is entitled, *Restructuring Schools for Linguistic Diversity: Linking Decision-Making to Effective Programs.*

Jean Nidorf is a Professor of Sociology at the University of California, San Diego. She is a specialist in adolescent delinquency, especially gang affiliations.

Valerie Ooka Pang is a Professor of Teacher Education at San Diego State University. She was a Spencer Foundation Postdoctoral Fellow and studied achievement and test anxiety in Asian American students. Her articles have appeared in publications like *Handbook of Research on Multicultural Education, Harvard Educational Review, The Kappan, Theory and Research in Social Education, Multicultural Education,* and *Social Education.* Pang received the 1997 Distinguished Scholar Award from the American Educational Research Association's Standing Committee on the Role and Status of Minorities in Education. Her interests include Asian Pacific American children, Multicultural Education, Teacher Education, and Race Relations.

Stanley Sue is a Professor of Psychology, Director of the Asian American Studies Program, and Director of the National Research Center on Asian American Mental Health, an NIMH-funded research center, at the University of California, Davis. He received a B.S. degree from the University of Oregon (1966) and the Ph.D. degree in psychology from UCLA (1971). From 1981–1996, he was a Professor of Psychology at UCLA, where he was also Associate Dean of the Graduate Division. Prior to his faculty appointment at UCLA, he served for ten years on the Psychology faculty at the University of Washington and from 1980–1981 was Director of Clinical-Community Psychology Training at the National Asian American Psychology Training Center in San Francisco, an APA-approved internship program.

MyLuong Tran is an Associate Professor in Teacher Education at San Diego State University. Tran developed a unique preservice teacher education program for Hmong teachers. In addition, she was honored with the Outstanding Educator Award from the Vietnamese Teachers and Parents Association. She is one of few tenured Vietnamese American female professors in the nation.

Enrique Henry T. Trueba is Co-Executive Director of the Institute on Urban Education at the University of Houston. He was honored with the Distinguished Research on Bilingual Education Award in 1990, American Educational Research Association's Outstanding Hispanic Education Award in 1987, and the Martin Luther King, Jr., Rosa Park and Cesar Chavez Distinguished Visiting Professorship at Michigan State University. His work focuses on bilingual education, international education, literacy, Asian Pacific Americans and Asians in China and Southeast Asia.

Addison Watanabe is an Associate Professor of Special Education at San Francisco State University where he teaches courses related to classroom management and organization, educating students with serious emotional and behavioral disturbances, as well as serving as a field supervisor for teachers in training. In addition to teaching at the university, Watanabe is an active member of the Council for Exceptional Children where he served as a member of the Ethnic and Multicultural Concerns Committee. Watanabe has also served as the treasurer for the Division of Culturally and Linguistically Diverse Exceptional Learners. He also provides technical assistance to education programs in Guam, Commonwealth of the Northern Mariana Islands, and the Republic of Palau. Watanabe has directed numerous federally-supported projects designed to improve services for students with disabilities.

Russell Young is currently an associate professor in the Department of Policy Studies in Language and Cross-Cultural Education. He teaches courses in multicultural education, language policy, and educational research. He is a third generation Chinese-American who spent six years in Hong Kong and Taiwan teaching, studying Chinese, and working with the Fulbright Foundation. His research interests include ethnic identity development, multicultural teacher training, and educational policy. His publications have appeared in journals like *Multicultural Education, Teaching Education Quarterly, Equity and Excellence,* and *Journal of Teacher Education.* He also enjoys writing multicultural children's literature.

Index